MOVIE BLOCKBUSTERS

Edited by
Julian Stringer

LONDON AND NEW YORK

FOR STEVE

First published 2003
by Routledge
11 New Fetter Lane, London EC4P 4EE

Simultaneously published in the USA and Canada
by Routledge
29 West 35th Street, New York, NY 10001

Routledge is an imprint of the Taylor & Francis Group

Typeset in Perpetua by
BOOK NOW Ltd
Printed and bound in Great Britain by
MPG Books Ltd, Bodmin, Cornwall

British Library Cataloguing in Publication Data
A catalogue record for this book is available from the British Library

Library of Congress Cataloging in Publication Data
A catalog record has been requested

ISBN 0-415-25608-9 (hbk)
ISBN 0-415-25609-7 (pbk)

CONTENTS

FIGURES

CONTRIBUTORS

Michael Allen teaches film, television, and new media at Birkbeck College, London. He is author of *Family Secrets: The Feature Films of D.W. Griffith* (British Film Institute, 2000), has contributed to *The Cinema Book* (BFI, 1999) and *Contemporary Hollywood Cinema* (Routledge, 1998), and has just completed a book on contemporary American cinema for McLean Press and Pearson International. He also designs multimedia materials for film and television studies use.

Chris Berry teaches in the Film Studies Program and Department of Theater, Dance and Performance Studies at the University of California, Berkeley. He is author of numerous articles on Chinese cinema, and editor of *Perspectives on Chinese Cinema* (British Film Institute, 1991). His current project is a book on Chinese cinema and the national (co-written with Mary Farquhar) for Cambridge University Press.

Warren Buckland is Associate Professor in Film Studies at Chapman University, California. He is editor of *The Film Spectator: From Sign to Mind* (Amsterdam University Press, 1995), author of *Teach Yourself Film Studies* (Hodder & Stoughton/NTC Press, 1998) and *The Cognitive Semiotics of Film* (Cambridge University Press, 2000), and co-author (with Thomas Elsaesser) of *Studying Contemporary American Film: A Guide to Movie Analysis* (Arnold, 2002).

Lucy Faire is a Research Associate in the Department of Geography at Loughborough University, working on the project "Modernizing the City: Experiences of Urban Change in Post-War Britain." She is co-author of *The Place of the Audience: Cultural Geographies of Film Consumption* (British Film Institute, 2003).

Tamara L. Falicov is Assistant Professor of Theatre and Film and Latin American Studies at the University of Kansas. She has been the recipient of a Fulbright Fellowship to Argentina and a Rockefeller Humanities Visiting Fellowship at the University of the Republic, Uruguay. She has published in *Media, Culture and Society*, *Southern Quarterly*, and *Studies in Latin American Popular Culture*. She is currently writing a book on the history of the film industry in Argentina and its relationships with Hollywood and European cinema.

Rebecca Feasey is a Ph.D student in the Institute of Film Studies at the University of Nottingham. Her research interests include star studies, reception studies, and the contemporary erotic thriller.

Douglas Gomery teaches at the University of Maryland, and is resident scholar at the Library of American Broadcasting. His previous publications include *Who Owns the Media?* (Erlbaum Publishers, 2000), *Shared Pleasures* (University of Wisconsin Press, 1992), and *The Hollywood Studio System* (Macmillan/BFI, 1986).

Matt Hills is a Lecturer in the School of Journalism, Media, and Cultural Studies at Cardiff University. He is the author of *Fan Cultures* (Routledge, 2002) and has written for *The Velvet Light Trap*, *Foundation: The International Review of Science Fiction*, and *New Media and Society*. He is co-editor of *Intensities: The Journal of Cult Media* (www.cult-media.com), and is currently researching and writing *The Pleasures of Horror* (Continuum, forthcoming 2003).

Mark Jancovich is Reader and Director of the Institute of Film Studies at the University of Nottingham. He is the author of several books, including *Horror* (Batsford, 1992), *The Cultural Politics of the New Criticism* (Cambridge University Press, 1993), *Approaches to Popular Film* (co-editor, Manchester University Press, 1995), *Rational Fears: American Horror in the 1950s* (Manchester University Press, 1996), *The Film Studies Reader* (co-editor, Arnold, 2000), and *Horror: The Film Reader* (Routledge, 2002).

Geoff King is Course Director, Film and TV Studies, Brunel University, London. His books include *New Hollywood Cinema: An Introduction* (I. B. Tauris, 2002), *Spectacular Narratives: Hollywood in the Age of the Blockbuster* (I. B. Tauris, 2000), *Film Comedy* (Wallflower Press, 2002), and, as co-editor, *ScreenPlay: Cinema/Videogames/Interfaces* (Wallflower Press, forthcoming).

Peter Krämer teaches film studies at the University of East Anglia. He has published essays on American film and media history in *Screen*, *The Velvet Light Trap*, *Theatre History Studies*, *Historical Journal of Film, Radio and Television*, *History Today*, *Film Studies*, and various edited collections. Together with Alan Lovell, he co-edited *Screen Acting* (Routledge, 1999). He is author of *The Big Picture: Hollywood Cinema from Star Wars to Titanic* (British Film Institute, 2003).

Jon Lewis is Professor of English at Oregon State University. He is the author of *The Road to Romance and Ruin: Teen Films and Youth Culture* (Routledge, 1992), *Whom God Wishes to Destroy: Francis Coppola and the New Hollywood* (Duke University Press, 1995), and *Hollywood v. Hard Core: How the Struggle over Censorship Saved the Modern Film Industry* (New York University Press, 2000).

Steve Neale is Research Professor in Film, Media, and Communication Studies at Sheffield Hallam University. He is author of *Genre and Hollywood* (Routledge, 2000), co-author of *Popular Film and Television Comedy* (Routledge, 1990), and co-editor of *Contemporary Hollywood Cinema* (Routledge, 1998). He has contributed articles to *Screen*, *Framework*, and *The Velvet Light Trap*.

Gillian Roberts is pursuing a Ph.D in English at the University of Leeds. She has published articles in *Canadian Review of American Studies* and *Essays on Canadian Writing*.

Thomas Schatz is Professor and Chair of the Radio-Television-Film Department at the University of Texas, where he has been on the faculty since 1976. He is the author of four books about Hollywood films and filmmaking and has also written for numerous magazines, newspapers, and academic journals, including the *New York Times*, *Premiere*, *The Nation*, and *Film Comment*. He is currently working on a history of MCA-Universal with co-author Thom Mount, former president of Universal Pictures.

Gianluca Sergi teaches film studies at the University of Staffordshire. He is particularly interested in film sound and performance and has published articles in the *Journal of Popular Film and Television* and chapters in *Contemporary Hollywood Cinema* (Routledge, 1998) and *Screen Acting* (Routledge, 1999). His most recent publication, in *Hollywood Spectatorship* (British Film Institute, 2001), discusses the figure of the spectator as listener. He is currently preparing a book on the working practices of contemporary Hollywood filmmakers.

Julian Stringer is Lecturer in Film Studies at the University of Nottingham, and an editorial board member of *Scope: An Online Journal of Film Studies* (www.nottingham.ac.uk/film). His recent publications include articles in *Countervisions: Asian American Film Criticism* (Temple University Press, 2000) and *Im Kwon-Taek: The Making of a Korean National Cinema* (Wayne State University Press, 2002). He is currently researching a Ph.D on film festivals at Indiana University.

Kirsten Moana Thompson is Assistant Professor of English at Wayne State University, Detroit. She is co-editor (with Terri Ginsberg) of *Perspectives on German Cinema* (G. K. Hall, 1996) and has published articles on animation and New Zealand cinema. She is currently working on a book on the Fleischer brothers.

Andrew Willis is Lecturer in Media and Performance at the University of Salford. He is co-author of *Media Studies: Texts, Institutions and Audiences* (Blackwell, 1999) and editor of *Film Stars: Hollywood and Beyond* (Manchester University Press, forthcoming).

INTRODUCTION

Julian Stringer

We are all experts on movie blockbusters. "Event movies" target the mass audience, making lack of knowledge of their existence virtually impossible. We may as individuals choose to consume them, or we may choose to avoid them, but either way we share in common the simple fact of knowing something about them. It is very difficult to imagine meeting someone on the street who did not possess some level of familiarity with blockbusters such as *Gone with the Wind* (1939), *The Sound of Music* (1965), *Star Wars* (1977), and *Titanic* (1997). If we were to meet such a person we might find their ignorance strange and disturbing.

Yet at the same time as we are all aware of the existence of movie blockbusters, we do not appear to spend much time actually thinking very hard about them. Why should we? The Hollywood film industry makes the process of consuming such films both easy and pleasurable. (If we can bank on anything in this uncertain world, it is that a new "must see" attraction will come along every once in a while to distract and entertain us.) In addition, critics, journalists, and scholars often claim an insidious superficiality and underlying awfulness for blockbusters, encouraging at the worst extreme blanket dismissals of some of the most popular forms of commercial cinema. Films labeled as blockbusters are frequently positioned as examples of the culturally retrograde, beneath serious consideration or analysis. Casual accusations are habitually thrown around regarding "lowest common denominator film-making," or the complaint that such-and-such a title is "a typical blockbuster" or "only a blockbuster." Supposedly depersonalized and "arrived at by corporate decisions" (*New York Times* on *Batman* [1989], quoted in Tanitch 2000: 136), blockbusters are more often than not dismissed as ostentatious and insubstantial – "as tastelessly impressive as a ten-ton marshmallow" (*Time* on *South Pacific* [1958], quoted in ibid.: 69). Given the prevalence of attitudes such as these, it is little wonder that, while they are usually the first films we get to hear about, blockbusters are among the very last we may end up reflecting further upon.

The central argument of this volume is that there is a need to talk with much greater clarity and deliberation about the subject of movie blockbusters. Aside from the importance of exploring the sheer social and cultural ubiquity of those titles which top box-office charts and attract intense media attention, the primary reason for this is because the meaning of the term "blockbuster" is itself far from self-evident. As a key word of contemporary culture, "blockbuster" is something of a moving target – its meaning is never fixed or clear, but changes according to who is speaking and what is being said. Analysis of the language used to describe blockbusters across time reveals contradictory beliefs and assumptions, because commentators have attached very different values to the films identified under this particular umbrella label. Moreover, many have held differing perceptions concerning periodization – in other words, when blockbusters were first made or named as such – and about the specific elements that need to be in place in order for any individual title to be defined along these lines.

As a way of tackling these kinds of problems, the contributors to *Movie Blockbusters* have proceeded by first retreating and taking stock. The seventeen original essays and one reprint published here work to advance the claim that the blockbuster has no essential characteristics. By contrast, the movie blockbuster is a multifaceted phenomenon whose meanings are contingent upon the presence of a range of discourses both internal and external to the Hollywood and indeed the non-US film industries. Across these pages, the term "blockbuster" reveals itself to be a method of classification, and not everyone describes it in quite the same way or proposes identical constitutive features. In seeking to open a more focused and expansive critical dialog around the subject, then, this book understands the blockbuster as a complex notion for categorizing and so thinking about certain kinds of films. In short, it understands the blockbuster as a genre.

In his important recent study *Film/Genre* (from which discussion of the blockbuster is nevertheless absent), Rick Altman points out that "generic practice and terminology are the sites of constant struggle. Instead of conflating the work of producers, exhibitors, viewers and critics, we need to recognize their differing purposes and the resultant differences in generic categories, labels and uses" (Altman 1999: 101). Such observations are borne out in the case of blockbusters. The press, film critics, and academics often hold very specific views on what the term "blockbuster" refers to, as do both fans and "ordinary" consumers, and these may or may not overlap with industrial definitions. Differing terminology can be shown to be in use in an array of diverse time periods and cultural contexts because of the "*discursive* status of all generic claims. Pronounced *by* someone and addressed *to* someone, statements about genre are always informed by the identity of speaker and audience" (ibid.: 102; italics in original). As a minor example of this process, consider the fact that in 1988 two comic authors published a satirical novel promisingly entitled *Blockbuster*. However, on closer inspection, the book proves to be of interest only to the extent that it talks about the subject indirectly, by exploring not what a blockbuster is, but rather *what it is not*. In order to fulfill its goal

of being funny, sophisticated, and clever, the novel turns out to be a cynical study of the so-called "failed" blockbuster. As such, it exposes a relational component to the tricky task of explaining what the word "blockbuster" actually does stand for. (*Blockbuster* tells the story of the production of "the flop of flops," or an attempt to produce a big-screen adaptation of John Bunyan's *The Pilgrim's Progress*, peopled with one-dimensional characters sporting names such as "Obstinate, Pliable, Sloth, etc." [Marx and McGrath 1988: 115].)

When trying to think through the significance of the term "blockbuster" as a site of constant struggle, other contemporary work on genre also proves highly instructive. In *More Than Night: Film Noir in its Contexts*, James Naremore refers to film noir as an "idea" and an amorphous category of cinema history: "[film noir] has less to do with a group of artifacts than with a discourse – a loose, evolving system of arguments and readings that helps to shape commercial strategies and aesthetic ideologies" (Naremore 1998: 11). Blockbusters might be thought of in much the same way. As a loose, evolving system of claims and counterclaims – or an influential and multifaceted idea – the blockbuster circulates diverse kinds of knowledge concerning titles deemed to be social events. Such discursive activity takes place on both textual and extra-textual levels. As a means of responding to the complexities of a variety of distinct circumstances, therefore, the essays in this volume explore culturally and historically specific aspects of film production, distribution, exhibition, and marketing, as well as critical and audience reception. By placing the blockbuster within such a wide variety of interpretative frames, it is to be hoped that simplistic statements concerning what the blockbuster "is" – at all times and in all places – have thus been avoided.

Given all this, one might be tempted to ask whether it is still possible to identify with any degree of precision what lies behind the blockbuster as an idea. If "night" is the key term structuring discussion of film noir, the blockbuster appears most frequently understood through repeated association with an alternative key term – namely, "size." Size is the central notion through which the blockbuster's generic identity comes to be identified. However, the exact connotations this notion will carry in specific historical contexts cannot be assumed or taken for granted. What may be termed a blockbuster's "size factor" operates to distinguish something unique in the case of each individual movie, but it does so in divergent ways, depending on who is speaking, who is being addressed, and the existence of a range of other variables against which an event movie's relative dimensions may be measured.

As Steve Neale's chapter in this volume demonstrates, the size factor has been present throughout Hollywood's history, and it has been deployed in numerous ways so as to differentiate some kinds of films from others. "In casting about for adjectives with which to describe the long-awaited movie version of *Ben-Hur*," wrote a critic for *Life* in 1926, "I find myself limited to that section of the thesaurus which

Figure 0.1 The bigness of *Ben-Hur* (1925). The Kobal Collection/MGM.

offers synonyms of 'big'" (Sherwood 1926: 170). Commentators have across the years responded likewise, perceiving *bigness* as the medium through which this size factor manifests itself. It may well be the case that certain blockbusters exist as a result of thinking small. However, it is much more common for the genre to be identified alongside those movies believed to be in some sense bigger – or of more noteworthy size – than the rest.

Size matters to the idea of the blockbuster primarily because such films are widely believed to garner a disproportionate amount of box-office income. (As Houston and Gillett [1963: 64] put it: "Block to be busted: audience resistance.") Yet there are many sides to the relationship between the amount of money a blockbuster costs, or generates, and its various other size differentials. Whichever factor is being advanced – money or something else – the language of superlatives appears most suited to the task of approximating the blockbuster's bigness. (Conversely, the language of "flop of flops" is used for "failed" blockbusters.) For example, in 1926 one critic described *The Black Pirate* as an example of the "so-called super-film" (Martin 1926: 172), while in later years others presented *Gone with the Wind* (1939) as a "super-picture" (Hoellering 1939: 370), *Duel in the Sun* (1946) as a "super-western" (Bazin 1971), and *Ben-Hur* (1959) as a "superspectacular" (*New York Herald Tribune*, quoted in Tanitch 2000: 71). Such rhetoric carries right on through to the present day, with extended critical interest in the "supersystem" of multimedia marketing that spins a web of commercial exploitation around contemporary movie franchises (Kinder 1991). In each of these examples, use of the word "super" implies excess: a going beyond of what had been the size norms of accepted or established practice; the adding on of something special; the presence of an extra dimension of some kind or other.

Two aspects of the blockbuster's extra dimensions or superlative nature are of particular importance. First, such films are distinct for the simple reason that they announce themselves as such. Blockbusters constitute the most public kind of popular cinema, and a key part of the genre's attractions has always been its ability to flaunt its assets and speak in a loud voice – in short, to create audience awareness. Public consciousness is achieved through the thrilling assurances held out to the blockbuster's spectator; this movie will excite you, expose you to something never before experienced, it will prick up your ears and make your eyes bulge out in awe. In this sense, the underlying philosophy behind the blockbuster as a distinct category of super movie is given in its most basic form by producer Irwin Allen, who once commented of *The Towering Inferno* (1975): "We were trying to make it as spectacular as we could" (quoted in Paskin 1975: 22).

Clearly, spectacle – herein defined as public display – is a characteristic of all forms of commercial cinema. While it cannot therefore be said to be the sole preserve of blockbusters, the perception that "big" films offer a version of outsize or extraordinary spectacle underlines many attempts to differentiate and so specify the blockbuster experience. Certainly, the promise of ever-increasing levels of audio-visual intemperance lies at the heart of the commercial film industry's ability to rejuvenate itself. To take just one familiar example, James Bond movies are consumed around the world on the basis of their lavish scale. Yet they also sell millions of tickets through the expectation that any new title in the series will go the rest one better – that the latest Bond will outstrip the spectacular achievements of the series' already highly extravagant past. "The Most Fantastic Bond Set Ever!" ran a typical article from the time on *You Only Live Twice* (1967). Director Lewis Gilbert is quoted as saying of SPECTRE's volcano compound that "[it is] . . . the most fantastic, most expensive and most ingenious prop we have ever had to play with," while production designer, Ken Adam, calls it a "nightmare" – the result of "suddenly realising that you have designed something that has never been done before in films, that is bigger than any set ever used before" (quoted in "The Most Fantastic Bond Set Ever!" 1967: 20). Of course, for the competitive advantage of excess size to be retained, subsequent Bond films would then have to top the high-water mark of *You Only Live Twice*'s fantastic bigness.

This constant superseding of hitherto available attractions offers a clue as to why blockbusters can simultaneously fascinate and delight us, yet also make us blasé and detached. On the one hand, they offer the possibility that there really might be

Figure 0.2 The most fantastic Bond set ever . . . until the next one: *You Only Live Twice* (1967). The Kobal Collection/EON/UA.

something new under the sun – something rare, something special. As far back as 1913, for instance, the *Moving Picture Herald* claimed that the "eight-reel photo-drama" *Quo Vadis?* (1913) "gives us a view of Rome, burning, one of the most impressive spectacles ever pictured. Nowhere else could this have been done with equal fidelity . . . Where else could the hiding places of the early Christians have been pictured so realistically?" (McQuade 1913: 64). One year later, *Cabiria* out-distanced even this impressive achievement: "with all due respect to its classic predecessors, I must confess that in the portrayal of the spectacular this film creates new records . . . all these and a hundred other marvels of the spectacular make this feature pre-eminent among the spectacular successes in all the history of spectacles" (Bush 1914: 80–1). Similarly, the *New Republic* wrote in 1915 that "as a spectacle, [*The Birth of a Nation*] is stupendous" (Hackett 1915: 89), while shortly thereafter the *New York Times* reported on one early example of blockbuster business competition:

> *Civilization*, Thomas H. Ince's effort to rival D. W. Griffith with a photo spectacle of the scale and scope of *The Birth of a Nation*, was displayed in New York for the first time last evening at the Criterion Theater. It is an excellently elaborate photo pageant on the physical horrors of war, a big motion picture marked by lavishness in production and beauty in photography.
>
> ("*Civilization*" 1916: 95)

On the other hand, and as the above quotes have begun to suggest, a genealogy of the history of the idea of the blockbuster confirms the suspicion that, when it comes to popular movies, everything has in fact already been done before. *Gladiator* (2000) boasts state-of-the-art special effects, yet it is also clearly modeled on *Ben-Hur* (1959) and *Spartacus* (1960), themselves hugely indebted to the 1925 *Ben Hur*. In addition, the *New Republic*'s jaded response to *Intolerance* in 1916 may strike chords of recognition for some modern audiences reeling from exposure to *Harry Potter and the Philosopher's Stone* (2001), *Lord of the Rings: Fellowship of the Ring* (2001), *Pearl Harbor* (2001), or *Star Wars II: Attack of the Clones* (2002):

> The surprising, the enormous, the daring, the sumptuous, in a terrific melee of attack on the sensations, eject one from the theater with the memory of no human emotion except visual amazement and wonder as to how it was done. The attempt is not to stimulate the imagination, but to gorge the senses. Even this attempt is unsuccessful, because the illusion is not played for honestly; one is astounded at the tricks, the expense, the machinery of production, more often than one is absorbed by their result.
>
> (Soule 1916: 101)

Indeed, a fine line has always separated the public's willingness to be seduced by the values of public showmanship from its impulse to recoil in the face of vulgar exhibitionism. More so than audiences for other genres, blockbuster spectators oscillate as a matter of course between moments of pure delight and moments of rank disappointment. "As a 'thriller'", wrote the *Philadelphia Inquirer* in 1904 about *The Great Train Robbery* (a key movie event of cinema's first decade), "[it is] a source of wonder as to how photographs of such a drama could have been taken in the Rocky Mountains." It continues:

> The men are good riders. In the pursuit by the sheriff one is shot in the back as he dashes madly downhill, and the way in which he tumbles from his horse and strikes the ground leaves the spectators wondering if he is not a dummy, for it does not seem possible that a man could take such a fall and live.
>
> ("*The Great Train Robbery*" 1904: 5)

Reporting on the release of *Earthquake* (1975) seven decades later, *Film Review* also articulated this same sense of dual consciousness: "you see buildings, many of them skyscrapers, keeling over, while highways break-up, shaking the cars off the road-surfaces and over the side. Of course, it's all an illusion but its realism is startling and horrifying" ("*Earthquake*" 1975: 11). Therein lies a point of defence for many who like blockbusters, and a point of dissent for those who do not.

Moving beyond the cultural politics of spectacle, the second important aspect of the blockbuster's extra dimensions or superlative nature is its perceived difference from "mainstream" or "normal" cinema. This is a very difficult subject to approach. If the blockbuster itself has no essential characteristics, how might one go about defining the "non-blockbuster"? What can be said is that every time an event movie is rhetorically differentiated from its Other – "average movies" – further evidence then exists of the relative nature of the "blockbuster" as a classificatory term. Whether articulated by the industry, critics, or audiences, such statements signal that perceptions of *blockbuster-ness* separate movies felt to be exceptional from an imaginary mass of indistinct, unspecified, or otherwise nonspecial titles. The important point to make concerning this situation is that it is precisely through such processes that the blockbuster reveals itself to be a moving target. In such cases, the meaning of the term will once again shift according to who is doing the looking and who is doing the labeling.

In sum, a number of key concepts may broadly be identified as of particular relevance to the idea of the blockbuster: namely, the money/spectacle nexus and, underpinning these two, the size factor and bigness and exceptionality as relational terms. It is the presence of these key concepts, in varying degrees of historically specific combination, that links the essays gathered together in this book.

The existence of these kinds of variables leads to one of the hardest questions for blockbuster studies. How should such films' cultural value (or lack thereof) be assessed? Simply put, the social stature of movie blockbusters is never guaranteed. A title may circulate at one moment as a prestige attraction, and then recirculate the next as a profoundly devalued object (or vice versa). Indeed, many commentators construct oppositions between certain forms of "quality" cinema (e.g. "art cinema") and blockbusters, or between "quality" blockbusters and "average blockbusters." For example, it is sometimes claimed that Hollywood's biggest productions of the 1950s and 1960s deservedly won Academy Awards for best picture (*The Greatest Show on Earth* [1952], *Around the World in Eighty Days* [1956], *The Bridge on the River Kwai* [1957], *Ben-Hur* [1959], *Lawrence of Arabia* [1962], *The Sound of Music*, *Oliver*! [1968]). Conversely, action blockbusters of the 1980s and 1990s are often believed to have been justifiably relegated to less showcase technical categories such as best sound (*The Empire Strikes Back*, 1980), original song (*Top Gun*, 1986), art direction (*Batman*, 1989), and visual effects (*Jurassic Park*, 1993).

In other words, just as being a best-seller does not automatically make a book culturally valuable or culturally worthless, movie blockbusters possess no intrinsic cultural status. Instead, this is something that has to be fought over. When it comes down to the most public kinds of commercial movies, intense struggles take place over questions of taste. One illustration of this can be seen in the description for a series of 70 mm gauge films shown at the National Film Theatre, London, in 1990. In his programme notes for "Bigger than Life: A Glorious Season of 70mm

Spectaculars," Andrew Britton asserts that "in the last ten or fifteen years remarkable advances in the fields of sound and special effects have given rise to a form of 70mm spectacle which is entirely dedicated to engulfing and overwhelming the spectator." Despite this, Britton goes on to claim that many of these films "fulfill [John] Keats' demand for a life of sensations rather than thoughts in a way with which, one feels, he would not have been entirely happy." As a result, Britton concludes by way of apology:

> Most of the films in this season are contemporary Hollywood blockbusters, and it should be pointed out that this emphasis has been determined by serious problems of film availability. When we started planning this season twelve months ago we intended . . . to pay tribute to its major *artistic* achievements: the original film list included, amongst other titles, *Exodus* [1960], *El Cid* [1961], *Cheyenne Autumn* [1964], *Lawrence of Arabia*, *Barabbas* [1961], *55 Days at Peking* [1962].
>
> (Britton 1990: 23; italics in original)

By contrast, the "less worthy" films selected for the actual season include *Aliens* (1986), *Batman*, *The Big Blue* (France, 1988), *Die Hard* (1988), *E.T.: The Extra-Terrestrial* (1982), *Hello, Dolly!* (1969), *Indiana Jones and the Temple of Doom* (1984), *Mad Max Beyond Thunderdome* (1985), and *Who Framed Roger Rabbit?* (1988).

Two instabilities are at work here. First, Britton advances the unsubstantiated, nay frankly illogical belief that blockbusters "then" were good but that blockbusters "now" are bad. Second, that compared to developments of the recent past, contemporary "remarkable advances" in the realms of technology and aesthetics are somehow "not enough." (For a more positive view on technological innovation across Hollywood's history, see the 1992 documentary film *Visions of Light*.) The majority of contributors to this volume explore the movie blockbuster by first bracketing these kinds of easy assumptions regarding questions of cultural value. However, this is an issue which does still need to be addressed. The term "blockbuster" has been used, and will continue to be used, to describe a veritable throng of extremely diverse cinematic products. Even picking on just a few random examples – *The Godfather* (1971), *Home Alone 2: Lost in New York* (1992), *Mary Poppins* (1964), *The Matrix* (1999) – how can any singular sense of cultural value possibly claim to incorporate all such films? Alternatively, on what basis may discriminations between such titles usefully be drawn?

The making of cultural distinctions based upon perceptions (negative and positive) of Hollywood's power and influence has proved especially important to overseas responses to the American blockbuster. More significantly, they have also been crucial to the production by non-US film industries of "local" blockbusters. Some English-language scholars continue to believe that as an idea and practice the movie blockbuster is unique to Hollywood. However, such views blow on an increasingly ill wind. One result of globalization is the revelation that filmmakers, critics, and audiences the world over are actively reconstructing the blockbuster as a generic category. Maybe they always did? China and India, for example, are two of the most populous nations on earth, and both possess large-scale and well-established commercial movie industries. Armed with such knowledge, it is difficult to imagine how anyone could seriously insist that domestic megahits such as *Big Shot's Funeral* (China/US, 2002), *The Burning of the Imperial Palace* (China/Hong Kong, 1983), *Live or Die* (China, 2000), *Mother India* (India, 1957), *Raja Hindustani* (India, 1996), and *Sangam* (India, 1964) could not and should not be conceptualized through the discourse of the blockbuster.

Moreover, it is perhaps time fully to acknowledge that the Hollywood blockbuster itself is very frequently a transnational product. In his exemplary work on *Lawrence of Arabia*, Steven C. Caton argues that the creation by international casts and crews of popular epics in the 1950s and 1960s reveals the Hollywood blockbuster to be an "allegory of anthropology" (Caton 1999: 142–71). The very production and narrative concerns of *Around the World in Eighty Days*, *Bridge on the River Kwai*, *Khartoum* (1966), and others, prioritize issues of cross-cultural contact and understanding. Similarly, the recurring fetishization of "exotic" overseas locations in many contemporary box-office hits, as well as the projection of anthropological themes in action-adventure titles such as *Raiders of the Lost Ark* (1981) and *The Mummy* (1999), both suggest that the Hollywood blockbuster continues to enjoy close and ongoing relations with the global culture that spawns and sustains it.

To conclude, it should be clear by now that anyone scouring these pages in search of a simple definition of the term "blockbuster" is going to be disappointed. (The entry provided by *The Oxford English Dictionary* – "thing of great power" – is hideously vague, albeit suggestively so.) Because the blockbuster has no essential characteristics, it can never be defined. However, within the purview of an expanded, yet always precisely focused angle of vision – one that acknowledges the need to consider the diversity of rhetorical claims made by real speakers for specific purposes in particular situations – the following general pronouncement can still be made: some movies are born blockbusters; some achieve blockbuster status; some have blockbuster status thrust upon them.

The essays in *Movie Blockbusters* are concerned to explore this particular genre by investigating the differences within and between these three critical positions. Acknowledging the public nature of blockbuster culture – in other words, the sense that we all know something about the subject matter at hand – the contributors have sought as much as possible to minimize their use of specialized academic jargon. When discussing blockbuster movies, the results of empirically verifiable research should be made accessible to all, and not just a small coterie of university-based "eggheads."

The book opens with a reprint of Thomas Schatz's 1993 essay "The New Hollywood," an authoritative and influential overview of the development of the blockbuster syndrome in the post-World War II US movie industry. Schatz's work has been widely cited and used in film studies, and "The New Hollywood" acts as an explicit point of reference for many of the other contributors to this volume.

Pursuing Schatz's emphasis on the need to be aware of the structural conditions that enable the systematic production and circulation of blockbusters, the first section of the book, "Industry Matters," considers various aspects of the political economy of Hollywood. In an essay which explicitly challenges Schatz's sense of periodization, Steve Neale provides a comprehensive historical re-evaluation of Hollywood's blockbuster traditions. Next, Jon Lewis engages the genre's association with excess wealth by offering a cautionary tale on the increased centrality to blockbuster culture of sophisticated forms of marketing "spin." Such concerns also animate Douglas Gomery's chapter, wherein contemporary Hollywood's distribution and marketing strategies are laid out in detail. Finally, Warren Buckland investigates the role of the auteur at the start of the twenty-first century by offering a case study of the activities of director Steven Spielberg and his DreamWorks studio.

The second section, "Exploring Spectacle," presents numerous points of view on one of the key terms animating discussion of the genre. In his opening chapter, Michael Allen examines how the blockbuster has been used by the industry to introduce new technological developments, such as sound, widescreen, and digital special effects. Geoff King then surveys the perceived relations between spectacle and narrative by examining a range of blockbusters from old and New Hollywood alike. Two essays on films of the 1990s round the section off. Peter Krämer analyses the ways in which the Jodie Foster star vehicle *Contact* (1997) provides an emotional and intellectual meditation on the blockbuster experience itself, while Gianluca Sergi tackles the underresearched question of aural spectacle. Focusing on the production of one extremely successful action movie, *The Fugitive* (1994), Sergi exposes the working practices of contemporary Hollywood by drawing on interviews with the sound designers involved in the film's actual creation.

The third section, "Establishing Cultural Status," takes a more discursive approach to the subject by unearthing the diversity of ways in which a sense of cultural value circulates around blockbusters. In their analysis of the construction of distinct taste formations, the contributors consider issues of critical and cultural reception, the activities of fans and other audiences, and some of the specific exhibition contexts within which blockbusting movies are consumed. Gillian Roberts opens this section with a discussion of *Titanic*'s relationship to the institution of the Academy Awards. Rebecca Feasey then reports on how two erotic-themed "controversial blockbusters" were written about by various sectors of the press; and Matt Hills explores *Star Wars*'s contradictory status as a so-called cult blockbuster. After that, Mark Jancovich and Lucy Faire provide discussion of the connotations that surround the multiplex cinema, while Julian Stringer examines the ambivalent place reserved for different kinds of blockbusters at some international film festivals.

The fourth section, "The Blockbuster in the International Frame," takes many of the fundamental concerns of the book into wholly new scholarly territory. Each of these essays perceives the genre as both global and culturally and nationally specific. Chris Berry argues for the blockbuster's de-Westernization by charting recent filmmaking and critical activity in both Korea and China. Kirsten Moana Thompson discusses *Once Were Warriors* (1994) as New Zealand's first bona fide event movie. Tamara L. Falicov then dissects the production and reception circumstances of the Argentinian megahit *Comodines* (1997). Finally, Andrew Willis closes the volume with a timely analysis of recent shifts in the global fortunes of the Hindi (or "Bollywood") blockbuster.

Historical events more than keep pace with critical thinking, and, just as this book argues the need to re-evaluate current perspectives on this most neglected of film genres, it is important that scholars also respond to contemporary developments in blockbuster culture. In the months during which final editorial work on this book was being completed, various events testified to the continuing currency of the blockbuster as an idea in both the US and elsewhere. On the one hand, each of these events passed itself off as new – each felt super and distinct and spectacular, and worked to supersede the high-water marks achieved by previous events. On the other hand, each also showed that, *vis-à-vis* blockbusters – and however much we might wish it otherwise – there really is nothing new under the sun.

Such thoughts might have come to readers as they considered the inevitable hype surrounding the much-anticipated opening weekend releases of *Men in Black 2*, *Lord of the Rings 2*, *Spider Man*, and *Star Wars II: Attack of the Clones* (all 2002). (Box-office figures do not tell the whole story though. A report produced by the Chicago-based outplacement firm Challenger, Gray, and Christmas estimated that the May 16, 2002, release date of *Star Wars II: Attack of the Clones* could cost the US economy more than $319 million in lost wages, as around 2.6 million workers were forecast to skip out for the day to catch its big city premieres.) Most startlingly, the spectacular destruction on live television of the World Trade Center, New York, on September 11, 2001, generated previously unimagined associations around Hollywood blockbusters. In the days and weeks following the attack, as millions of people throughout the world sought to make sense of the traumatic events they had witnessed as if "watching a movie," innumerable comparisons were made to films such as *The Towering Inferno*, the *Die Hard* series, *Godzilla* (1998), *Independence Day* (1996), *The Siege* (1998), and *True Lies* (1994). (It is worth mentioning, too, that international terrorism had figured prominently in big-budget and high-profile examples of non-US blockbuster cinema of the 1990s, such as *Shiri* [South Korea, 1999], *Gen-X Cops* [Hong Kong, 1999], and *Purple Storm* [Hong Kong, 1999].)

As what has become known as 9/11, and other events, so graphically demonstrate, movie blockbusters continue to do what they have always done – namely, occupy a central part of our mental landscape. In the current cultural climate, they simply cannot be avoided. Indeed, it is the blockbuster's heightened public presence that perhaps best accounts for why to date so little sustained scholarly attention has been paid to them. Because "event movies" seem always to be *there*, in the public eye, we have thought about them less than we should. The essays in this volume aim to challenge the easy assumptions that too often plague discussion of these most noticeable, yet taken-for-granted, examples of popular culture. They stand as a point of departure for the future work that will hopefully engage further with the movie blockbuster's varied shapes and sizes.

References

Altman, Rick (1999) *Film/Genre*, London: British Film Institute.

Bazin, André (1971) "The Evolution of the Western," in *What is Cinema?*, vol. 2, ed. and trans. Hugh Gray, Berkeley: University of California Press: 149–57.

Britton, Andrew (1990) "Bigger than Life: A Glorious Season of 70mm Spectaculars," National Film Theatre, London: 22–7 [programme booklet].

Bush, Stephen W. (1914) "*Cabiria*," *Moving Picture World*, May 23 [reprinted in Kauffman with Henstell 1972: 80–2].

Caton, Steven C. (1999) *Lawrence of Arabia: A Film's Anthropology*, Berkeley: University of California Press.

"*Civilization*" (1916), *New York Times*, June 3 [reprinted in Kauffman with Henstell 1972: 95–6].

"*Earthquake*" (1975), *Film Review*, 25, 4: 10–11.

"*The Great Train Robbery*" (1904), *Philadelphia Inquirer*, June 26 [reprinted in Kauffman with Henstell 1972: 5].

Hackett, Francis (1915) "*The Birth of a Nation*," *New Republic*, March 20 [reprinted in Kauffman with Henstell 1972: 89–92].

Hoellering, Franz (1939) "*Gone with the Wind*," *The Nation*, December 30 [reprinted in Kauffman with Henstell 1972: 370–1].

Houston, Penelope, and Gillett, John (1963) "The Theory and Practice of Blockbusting," *Sight and Sound*, 32, 2: 68–74.

Kauffmann, Stanley with Henstell, Bruce (eds) (1972) *American Film Criticism: From the Beginnings to Citizen Kane: Reviews of Significant Films at the Time They First Appeared*, New York: Liveright.

Kinder, Marsha (1991) *Playing with Power in Movies, Television and Video Games: From Muppet Babies to Teenage Mutant Ninja Turtles*, Berkeley: University of California Press.

Martin, Quinn (1926) "*The Black Pirate*," *The Arts*, April [reprinted in Kauffman with Henstell 1972: 172–4].

Marx, Patricia, and McGrath, Douglas G. (1988) *Blockbuster*, New York: Bantam Books.

McQuade, James S. (1913) "*Quo Vadis?*," *Motion Picture World*, May 17 [reprinted in Kauffman with Henstell 1972: 64–6].

"The Most Fantastic Bond Set Ever!" (1967) *Photoplay*, 18, 3: 20–1.

Naremore, James (1998) *More Than Night: Film Noir in its Contexts*, Berkeley: University of California Press.

Paskin, Barbra (1975) "The Terrifying Message of *Towering Inferno*," *Film Review*, 25, 7: 22–3.

Sherwood, Robert E. (1926) "*Ben Hur*", *Life*, January 26 [reprinted in Kauffmann with Henstell 1972: 170].

Soule, George (1916) "*Intolerance*," *New Republic*, September 30 [reprinted in Kauffman with Henstell 1972: 99–101].

Tanitch, Robert (2000) *Blockbusters!: 70 Years of Best-Selling Movies*, London: B. T. Batsford.

THE NEW HOLLYWOOD

Thomas Schatz

Reprinted from Jim Collins, Hilary Radner, and Ava Preacher Collins (eds), *Film Theory Goes to the Movies* (New York and London: Routledge, 1993): 8–36. Reproduced by permission of Routledge, Inc., part of the Taylor & Francis Group.

Among the more curious and confounding terms in media studies is "the New Hollywood." In its broadest historical sense the term applies to the American cinema after World War II, when Hollywood's entrenched "studio system" collapsed and commercial television began to sweep the newly suburbanized national landscape. That marked the end of Hollywood's "classical" era of the 1920s, 1930s, and early 1940s, when movies were mass produced by a cartel of studios for a virtually guaranteed market. All that changed in the postwar decade, as motion pictures came to be produced and sold on a film-by-film basis and as "watching TV" rapidly replaced "going to the movies" as America's preferred ritual of habituated, mass-mediated narrative entertainment.[1]

Ensuing pronouncements of the "death of Hollywood" proved to be greatly exaggerated, however; the industry not only survived but flourished in a changing media marketplace. Among the more remarkable developments in recent media history, in fact, is the staying power of the major studios (Paramount, MGM, Warners, *et al.*) and of the movie itself – that is, the theatrically released feature film – in an increasingly vast and complex "entertainment industry." This is no small feat, considering the changes Hollywood has faced since the late 1940s. The industry adjusted to those changes, and in the process its ways of doing business and of making movies changed as well – and thus the difficulty in defining the New Hollywood, which has meant something different from one period of adjustment to another.

The key to Hollywood's survival and the one abiding aspect of its postwar transformation has been the steady rise of the movie blockbuster. In terms of budgets, production values, and market strategy, Hollywood has been increasingly hit-driven since the early 1950s. This marks a significant departure from the classical era, when the studios turned out a few "prestige" pictures each year and relished the occasional runaway box-office hit, but relied primarily on routine A-class features to generate revenues. The exceptional became the rule in postwar Hollywood, as the occasional hit gave way to the calculated blockbuster.

The most obvious measure of this blockbuster syndrome is box-office revenues, which have indeed surged over the past forty years.[2] In 1983, *Variety* commissioned a study of the industry's all-time commercial hits in "constant dollars" – that is, in figures adjusted for inflation – which placed only two films made before 1950, *Gone with the Wind* (1939) and *Snow White and the Seven Dwarfs* (1937), in the top 75.[3] In other words, of the 7,000 or so Hollywood features released before 1950, only two enjoyed the kind of success that has become routine since then – and particularly in the past two decades. According to *Variety*'s January, 1992, update of the all-time "film rental champs," 90 of the top 100 hits had been produced since 1970, and all of the top 20 since *Jaws* in 1975.[4]

The blockbuster syndrome went into high gear in the mid-1970s, despite (and in some ways because of) the concurrent emergence of competing media technologies and new delivery systems, notably pay-cable TV and home video (VCRs). This was the first period of sustained economic vitality and industry stability since the classical era. Thus this post-1975 era best warrants the term "the New Hollywood," and for essentially the same reasons associated with the "classical" era. Both terms connote not only specific historical periods, but also characteristic qualities of the movie industry at the time – particularly its economic and institutional structure, its mode of production, and its system of narrative conventions.

This is not to say that the New Hollywood is as stable or well integrated as the classical Hollywood, however. As we will see, the government's postwar dismantling of the "vertically integrated" studio system ensured a more competitive movie marketplace, and a more fundamentally disintegrated industry as well. The marketplace became even more fragmented and uncertain with the emergence of TV and other media industries, and with the massive changes in lifestyle accompanying suburban migration and the related family/housing/baby boom. In one sense the mid-1970s ascent of the New Hollywood marks the studios' eventual coming to terms with an increasingly fragmented entertainment industry – with its demographics and target audiences, its diversified "multimedia" conglomerates, its global(ized) markets and new delivery systems. And equally fragmented, perhaps, are the movies themselves, especially the high-cost, high-tech, high-stakes blockbusters, those multipurpose entertainment machines that breed music videos and soundtrack albums, TV series and videocassettes, video games and theme park rides, novelizations and comic books.

Hollywood's mid-1970s restabilization came after some thirty years of uncertainty and disarray. I would suggest, in fact, that the movie industry underwent three fairly distinct decade-long phases after the war – from 1946 to 1955, from 1956 to 1965, and from 1966 to 1975. These phases were distinguished by various developments both inside and outside the industry, and four in particular: the shift to independent motion picture production, the changing role of the studios, the emergence of commercial TV, and changes in American lifestyle and patterns of media consumption. The key markers in these phases were huge hits such as *The Ten Commandments* in 1956, *The Sound of Music* in 1965, and *Jaws* in 1975, which redefined the nature, scope, and profit potential of the blockbuster movie, and which laid the foundation for the films and filmmaking practices of the New Hollywood.

To understand the New Hollywood, we need to chart these postwar phases and the concurrent emergence of the blockbuster syndrome in American filmmaking. Our ultimate focus, though, will be on the post-1975 New Hollywood and its complex interplay of economic, aesthetic, and technological forces. If recent studies of classical Hollywood have taught us anything, it is that we cannot consider either the filmmaking process or films themselves in isolation from their economic, technological, and industrial context. As we will see, this interplay of forces is in many ways even more complex in the New Hollywood, especially when blockbusters are involved. In today's media marketplace, it has become virtually impossible to identify or isolate the "text" itself, or to distinguish a film's aesthetic or narrative quality from its commercial imperatives. As Eileen Meehan suggests in a perceptive study of *Batman*, to analyze contemporary movies "we must be able to understand them as always and simultaneously text and commodity, intertext and product line."[5]

The goal of this essay is to situate that "understanding" historically, tracing the emergence and the complex workings of the New Hollywood. The emphasis throughout will be on the high-cost, high-tech, high-stakes productions that have driven the postwar movie industry – and that now drive the global multimedia marketplace at large. While one crucial dimension of the New Hollywood is the "space" that has been opened for independent and alternative cinema, the fact is that these mainstream hits are where stars, genres, and cinematic innovations invariably are established, where the "grammar" of cinema is most likely to be refined, and where the essential qualities of the medium – its popular and commercial character – are most evident. These blockbuster hits are, for better or worse, what the New Hollywood is about, and thus are the necessary starting point for any analysis of contemporary American cinema.

Hollywood in transition

The year 1946 marked the culmination of a five-year "war boom" for Hollywood, with record revenues of over $1.5 billion and weekly ticket sales of 90 to 100 million.[6] The two biggest hits in 1946 were "major independent" productions: Sam Goldwyn's *The Best Years of Our Lives* and David O. Selznick's *Duel in the Sun*. Both returned $11.3 million in rentals, a huge sum at the time, and signaled important changes in the industry – though Selznick's *Duel* was the more telling of the two.[7] Like his *Gone with the Wind*, it was a prototype New Hollywood blockbuster: a "pre-sold" spectacle (based on a popular historical novel) with top stars, an excessive budget, a sprawling story, and state-of-the-art production values. Selznick himself termed *Duel* "an exercise in making a big-grossing film," gambling on a nationwide promotion-and-release campaign after weak sneak previews.[8] When the gamble paid off, he proclaimed it a "tremendous milestone in motion picture merchandising and exhibition."[9]

That proved to be prophetic, given Hollywood's wholesale postwar transformation, which was actually well under way in 1946. The Justice Department's pursuit of Hollywood's major powers for antitrust practices began to show results in the courts that year, and culminated in the Supreme Court's May 1948 *Paramount* decree, which forced the major studios to divest their theater chains and to cease various tactics which had enabled them to control the market. Without the cash flow from their theaters and a guaranteed outlet for their product, the established studio system was effectively finished. The studios gradually fired their contract personnel and phased out active production, and began leasing their facilities for independent projects, generally providing re-financing and distribution as well. This shift to "one-film deals" also affected the established relations of power, with top talent (and their agents and attorneys) gaining more authority over production.[10]

The studios' new role as financing-and-distribution entities also jibed with other industry developments. The war boom had ended rather suddenly in 1947 as the economy slumped and, more importantly, as millions of couples married, settled down, and started families – many of them moving to the suburbs and away from urban centers, where movie business thrived. Declining attendance at home was complemented by a decline in international trade in 1947–8, notably in the newly reopened European markets, where "protectionist" policies were initiated to foster domestic production and to restrict the revenues that could be taken out of the country. This encouraged the studios to enter into co-financing and co-production deals overseas, which complemented the changing strategy at home and fueled the general postwar rise in motion picture imports as well as independent production.

Another crucial factor on the domestic front was, of course, television. Early on, the major studios had met the competition head on with efforts to differentiate movies from TV programs. There was a marked increase in historical spectacles, westerns, and biblical epics, invariably designed for a global market and shot on location with international casts. These were enhanced by the increased use of Technicolor and by innovations in technology, notably widescreen formats and 3-D. These efforts soon began paying off despite TV's continued growth, as *Fortune's* Freeman Lincoln pointed out in a 1955 piece aptly titled "The Comeback of the Movies." Lincoln noted that, traditionally, "any picture that topped $5 million worldwide was a smash hit," and he estimated that only about 100 Hollywood releases had ever reached that total. "In September, 1953, 20th Century-Fox released *The Robe*, which has since grossed better than $20 million around the world and is expected to surpass $30 million," wrote Lincoln, and pointed out that "in the 17 months since *The Robe* was turned loose nearly 30 pictures have grossed more than the previously magic $5 million."[11]

As Hollywood's blockbuster mentality took hold in 1955, the majors finally ventured into television. MGM, Warners, and Fox, taking a cue from Disney and the lesser Hollywood powers already involved in "telefilm" series production, began producing filmed series of their own in the fall of 1955.[12] And late that year the majors also began to sell or lease their pre-1948 features to TV syndicators. In 1956 alone, some 3,000 feature films went into syndication; by 1958, all of the majors had unloaded hundreds of pre-1948 films.[13] In 1960, the studios and talent guilds agreed on residual payments for post-1948 films, leading to another wave of movie syndication and to Hollywood movies being scheduled in regular prime time. Telefilm production was also on the rise in the late 1950s, as the studios relied increasingly on TV series to keep their facilities in constant operation, since more and more feature films were shot on location. The studios also had begun realizing sizable profits from the syndication of hit TV series, both as reruns in the US and as first-run series abroad. As the studios upgraded series production and as the preferred programming format shifted from live video to telefilm – despite the introduction of videotape in 1957 – the networks steadily shifted their production operations from New York to Los Angeles. By 1960 virtually all prime-time fictional series were produced on film in Hollywood, with the traditional studio powers dominating this trend.

Meanwhile the blockbuster mentality intensified. Lincoln had suggested in his 1955 *Fortune* piece, "The beauty of the big picture nowadays is, of course, that there seems to be no limit to what the box office return may be."[14] The ensuing decade bore this out with a vengeance, bracketed by two colossal hits: *The Ten Commandments* in 1956, with domestic rentals of $43 million (versus *The Robe's* $17.5 million), and *The Sound of Music* in 1965, with rentals of $79.9 million. Other top hits from the decade included similarly "big" all-star projects, most of them shot on location for an international market:

Around the World in 80 Days (1956; $23 million in rentals)
The Bridge on the River Kwai (1957; $17.2 million)
South Pacific (1958; $17.5 million)
Ben-Hur (1959; $36.5 million)
Lawrence of Arabia (1962; $17.7 million)
The Longest Day (1962; $17.6 million)
Cleopatra (1963; $26 million)

Figure 0.3 The Ten Commandments (1956): the parting of the Red Sea. The Kobal Collection/Paramount.

Goldfinger (1964; $23 million)
Thunderball (1965; $28.5 million)
Dr. Zhivago (1965; $46.5 million).

While these megahits dominated the high end of Hollywood's output, the studios looked for ways beyond TV series production to diversify their media interests. Besides the need to hedge their bets on high-stakes blockbusters, this impulse to diversify was a response to the postwar boom in entertainment and leisure activities, the increasing segmentation of media audiences in a period of general prosperity and population growth, and the sophisticated new advertising and marketing strategies used to measure and attract those audiences. MCA was the clear industry leader in terms of diversification, having expanded from a music booking and talent agency in the 1930s and 1940s into telefilm production and syndication in the 1950s, eventually buying Decca Records and then Universal Pictures in the early 1960s.

The 1950s and 1960s also saw diversified, segmented moviegoing trends, most of them keyed to the immense, emergent "youth market." With the baby-boom generation reaching active consumer status and developing distinctive interests and tastes, there was a marked surge in drive-in moviegoing, itself a phenomenon directly associated with postwar suburbanization and the family boom. With the emergent youth market, drive-in viewing fare turned increasingly to low-budget "teenpics" and "exploitation" films. The "art cinema" and foreign film movements also took off in the late 1950s and early 1960s, as neighborhood movie houses and campus film societies screened alternatives to mainstream Hollywood and as film courses began springing up on college campuses. These indicated a more "cine-literate" generation – with that literacy actually enhanced by TV, which had become a veritable archive of American film history.

While the exploitation and art cinema movements produced a few commercial hits – Hitchcock's *Psycho* and Fellini's *La Dolce Vita* in 1960, for instance – the box office was dominated well into the 1960s by much the same blockbuster mentality as in previous decades. Indeed, the biopics, historical and biblical epics, literary adaptations, and transplanted stage musicals of the 1950s and 1960s differed from the prestige pictures of the classical era only in their oversized budgets, casts, running times, and screen width. If the emergent youth culture and increasingly diversified media marketplace were danger signs, they were lost on the studios – particularly after the huge commercial success of two very traditional mainstream films in 1965, *The Sound of Music* and *Dr Zhivago*.

Actually, Hollywood was on the verge of its worst economic slump since the war – fueled to a degree by those two 1965 hits, because they led to a cycle of expensive, heavily promoted commercial flops. Fox, for instance, went on a blockbuster musical binge in an effort to replicate its success with *The Sound of Music*, and the results were disastrous: losses of $11 million on *Dr Dolittle* in 1967, $15 million on *Star!* in 1968, and $16 million in 1969 on *Hello Dolly*, at the time the most expensive film ever made.[15] Fox then tightened its belt, avoiding bankruptcy thanks to two relatively inexpensive, offbeat films: *Butch Cassidy and the Sundance Kid* (1969; $46 million in rentals) and *MASH* (1970; $36.7 million).

Those two hits were significant for a number of reasons besides the reversal of Fox's fortunes, reasons which signaled changes of aesthetic as well as economic direction in late-1960s Hollywood. With the blockbuster strategy stalled, the industry saw a period of widespread and unprecedented innovation, due largely to a new "generation" of Hollywood filmmakers such as Robert Altman, Arthur Penn, Mike Nichols, and Bob Rafelson, who were turning out films that had as much in common with the European art cinema as with classical Hollywood. There was also a growing contingent of international auteurs – Bergman, Fellini, Truffaut, Bertolucci, Polanski, Kubrick – who, in the wake of the 1966 success of Antonioni's *Blow-Up* and Claude Lelouch's *A Man and a Woman*, developed a quasi-independent rapport with Hollywood, making films for a Euro-American market and bringing art cinema into the mainstream.

Thus an "American film renaissance" of sorts was induced by a succession of big-budget flops and successful imports. Its key constituency was the American youth, by now the most dependable segment of regular moviegoers as attendance continued to fall despite the overall increase in population. Younger viewers contributed heavily to the success of sizable hits such as *Bonnie and Clyde* (1967; rentals of $22.8 million), *2001: A Space Odyssey* (1968; $25.5 million), and *The Graduate* (1968; $43 million), and they were almost solely responsible for modest hits such as *Easy Rider* (1969; $19 million) and *Woodstock* (1970; $16.4 million). As these films suggest, the older baby boomers were reaching critical mass as a target market and were something of a countercultural force as well, caught up in the antiwar movement, civil rights, the sexual revolution, and so on. And with the 1966 breakdown of Hollywood's Production Code and the emergence in 1968 of the new ratings system – itself a further indication of the segmented movie audiences – filmmakers were experimenting with more politically subversive, sexually explicit, and/or graphically violent material.

As one might suspect, Hollywood's cultivation of the youth market and penchant for innovation in the late 1960s and early 1970s scarcely indicated a favorable market climate. On the contrary, they reflected the studios' uncertainty and growing desperation. Film historian Tino Balio has written about "the Recession of 1969" and its aftermath, when "Hollywood nearly collapsed."[16] *Variety* at the time pegged combined industry losses for 1969–71 at $600 million, and, according to an economic study by Joseph Dominick, studio profits fell from an average of $64 million in the five-year span from 1964 to 1968, to $13 million from 1969 to 1973.[17] Market conditions rendered the studios ripe for takeover, and in fact a number of the studios were absorbed in a post-1965 conglomerate wave. Paramount was taken over by Gulf & Western in 1966, United Artists by Transamerica in 1967, and Warner Bros. by Kinney National Services in 1969, the same year MGM was bought out by real-estate tycoon Kirk Kerkorian. This trend proved to be a mixed blessing for the studios. The cash-rich parent company relieved much of the financial pressures and spurred diversification, but the new owners knew little about the movie business and, as the market worsened, tended to view their Hollywood subsidiaries as troublesome tax write-offs.

One bright spot during this period was the surge in network prices paid for hit movies. Back in 1961, NBC had paid Fox an average of $180,000 for each feature shown on *Saturday Night at the Movies*; that year forty-five features were broadcast in prime time. By 1970, the average price tag per feature was up to $800,000, with the networks spending $65 million on a total of 166 feature films. That total jumped to 227 for the 1971–2 season, when movies comprised over one-quarter of all prime-time programming. The average price went up as well, due largely to ABC's paying $50 million in the summer of 1971 for a package of blockbusters, including $5 million for *Lawrence of Arabia*, $3 million for the 1970 hit *Love Story*, and $2.5 million each for seven James Bond films.[18] Significantly enough, however, these big payoffs were going only to top Hollywood hits as all three networks began producing their own TV movies. Hollywood features comprised only half of the movies shown on network TV in the 1971–2 season, and that percentage declined further in subsequent years, as made-for-TV movie production increased.

The network payoff for top movie hits scarcely reversed the late-sixties downturn, as *The Graduate* in 1968 was the only release between 1965 and 1969 to surpass even $30 million in rentals. *Butch Cassidy*, *Airport*, and *Love Story* in 1969–70 all earned $45 to $50 million, carrying much of the freight in those otherwise bleak economic years. *Airport* was especially important in that it generated a cycle of successful "disaster pictures" such as *The Poseidon Adventure*, *The Towering Inferno*, and *Earthquake*, all solid performers in the $40 to $50 million range, though they were fairly expensive to produce and not quite the breakaway hits that the industry so desperately needed.

The first real sign of a reversal of the industry's sagging fortunes came with *The Godfather*, a 1972 Paramount release that returned over $86 million. *The Godfather* was that rarest of movies, a critical and commercial smash with widespread appeal, drawing art cinema connoisseurs and disaffected youth as well as mainstream moviegoers. Adapted from Mario Puzo's novel while it was still in galleys, the project was scarcely mounted as a surefire hit. Director Francis Ford Coppola was a debt-ridden film school product with far more success as a writer, and star Marlon Brando hadn't had a hit in over a decade. The huge sales of the novel, published while the film was in production, generated interest, as did well-publicized stories of problems on the set, cost overruns, and protests from Italian-American groups. By the time of its release, *The Godfather* had attained "event" status, and audiences responded to Coppola's stylish and highly stylized hybrid of the gangster genre and family melodrama. Like so many 1970s films, *The Godfather* had a strong nostalgic quality, invoking the male ethos and patriarchal order of a bygone era – and putting its three male co-stars, Al Pacino, James Caan, and Robert Duvall, on the industry map.

The Godfather also did well in the international market, thus spurring an upturn in the overseas as well as the domestic market. Domestic theater admissions in 1972 were up roughly 20 percent over 1971, reversing a seven-year slide, and total box-office revenues surged from the $1 billion range, where they had stagnated for several years, to $1.64 billion. While *The Godfather* alone accounted for nearly 10 percent of those gross proceeds, other films clearly were contributing; revenues for the top ten box-office hits of 1972 were up nearly 70 percent over the previous year. That momentum held through 1973 and then the market surged again in 1974, nearing the $2 billion mark – and thus finally surpassing Hollywood's postwar box-office peak. Key to the upturn were the now predictable spate of disaster films, though these were far outdistanced by three hits which, in different ways, were sure signs of a changing industry.

One was *American Graffiti*, a surprise summer 1973 hit written and directed by

Coppola protégé George Lucas. A coming-of-age film with strong commercial tie-ins to both TV and rock music, its story's 1962 setting enabled Lucas to circumvent (or rather to predate) the current sociopolitical climate and broadened its appeal to older viewers. Two even bigger hits were late 1973 releases, *The Sting* and *The Exorcist* ($78 million and $86 million, respectively). *The Sting* was yet another nostalgia piece, a 1930s-era gangster/buddy/caper hybrid, reprising the Newman–Redford pairing of five years earlier – something like "Butch and Sundance meet the Godfather." The nostalgia and studied innocence of both *The Sting* and *American Graffiti* were hardly evident in *The Exorcist*, William Friedkin's kinetic, gut-wrenching, effects-laden exercise in screen violence and horror. While *Psycho* and *Rosemary's Baby* had proved that horror thrillers could attain hit status, *The Exorcist* pushed the logic and limits of the genre (and the viewer's capacity for masochistic pleasure) to new extremes, resulting in a truly monstrous hit and perhaps the clearest indication of the emergent New Hollywood.

Jaws and the New Hollywood

If any single film marked the arrival of the New Hollywood, it was *Jaws*, the Spielberg-directed thriller that recalibrated the profit potential of the Hollywood hit, and redefined its status as a marketable commodity and cultural phenomenon as well. The film brought an emphatic end to Hollywood's five-year recession, while ushering in an era of high-cost, high-tech, high-speed thrillers. The release of *Jaws* also happened to coincide with developments both inside and outside the movie industry in the mid-1970s which, while having little or nothing to do with that particular film, were equally important to the emergent New Hollywood.

Jaws, like *Love Story*, *The Godfather*, *The Exorcist*, and several other recent hits, was presold via a current best-selling novel. And, like *The Godfather*, movie rights to the novel were purchased before it was published, and publicity from the deal and from the subsequent production helped spur the initial book sales – of a reported 7.6 million copies before the film's release in this case – which in turn fueled public interest in the film.[19] The *Jaws* deal was packaged by International Creative Management (ICM), which represented author Peter Benchley and handled the sale of the movie rights. ICM also represented the producing team of Richard Zanuck and David Brown, whose recent hits included *Butch Cassidy* and *The Sting*, and who worked with ICM to put together the movie project with MCA/Universal and *wunderkind* director Steven Spielberg.[20]

Initially budgeted at $3.5 million, *Jaws* was expensive by contemporary standards (average production costs in 1975 were $2.5 million), but it was scarcely a big-ticket project in that age of $10 million musicals and $20 million disaster epics.[21] The budget did steadily escalate due to logistical problems and Spielberg's ever-expanding vision and confidence; in fact problems with the mechanical shark pushed the effects budget alone to over $3 million. The producers managed to parlay those problems into positive publicity, however, and continued to hype the film during post-production. The movie was planned for a summer 1975 release due to its subject matter, even though in those years most calculated hits were released during the Christmas holidays. Zanuck and Brown compensated by spending $2.5 million on promotion, much of it invested in a media blitz during the week before the film's 464-screen opening.[22]

The print campaign featured a poster depicting a huge shark rising through the water toward an unsuspecting swimmer, while the radio and TV ads exploited John Williams's now-famous "Jaws theme." The provocative poster art and Williams's pulsating, foreboding theme conveyed the essence of the film experience and worked their way into the national consciousness, setting new standards for motion picture promotion. With the public's appetite sufficiently whetted, the release of *Jaws* set off a feeding frenzy as 25 million tickets were sold in the film's first 38 days of public viewing. After this quick start, the shark proved to have "good legs" at the box office, running strong throughout the summer en route to a record $102.5 million in rentals in 1975. In the process, *Jaws* became a veritable sub-industry unto itself via commercial tie-ins and merchandising ploys. But hype and promotion aside, the success of *Jaws* ultimately centered on the appeal of the film itself; one enduring verity in the movie business is that, whatever the marketing efforts, only positive audience response and favorable word of mouth can propel a film to genuine hit status.

Jaws was essentially an action film and a thriller, of course, though it effectively melded various genres and story types. It tapped into the monster movie tradition with a revenge-of-nature subtext (like *King Kong*, *The Birds*, *et al.*), and in the film's latter stages the shark begins to take on supernatural, even Satanic, qualities à la *Rosemary's Baby* and *The Exorcist*. And, given the fact that the initial victims are women and children, *Jaws* also had ties to the high-gore "slasher" film, which had been given considerable impetus a year earlier by *The Texas Chainsaw Massacre*. The seagoing chase in the latter half is also a buddy film and a male initiation story, with Brodie the cop, Hooper the scientist, and Quint the sea captain providing different strategies for dealing with the shark and different takes on male heroic behavior.

Technically, *Jaws* is an adept "chase film" that takes the viewer on an emotional roller coaster, first in awaiting the subsequent (and increasingly graphic) shark attacks, then in the actual pursuit of the shark. The narrative is precise and effectively paced, with each stage building to a climactic peak, then dissipating, then building again until the explosive finale. The performances, camera work, and editing are all crucial to this effect, as is John Williams's score. This was in fact the breakthrough film for Williams, the first in a run of huge hits that he scored (including *Star Wars*, *Close Encounters of the Third Kind*, *Raiders of the Lost Ark*, and *E.T.*) whose music is absolutely essential to the emotional impact of the film.

Many critics disparaged that impact, dismissing *Jaws* as an utterly mechanical (if technically flawless) exercise in viewer manipulation. James Monaco cites *Jaws* itself as the basis for the "Bruce aesthetic" (named after the film crew's pet name for the marauding robotic shark), whose ultimate cinematic effect is "visceral – mechanical rather than human." More exciting than interesting, more style than substance, *Jaws* and its myriad offspring, argues Monaco, are mere "machines of entertainment, precisely calculated to achieve their effect."[23] Others have argued, however, that *Jaws* is redeemed by several factors, notably the political critique in the film's first half, the essential humanity of Brodie, and the growing camaraderie of the three pursuers.

Critical debate aside, *Jaws* was a social, industrial, and economic phenomenon of the first order, a cinematic idea and cultural commodity whose time had come. In many ways, the film simply confirmed or consolidated various existing industry trends and practices. In terms of marketing, its nationwide release and concurrent ad campaign underscored the value of saturation booking and advertising, which placed increased importance on a film's box-office performance in its opening weeks of release. "Front-loading" the audience became a widespread marketing ploy, since it maximized a movie's event status while diminishing the potential damage done to weak pictures by negative reviews and poor word of mouth. *Jaws* also confirmed the viability of the "summer hit," indicating an adjustment in seasonal release tactics and a few other new moviegoing trends as well. One involved the composition and industry conceptualization of the youth market, which was shifting from the politically hip, cineliterate viewers of a few years earlier to even younger viewers with more conservative tastes and sensibilities. Demographically, this trend reflected the aging of the front-end baby boomers and the ascendence not only of their younger siblings but of their children as well – a new generation with time and spending money and a penchant for wandering suburban shopping malls and for repeated viewings of their favorite films.

This signaled a crucial shift in moviegoing and exhibition that accompanied the rise of the modern "shopping center." Until the mid-1970s, despite suburbanization and the rise of the drive-in, movie exhibition was still dominated by a select group of so-called key run bookings in major markets. According to Axel Madsen's 1975 study of the industry, over 60 percent of box-office revenues were generated by 1,900 key-run indoor theaters – out of a total of roughly 11,500 indoor and 3,500 outdoor theaters in the US.[24] Though Madsen scarcely saw it at the time, this was about to change dramatically. Between 1965 and 1970, the number of shopping malls in the US increased from about 1,500 to 12,500; by 1980 the number would reach 22,500.[25] The number of indoor theaters, which had held remarkably steady from 1965 to 1974 at just over 10,000, began to increase sharply in 1975 and reached a total of 22,750 by 1990, due largely to the surge of mall-based "multiplex" theaters.[26]

With the shifting market patterns and changing conception of youth culture, the mid-1970s also saw the rapid decline of the art cinema movement as a significant industry force. A number of films in 1974–5 marked both the peak and, as it turned out, the waning of the Hollywood renaissance – Altman's *Nashville*, Penn's *Night Moves*, Polanski's *Chinatown*, and, most notably perhaps, Coppola's *The Conversation*. Although Coppola was the consummate American auteur and "godfather" to a generation of filmmakers, his own artistic bent and maverick filmmaking left him oddly out of step with the times. While he was in the Philippines filming *Apocalypse Now*, a brilliant though self-indulgent, self-destructive venture of Wellesian proportions, his proteges Lucas and Spielberg were busy refining the New Hollywood's Bruce aesthetic (via *Star Wars* and *Close Encounters*), while replacing the director-as-author with a director-as-superstar ethos.

The emergence of star directors like Lucas and Spielberg evinced not only the growing salaries and leverage of top talent, but also the increasing influence of Hollywood's top agents and talent agencies. The kind of packaging done by ICM on *Jaws* was fast becoming the rule on high-stakes projects, with ICM and another powerful agency, Creative Artists Associates (CAA), relying on aggressive packaging to compete with the venerable William Morris Agency. Interestingly enough, both ICM and CAA were created in 1974 – ICM via merger and CAA by five young agents who bolted William Morris and, led by Michael Ovitz, set out to revamp the industry and upgrade the power and status of the agent-packager. For the most part they succeeded, and consequently top agents, most often from CAA or ICM, became even more important than studio executives in putting together movie projects. And not surprisingly, given this shift in the power structure, an increasing number of top studio executives after the mid-1970s came from the agency ranks.

Yet another significant mid-1970s industry trend was the elimination of tax loopholes and write-offs which had provided incentives for investors, especially those financing independent films. This cut down the number of innovative and offbeat films, although by now the critical mass of cinephiles and art cinema theaters was sufficient to sustain a vigorous alternative cinema. This conservative turn coincided with an upswing in defensive market tactics, notably an increase in sequels, series, reissues, and remakes. From 1964 to 1968, sequels and reissues combined accounted for just under 5 percent of all Hollywood releases. From 1974 to 1978, they comprised 17.5 percent. *Jaws*, for instance, was reissued in 1976 (as was *The Exorcist*), generating another $16 million in rentals, and in 1978 the first of several sequels, *Jaws 2*, was released, returning $49.3 million in rentals and clearly securing the Jaws "franchise."[27]

Another crucial dimension of the New Hollywood's mid-1970s emergence was the relationship between cinema and television, which was redefined altogether by three distinct developments. The first involved TV advertising which, incredibly enough, had not been an important factor in movie marketing up to that time. A breakthrough of sorts occurred in 1974 with the reissue of a low-budget independent 1971 feature, *Billy Jack*, whose director and star, Tom Laughlin, successfully sued Warner Bros. for not sufficiently promoting the film on its initial release. For the 1974 reissue, according to *Variety*, "Laughlin compelled Warners to try what was then a revolutionary marketing tactic: 'Billy Jack' received massive amounts of tv advertising support, an unheard of practice at the time."[28] The film went on to earn $32.5 million in rentals, after generating only $4 million in its initial release. This tactic gained further credibility with the *Jaws* campaign and others, soon becoming standard practice and taking motion picture marketing into a new era.

A second crucial development grew out of the FCC's 1972 Report and Order on Cable Television and the 1975 launch of SATCOM I, which effectively ended the three-network stranglehold over commercial television.[29] Pay-cable services started slowly after the 1972 ruling, but the launching of America's first commercially available geo-stationary orbit satellite – and the August 1975 decision by Home Box Office (HBO) to go onto SATCOM – changed all that. HBO immediately became a truly nationwide "movie channel" and a key player in the ancillary movie market. Cable TV proved to be a boon to Hollywood in another way as well, thanks to the FCC's "Must Carry" and "Prime Time Access" rules which increased the demand for syndicated series and movies. That in turn sent syndication prices soaring, providing another windfall for those studios producing TV series.

An even more radical change in Hollywood's relationship with television came with the introduction in 1975 of Sony's Betamax videotape recorder, thus initiating the "home-video revolution." In 1977 Matsushita, the Japanese parent company of Pioneer, JVC, and other consumer electronics companies, introduced its "video home system" (VHS), setting off a battle for the home-video market. Matsushita's VHS format prevailed for several reasons: VHS was less expensive (though technically inferior) and more flexible and efficient in off-the-air recording, and Matsushita was more savvy and aggressive in acquiring "software" (i.e. the rights to movie titles) as a means of pushing its hardware.[30]

While Hollywood's initial response to the "Japanese threat" was predictably (and characteristically) negative, it became increasingly evident that the key home-video commodity was the Hollywood film – and particularly the blockbuster hit with its vast multi-media potential. And there was plenty to drive these new media industries, as Hollywood's blockbuster mentality re-established itself with a vengeance in 1977–8. Total domestic grosses, which had reached $2 billion for the first time in 1975, surged to $2.65 billion in 1977 and $2.8 billion in 1978, a 40 percent climb in only three years, with hits such as *Star Wars*, *Grease*, *Close Encounters*, *Superman*, and *Saturday Night Fever* doing record business. From *The Sound of Music* in 1965 through 1976, only seven pictures (including *Jaws*) had returned $50 million in rentals; in 1977–8 nine films surpassed that mark.

While *Star Wars* was the top hit of the period, doing $127 million in rentals in 1977 and then another $38 million as a reissue in 1978, *Saturday Night Fever* was, in its own way, an equally significant and symptomatic New Hollywood blockbuster. The film did well at the box office ($74 million in rentals) and signaled both the erosion of various industry barriers and also the multimedia potential of movie hits. The film starred TV sitcom star John Travolta, the first of many "crossover" stars of the late seventies and eighties. The Bee Gees soundtrack dominated the pop charts and album sales, and along with the film helped spur the "disco craze" in the club scene and recording industry. *Saturday Night Fever* also keyed the shift from the traditional Hollywood musical to the "music movie," a dominant eighties form, and was an obvious precursor to MTV.

In terms of story, *Saturday Night Fever* was yet another male coming-of-age film, centering on the Travolta character's quest for freedom, self-expression, and the Big Time as a dancer on Broadway. The age-old male initiation rite had found new life in Hollywood with the success of *The Graduate* and the emergent youth market, and proved exceptionally well suited to changes in the industry and the marketplace during the 1970s. One measure of its adaptability and appeal was *Star Wars*, which charts Luke Skywalker's initiation into manhood in altogether different terms – though here too the coming-of-age story, while providing the spine of the film, is developed in remarkably superficial terms. Indeed, *Star Wars* is so fast-paced ("breathtaking," in movie ad-speak) and resolutely plot-driven that character depth and development are scarcely on the narrative agenda.

This emphasis on plot over character marks a significant departure from classical Hollywood films, including *The Godfather* and even *Jaws*, wherein plot tended to emerge more organically as a function of the drives, desires, motivations, and goals of the central characters. In *Star Wars* and its myriad successors, however, particularly male action-adventure films, characters (even "the hero") are essentially plot functions. *The Godfather* and *Star Wars*, for example, are in many ways quite similar but ultimately very different kinds of stories. Like *Star Wars*, *The Godfather* is itself a male action film, a drama of succession, and a coming-of-age story centering on Michael's ascension to warrior status by fighting the "gang wars." Both films have a mythic dimension, and are in fact variations on the Arthurian legend. But where *Star Wars* is so obviously and inexorably plot-driven, *The Godfather* develops its story in terms of character – initially Don Corleone, then sons Sonny and Michael, and finally Michael alone – whose decisions and actions define the narrative trajectory of the film.

This is not to say that *Star Wars* does not "work" as a narrative, but that the way it works may indicate a shift in the nature of film narrative. From *The Godfather* to *Jaws* to *Star Wars*, we see films that are increasingly plot-driven, increasingly visceral, kinetic, and fast-paced, increasingly reliant on special effects, increasingly "fantastic" (and thus apolitical), and increasingly targeted at younger audiences. And, significantly enough, the lack of complex characters or plot in *Star Wars* opens the film to other possibilities, notably its radical amalgamation of genre conventions and its elaborate play of cinematic references. The film, as J. Hoberman has said, "pioneered the genre pastiche – synthesizing a mythology so soulless that its most human characters were a pair of robots."[31] The hell-bent narrative careens from one genre-coded episode to another – from western to war film to vine-swinging adventure – and also effectively melds different styles and genres in individual sequences. The bar scene early on which introduces Han Solo's character, for instance, is an inspired amalgam of western, film noir, hardboiled detective, and sci-fi. Thus the seemingly one-dimensional characters and ruthlessly linear chase-film plotting are offset by a purposeful incoherence which actually "opens" the film to different readings (and readers), allowing for multiple interpretive strategies and thus broadening the potential audience appeal. This is reinforced by the film's oddly nostalgic quality, due mainly to its evocations of old movie serials and TV series (*Flash Gordon*, *Captain Video*, and so on), references that undoubtedly are lost on younger viewers but relished by their cineliterate parents and senior siblings.

Like *Jaws,* Lucas's space epic is a masterwork of narrative technique and film technology. It too features an excessive John Williams score and signature musical theme, and Lucas's general attention to sound and audio effects was as widely praised as the visuals. Indeed, while the film was shut out in its major Oscar nominations (best picture, director, and screenplay), it won Academy Awards for editing, art direction, costume design, visual effects, and musical score, along with a special achievement award for sound effects editing. And although *Star Wars* was the twenty-first feature to be released with a Dolby soundtrack, it was the first to induce theater owners to install Dolby sound systems.[32] There were countless commercial tie-ins, as well as a multi-billion dollar licensing and merchandising bonanza. And strictly as a movie franchise it had tremendous legs, as this inventory of its first decade well indicates:

May 1977	*Star Wars* released
July 1978	*Star Wars* reissue # I
May 1979	*Star Wars* reissue #2
May 1980	*Star Wars* sequel #1: *The Empire Strikes Back*
April 1981	*Star Wars* reissue #3
May 1982	*Star Wars* available on videocassette
August 1982	*Star Wars* reissue #4
February 1983	*Star Wars* appears on pay-cable TV
May 1983	*Star Wars* sequel #2: *Return of the Jedi*
February 1984	*Star Wars* on network TV
March 1985	*Star Wars* trilogy screened in eight cities
January 1987	"Star Tours" opens at Disneyland.[33]

The promise of *Jaws* was confirmed by *Star Wars*, the only other film at the time to surpass $100 million in rentals. *Star Wars* also secured Lucas's place with Spielberg as charter member of "Hollywood's delayed New Wave," as J. Hoberman put it, a group of brash young filmmakers (Brian DePalma, John Landis, Lawrence Kasdan, John Carpenter, *et al.*) steeped in movie lore whose "cult blockbusters" and genre hybrids elevated "the most vital and disreputable genres of their youth . . . to cosmic heights."[34] Perhaps inevitably, Lucas and Spielberg decided to join forces – a decision they made, as legend has it, while vacationing in Hawaii in May 1977, a week before the release *of Star Wars*, and during a break between the shooting and editing of *Close Encounters*. Lucas was mulling over an idea for a movie serial about the exploits of an adventurer-anthropologist; Spielberg loved the idea, and he convinced Lucas to write and produce the first installment, and to let him direct.[35]

The result, of course, was *Raiders of the Lost Ark*, the huge 1981 hit that established the billion-dollar Indiana Jones franchise and further solidified the two filmmakers in the New Hollywood pantheon. Indeed, whether working together or on their own projects – notably Spielberg on *E.T.* and Lucas on the *Star Wars* sequels – the two virtually rewrote the box-office record books in the late 1970s and the 1980s. With the release of their third Indiana Jones collaboration in 1989, Lucas and Spielberg could claim eight of the ten biggest hits in movie history, all of them surpassing $100 million in rentals.[36] Seven of those hits came out in the decade following the release of *Jaws*, a period that Hoberman has aptly termed "ten years that shook the world" of cinema, and that A. D. Murphy calls "the modern era of super-blockbuster films."[37]

Into the 1980s

The importance of the Lucas and Spielberg super-blockbusters can hardly be overstated, considering their impact on theatrical and video markets in the US, which along with the rapidly expanding global entertainment market went into overdrive in the 1980s. After surpassing $2 billion in 1975, Hollywood's domestic theatrical revenues climbed steadily from $2.75 billion in 1980 to $5 billion in both 1989 and 1990. And remarkably enough, this steady theatrical growth throughout the 1980s was outpaced rather dramatically by various "secondary markets," particularly pay-cable and home video. During the 1980s, the number of US households with VCRs climbed from 1.85 million (one home in forty) to 62 million (two-thirds of all homes). Pre-recorded videocassette sales rose from only 3 million in 1980 to 220 million in 1990 – an increase of 6,500 percent – while the number of cable households rose from 19.6 million in 1980 to 55 million in 1990, with pay subscriptions increasing from 9 million to 42 million during the decade.[38]

This growth has been a tremendous windfall for Hollywood, since both the pay-cable and home-video industries have been driven primarily by feature films, and in fact have been as hit-driven as the theatrical market. Through all the changes during the 1980s, domestic theatrical release remained the launching pad for blockbuster hits, and it established a movie's value in virtually all other secondary or ancillary markets. Yet even with the record-setting box-office revenues throughout the 1980s, the portion of the Hollywood majors' income from theater rentals actually declined, while total revenues soared. According to Robert Levin, president of international motion picture marketing for Disney, the domestic box office in 1978 comprised just over half (54 percent) of the majors' overall income, with a mere 4 percent coming from pay-cable and home video combined. By 1986, box-office revenues comprised barely one-quarter (28 percent) of the majors' total, with pay-cable and home video combining for over half (12 percent and 40 percent, respectively).[39] Home-video revenues actually exceeded worldwide theatrical revenues that year, 1986, and by decade's end cassette revenues alone actually doubled domestic box-office revenues.[40]

Another crucial secondary market for Hollywood has been the box office overseas, particularly in Europe. While the overseas pay-TV and home-video markets are still taking shape, European theatrical began surging in 1985 and reached record levels in 1990, when a number of top hits – including *Pretty Woman*, *Total Recall*, *The Little Mermaid*, and *Dances With Wolves* – actually did better box office in Europe than in the US.[41] And *Forbes* magazine has estimated that the European theatrical market will double by 1995, as multiplexing picks up in Western Europe and as new markets open in Eastern Europe.[42]

With the astounding growth of both theatrical and video markets and the continued stature of the Hollywood-produced feature, the American movie industry became increasingly stable in the late 1980s. What's more, the blockbuster mentality seemed to have leveled off somewhat. In the early 1980s, one or two huge hits tended to dominate the marketplace, doing well over $100 million and far outdistancing other top hits. From 1986 to 1990, however, the number of super-blockbuster hits dropped while the number of mid-range hits earning $10 million or more in rentals increased significantly, as did the number returning $50 million or more – still the measure of blockbuster-hit status. From 1975 to 1985 ten films earned $100 million or more in rentals. Meanwhile, the number of films earning $50 million or more has climbed considerably. From 1965 to 1975, only six reached this mark; from 1976 to 1980 there were thirteen; from 1981 to 1985 there were seventeen. From 1986 to 1990, thirty films surpassed $50 million in rentals.

As the economic stakes have risen so have production and marketing costs. The average "negative cost" (i.e. money spent to complete the actual film) on all major studio releases climbed from $9.4 million in 1980 to $26.8 million in 1990. Over the same period, average costs for prints and advertising rose from $4.3 million per film in 1980 to $1 1.6 million in 1990.[43] The rise in production costs is due largely to two dominant factors: an increased reliance on special effects and the soaring salaries paid to top talent, especially stars. The rise in marketing costs reflects Hollywood's deepening commitment to saturation booking and advertising, which has grown more expensive with the continued multiplex phenomenon and the increased ad opportunities due to cable and VCRs. The number of indoor theaters in the US increased from about 14,000 in 1980 to over 22,000 in 1990, which meant that widespread nationwide release required anywhere from 1,000 to 2,700 prints, at roughly $2,500 per print. But the primary reason for rising marketing costs is TV advertising, particularly for high-stakes blockbusters. In 1990, for example, well over $20 million was spent on TV ads alone for *Dick Tracy*, *Total Recall*, and *Die Hard 2*.[44]

While this may seem like fiscal madness, there is method in it. Consider the performance of the three top hits of the "blockbuster summer" in 1989, Hollywood's single biggest season ever. In a four-week span beginning Memorial Day weekend, *Indiana Jones and the Last Crusade*, *Ghostbusters II*, and *Batman* enjoyed successive weekend releases in at least 2,300 theaters in the US and Canada after heavy TV advertising. Each of these pre-sold entertainment machines set a new box-office record for its opening weekend, culminating in *Batman*'s three-day ticket sales of $40.5 million. In an era when $100 million in gross revenues is one measure of a blockbuster hit, it took *Indiana Jones* just nineteen days to reach that total; it took *Batman* eleven. And, like so many recent hits, all three underwent a "fast burn" at the box office. Compare the week-to-week box-office revenues on Hollywood's two all-time summer hits, *E.T.* (1982) *and Batman*, which well indicate certain crucial 1980s market trends.[45]

	week 1	*2*	*3*	*4*	*5*	*6*	*7*	*8*	*9*	*10*
E.T.	$22m	22	26	24	23	23	19	19	16	15
Batman	$70m	52	30	24	18	13	11	8	5	4

E.T. earned another $100 million at the box office, which in 1982 was its only serious source of domestic income, while *Batman* was pulled from domestic theatrical for the home-video market – where it generated another $179 million in revenues.[46] Few recent films match *Batman's* home-video performance and, for that matter, few match its box-office legs, either. In 1990, no saturation summer releases except *Ghost* and *Pretty Woman* had any real pull beyond five weeks, although a number of films (*Total Recall*, *Die Hard 2*, *Dick Tracy*) grossed over $100 million at the box office.

The three top hits of 1990, *Home Alone*, *Ghost*, and *Pretty Woman*, bucked the calculated blockbuster trend and demonstrated why Hollywood relies on a steady output of "smaller" (i.e. less expensive) films which, mainly via word of mouth rather than massive preselling and promotion, might emerge as surprise hits. Such "sleepers" are most welcome, of course, even in this age of high-cost, high-tech, high-volume behemoths, and they are invariably well exploited once they begin to take off – as were those three surprise hits of 1990. And each undoubtedly will spawn a sequel of calculated blockbuster proportions, with the studio hoping not only for a profitable follow-up but for the kind of success that MGM/UA had with *Rocky*, a modest, offbeat sleeper in 1976 that became a billion-dollar entertainment franchise.

Many have touted the three 1990 hits as a return to reason in Hollywood filmmaking, including Disney production chief Jeffrey Katzenberg in a now legendary interoffice memo of January 1991. Katzenberg warned of "the 'blockbuster mentality' that has gripped our industry," and encouraged a return to "the kind of modest, story-driven movie we tended to make in our salad days."[47] The memo was leaked to the press and caused quite a stir, but scarcely signaled any real change at Disney or anywhere else. *Variety* subtly underscored this point by running excerpts from the memo directly below an even more prominent story with the banner headline "Megabudgets Boom Despite Talk of Doom." That story inventoried the numerous high-cost Hollywood films "still being greenlighted," including several at Disney.[48]

In one sense, Katzenberg's memo was a rationale for *Dick Tracy*, the 1990 Disney blockbuster that cost $46 million to produce and another $55 million to market and release, with $44 million spent on advertising and promotion alone. Those figures were disclosed some two months before Katzenberg's memo and startled many industry observers, since by then the film had run its theatrical course and returned only about $60 million to Disney in rentals. But Hollywood insiders (including Katzenberg, no doubt) well understood the logic, given today's entertainment marketplace. As one competing executive told the *New York Times*, Disney had to "build awareness" of the Tracy story and character not simply to sell the film, but to establish "the value of a new character in the Disney family . . . so that it could be brought back in a sequel and used in Disney's theme parks."[49]

The future of the Tracy franchise remains to be seen, but one can hardly fault Disney for making the investment. Lip service to scaled-down moviemaking aside, Hollywood's blockbuster mentality is more entrenched now than ever, the industry is more secure, and certain rules of the movie marketplace are virtually set in stone. The first is William Goldman's 1983 axiom "nobody knows anything," which is quoted with increasing frequency these years as it grows ever more evident that, despite all the market studies and promotional strategies, the kind of public response that generates a bona fide hit simply cannot be manufactured, calculated, or predicted.[50] The studios have learned to hedge their bets and increase the odds, however, and thus these other rules – all designed not only to complement but to counter the Goldman Rule.

The most basic of these rules is that only star vehicles with solid production values have any real chance at the box office (and thus in secondary markets as well). Such films nowadays cost $20 to $30 million, and will push $50 million if top stars, special effects, and/or logistical difficulties are involved. The next rule concerns what is termed the "reward risk" factor, and holds that reaping the potential benefits of a hit requires heavy up-front spending on marketing as well as production. A corollary to this is that risk can be minimized via presold pictures, and today the most effective preselling involves previous movie hits or other familiar media products (TV series, pop songs, comic books). An aesthetic corollary holds that films with minimal character complexity or development and by-the-numbers plotting (especially male action pictures) are the most readily reformulated and thus the most likely to be parlayed into a full-blown franchise.

Another cardinal rule is that a film's theatrical release, with its attendant media exposure, creates a cultural commodity that might be regenerated in any number of media forms: perhaps in pop music, and not only as a hit single or musical score (note that *Batman* had two soundtrack albums and *Dick Tracy* had three); perhaps as an arcade game, a $7 billion industry in 1990 (note that *Hook* and *Terminator 2* both were released simultaneously as movies and video games); perhaps as a theme park ride (note that Disney earns far more on its theme parks than on motion pictures and television, and that the hottest new Disney World attraction is "Toon Town," adapted from *Who Framed Roger Rabbit?*);[51] perhaps as a comic book or related item (note that the Advance Comics Special Batlist offered 214 separate pieces of Batman-related paraphernalia);[52] perhaps in "novelized" form, with print (and audiocassette) versions of movie hits regularly becoming worldwide best-sellers (note that Simon and Schuster, a Paramount subdivision and the nation's largest bookseller, has devoted an entire division to its Star Trek publications).

These rules are evident not only in today's multimedia worldwide blockbusters, but also in the structure and operations of international corporate giants that produce and market them. Competing successfully in today's high-stakes entertainment marketplace requires an operation that is not only well financed and productive, but also diversified and well coordinated. John Mickelthwait of *The Economist* has written that an entertainment company "needs financial muscle to produce enough software to give itself a decent chance for bringing in a hit, and marketing muscle to make the most of that hit when it happens."[53] Thus there has been a trend toward "tight diversification" and "synergy" in the recent merger-and-acquisitions wave, bringing movie studios into direct play with television production companies, network and cable TV, music and recording companies, and book, magazine, and newspaper publishers, and possibly even with games, toys, theme parks, and electronics hardware manufacturers as well.

So obviously enough, diversification and conglomeration remain key factors in the entertainment industry, though today's media empires are much different than those of the 1960s and 1970s such as Gulf & Western, Kinney, and Transamerica. Those top-heavy, widely diversified conglomerates sold out, "downsized," or otherwise regrouped to achieve tighter diversification. Gulf & Western, for instance, sold all of its media holdings by the late 1980s and changed its corporate name to Paramount Communications. Kinney created a media subsidiary in Warner Communications, which also downsized in the early 1980s – only to expand via a $13 billion marriage with Time in 1989 (to avoid a hostile $12 billion takeover by Paramount), thereby creating Time Warner, the world's largest multimedia company and a model of synergy, with holdings in movies, TV production, cable, records, and book and magazine publishing. Because movies drive the global multimedia marketplace, a key holding for any media conglomerate is a motion picture studio; but there is no typical media conglomerate these days due to the widening range of entertainment markets and rapid changes in media technology.

Conglomeration has taken on another new dimension in that several studios have been purchased by foreign media companies: Fox by Rupert Murdoch's News Corporation in 1985, Columbia by Sony in 1989, and MCA/Universal by Matsushita in 1990. The Fox purchase may have greater implications for TV than cinema, given the creation of a "fourth network" in America and its expansion into Europe. The Sony and Matsushita buyouts take the cinema–television synergy in yet another direction, since this time the two consumer electronics giants are battling over domination of the multibillion-dollar high definition television (HDTV) market. Columbia and MCA gave the two firms sizable media libraries and active production companies, which may well give them an edge in the race not only to develop but to sell HDTV.

The Sony–Columbia and Matsushita–MCA deals are significant in terms of "talent" as well. Beyond the $3.5 billion Sony paid for Columbia, the company also spent roughly $750 million for the services of Peter Guber and Jon Peters, two successful producers (*Batman*, *Rain Man*, *et al.*) then under contact to Warners. This underscored the importance of corporate and studio management in the diversified, globalized, synergized marketplace. Indeed, the most successful companies in the mid to late 1980s – Paramount, Disney, Warners, and Universal – all enjoyed consistent, capable executive leadership. Successful studio management involves not only positioning movies in a global multimedia market, but also dealing effectively with top talent and their agents, which introduces other human factors into the New Hollywood equation. These factors were best indicated by the role of Michael Ovitz in both the Sony and Matsushita deals. Co-founder and chief executive of CAA, Ovitz is the most powerful agent in Hollywood's premiere agency. He was a key advisor in the Sony–Columbia deal, and in fact he packaged *Rain Man* during the negotiations and later helped arrange the Guber–Peters transaction. And Ovitz quite literally brokered the Matsushita–MCA deal, acting as the sole go-between during the year-long negotiations.[54]

Ovtiz's rise to power in the New Hollywood has been due to various factors: CAA's steadily expanding client list, its packaging of top talent in highly desirable movie packages, and its capacity to secure favorable terms for its clients when cutting movie deals. In perhaps no other industry is the "art of the deal" so important, and in that regard Ovitz is Hollywood's consummate artist. He also is a master at managing relationships – whether interpersonal, institutional, or corporate, as the Columbia and MCA deals both demonstrate. And, more than any other single factor, Ovitz's and CAA's success has hinged on the increasingly hit-driven nature of the entertainment industry, and in turn on the star-driven nature of top industry products.

The "star system" is as old as the movie industry itself, of course. "Marquee value," "bankable" talent, and "star vehicles" have always been vital to Hollywood's market strategy, just as the "star persona" has keyed both the narrative and production economies of moviemaking. In the classical era, in fact, studios built their entire production and marketing operations around a few prime star-genre formulas. In the New Hollywood, however, where fewer films carry much wider commercial and cultural impact, and where personas are prone to multimedia reincarnation, the star's commercial value, cultural cache, and creative clout have increased enormously. The most obvious indication of this was the rampant escalation of star salaries during the 1980s – a phenomenon often traced to Sylvester Stallone's $15 million paycheck in 1983 for *Rocky IV*.[55] Interestingly enough, many (if not most) of the seminal New Hollywood blockbusters were not star-driven; in fact many secured stardom for their lead actors. But as the blockbuster sequels and multimedia markets coalesced in the early 1980s, both the salary scale and narrative agency of top stars rose dramatically – to a point where Stallone, Arnold Schwarzenegger, Bruce Willis, Michael Douglas, Eddie Murphy, Sean Connery, and Kevin Costner earn seven or even eight figures per film, having become not only genres but franchises unto themselves, and where "star vehicles" are often simply that: stylish, careening machines designed for their star-drivers which, in terms of plot and character development, tend to go nowhere fast.

Not surprisingly, the studios bemoan their dwindling profit margins due to increased talent costs while top talent demand – and often get – "participation" deals on potential blockbusters. CAA's package for *Hook* gave Dustin Hoffman, Robin Williams, and Steven Spielberg a reported 40 percent of the box-office take, and Jack Nicholson's escalating 15 to 20 percent of the gross on *Batman* paid him upwards of $50 million.[56]

While studio laments about narrowing margins are understandable, so too are agency efforts to secure a piece of the box-office take for their clients, particularly in light of the limited payoff for stars and other talent in ancillary markets and in licensing and merchandizing deals. And given the potential long-term payoff of a franchise-scale blockbuster, the stars' demands are as inevitable as the studios' grudging willingness to accommodate them. As Geraldine Fabrikant suggests in a *New York Times* piece on soaring production costs:

> Some studios can more easily justify paying higher prices for talent these days because, with the consolidation of the media industry and the rise of integrated entertainment conglomerates that distribute movies, books, recordings, television programming and magazines, they have more outlets through which to recoup their investments.[57]

The economics and aesthetics of the New Hollywood

This brings us back, yet again, to the New Hollywood blockbuster's peculiar status as what Eileen Meehan has aptly termed a "commercial intertext." As Meehan suggests, today's conglomerates "view every project as a multimedia production line," and thus *Batman* "is best understood as a multimedia, multimarket sales campaign."[58] Others have noted the increased interplay of moviemaking and advertising, notably Mark Crispin Miller in a cover story for *Atlantic Monthly*, "Hollywood: The Ad." Miller opens with an indictment of the "product placement" trend in movies (a means of offsetting production costs which, as he suggests, often brings the narrative to a dead halt), and he goes on to discuss other areas where movies and advertising – especially TV advertising – have begun to merge. Like TV ads, says Miller, movies today aspire to a total "look" and seem more designed than directed, often by filmmakers segueing from studio to ad agency. And now that movies are more likely to be seen on a VCR than a theater screen, cinematic technique is adjusted accordingly, conforming with the small screen's "most hypnotic images," its ads. Visual and spatial scale are downsized, action is repetitiously foregrounded and centered, pace and transitions are quicker, music and montage are more prevalent, and slick production values and special effects abound.[59]

While Miller's view of the cinema as the last bastion of high culture under siege by the twin evils of TV and advertising displays a rather limited understanding of the contemporary culture industries, there is no question but that movie and ad techniques are intermingling. In fact, one might argue that the New Hollywood's calculated blockbusters are themselves massive advertisements for their product lines – a notion that places a very different value on their one-dimensional characters, mechanical plots, and high-gloss style. This evokes that New Hollywood buzzword "high concept," a term best defined perhaps by its chief progenitor, Steven Spielberg, in an interview back in 1978: "What interests me more than anything else is the idea. If a person can tell me the idea in twenty-five words or less, it's going to be a good movie."[60] And a pretty good ad campaign as well – whether condensed into a thirty-second movie trailer or as a feature-length plug for any number of multimedia reiterations.

This paradoxical reduction and reiteration of blockbuster movie narratives points up the central, governing contradiction in contemporary cinema. On the one hand, the seemingly infinite capacity for multimedia reiteration of a movie hit redefines textual boundaries, creates a dynamic commercial intertext that is more process than product, and involves the audience(s) in the creative process – not only as multimarket consumers but also as mediators in the play of narrative signification. On the other hand, the actual movie "itself," if indeed it can be isolated and understood as such (which is questionable at best), often has been reduced and stylized to a point where, for some observers, it scarcely even qualifies as a narrative.

Critic Richard Schickel, for instance, has stated: "In the best of all possible marketing worlds the movie will inspire some simple summarizing graphic treatment, adaptable to all media, by which it can be instantly recognized the world over, even by subliterates."[61] The assembly-line process in the studio era demanded that story ideas be progressively refined into a classical three-act structure of exposition, complication, and resolution. But nowadays, says Schickel:

> Hollywood seems to have lost or abandoned the art of narrative. . . . [Filmmakers] are generally not refining stories at all, they are spicing up "concepts" (as they like to call them), refining gimmicks, making sure there are no complexities to fur our tongues when it comes time to spread the word of mouth.

Schickel argues that all genres have merged into two metacategories, comedies and action-adventure films, both of which offer "a succession of undifferentiated sensations, lucky or unlucky accidents, that have little or nothing to do with whatever went before or is about to come next," with a mere "illusion of forward motion" created via music and editing.[62]

Schickel excuses his "geriatric grumble" while demeaning "youthful" moviegoers for their lack of "very sophisticated tastes or expectations when it comes to narrative," and his nod to audience fragmentation along generational lines raises a few important issues.[63] To begin with, younger viewers – despite "grown-up" biases about limited attention spans, depth of feeling, and intellectual development – are far more likely to be active multimedia players, consumers, and semioticians, and thus to gauge a movie in intertextual terms and to appreciate in it a richness and complexity that may well be lost on middle-aged movie critics. In fact, given the penchant these years to presell movies via other popular culture products (rock songs, comic books, TV series, etc.), chances are that younger, media-literate viewers encounter a movie in an already activated narrative process. The size, scope, and emotional charge of the movie and its concurrent ad campaign certainly privilege the big screen "version" of the story, but the movie itself scarcely begins or ends the textual cycle.

This in turn raises the issue of narrative "integrity," which in classical Hollywood was a textual feature directly related to the integrity of both the "art form" and the system of production. While movies during the studio era certainly had their intertextual qualities, these were incidental and rarely undermined the internal coherence of the narrative itself. While many (perhaps most) New Hollywood films still aspire to this kind of narrative integrity, the blockbuster tends to be intertextual and purposefully incoherent – virtually of necessity, given the current conditions of cultural production and consumption. Put another way, the vertical integration of classical Hollywood, which ensured a closed industrial system and coherent narrative, has given way to "horizontal integration" of the New Hollywood's tightly diversified media conglomerates, which favors texts strategically "open" to multiple readings and multimedia reiteration.

These calculated blockbusters utterly dominate the movie industry, but they also promote alternative films and filmmaking practices in a number of ways. Because the majors' high-cost, high-stakes projects require a concentration of resources and limit overall output, they tend to foster product demand. This demand is satisfied, for the most part, by moderately priced star vehicles financed and distributed by the majors, which may emerge as surprise hits but essentially serve to keep the industry machinery running, to develop new talent, and to maintain a steady supply of dependable mainstream product. Complementing these routine features, and far more interesting from a critical and cultural perspective, are the low-cost films from independent outfits such as Miramax and New Line Cinema. In fact, the very market fragmentation which the studios' franchise projects are designed to exploit and overcome, these independents are exploiting in a very different way via their small-is-beautiful, market-niche approach.

Miramax, for instance, has carved out a niche by financing or buying and then distributing low-budget art films and imports such as *Sex, Lies and Videotape*, *My Left Foot*, *Cinema Paradiso*, and *Tie Me Up, Tie Me Down* to a fairly consistent art film crowd. New Line's strategy is more wideranging, targeting an array of demographic groups and taste cultures from art film aficionados and environmentalists to born-again Christians and wrestling fans. If any one of New Line's products takes off at the box office, it is liable to be a teen pic such as *Teenage Mutant Ninja Turtles*, which returned $67 million in rentals in 1990. While fully exploiting that hit was a real challenge for a company like New Line, an even bigger challenge, no doubt, was resisting the urge to expand their operations, upgrade their product, and compete with the majors – an impulse that proved disastrous for many independent companies during the 1980s.[64]

Thus we might see the New Hollywood as producing three different classes of movie: the calculated blockbuster designed with the multimedia marketplace and franchise status in mind, the mainstream A-class star vehicle with sleeper-hit potential, and the low-cost independent feature targeted for a specific market and with little chance of anything more than "cult film" status. These three classes of movie have corresponding ranks of auteurs, from the superstar directors at the "high end" such as Spielberg and Lucas, whose knack for engineering hits has transformed their names into virtual trademarks, to those filmmakers on the margins such as Gus Van Sant, John Sayles, and the Coen brothers, whose creative control and personal style are considerably less constrained by commercial imperatives. And then there are the established genre auteurs such as Jonathan Demme, Martin Scorsese, David Lynch, and Woody Allen who, like Ford and Hitchcock and the other top studio directors of old, are the most perplexing and intriguing cases – each of them part visionary cineaste and part commercial hack, whose best films flirt with hit status and critique the very genres (and audiences) they exploit.

Despite its stratification, the New Hollywood is scarcely a Balkanized or rigidly class-bound system. On the contrary, these classes of films and filmmakers are in a state of dynamic tension with one another and continually intermingle. Consider, for instance, the two recent forays into that most contemptible of genres, the psycho-killer/stalk-and-slash film, by Jonathan Demme in *The Silence of the Lambs* and Martin Scorsese in *Cape Fear*. Each film took the genre into uncharted narrative and thematic territory; each was a cinematic tour-de-force, enhancing both the aesthetic and commercial value of the form; and each thoroughly terrified audiences, thereby reinforcing the genre's capacity to explore the dark recesses of the collective American psyche and underscoring the cinema's vital contact with its public.

Besides winning the Oscar for "Best Picture of 1991," *Silence of the Lambs* emerged as a solid international hit, indicating the potential global currency of the genre while raising some interesting questions about the New Hollywood's high-end products *vis-à-vis* the American cultural experience. With the rapid development of multiplex theaters and home video in Europe and the Far East, and the concurrent advances in advertising and marketing, one can readily foresee the "global release" of calculated blockbusters far beyond the scale of a *Batman* or *Terminator 2*, let alone a surprise hit such as *The Silence of the Lambs*. This may require a very different kind of product, effectively segregating the calculated blockbuster from the studios' other feature output and redefining the Hollywood cinema as an American culture industry. But it is much more likely that the New Hollywood and its characteristic blockbuster product will endure, given the social and economic development in the major overseas markets, the survival instincts and overall economic stability of the Hollywood studios, and the established global appeal of its products.

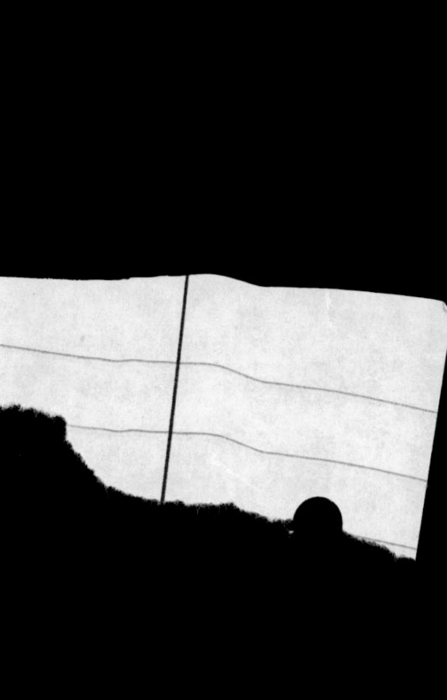

Notes

1 Recent studies of "classical" Hollywood and the "studio system" include *The Classical Hollywood Cinema: Film Style and Mode of Production to 1960*, David Bordwell, Janet

Staiger, and Kristin Thompson (New York: Columbia University Press, 1985); *The Hollywood Studio System*, Douglas Gomery (New York: St Martin, 1986); and *The Genius of the System: Hollywood Filmmaking in the Studio Era*, Thomas Schatz (New York: Pantheon, 1988).

2 Here and throughout this essay, I will be referring to "*rentals*" (or "rental receipts") and also to "*gross revenues*" (or "box-office revenues"). This is a crucial distinction, since the gross revenues indicate the amount of money actually spent at the box office, whereas rental receipts refer, as *Variety* puts it, to "actual amounts received by the distributor" – i.e. to the moneys returned by theaters to the company (usually a "studio") that released the movie. Unless otherwise indicated, both the rentals and gross revenues involve only the "domestic box office" – i.e. theatrical release in the US and Canada.

All of the references to box-office performance and rental receipts in this essay are taken from *Variety*, most of them from its (January 11–17, 1989; pp. 28–74) survey of "All-Time Film Rental Champs," which includes all motion pictures returning at least $4 million in rentals. Because this survey is continually updated, the totals include reissues and thus may be considerably higher than the rentals from initial release. In these cases I try to use figures from earlier *Variety* surveys for purposes of accuracy.

3 "'Gone with the Wind' Again Tops All-Time List," *Variety* (May 4, 1983), p. 15.

4 "Top 100 All-Time Film Rental Champs," *Variety* (January 6, 1992), p. 86.

5 Eileen R. Meehan, "'Holy Commodity Fetish, Batman!': The Political Economy of a Commercial Intertext," in *The Many Lives of the Batman*, Roberta E. Pearson and William Uricchio, eds (New York: BFI-Routledge, 1991), p. 62.

6 Christopher H. Sterling and Timothy R. Haight, *The Mass Media: Aspen Institute Guide to Communications Industry Trends* (New York: Praeger, 1978), pp. 187 and 352. Unless otherwise noted, the statistics on attendance, ticket sales, etc., are from this reliable compendium of statistical data on the movie industry.

7 "All-Time Film Rental Champs," *Variety* (January 11–17, 1989), pp. 28–74.

8 Personal correspondence from Selznick to Louis B. Mayer, September 16, 1953; David O. Selznick Collection, Humanities Research Center, University of Texas at Austin.

9 Rudy Behlmer, ed., *Memo from David O. Selznick* (New York: Viking, 1972), p. 373.

10 See Janet Staiger, "Individualism Versus Collectivism," *Screen* 24 (July–October 1983), pp. 68–79.

11 Freeman Lincoln, "The Comeback of the Movies," *Fortune* (February, 1955), p. 127.

12 See Robert Vianello, "The Rise of the Telefilm and the Networks' Hegemony over the Motion Picture Industry," *Quarterly Review of Film Studies* (Summer, 1984), pp. 204–18.

13 See William Lafferty, "Feature Films on Prime-Time Television," in *Hollywood in the Age of Television*, Tino Balio, ed. (Boston: Unwin Hyman, 1990), pp. 235–56.

14 Lincoln, "Comeback," p. 131.

15 Stephen M. Silverman, *The Fox That Got Away* (Secaucus, NJ: Lyle Stuart Inc., 1988), pp. 323–9.

16 Tino Balio, "Introduction to Part II" of *Hollywood in the Age of Television*, pp. 259–60.

17 Joseph R. Dominick, "Film Economics and Film Content: 1964–1983," in *Current Research in Film* (Norwood, NJ: Ablex, 1987), p. 144.

18 Lafferty, "Feature Films," pp. 245–8.

19 Michael Pye and Lynda Myles, *The Movie Brats* (New York: Holt, Rinehart & Winston, 1979), p. 236.

20 Carl Gottlieb, *The Jaws Log* (New York: Dell, 1975), pp. 15–19. Note that Dell is a subdivision of MCA.

21 Gottlieb, *Jaws Log*, p. 62.
22 Pye and Myles, *Movie Brats*, p. 232.
23 James Monaco, *American Film Now* (New York: New American Library, 1979), p. 50.
24 Axel Madsen, *The New Hollywood* (New York: Thomas Y. Crowell, 1975), p. 94.
25 Balio, "Introduction to Part I," *Hollywood in the Age of Television*, p. 29.
26 "Theatrical Data" section in "1990 U.S. Economic Review" (New York: Motion Picture Association of America, 1991), p. 3.
27 Dominick, "Film Economics," p. 146.
28 Jennifer Pendleton, "Fast Forward, Reverse," *Daily Variety* (58th Anniversary Issue, "Focus on Entertainment Marketing," October, 1991), p. 14.
29 Michelle Hilmes, "Breaking the Broadcast Bottleneck," in Balio, *Hollywood*, p. 299–300.
30 See Hilmes, "Breaking," and also Bruce A. Austin, "Home Video: The Second-Run 'Theater' of the 1990s," in Balio, *Hollywood*, pp. 319–49.
31 J. Hoberman, "Ten Years That Shook the World," *American Film* 10 (June, 1985), p. 42.
32 Jim McCullaugh, "*Star Wars* Hikes Demand for Dolby," *Billboard* (July 9, 1977), p. 4.
33 "*Star Wars*: A Cultural Phenomenon," *Box Office* (July, 1987), pp. 36–8.
34 Hoberman, "Ten Years," pp. 36–7.
35 "Behind the Scenes on *Raiders of the Lost Ark*," *American Cinematographer* (November, 1981), p. 1096. See also Tony Crawley, *The Steven Spielberg Story* (New York: Quill, 1983), p. 90.
36 "Top 100 All-Time Film Rental Champs," *Variety* (January 11–17, 1989), p. 26.
37 Hoberman, "Ten Years," and A. D. Murphy, "Twenty Years of Weekly Film Ticket Sales in U.S. Theaters," *Variety* (March 15–21, 1989), p. 26.
38 Figures from "Theatrical Data" and "VCR and Cable" sections in MPAA's "1990 U.S. Economic Review."
39 Robert B. Levin and John H. Murphy, unpublished case study of Walt Disney Pictures' 1986 marketing strategies, for use in an advertising course taught by Professor Murphy.
40 Richard Natale, "Hollywood's 'New Math': Does it Still Add Up?," *Variety* (September 23, 1991), pp. 1, 95.
41 Terry Ilott, "Yank Pix Flex Pecs in New Euro Arena," *Variety* (August 19, 1991), pp. 1, 60.
42 John Marcon, Jr., "Dream Factory to the World," *Forbes* (April 29, 1991), p. 100.
43 Figures from "Prints and Advertising Costs of New Features" in MPAA's "1990 U.S. Economic Review."
44 Charles Fleming, "Pitching Costs out of Ballpark: Record Pic-Spending Spells Windfall for TV," *Variety* (June 27, 1990), p. 1.
45 "Week-by-week domestic b.o. gross," *Variety* (January 7, 1991), p. 10.
46 "Video and Theatrical Revenues," *Variety* (September 24, 1990), p. 108.
47 "The Teachings of Chairman Jeff," *Variety* (February 4, 1991), p. 24. Article contains excerpts of the January 11 memo.
48 Charles Fleming, "Megabudgets Boom Despite Talk of Doom," *Variety* (February 4, 1991), pp. 5ff.
49 Geraldine Fabrikant, "In Land of Big Bucks, Even Bigger Bucks," *New York Times* (October 18, 1990), p. C5.
50 William Goldman, *Adventures in the Screen Trade* (New York: Warner Books, 1983), p. 39.
51 "Disney's Profits in Park: Off 23%," *Hollywood Reporter* (November 15, 1991), pp. 1, 6.

52 Meehan, "Holy Commodity," p. 47.
53 John Mickelthwait, "A Survey of the Entertainment Industry," *The Economist* (December 23, 1989), p. 5.
54 For an excellent overview of both the Sony and Matsushita deals, and Ovitz's role in each, see Connie Bruck, "Leap of Faith," *New Yorker* (September 9, 1991), pp. 38–74.
55 Lawrence Cohn, "Stars' Rocketing Salaries Keep Pushing Envelope," *Variety* (September 24, 1990), p. 3.
56 Spielberg/Hoffman/Williams deal reported in Geraldine Fabrikant, "The Hole in Hollywood's Pocket," *New York* Times (December 10, 1990), p. C7. Nicholson deal in Ben Stein, "Holy Bat-Debt!," *Entertainment Weekly* (April 26, 1991), p. 12.
57 Fabrikant, "The Hole in Hollywood's Pocket," p. C7.
58 Meehan, "Holy Commodity," p. 52.
59 Mark Crispin Miller, "Hollywood: The Ad," *Atlantic Monthly* (April, 1990), pp. 49–52.
60 Quoted in Hoberman, "Ten Years," p. 36.
61 Richard Schickel, "The Crisis in Movie Narrative," *Gannett Center Journal* 3 (Summer, 1989), p. 2.
62 Ibid., pp. 3–4.
63 Ibid., p. 3.
64 See Joshua Hammer, "Small is Beautiful," *Newsweek* (November 26, 1990), pp. 52–3, and William Grimes, "Film Maker's Secret Is Knowing What's Not for Everyone," *New York Times* (December 2, 1991), p. B1.

Part I

INDUSTRY MATTERS

1

HOLLYWOOD BLOCKBUSTERS

Historical dimensions

Steve Neale

Many commentators give the impression that blockbusters are particular to or peculiarly characteristic of New Hollywood cinema – of Hollywood since the advent of *Jaws* (1975), *Superman* (1978), *Star Trek–The Motion Picture* (1979), and *Raiders of the Lost Ark* (1981) in the mid- to late 1970s and early 1980s.[1] They also give the impression that New Hollywood blockbusters consist almost solely, from a generic point of view, of action-adventure, science-fiction, and disaster films. This chapter seeks among other things to qualify these impressions by locating the New Hollywood blockbuster within a series of historical contexts, both aesthetic and industrial. In doing so, attention will be drawn to the continuities – as well as the discontinuities – between pre- and post-1970s Hollywood cinema, and to some of the films and trends in the New Hollywood blockbuster tradition that run counter to prevailing generic accounts. In this way I hope not only to contest a number of current orthodoxies, but also to lay out the terms for a multidimensional definition of the blockbuster, a definition that encompasses films made before the 1970s as well as films made since then.

The first point to make here is that "blockbuster" as a term has been used both inside and outside the film industry to mean two different things. Originally coined to describe a large-scale bomb in World War II, the term was taken up and used by Hollywood from the early 1950s on to refer on the one hand to large-scale productions and on the other to large-scale box-office hits (Hall 1999: 1–2; Blandford, Grant and Hillier 2001: 26–7).[2] The two, of course, are by no means synonymous, as the box-office failure of large-scale productions such as *The Fall of the Roman Empire* (1964), *Ishtar* (1987), and *The Postman* (1997), and as the box-office success of small or medium-sized productions such as *Easy Rider* (1969), *Star Wars* (1977), and *Ghost* (1990) all make clear.[3] Thus while some films are produced and marketed as "event films" (to use current industry terminology), others become event films by dint of their growing and unexpected success. Although both can achieve must-see status for contemporary audiences, the distinction remains important. Others will take up the role of audiences in the determination of a film's blockbuster status elsewhere in this book. Here, to repeat, the focus will be on the industry, on the production of large-scale movies as a matter of industrial policy, on their modes of distribution and exhibition, and on some of the textual and extra-textual features of the movies themselves.

Largeness of scale is a multidimensional – as well as a relative – characteristic. It includes such factors as running time and length, the size of a film's cast, and the nature, scope, and mode of cinematic presentation of the events and situations depicted. These factors are nearly always related to the size of a film's budget – large-scale nearly always means high-cost. As is well documented, New Hollywood's major studios have spent more and more money each year on a handful of large-scale films, calculating that blockbuster productions are likely to become blockbuster hits. (By 1996, $100 million productions, once unheard of, were becoming more common. See "T2 Ushered in $100 mil Era," *Variety*, 29 April–5 May, 1996: 153.)[4] As is also well documented, these films tend to be heavily pre-advertised and widely released, opening on at least 500 screens either in the summer or during the course of the Christmas period.[5] Their blockbuster status is thus marked not only by their scale and their cost, but also by the amount and type of publicity they receive and by the ways in which they are distributed and shown. One of the elements that affects both their cost and their presentation is their deployment of expensive, up-to-date technology. In addition to special effects, I am thinking here of the sound technologies that have been introduced since the mid–1970s, notably Dolby and digital stereo and their various refinements. As Gianluca Sergi in particular has argued, these technologies have transformed the aural (and hence the audio-visual) nature of contemporary Hollywood cinema, adding new aesthetic and sensual dimensions to the "spectacle" and experience of Hollywood movies.[6]

However, the New Hollywood era is by no means the first in which Hollywood has invested in high-cost, large-scale films. Nor is it the first in which specially made, unusually lavish, and hence unusually spectacular productions have been marked by special modes of promotion, distribution, and exhibition. Nor, for that matter, is it the first in which expensive technologies – including aural ones – have been deployed to enhance their status, experience, and profits. The introduction of "blockbuster" as a term in the early 1950s coincided with the beginnings of a period of sustained and increased investment in productions of this kind and with the increasing use of an additional term, "epic," to mark, describe, and sell them. In its review section, *Variety* labeled *Quo Vadis* (1951) "A boxoffice blockbuster" (November 14, 1951: 6).[7] On its front page on August 1, 1951, under the heading "Back to Multi-Million $ Pix," it reported that "Hollywood is returning – on a

Figure 1.1 A box-office blockbuster: *Quo Vadis* (1951). The Kobal Collection/MGM.

limited scale at least – to the multi-million dollar epic." "The 'colossals,'" it continued, "include Warner Bros.' 'Captain Horatio Hornblower,' Metro's 'Quo Vadis' and 20th's 'David and Bathesheba'." What the report was marking was the start of a twenty-year era in which, in the wake of the Paramount case, the break-up of the studio system, declining attendances, and competition from television and other leisure pursuits, the major studios and those new independents whose productions the majors helped to finance and distribute became increasingly involved in the production of films of this kind.

There were several reasons for this. The Paramount antitrust case meant that the major Hollywood companies were forced to sell off their cinemas and to abandon block-booking their films. Although in some cases the selling-off of cinemas took several years to complete, the combined effects of these rulings meant that companies could no longer guarantee exhibition of all their films and hence could no longer sustain the overheads and levels of production that had marked the studio era. Rapidly declining cinema attendances after the war had in any case already brought about market uncertainty, a downturn in profits, and a series of cuts in studio overheads. Although wage-levels rose for most sectors of the population, newly established families, often in newly established homes in newly established suburbs away from traditionally located cinemas, often chose to spend their money on domestic leisure pursuits, consumer durables, and forms of entertainment other than the cinema. The advent and spread of television, from ownership of whose networks Hollywood's companies had been legally barred, merely augmented these developments.

As it happened, however, their coincidence for the most part strengthened the position of Hollywood's major companies. (RKO collapsed in 1957, but by then hitherto smaller companies such as Columbia, United Artists, and Universal had taken its place at the apex of the industry.) The selling-off of increasingly unprofitable cinemas proved a blessing in disguise. The retention of national and international distribution facilities enabled them to garner large shares in the profits available. Freed from the need to service their cinemas, they were able to cut back on the number of films they produced and to share the risks and the profits of production with the new independents who stepped in to fill the gaps opened up by declining studio output and whose ranks were swelled by personnel who no longer were, or who no longer wished to be, studio employees (Balio 1985: 401–573; Belton 1994: 257–60; Schatz 1999: 323–52). At the same time, as a means of sustaining profit and competing for the leisure dollar, they were able to lavish more money on the films they did produce or finance, to invest in new technologies in order to upgrade their product, and in various ways to use the exhibition sector as an enhanced source of income and as a means of upgrading the cinemagoing experience.

By no means all of the films produced at this time were epics, colossals, or blockbusters. But their numbers increased markedly through the 1950s and 1960s as they proved central to most of these strategies. In addition to those cited above, they included *The Robe* (1953), *The Ten Commandments* (1956), *The King and I* (1956), *Raintree County* (1957), *Ben-Hur* (1959), *Exodus* (1960), *Spartacus* (1960), *The Alamo* (1960), *The Longest Day* (1962), *Lawrence of Arabia* (1962), *How the West Was Won* (1963), *It's a Mad, Mad, Mad, Mad World* (1963), *Battle of the Bulge* (1965), *The Sound of Music* (1965), *Grand Prix* (1967), *Krakatoa, East of Java* (1969), *Hello, Dolly* (1969), *Paint Your Wagon* (1969), and *Patton* (1970). All of them were expensive, at least three times the cost of the average Hollywood feature at the time they were made.[8] Nearly all of them deployed the latest technology, not just widescreen, large-screen or large-gauge processes such as Cinemera (*How the West Was Won*), CinemaScope (*The Robe*), VistaVision (*The Ten Commandments*), Todd-AO (*The Alamo*, *The Sound of Music*, *Krakatoa, East of Java*), Camera 65 (*Raintree County*, *Ben-Hur*), Super Technirama 70 (*Spartacus*), Super Panavision 70 (*Lawrence of Arabia*, *Grand Prix*), Ultra Panavision 70 (*It's a Mad, Mad, Mad, Mad World*), and Dimension 150 (*Patton*), but four-, six-, or eight-track stereo as well (Belton 1992: 113–82).[9] Nearly all of them were longer – in some cases much longer – than the average feature (*Lawrence of Arabia* ran for 216 minutes, *Exodus* for 213 minutes, *Ben-Hur* for 212 minutes, and *The Ten Commandments* for 220 minutes).[10] And nearly all of them were either roadshown – "first released to a select few theatres . . . for separate (rather than continuous) performances, with higher ticket prices and reserved seats" (Blandford, Grant and Hillier 2001: 201) – or distributed and exhibited in other exceptional ways in order to enhance their profitability, showcase their aesthetic and technological features, and highlight their special status.[11]

Large-scale roadshown productions were by no means unknown in the studio era – indeed at least two of them, *Noah's Ark* (1929) and *Gone with the Wind* (1939), were re-released in the 1950s (the former in a re-edited version with a commentary and soundtrack, the latter in an ersatz widescreen form). There was a flurry of roadshown productions in the late 1920s and very early 1930s. In keeping with the traditions I have sought to underline here, some of them showcased new aural and visual technologies, notably pre-recorded sound and such widescreen and large-screen formats as Magnascope, Vitascope and Grandeur. These films included *The Jazz Singer* (1927), *Four Devils* (1928) and *The Air Circus* (1928), and *Old Ironsides* (1926), *The Four Feathers* (1929), *Hell's Angels* (1930), *The Big Trail* (1930), and *Kismet* (1930) (Belton 1992: 34–64; Hall 1999: 48–56).[12] Others, usually also "specials" of one kind or another – most of them showcasing sound as well – were roadshown on Broadway as a means, prior to making distribution deals, of drawing them to the attention of potential exhibitors (Hall 1999: 43).

However, as the Depression began to affect attendances, profits and the relative costs of production, and as the subsequent stabilization of the industry placed a premium on conventional first-run cinemas and the routine weekly provision of A and B features and shorts, high-cost roadshown productions were by comparison few and far between. They consisted for the most part, as Hall points out (1999: 60–6), of "prestige" biopics, musicals, and literary adaptations, of films such as *A Midsummer Night's Dream* (1935), *The Great Ziegfeld* (1936), *The Good Earth* (1937), *The Hurricane* (1937), *The Life of Emile Zola* (1937), and *Lost Horizon* (1937), and they were often only roadshown for a limited period in first-run cinemas. In the era of the double-bill, only a few of these films – notably *The Great Ziegfeld* at 180 minutes – were much longer than average, and expensive new technologies were rare. But it is worth pointing out that *Becky Sharp* (1935), the first three-color Technicolor feature, and *Snow White and the Seven Dwarves* (1937), the first feature-length cartoon, were both roadshown in the mid-1930s. Subsequently, despite the enormous success of *Gone with the Wind* – a 1930s prestige "superspecial" which, in terms of its cost, length and lavishness, in terms of its status as independent-studio product, and in terms of its patterns of distribution and exhibition, anticipated many of the features of the postwar blockbuster (Hall 1999: 66–70) – only a few films, such as *For Whom the Bell Tolls* (1943), *The Song of Bernadette* (1943), *An American Romance* (1944), and David O. Selznick's wartime follow-up to *Gone with the Wind*, *Since You Went Away* (1943), sought or were able in wartime industrial conditions to build on the example it set.

While negotiating with MGM to roadshow *Gone with the Wind*, Selznick wrote an unsent memo to Al Lichtman, MGM's vice-president. "I think it is as wrong not to road show *Gone with the Wind*," he wrote, "as it would have been not to road show *The Birth of a Nation* [1915]" (Behlmer 1989: 223). In doing so, and in going on to refer in his memo to *Ben-Hur* (1925), and *The Big Parade* (1925) as well, Selznick evoked the traditions of the silent roadshown superspecial, traditions which have their roots in the early 1910s. At this point in its history, when the industry in America was geared to the routine production, distribution, and exhibition of daily programmes of single-reel films, roadshowing, along with states rights distribution, was adopted as a means of circulating nonstandard, multireel features.[13] According to Balio (1976: 8–9), some 300 films were distributed in this way between 1912 and 1914. Approximately half were American, the other half European (mainly from Italy and France). Among the former were *The Coming of Columbus* (1912), *Tess of the D'Urbevilles* (1913), and *Judith of Bethulia* (1914), among the latter *Queen Elizabeth* (1912), *Quo Vadis?* (1913), and *Cabiria* (1914). Two discernible though often overlapping trends are apparent here: prestige literary or theatrical adaptations on the one hand, and "spectacles" on the other.[14] These were to continue into the 1920s (and, as we have seen, into the 1930s, 1940s, and beyond). A year later *The Birth of a Nation*, whose cost, scale, and earnings are legendary, and whose initial roadshow run lasted through until the early 1920s, helped, as features began to become more routine, to up the stakes and establish the superspecial as an additional type of industrial product.

Among the features of roadshow productions and, increasingly, premieres and first-run presentations in metropolitan movie palaces too, were especially composed or compiled music scores.[15] The experience contributed by the performance of these scores augmented the visual spectacle provided not just by the films themselves, but also by the stage performances with which they were often accompanied. This in turn was augmented not just by the tinting and toning of prints (a conventional element in most films by the 1920s), but also by the use of such new color processes as Prizmacolor (used for sequences in *Way Down East* in 1920) and two-color Technicolor (used for *The Black Pirate* [1926] and for sequences in *The Ten Commandments* [1923], *Ben-Hur*, and *The Big Parade*, among others). To that extent, these and the other elements I have mentioned exemplify traits characteristic not just of silent roadshown superspecials, but of Hollywood's blockbuster tradition – or traditions – as a whole. To that extent too, while it would be foolish to minimize the differences between New and old Hollywood blockbusters, it would be equally foolish to ignore some of the features they share. In this context, and in conclusion, I would like to draw attention to some of the cyclic, generic, and textual characteristics that have, at times at least, marked them both.

It is generally argued that the New Hollywood blockbuster is dominated by genres, such as science-fiction and action-adventure, which would in the past have been the province of the B film, the serial, and the program picture. As a corollary, the prestige tradition has been swept aside, and with it the Broadway-oriented musical, the epic western and war film, the ancient-world epic, the prestige biopic, the literary adaptation, and the prestige costume film. There is clearly a considerable degree of truth in this; the generic balance among and between old and New Hollywood blockbusters has indeed clearly changed. However, it is worth pointing out that older genres and traditions have not entirely disappeared, as such 1980s films as *Reds* (1981), *Annie* (1982), *The Right Stuff* (1983), *Out of Africa* (1985), and *Empire of the Sun* (1987), and as such 1990s (and post–1990s) films as *Dances with Wolves* (1990), *Far and Away* (1992), *1492* (1992), *Schindler's List* (1993), *Nixon* (1995), *Saving Private Ryan* (1998), and *Gladiator* (2000) all illustrate. At the same same, contemporary disaster films such as *Twister* (1996), *Deep Impact* (1998), and *The Perfect Storm* (2000) clearly recall not just *The Towering Inferno* (1974), and *Earthquake* (1974), but also *San Francisco* (1936) and *The Hurricane*, and indeed, if more indirectly, all those sequences in biblical films in particular whose theatrical origins lie in the turn-of-the-century "disaster spectacle" (Dennett and Warnke 1990). Largely unnoted, meanwhile, at least in film studies, the animated blockbuster feature has, in its own specific and particular way, helped revive not just the

Figure 1.2 The spectacle of destruction: *Earthquake* (1974). The Kobal Collection/ Universal.

biblical epic – in the form of *The Prince of Egypt* (1998) – but, in films such as *Beauty and the Beast* (1991), *The Hunchback of Notre Dame* (1996), and *The King and I* (1999), the traditions of the Broadway-oriented musical as well.

The most obvious of features linking most of the genres, cycles, and presentational traditions of Hollywood blockbusters, old and New, are specialness and spectacle. Specialness, as we have seen, is at least in part a function of the industry's practices of distribution and exhibition. Spectacle, while it encompasses exhibition as well, is first and foremost a textual feature. It has, however, proved notoriously resistant to analysis. (Visual spectacle is at least commonly acknowledged; "aural spectacle" has hardly been recognized. For recent discussions of visual spectacle in the blockbuster context, see Arroyo [2000] and King [2000].) Ted Hovet's expression, "representational prowess," advanced in an as yet unpublished essay, conveys something of the power, scope, and scale the term implies. It can encompass the aural as well as the visual dimensions of film, and films as otherwise diverse as *The Ten Commandments*, *Gone with the Wind*, and *Independence Day* (1996) (as Klady [1996], among others, has noted). The term "representational" tends perhaps to underplay the *non*representational aspects of spectacle – the overwhelming sensual experience of images and sounds. For that reason, and because it links the films themselves to their conditions of exhibition, "presentational prowess" might be preferred. Either way Hollywood's blockbusters, whether in historical, musical, or science-fictional form, have been dedicated to its demonstration for a lot longer than the last twenty-five years.

Notes

1 As Peter Krämer (1998) has explained, the term "New Hollywood" was initially associated with what Diane Jacobs (1977) called the "Hollywood Renaissance" – the period of industrial crisis and stylistic and thematic innovation (and uncertainty) that marked the late 1960s and early 1970s. Since then, the term has either changed to refer to Hollywood since *Star Wars* (1977) and *Jaws*, or expanded to include both of these periods. Sometimes the years since 1948, since government antitrust legislation – in the form of the Paramount decision – forced the major film companies to abandon block-booking, to sell the cinemas they owned, and thus to dismantle the cornerstones of the studio system, are included as well. For further discussion, see Balio (1985: 401–630); Blandford, Grant, and Hillier (2001: 166–7); Bordwell, Staiger and Thompson (1985: 367–77); Gomery (1996); Hillier (1992: 6–37); Maltby (1998); Neale (2000: 242–4); Schatz (1993); and Smith (1998). For the evolution of the New Hollywood blockbuster in the 1970s, see Cook (2000: 25–65).

2 Peter Bart (1995: 6) uses the term in its former sense and Robert Tanitch (2000) in its latter sense. Steven Bach (1985) uses it in its former sense on page 128 of *Final Cut: Dreams and Disasters in the Making of Heaven's Gate* and in its latter sense on page 109. As Bach's book makes clear, *Heaven's Gate* (1980) itself is an interesting case. Initially envisaged as a medium- to low-budget film, it became a blockbuster production but failed disastrously to become a blockbuster hit.

3 *The Fall of the Roman Empire* cost $20 million and grossed only $1.9 million (Finler 1988: 154), *Ishtar* cost $45 million and grossed only $7.4 million (*Variety*, 20 January, 1988: 20), and *The Postman* cost $80 million (Hopp 2000: 162) and grossed only $18 million (Bart 2000: 42). On the other hand, *Easy Rider* cost $400,000 and grossed $16.9 million (Finler: 77), and *Ghost* cost between $20 and 25 million and grossed nearly $100 million ("Modestly Budgeted Pix Had a Hard Time in 1990," *Variety*, 4 March, 1991: 10). *Star Wars*, which of course became a massive blockbuster hit grossing over $185 million (Finler: 99), cost only $9.5 million and was never planned by 20th Century-Fox as a blockbuster production (Biskind 1998: 318–21). It is worth noting that some blockbuster productions can fail in the domestic market but perform well abroad. (The gross figures quoted above relate to initial release in the US.) *Waterworld* (1995) is a well-known case in point. Costing approximately $175 million, its overseas gross of over $150 million exceeded its domestic gross by more than 50 percent, thus helping the film make a profit ("'Waterworld's' Wordly B.O.," *Variety*, 25 September–1 October, 1995: 15. For other examples, see "Foreign B.O. in '95 Proves All the World's a Screen," *Variety*, 15–21 January, 1996: 1, 139.) Blockbusters in the New Hollywood era have, of course, always been produced with the global as well as the domestic market in mind. Their importance in the global market is discussed in Balio (1998) and Hillier (1992: 32–3). The nature of their global appeal is discussed in Olson (1999).

4 It should not be forgotten, however, that Hollywood continues, as it has always done, to invest in medium- and low-budget features as well, not least because such films are often more profitable and because, as noted above, they can always unpredictably become blockbuster hits. (See "Profit's the Thing, Not the Box Office Tally," *Variety*, 5 October, 1992: 5, 8; "H'Wood Tries to Think Small," *Variety*, 16–22 January, 1995: 1, 107; "Summer's Niche Pix Nip at Blockbusters," *Variety*, 4–10 September, 1995: 1, 80; "Size Doesn't Matter," *Variety*, 17–23 November, 1997: 1, 82; and "Smaller Pix Enjoy Happier Returns than Blockbusters," *Variety*, 23 February–1 March, 1998: 1, 66, 72.)

5 The summer period generally runs from mid-May through to the Labor Day weekend in early September, the Christmas period from the Friday preceding Thanksgiving through to New Year's weekend. (See "Hollywood's Fright Before Christmas," *Variety*, 11 November, 1991: 76; "Surviving Summer Screen Crunch Time," *Variety*, 15–21 August, 1994: 7, 12; "Studios Overstuff Xmas Stockings," *Variety*, 26 September–2 October, 1994: 1, 74; and "Fast Fades Follow Wow Bows," *Variety*, 26 June–9 July, 1995: 1.) As these cited reports all make clear, the increasing competition for screens and playdates among blockbuster productions at these times often results not just in the squeezing out of small and medium-sized films, films which would generally depend for their commercial success on long runs, word of mouth, and the gradual build-up of a positive reputation, but also in the curtailing of longer runs for blockbusters too. Wide releases (also known as "saturation" or "blanket" releases) are partial compensation for this last, though in tying up more and more screens they can be part of the problem as well. So great was the competition for screens in 1997 that blockbusters such as *Dante's Peak* and *Volcano* were released at other points in the year.

The number of screens defining wide releases has varied over time and in proportion to the number of screens available. It was reported that in 1996, 43 percent of wide releases played on 2,000 screens or more and that since 1990 screen counts for wide releases had increased by 33 percent, partly as a result of an increase in the number of screens ("Really Wide Releases," "Wide Releases Keep Getting Wider," and "New Screens in 1996," *Variety*, 6–12 January, 1997: 18. See also "Box Office News: 1998

Stats," *Variety*, 4–10 January, 1999: 28; and "Box Office News: 1999 Screen Profile," *Variety*, 10–16 January, 2000). What is clear is that "really wide releases" serve to differentiate particularly special (usually particularly expensive) wide releases from others.

Wide releases are distinguished on the one hand from "limited" releases, which by 1998 meant anything up to 600 screens ("A Decade of Limited Releases," *Variety*, 23 February–1 March, 1998: 4), and on the other from "platform" releases, which since 1995 has meant films that open "on 150 screens or less for at least two weeks before expanding to more than 500 theaters" ("Productive Platform Launches," *Variety*, 9–15 November, 1998: 18). It is worth noting that, on its initial release, *Star Wars* opened "in only forty-two theaters in twenty-eight cities" (Cook 2000: 50). In terms, therefore, of its distribution and exhibition – as well as of its cost and its initial 70 mm print gauge – it was not the paradigm it is often claimed to be. It is also worth noting that, during the studio era, the summer was regarded as a slack period, a period in which "outdoor recreation took patrons away from the movie theaters. (Traditionally-speaking, the slow summer months were also a distant hold-over from the early silent days when film companies spent their time making films during the favorable summer weather, and distributing them throughout the other months of the year.)" However, "As audiences got younger, movie grosses expanded during vacation periods. Summer became the most important blockbuster season, followed by the Christmas holiday" (Aberdeen 2000: 245). Early indications of the change are noted in "Summer B.O. Key to Pix Future," *Daily Variety*, 26 June, 1957: 1; and "ABPT's Hyman Deplores Concentration of Pix Blockbusters For Yule Release," *Daily Variety*, 14 November, 1957: 3.

It is generally – and rightly – argued that wide releasing replaced more exclusive modes of distribution for blockbuster films in the 1970s, and that, hitherto, wide releasing had been used almost exclusively for low-budget exploitation material (Wyatt 1998). However, it is worth pointing out that David O. Selznick experimented with various forms of wide releasing, in particular for *Duel in the Sun* (1946) in the 1940s (Hall 1999: 78–80), and that *The Carpetbaggers* (1964) had been wide released in the 1960s (Cook 2000: 42).

6 See Sergi (1998a and 1998b). For an overview of technological developments in the New Hollywood era, see Allen (1998). For further accounts, see Cook (2000: 383–96) and Prince (2000: 290–5).

7 "Blockbuster" as a term seems to have been used to refer to box-office hits first of all, as here, and to big productions soon after. In addition to examples already cited, see "No Fan Has Yet Stopt to Ask a Mgr., 'How Much Did this Film Cost?,'" *Variety*, 2 January, 1952: 7; and "Vogel Pledges Full MGM Prod'n: Allied States Told Small Pix, with 'Special Appeal,' on Slate with 'Blockbusters,'" *Daily Variety*, 14 February, 1958: 1.

8 Finler indicates that the average cost of a Hollywood feature was \$1 million in 1951, \$1.5 million in 1955, \$2 million in 1961, and \$1.5 million in 1965 (1988: 36). Brown indicates that the overage cost of a Hollywood feature by 1972 was \$1.89 million (1995: 311). Of the films cited here, the least expensive include *The Robe* at \$4 million (Custen 1997: 241), *The King and I* at \$4.55 million (Solomon 1988: 249), and *The Sound of Music* at \$8 million (Finler: 99). The most expensive include *Ben-Hur* at \$15 million (ibid.: 126), *The Alamo* at \$12 million (ibid.: 197), and *Paint Your Wagon* at \$20 million (ibid.: 153), all of them over seven times the cost of an average feature. New Hollywood blockbusters, in contrast, have rarely cost more than three times the average. *The Empire Strikes Back* (1980), for example, cost \$22 million (ibid.: 99) when the average was \$8.5 million (ibid.: 36), *Indiana Jones and the Temple of Doom* (1984) \$27 million (ibid.: 153)

when the average was $14.4 million (Brown 1995: 363), and *Jurassic Park* (1993) $65 million (Sackett 1996: 353) when the average was $29.9 million (Brown: 403). According to figures provided by Bart (1995: 16), even *Titanic* (1997) was only four to five times more expensive than the average feature that year. It could be argued that the New Hollywood produces a higher proportion of big-budget features than the Hollywood of the 1950s and 1960s, and that this pushes up the average. Even so, the cost differential – and, I would argue, the other modes of differentiation discussed in this chapter: special modes of distribution and exhibition, running time, the deployment of innovative technologies, and so on – are less heavily marked in the New Hollywood than they were in earlier periods of Hollywood's history.

9 As Belton makes clear, only a relatively small proportion of cinemas were equipped to showcase these technologies in full. As a result, multiple versions of films using different gauges and formats were sometimes shot, and multiple versions of prints were often struck. It should be noted that 65 mm shooting processes and 70 mm prints have been much more sparingly used in the New Hollywood era, for reasons of cost, but also because it became possible in the early 1990s to produce 35 mm prints with six track stereo soundtracks – a major development in an era so geared to spectacular sound ("Digital Demise for 70mm?," *Variety*, 29 July, 1991: 1, 48; and "The 65 mm Film's Future is Fuzzy," *Variety*, 18 May, 1992: 4, 15). Among the few New Hollywood films shot either in 35 mm or 65 mm and shown in 70 mm – aside from *Star Wars* – are *Apocalypse Now* (1979), *Hurricane* (1979), *Heaven's Gate* (1980), *Tron* (1981), and *Far and Away* (1992).

10 The provision of running times for films such as these is complicated by the fact that they were usually first shown with an intermission (whose length was likely, in practice, to vary) and with a pre-recorded overture, entre'acte (a piece of music preceding the second half), and recessional (a piece of music designed to play as the audience left the cinema). It is also complicated by the fact that they were often cut for subsequent runs or releases. *The Alamo*, for example, is listed by Hayes (1998: 189) as having an initial running time of 201 minutes (208 with an intermission) and subsequent running times of 161 minutes (for shorter roadshow versions) and 140 minutes for general release. New Hollywood blockbusters have rarely been as long or as elaborately presented as films such as this. *Titanic* at 194 minutes and *Schindler's List* (1993) at 195 minutes, neither of which were shown with an intermission (let alone an overture or an entre'acte), are the exception rather than the rule. One of the reasons for this is that the wide-release distribution mode tends to place a premium on audience turnover, and hence on as many performances as possible. This contrasts strongly with the roadshow tradition, discussed below, which depends very heavily on the exclusivity of the venue, its exhibition facilities, its prices, and the number of its performances (usually two a day). In this context, it is worth noting that roadshowing was discussed briefly as an option for releasing at least some blockbusters in *Variety* ("Get the Show Back on the Road," 20 June: 1, 27) in 1990, and again, precisely in response to a cycle of longer films ("Lengthy Pix Turn Heat on Exhibs, Auds," 15–21 January) in 1996. It is also worth noting that Disney roadshowed 70 mm prints of *The Lion King* (1994), *Pocahontas* (1995), and *Mulan* (1997) in the mid- to late 1990s. At 88 minutes, 82 minutes, and 88 minutes respectively, these films are, if anything, fairly short. As far as I am aware, they were shown without an intermission.

11 In addition to roadshowing proper, some films were shown at higher ticket prices in first-run cinemas. Some were also sometimes initially "pre-released" in a limited number of cinemas in specified regions. Shorter films, those running between two and

two and a half hours, were sometimes screened four times a day rather than two. These were all means of increasing rental charges, prices, and income in otherwise inhospitable market conditions (Hall 1999: 90–9).

12 Some of these films also used two-color Technicolor, which was initially showcased in the silent era, as noted below. Some also mixed the new sound technology with the presentation modes of the roadshown silent superspecial. *Lilac Time* (1928), for instance, deployed sound effects and music on its Movietone soundtrack and was presented on its roadshow run in New York with sprayed lilac scent and additional live sound effects and vocals.

13 As Eileen Bowser (1990: 192) notes, "The states rights system meant that an individual or a small company could buy the rights for a specific territory and then go out and get whatever the market would bear from the special exhibition places or from ordinary movie houses." As she also notes, "The term 'feature' was an inheritance of the vaudeville program. When the 'feature film' was first marketed, it meant a special film, a film with something that could be featured in advertising as something out of the ordinary" (ibid.: 191). It was thus initially not simply synonymous with longer, multi-reel films. Michael Quinn (2001: 37) picks up on this point, arguing that "In the first years of feature cinema . . . the feature was not defined exclusively, or even primarily, with respect to production. For a film to be a feature, it needed first and foremost to be differentiated from other films, and, particularly in the early 1910s, distribution and exhibition played a primary role in that process." He goes on to note in particular the role of advertising, state rights distribution, longer runs, and special presentational practices, and to argue that Famous Players, which specialized in the production of multireel features, began as early as 1913 further to differentiate its "regular features" from its prestigious class A films (2001: 50). As Quinn has detailed in an earlier article (1999), this process of differentiation continued into the late 1910s and the 1920s. (It is here that the category of the "superspecial" comes into play.) The emphasis he places both on differentiation and on its multidimensional nature is clearly consonant with the emphasis I have sought to place here on the differential and multidimensional nature of blockbuster films.

14 These two categories overlap so often because roadshown spectacles in the old Hollywood era, even those which did not derive from prestige literary, theatrical, or cultural sources, were given prestige treatment, and were almost automatically accorded prestige status by being showcased as special. Although there are more exceptions than are sometimes acknowledged, as noted below, one of the hallmarks of the New Hollywood era is that blockbusters and prestige are no longer as synonymous as they were.

15 For music and the silent roadshown feature, see Berg (1976: 147–66), Bowser (1990: 211–13), Koszarski, who also includes details of stage presentations and programs in picture palaces and in first-run cinemas in general (1990: 41–56), and Marks (1997: 62–166).

References

Aberdeen, J. A. (2000) *Hollywood Renegades: The Society of Independent Motion Picture Producers*, Los Angeles: Cobblestone.

Allen, Michael (1998) "From *Bwana Devil* to *Batman Forever*: Technology in Contemporary Hollywood Cinema," in Neale and Smith 1998: 108–29.

Arroyo, José (ed.) (2000) *Action / Spectacle Cinema: A Sight and Sound Reader*, London: British Film Institute.

Bach, Steven (1985) *Final Cut: Dreams and Disasters in the Making of Heaven's Gate*, London: Jonathan Cape.

Balio, Tino (1976) *United Artists: The Company Built by the Stars*, Madison: University of Wisconsin Press.

—— (ed.) (1985) *The American Film Industry*, rev. edn., Madison: University of Wisconsin Press.

—— (1998) "'A Major Presence in All the World's Most Important Markets': The Globalization of Hollywood in the 1990s," in Neale and Smith 1998: 58–73.

Bart, Peter (1995) "The Blockbuster Binge," *Variety*, 24–30 July: 1.

—— (2000) *The Gross: The Hits, The Flops – The Summer that Ate Hollywood*, New York and London: St Martin's Press.

Behlmer, Rudy (ed.) (1989) *Memo from David O. Selznick*, Los Angeles: Samuel French.

Belton, John (1992) *Widescreen Cinema*, Cambridge, MA: Harvard University Press.

—— (1994) *American Cinema / American Culture*, New York: McGraw-Hill.

Berg, Charles Merrell (1976) *An Investigation of the Motives for and Realization of Music to Accompany the American Silent Film, 1896–1927*, New York: Arno Press.

Biskind, Peter (1998) *Easy Riders and Raging Bulls: How the Sex-Drugs-and Rock 'n' Roll Generation Saved Hollywood*, New York: Touchstone.

Blandford, Steve, Grant, Barry Keith, and Hillier, Jim (2001) *The Film Studies Dictionary*, London: Arnold.

Bordwell, David, Staiger, Janet, and Thompson, Kristin (1985) *The Classical Hollywood Cinema: Film Style and Mode of Production to 1960*, London: Routledge & Kegan Paul.

Bowser, Eileen (1990) *The Transformation of Cinema 1907–1915*, Berkeley: University of California Press.

Brown, Gene (1995) *Movie Time: A Chronology of Hollywood and the Movie Industry from Its Beginnings to the Present*, New York: Macmillan.

Cook, David A. (2000) *Lost Illusions: American Cinema in the Shadow of Watergate and Vietnam, 1970–1979*, New York: Scribners.

Custen, George F. (1997) *Twentieth Century's Fox: Darryl F. Zanuck and the Culture of Hollywood*, New York: Basic Books.

Dennett, Andrea Stulman and Warnke, Nina (1990) "Disaster Spectacles at the Turn of the Century," *Film History*, 4, 2: 101–11.

Finler, Joel (1988) *The Hollwood Story*, London: Octopus Books.

Gomery, Douglas (1996) "The New Hollywood," in Geoffrey Nowell-Smith (ed.), *The Oxford History of World Cinema*, Oxford: Oxford University Press: 475–82.

Hall, Sheldon (1999) *Hard-Ticket Giants: Hollywood Blockbusters in the Wide Screen Era*, unpublished Ph.D Thesis, University of East Anglia.

Hayes, R. Michael (1998) "Roadshow Movies: A Review of Disk Versions of Hard Ticket Features," *Widescreen Review*: 186–93.

Hillier, Jim (1992) *The New Hollywood*, London: Studio Vista.

Hopp, Glenn (2000) *Videohound's Epics: Giants of the Screen*, Detroit: Visible Ink Press.

Hovet, Ted (unpublished) "Representing the Whole World: Narrative and 'Difference' in *Ben-Hur* (1925)."

Jacobs, Diane (1977) *Hollywood Renaissance: The New Generation of Filmmakers and their Work*, New York: Delta Books.

King, Geoff (2000) *Spectacular Narratives: Hollywood in the Age of the Blockbuster*, London and New York: I. B. Tauris.

Klady, Leonard (1996) "B.busters: boffo B.O. for Changing Tastes," *Variety*, 28 October–3 November: 11, 16.

Koszarski, Richard (1990) *An Evening's Entertainment: The Age of the Silent Feature Picture, 1915–1928*, Berkeley: University of California Press.

Krämer, Peter (1998) "Post-Classical Hollywood," in John Hill and Pamela Church Gibson (eds), *The Oxford Guide to Film Studies*, Oxford: Oxford University Press: 289–309.

Maltby, Richard (1998) "'Nobody Knows Everything': Post-Classical Historiographies and Consolidated Entertainment," in Neale and Smith 1998: 21–44.

Marks, Martin Miller (1997) *Music and the Silent Film: Contexts and Case Studies, 1895–1924*, New York: Oxford University Press.

Neale, Steve (2000) *Genre and Hollywood*, London: Routledge.

Neale, Steve, and Smith, Murray (eds) (1998) *Contemporary Hollywood Cinema*, London: Routledge.

Olson, Scott Robert (1999) *Hollywood Planet: Global Media and the Competitive Advantage of Narrative Transparency*, Mahwah, NJ: Lawrence Erlbaum Associates.

Prince, Stephen (2000) *A New Pot of Gold: Hollywood Under the Electronic Rainbow, 1980–1989*, New York: Scribners.

Quinn, Michael J. (1999) "Paramount and Early Feature Distribution: 1914–1921," *Film History*, 11, 1: 98–113.

——(2001) "Distribution, the Transient Audience, and the Transition to the Feature Film," *Cinema Journal*, 40, 2: 35–56.

Sackett, Susan (1996) *The Hollywood Reporter Book of Box-Office Hits*, New York: Billboard Books.

Schatz, Thomas (1993) "The New Hollywood," in Jim Collins, Hilary Radner, and Ava Preacher Collins (eds), *Film Theory Goes to the Movies*, New York and London: Routledge: 8–36 [reprinted in this volume].

——[1997] (1999) *Boom and Bust: American Cinema in the 1940s*, Berkeley: University of California Press.

Sergi, Gianluca (1998a) "A Cry in the Dark: The Role of Post-Classical Film Sound," in Neale and Smith 1998: 156–65.

——(1998b) "Tales of the Silent Blast: *Star Wars* and Sound," *Journal of Popular Film and Television*, 26, 1: 12–22.

Smith, Murray (1998) "Theses on the Philosophy of Hollywood History," in Neale and Smith 1998: 3–20.

Solomon, Aubrey (1988) *Twentieth Century-Fox: A Corporate and Financial History*, Metuchen, NJ: Scarecrow Press.

Tanitch, Robert (2000) *Blockbusters!: 70 Years of Best-Selling Movies*, London: B. T. Batsford.

Wyatt, Justin (1998) "From Roadshowing to Saturation Release: Majors, Independents, and Marketing/Distribution Innovations," in Jon Lewis (ed.), *The New American Cinema*, Durham, NC: Duke University Press: 64–86.

2

FOLLOWING THE MONEY IN AMERICA'S SUNNIEST COMPANY TOWN

Some notes on the political economy of the Hollywood blockbuster

Jon Lewis

Every week the *Los Angeles Times* issues its "Company Town Film Profit Report," a must-read compilation of estimates on costs and box-office revenues for high profile movies. In this report, the *Times*'s media experts evaluate a number of economic indicators, many of which are supplied by the studios. Using a complex formula, the *Times* boldly predicts success or failure – a thumbs-up or thumbs-down that is taken very seriously industry-wide. Films are categorized according to projected domestic box-office performance: "megamoneymakers" (at least $50 million in expected profits), "moneymakers" ($10 million in expected profits), "tossups" ($5 million in expected profits or losses), and "losers" (more than $5 million in expected losses). *Times* staff writer David Shaw puts the popularity of the "Report" in context: "It's like a scorecard. It is a scorecard. And Americans like to keep score, whether on the athletic field, at the polls or – especially in this company town – at the box office" (Shaw 2001).

How films are made and consumed has shifted in lock step with certain fundamental changes in industrial policies and procedures. Over the last thirty years, the revamped conglomerate, multinational, vastly diversified studio owners have more and more completely devoted their time, energy, and, most importantly, money to the production of formulaic blockbuster-style movies. Any attempt to evaluate or otherwise intellectually account for these films seems to begin and end with a larger Hollywood story regarding recovery, conglomeration, multinationalization, and vertical and horizontal integration (a.k.a. synergy).

The studios have always measured success in terms of dollars and cents. But these days, filmgoers seem content to follow the money as well, very much at the expense

Figure 2.1 Follow the money: *Batman* (1989). The Kobal Collection/Warner Bros./DC Comics.

of other criteria. If we are to lament the end of film culture here in the United States, and lots of us who teach film do so daily, the blame is rather easy to affix.

In these first few years of the new century, blockbuster Hollywood persists, now having lasted well over twice as long as the golden age, the so-called auteur renaissance it replaced. Questions regarding the relative importance of these two successive eras – questions regarding quality versus duration, artistic versus economic significance – drive New Hollywood history.

The auteur theory which was so popular in the early 1970s during those last few years before Hollywood so completely gave itself over to the blockbuster has become as outdated as the very "auteur films" many of us still so deeply admire. This progressive loss of film culture troubles many important critics and historians who, as the late Pauline Kael once described it, "lost it at the movies" in the glory years of the early 1970s. As Kael's contemporary David Thomson remarked in a recent essay entitled "Who Killed the Movies?":

> Lucas and Spielberg [whom Thomson regards as the principal villains of this Hollywood story] have changed everything, not just the way the industry functions and directs its own ambitions but the scheme by which film history is now perceived . . . This is not just a lamentation that movies are in a very bad state. Rather, I fear the medium has sunk beyond anything

> we dreamed of, leaving us stranded, a race of dreamers. This is more and worse than a bad cycle. This is something like a loss of feeling, and I blame Spielberg and Lucas.
>
> (Thomson 1996: 56)[1]

The swift and sure adoption of the blockbuster regards and reveals a simple Hollywood history. From 1948 to 1974, studio revenues and profits slumped, so much so that the conglomerate owners of the studios began to contemplate shutting down film production altogether. Gulf and Western went so far as to negotiate the sale of the Paramount studio lot, a sale nixed only when developers failed to get an adjacent lot (in an amusing foreshadowing of Spielberg's *Poltergeist* [1982], a cemetery) rezoned for new construction. The studios pulled out of their slump in the early 1970s by financing what historians now call the auteur renaissance. But the studios' embrace of the auteur theory was by design temporary. And film executives did not need to wait long for a viable and, from where they sit, superior alternative. The mid-decade release of *Jaws* (1975) and *Star Wars* (1977) promised the studios profits of previously unthinkable proportions in markets theretofore untapped. It changed not only the way films were made, but how they were promoted, distributed, and exhibited to American and international audiences.

The present public fascination with following the money in Hollywood seems a significant consequence of the industry's blockbuster mindset. Today, national media magazines and newspapers such as *Entertainment Weekly*, *Premiere*, *Vanity Fair*, and *USA Today*; Net sites such as Inside.com, IMDb, and Hollywoodpro; television programs such as *Entertainment Tonight* and virtually all of the gossip shows on the E! Channel; even local newspapers as small as the one that serves my home town (the *Gazette Times* of Corvallis, Oregon) highlight first and foremost the performance of films at the box office. It's the stuff of which feature story-lines are now made.

The focus on box office tells us a lot about the interconnectedness of the mass media these days – a lot about the ways in which popular print and electronic media participate in the marketing of motion pictures. This fetishization of financial data limits the ways in which films enter any sort of intellectual, critical, or historical dialog. Keeping track of the numbers – at the box office here and overseas, in ancillary markets such as videocassette, DVD, pay television and merchandise – is where the discussion of films in the popular media begins and ends. Importance and significance are now just a matter of keeping score.

The statistical or mathematical basis for importance and value of filmed products in the New Hollywood is to a large extent produced and promoted by companies with a vested interest not only in the medium's continued success but in the particular success of specific, astoundingly expensive products. Interestingly enough, despite all the coverage, box-office data is still not compiled scientifically (as it is now in the recording industry). Instead, theatrical revenues are routinely "cooked" by studio marketing and distribution departments. The notion that a movie's success could ever be mathematically determined is at once intellectually lazy and factually misleading.

In *The Gross: The Hits, The Flops – The Summer that Ate Hollywood*, *Variety* editor (and former Paramount executive) Peter Bart asserts that film audiences tend to believe and remember only what they read first. When box-office numbers are later revised and reduced, when something approximating facts are introduced, few readers seem to notice or care. As Bart writes:

> By Sunday morning the distribution chiefs, having filled in their colleagues, start calling key members of the press to spread the word. Often the process of achieving the number one position becomes a test of gamesmanship. A distribution chief, for example, may call *Variety*'s box office reporter, Andrew Hindes, and inquire what his rivals at other studios have reported. If his film is running neck-and-neck with a competitor, he will offer a higher number. Not until Tuesday morning are the official numbers announced . . . By that time the ads would already be in newspapers claiming that the film in question is "the number one movie in America." Given the herd instincts of the moviegoing public, this information helps build momentum, even if the basic data itself may be exaggerated. The machinery of hitmaking has been set in motion.
>
> (Bart 1999: 177–8)

That this machinery is driven by guesswork, bravado, and deliberately told falsehoods is consistent with the character and nature of business dealings in the New Hollywood. Patrick Goldstein, a movie reporter for the *LA Times*, quips that people in Hollywood "see truth in a different way than most people do . . . To them, truth is a good story, period." *Hollywood Reporter* editor Anita Busch adds, "If I talk to 100 people in a day, 99 of them are lying and the other one is my mom" (quoted in Shaw 2001).

Given how the conglomerate owners of the studios have diversified into various intersecting popular information and entertainment media, data on a film can now be fully controlled to suit the studio's needs. Box-office and inside(r) business information formerly unique to the trades reaches a far wider and less specialized readership thanks to popular magazines such as *Entertainment Weekly*. *Entertainment Weekly* is owned by media conglomerate AOL/Time Warner. This conflict of interest, or synergy, not only benefits products emanating from the Time publishing empire, the Warner Bros. film studio (and its various subsidiary and satellite film companies such as New Line and Fine Line), and the conglomerate's television holdings (TBS, TNT, CNN, HBO, etc.), but the industry as a whole. Indeed, the health of the industry that is so promoted and celebrated by the magazine reveals a glib truth about the contemporary entertainment industries: that what is good for AOL Time Warner is good for Hollywood – and what's good for Hollywood is, of course, good for America.

The other major studio owners – the News Corporation, Viacom, Sony, Vivendi, and Disney – all sport vast vertical and horizontal monopolies that include newspaper and magazine publishing, cable TV software and hardware, and video and music production, distribution, and sales. In order to succeed in the New Hollywood, such synergies, such strategic relationships and alliances and interdependencies, are not only useful but also necessary.

Conglomerate ownership has not only changed the sorts of films made in the New Hollywood but also the way these films are produced, advertised, distributed, and exhibited to the public. A film's initial success in 2001 depends on how a studio "positions" it in the marketplace, how various print and other audio-visual media are used to define, advertise, and promote the picture well in advance of its release. All the major studios are so diversified and flexible these days they need look no further than their own network of subsidiaries to position their films, and no further than their own chain of theaters and/or premium cable television channels to distribute and exhibit their films into the marketplace.

The growing importance of marketing has to a large extent driven production at the New Hollywood studios. Contemporary studio marketers talk a lot about playability and marketability: the former a category of films the studio can safely pre-screen for critics and depend on for good "word of mouth" from audiences; the latter a polite term for films that *need* to be well positioned or platformed in the media to succeed. As studios have discovered over the past several years, it doesn't matter whether or not blockbusters have playability. The key to their promotion and release is a marketability that is factored into the project from the very start of development.

The new studio owners prefer to treat Hollywood movies as products. When I worked for a market research firm contracted by the Coca-Cola corporation, which at the time owned Columbia Pictures Industries, we surveyed consumers and analyzed their reactions to a variety of products: Coca-Cola soft drinks, Frito-Lay snack foods, Hunts ketchup, and Columbia's motion pictures. Though food and filmed products are different in fundamental ways, we used the same methods and materials for all of Coke's product lines.[2] Films, so far as the executives at Coca-Cola and its marketing firm were concerned, were, like soft drinks, consumables, unique only in the amount of money at stake in their production and distribution.

According to the industrial economist Art DeVany, Hollywood is a place "poised between order and chaos." So much is riding on the success of a single product that executives are disinclined to take risks. To protect their positions (of privilege, by most criteria), these executives are quite practically attracted to "simple rules" and industry formulas that enhance or promise predictability and stability (Cassidy

1997: 36). An effort to standardize and thus more accurately and more completely control product lines in the New Hollywood is at the root of the blockbuster mindset at the studios.

Take, for example, the following movie-development formula that has been adopted in one form or another at all the major studios. Development executives and market researchers now routinely credit certain variables in the development of a film project with numerical values and predicted-revenue amounts. A film project needs to obtain a certain numerical total in order to get a green light for production.

First among the variables is casting. The casting of an Academy Award winner, for example, is given a numerical value slightly higher than the casting of nominees or winners of lesser awards. Movie stars and other celebrities with significant Q- or power ratings are also handicapped in these early accountings. Star directors carry some clout. But unlike thirty years ago, when blockbusters were produced and/or directed by auteurs, most successful blockbuster directors these days (for example, Michael Bay or Jan De Bont) are significantly less well known than the films they've made.

Different genres are handicapped differently and the odds vary in accordance with fads and industry trends. In the early 1980s, for example, science-fiction might have gotten a fairly high numerical value, while musicals would have scored significantly lower, and westerns may well have been given a negative number. In 2001, marketers remain convinced that certain types of films are marketable and others are not. While genres go in and out of style, action-adventure, it seems, is always in play. Action-adventure depends almost entirely on casting and special effects, two keys to blockbuster entertainment.

Blockbusters are positioned within the larger film marketplace through "sequelization." This applies not only to franchise product lines such as *Jurassic Park*, *Batman*, *Star Wars,* and *Raiders of the Lost Ark* but to films that borrow from these popular products as well. For example, though they are not precisely sequels to Spielberg's Indiana Jones films, distinctions between the two recent *Mummy* pictures (*The Mummy* [1999]; *The Mummy Returns* [2001]), the computer game spin-off *Lara Croft, Tomb Raider* (2001), and the genre prototype, *Raiders of the Lost Ark* (1981), are subtle. Newspaper coverage acknowledging just how closely these films ape Spielberg's contributes to marketability. Imitation here is not necessarily flattery. It's just a smart way to do business. Development executives and studio marketers thus give a lot of weight to film projects that sound like or promise to be like other, previously released, "megamoneymakers."

Another variable involves the carefully executed seasonal release. Though premature – such strategies look months or even years into the future of a film project – release patterns now figure prominently during the development stage. Here some simple rules apply. A summer release is more valuable than a mid-February date when you've got a big, loud, expensive film on your hands. Then again, you don't want to get crowded out at summertime with a film that might actually have playability.

Marketing plans are also essential, and it's never too early to think about how to sell a movie to the press and the public at large. Newspaper "advertising intensity" is calculated and budgeted well in advance of release, and there is a formula that links the number and size of motion picture ads to the future box-office numbers of a given film.

The number and type of trailers produced and where and when these trailers are aired or screened is also an important variable. There are two types of trailers used for big films. The "teaser" trailer is released as much as six months before the film is scheduled to reach theaters. This enables studios to advertise summer blockbusters during the Christmas season. During the summer, teasers allow studios to promote the films they've targeted for Academy Award consideration or holiday vacation-time family viewing. Teaser trailers are designed to reveal little about a movie's actual content. Bob Israel, the CEO and co-founder of Aspect Ratio, a Hollywood advertising agency, notes that it doesn't pay to "reveal too much in [a] teaser; [all you need is] a great piece of music and big images" (Tough 1993: 38). The story trailer that accompanies the release of the film some months later more fully positions the product in the marketplace. The teaser tells audiences that a certain film is so big they need to know about it half a year in advance. The story trailer is designed by the studios' market researchers to tell audiences what the film is about and specifically why they should or *need* to see it.[3]

The studios seldom pre-screen films for exhibitors anymore and when they do it's more a perk or courtesy than an attempt to sell theater owners on the virtues of a given motion picture. Thanks to a 1985 decision in *United States* v. *Capitol Service*, the strategic placement of films in theaters nationwide, another variable factored into the mix before a film is produced, has been made easy.[4]

The *Capitol Service* case involved a civil antitrust action filed against four theater chains – Capitol Service, Kohlberg, Marcus, and United Artists – which together controlled 90 percent of the exhibition business in the Milwaukee area. According to the government's case, the four theater chains entered into a collusive arrangement, what's called in the business a "split" or "split agreement." The theaters in the split agreed not to bid against each other – they agreed to take turns contracting for exclusive runs of studio films in order to keep rental prices down.[5]

A United States circuit court found against the theater owners, deciding with a lower court that the split unfairly fixed prices on rentals of studio films. The decision in the *Capitol Service* case proved devastating for the nation's exhibitors. As Capitol Service *et al.* had claimed in the suit, splits and other such collusive arrangements were essential to many theater owners' profitability and independence. In 1986 alone, 4,357 screens changed hands, and the studios were involved in a vast majority of the purchases. In a two-year period (1986–7), MCA/Universal purchased the Plitt, Septum, Essaness, Sterling and Neighborhood Theater chains as well as a 50 percent stake in Cineplex Odeon – a total of 2,500 screens. Columbia purchased the Walter Reade Theaters. TriStar (then owned in large part by Columbia) picked up the Loew's, Music Makers, and United Artists Theaters. Gulf and Western/ Paramount bought the Trans-Lux, Festival, and Mann Theaters (which it added to its ownership of the Famous Players chain and its co-ownership, with MCA, of Cinema International).

By the end of 1987, ten companies controlled 50 percent of the nation's first-run showcase screens. As Richard Trainor concluded in *Sight and Sound* at the end of 1987, "Representatives of the new Hollywood may insist that monopoly is the last thought on their minds, but many independent producers and exhibitors remain skeptical. They see further theater acquisitions on the horizon, fewer independently produced and distributed pictures, a re-establishment of the majors' power over all aspects of the industry" (Trainor 1987–8: 26). Trainor's dire prediction has come to pass. In 2001, we find a weakened and irrelevant FTC (Federal Trade Commission) and FCC (Federal Communications Commission) and a Justice Department disinclined to pursue antitrust cases against the conglomerate owners of the studios. How else can we explain the existence of such merged companies as AOL Time Warner Turner, Viacom Paramount CBS, or Disney Capital Cities ABC? In twenty-first-century Hollywood it's just like the old days, only better.

Big-budget films are now routinely presold into theaters that are owned outright by their studio distributors. Whether or not these films have playability is irrelevant, because the studios can secure a staggering number of venues and screens nationwide for any film they choose to market as an event or blockbuster. For example, consider the newspaper ads announcing the release of the 1996 summer hit *Independence Day*. The full-page ads said nothing about the film or its initial reception by critics. Instead it touted: "*Independence Day*: opening at theaters EVERYWHERE." However awful (or good) the film might have been, the sheer number of prints in circulation and screens devoted to its exhibition virtually guaranteed a successful opening weekend.[6]

In the contemporary film marketplace, the opening weekend has acquired a kind of singular importance. Contracting with a vast number of theaters is easy enough these days. And getting people into those theaters isn't all that difficult either, so long as you've got marketability. The relative quality of the film itself – its playability – is irrelevant. The only variables of any concern to studio ownership involve the way studio executives have handled the promotion and release, the degree of control these executives have exerted over the media attending the film. The auteurs of this New Hollywood are executive-level specialists and professionals who in many cases never bother actually to see the film they're promoting.

Studios are subsidiaries of huge publicly traded corporations. Projections of earnings of films in development or just beginning a general release are important to

Wall Street investors. Studio ownership and management focus a lot of attention on the opening weekend because their investors want and need them to. The degree to which the first weekend foretells a film's success – and the astonishing percentage of a film's total domestic gross that can be attributed to those first three days in release – is a recent phenomenon. And, as such, it reveals just how completely the industry has come to depend on marketable as opposed to playable movies.

In 1982, for example, Spielberg's *E.T.: The Extra-Terrestrial* took in $4,776,000 in its initial week in release. The film grossed $6,014,000 in its second week, a change of +26 percent. The number 2 film for the year, *Tootsie*, opened at $2,444,000 and then went up 63 percent in its second week to $3,978,000. Of the top ten films for 1982, only two dropped off from week 1 to week 2: *Rocky 3*, which fell 2 percent, and *Star Trek 2*, which fell 9 percent. *Rocky 3* and *Star Trek 2* are similar properties: both are high-concept franchise films from big studios, films with far more marketability than playability. Both performed predictably if not all that impressively at the box office.

Compare the success of the two sequels to two other top films from 1982, *Porky's* and *An Officer and a Gentleman*. Neither film seemed to fit the marketability model in advance of its release. The box office for *Porky's*, the number 4 film for the year, and *An Officer and a Gentleman*, number 5, took off weeks after their respective initial playoff at theaters. They became marketable because they were playable. But playability, studio executives are inclined to believe, is a matter of luck. There is, after all, no formula for making good films or for making films that exceed market expectations. The more formulaic *Rocky* and *Star Trek* sequels were significantly easier to handicap in advance and significantly easier to reproduce.

In 1992, every one of the top ten films fell off from the first week to the second. *Aladdin*, the number 1 film, sported a negative 48 percent change from week 1 to week 2. The three sequels that placed second, third, and fourth for the year – *Home Alone 2*, *Batman Returns*, and *Lethal Weapon 3* – dropped off significantly as well, 28 percent, 45 percent, and 25 percent respectively. All three films did well enough at the box office by year's end ($173.5 million, $163 million, and $144.7 million respectively), and all three turned a profit in the various ancillary markets available in 1992, this despite an apparent lack of playability.

The three big films released in the summer of 2001 reveal a continued industry reliance on marketability over playability. *Pearl Harbor*, *Planet of the Apes*, and *Jurassic Park 3* succeeded primarily because of well-executed pre-release marketing campaigns and saturation release platforms; the films were indeed *everywhere*, for a week or two at least. The drop off from the opening weekend to the second week in release was, with all three titles, dramatic and revealing. *Pearl Harbor*, which was budgeted at $152 million, grossed $75 million in its opening weekend. It dropped off to $29 million in its second week, $14 million in its third, and $9 million in its fourth. Of its total first-run gross of $195 million, almost 40 percent was earned in the first three days of general release. The implication here is that the film isn't very good, that once people actually saw it and told their friends what they thought about it, interest died off. But because the film had marketability, because it was developed, marketed, and released as a blockbuster, it made money anyway.

The $93 million *Jurassic Park 3* opened at $50.7 million. It then dropped off steadily to $22.5 million, $12 million, and $7 million. As of September 1, 2001, with the film playing in just a handful of sub-run theaters, the film had grossed $173 million, 29 percent of which was earned in the first weekend. The most anxiously awaited film of the summer, *Planet of the Apes*, was produced for $100 million. It opened big at $68.5 million, then dropped off to $27.5 million, $13 million, and $7 million, for a total gross (again as of September 1, 2001) of $168 million. Like *Pearl Harbor* and *Jurassic Park 3*, a significant portion, in this case 41 percent, of the total domestic box-office gross earned by *Planet of the Apes* can be credited to the crucial first weekend. Such are the mathematics of marketability.

Opening weekend numbers tend to be the key to the public's perception of whether or not a film is a hit. But these early numbers are hardly the whole story. In blockbuster Hollywood, box office is only the first and fastest money that is counted. A more accurate and complete accounting reveals that in the New Hollywood every studio film is a hit. In 1994, for example, on average, domestic theatrical revenues – that is, box-office numbers in the US and Canada – accounted for only 16 percent of the total revenue of a studio film. The remaining 84 percent was comprised of domestic home video (26 percent), international theatrical box office (16 percent), international home video (19.9 percent), domestic television (11 percent), and licensing and merchandising (11.1 percent) (Rice-Barker 1996: 19). Success at the box office insures continued profitability across these other ancillary markets. But even a dramatic box-office failure – think *Waterworld* (1995) or *Last Action Hero* (1993) – can eventually turn a profit, because there are now so many different ways for the studio to make money on a movie.

However inaccurate, however the information is spun, situated, or simply made up, the media's attention to box office and the business of entertainment has fundamentally changed how the filmgoing public has come to think about a film's and a filmmaker's success, importance, and value. The public, thanks in no small part to the success of the complexly integrated media that reports on films, can be counted on to consume movies that are big, that cost and make a lot of money, that get covered extensively and exhaustively in print and on television. The studios are driven to a certain extent by audience demand. Filmgoers no longer seem to clamor for the supply of good or meaningful films. Instead, what "they" want – what all the market research seems to say they want – are successful films – "megamoneymakers" to use the *Los Angeles Times*'s term. The studios are, of course, anxious to comply.

Notes

1 Regarding the decline or demise in film culture among this new generation of filmgoers, Thomson adds: "for the generation in its twenties today, it is possible to believe that movies began twenty years ago with the phenomenal impact of *Jaws* and *Star Wars.*" Such is the challenge of teaching film history and of somehow resurrecting film culture today.

2 I worked for Lieberman Research West, based in Century City, California, from 1979 to 1982.

3 Story trailers can be infuriatingly specific and complete – so much so that in ninety seconds they pretty much tell the entire story of the film they advertise. Hollywood directors, and most everyone I know for that matter, complain that these trailers make seeing the film redundant, even unnecessary. But the studios are convinced story trailers (that reveal much of a film's plot) are necessary. Plot, of course, isn't all that important to blockbusters; the studios appreciate the fact that blockbusters all follow the same narrow story track. More importantly, studio marketers are convinced that the single most important question for prospective audiences is: "what's the film about?" The story trailer is designed to answer that question.

4 *United States* v. *Capitol Service, Inc.*, 756 F 2nd 502 (7th Cir.), cert. Denied, 474 US 945 (1985).

5 For more on the *Capitol Service* case in particular and antitrust issues in general, see Lewis (2000: 50–85).

6 *Independence Day* grossed $50 million on its opening weekend. By the end of its first run, its domestic gross topped $300 million. As of September 2001, its total theatrical gross worldwide was a breathtaking $797 million (against a production budget estimated at $75 million).

References

Bart, Peter (1999) *The Gross: The Hits, The Flops – The Summer that Ate Hollywood*, New York and London: St Martin's Press.

Cassidy, John (1997) "Chaos in Hollywood: Can Science Explain Why a Movie is a Hit or a Flop?," *New Yorker*, March 31: 36.

Lewis, Jon (2000) *Hard Core: How the Struggle over Censorship Saved the Modern Film Industry*, New York: New York University Press.

Rice-Barker, Leo (1996) "Industry Banks on New Technology, Expanded Slates," *Playback*, May 6: 19.

Shaw, David (2001) "Tinseltown Spins Yarns – Media Takes Bait," *Los Angeles Times*, February 15: Calendar section; online: www.latimes.com/images/Blackpix.gif.

Thomson, David (1996) "Who Killed the Movies?," *Esquire*, December: 56.

Tough, Paul (1993) "The New Auteurs," *Harpers*, June: 38.

Trainor, Richard (1987–8) "Major Powers," *Sight and Sound* (winter): 26.

3

THE HOLLYWOOD BLOCKBUSTER

Industrial analysis and practice

Douglas Gomery

The first cinema century ended symbolically on 19 May, 1999, with the premiere of George Lucas's blockbuster *Star Wars: Episode 1 – The Phantom Menace*. More than one month before its 19 May premiere, 20th Century-Fox – twenty-two years after Lucas's *Star Wars* (1977) – began its TV ad blitz. While Lucas spent $115 million to produce *The Phantom Menace*, Fox spent about $50 million to make anyone who lived in the US know "Star Wars" was back. Fox also lined up deals for further merchandising and publicity. Toy-maker Hasbro paid a quarter of a billion dollars for toy rights; Pepsi agreed to spend $2 billion to promote *The Phantom Menace* – and two future sequels – along with its soft drinks. *Star Wars: Episode 1 – The Phantom Menace* opened to a record $28.5 million-worth of tickets sold on its first day, setting a new record. The twentieth century's final blockbuster was born.

Nothing better than this success of *The Phantom Menace* defined the continuing importance and economic power of the blockbuster as distributed by one of Hollywood's six major studios. George Lucas alone could not distribute his epic; he needed 20th Century-Fox to guarantee sales to foreign cinema circuits, pay-TV networks, and home-video retailers. Fox did its job, milking millions from domestic and foreign home video sales and rentals, and pay-TV, and *The Phantom Menace* became a member of the elite all-time Top Fifty "blockbuster list" – once all the monies were counted. All of the above traits represented the blockbuster, fully and completely, as an industry business strategy.

The big bang: the blockbuster's origins

In June 1975 *Jaws* initiated the era of the Hollywood blockbuster. This tale of shark terror, which earned more than $100 million at the box office in six months, easily surpassed *The Godfather* (1972) as the all-time Hollywood box-office champ by the

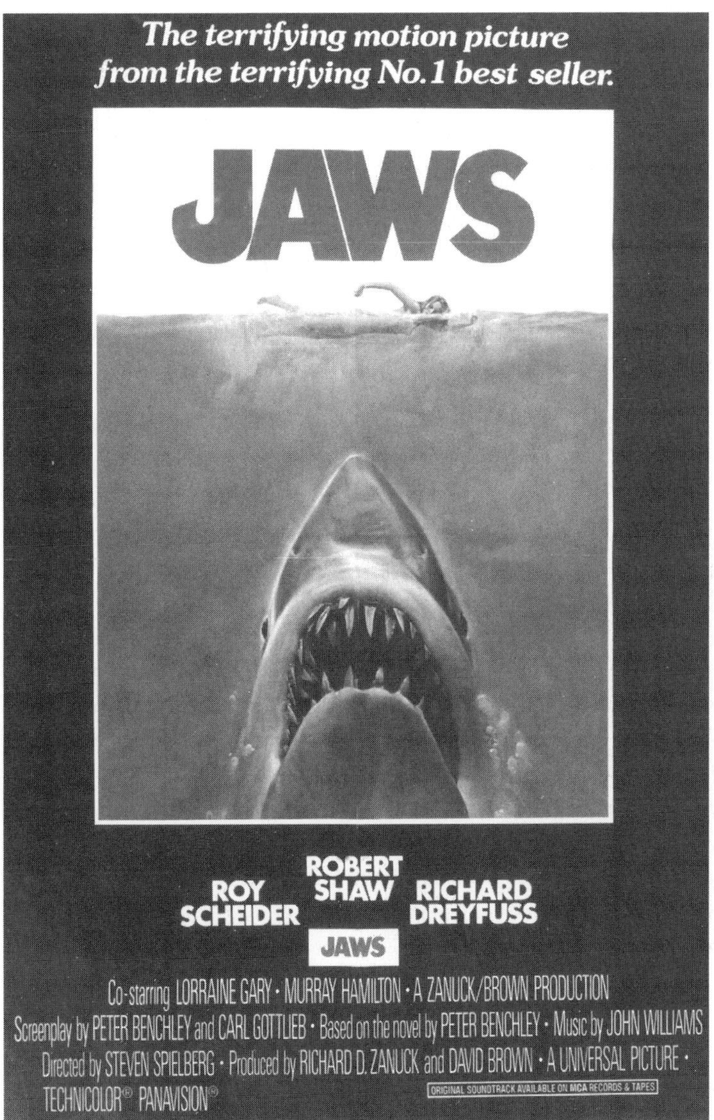

Figure 3.1 *Jaws* (1975). The Kobal Collection/Universal.

end of summer 1975. Although *Star Wars* and *E.T.: The Extra-Terrestrial* (1982) would go on to better *Jaws*'s record, it was *Jaws* which rendered the TV marketing precedents that have became key to the Hollywood blockbuster as an industry practice. *Jaws* proved that one film under careful guidance from its distributor, in this case Universal, could precipitate a national pop cultural "event," and make millions upon millions of dollars for a single studio with but a single film.

Universal opened *Jaws* in 409 American movie houses in June 1975, after its distributor, Universal, fully saturated prime-time US television with promotional ads. Universal, under Lew Wasserman's guidance, purchased at least one thirty-second ad on every prime time network television program (on then ABC, CBS, and NBC) during the evenings of the three days preceding the premiere at a cost of $1 million. So successful was this TV advertising campaign that it has become standard operating procedure in the American film industry. Gone were the days of a glamorous New York City or Hollywood premiere, critical reaction, and then gradual release first across the US. *Jaws* convinced Hollywood movie executives that television should be the centerpiece of the launch of a blockbuster. The rivalry with TV was over: Hollywood learned to use television; avoiding TV as a means of advertising became a practice of the past.

In seventeen days, *Jaws* earned an extraordinary $36 million at the US domestic box office. House records were broken in city after city. To the general public, Universal turned the June, July and August of 1975 into the "summer of the shark." The film inspired false sightings, pop songs, and brisk sales of posters, T-shirts, beach towels, and shark-tooth pendants. The stock of Universal's parent company, MCA, doubled – solely based on *Jaws*.

Suddenly one film, marketed through a "rival" medium of television, could break box-office records, generate millions of dollars in ancillary sales, fashion a profitable year for its distributor studio, and generate a rise in stock price which made everyone invested an "instant" millionaire and celebrity. Hollywood initiated a new way of doing business, one never "killed" by TV, but rather aided by it. A new era for industry practice had begun, as studios since then have looked for that single film which can convert a poor year into a record one. Movies became special "pop culture" attractions, predicating predictable cash flows that in the long-run needed ten figures to tally their total revenue intake.

Why Universal?

Universal's boss, Lew Wasserman, innovated the blockbuster business practices that would transform Hollywood. Beginning as an agent, in the 1950s, Wasserman moved into independent television and film production, in the 1960s took over Universal, and by the mid-1970s was ready to use his knowledge of television to redefine film production, distribution, and presentation with the blockbuster. In the process he reinvented Hollywood. George Lucas and Steven Spielberg may have gotten credit as the filmmakers, but it was Lew Wasserman who reinvented the system which enabled their films to become blockbusters.

In what would be his final innovation in studio business practice, Wasserman reasoned something new had to be done to add more profitability to feature film-making. He coupled mass saturated advertising on prime-time television with simultaneous saturation bookings in new shopping mall cineplexes across the US. Advertising on hit broadcast television shows became the key to turning a feature film into a blockbuster. Milking millions and millions of dollars from "ancillary rights" redefined a seemingly limitless upper bound of profit possibilities.

Jaws was not the first film sold by and through broadcast television, but its million-dollar success proved that strategy was the one that would redefine Hollywood through saturation advertising. The Wasserman-led Universal money-making machine reached it climax and closure with *E.T.* in 1982, bring the company that was languishing two decades earlier revenues that needed to be measured in the billions of dollars. Again Hollywood – as filmmaker, not the source of most prime time television – stood atop the pop culture hierarchy, able with a single film to initiate a true widespread popular-culture phenomenon leading to infusions of dollars.

With the innovation of the blockbuster *Jaws*, Wasserman led the Hollywood industry to and beyond a key transitional moment. The business has never been the same since. Hollywood already had world theatrical distribution under its control, but was still uncomfortable with its relationship with television. The blockbuster changed all that, allying with television to promote a "product" so efficiently that, while up-front costs of production could soar, profits rose even faster. In turn, this symbiotic linkage to television changed all phases of the Hollywood film industry.

Through the late 1970s, Lew Wasserman stood atop a renewed Hollywood moving-image business. Yet his success would last but seven years – through *E.T.* – as others were quick to copy his innovations. By 1990 Wasserman was an aging mogul working on the edge of a system he had created, still respected as an industry "godfather," but no longer a pioneer.

The effects of what Wasserman wrought

The innovation of the blockbuster affected all aspects of the film industry. With an upside profit so high, producers began spending more, but with constraints. Potential blockbusters had to be tied to how well the "product" could be hawked on television and simultaneously merchandized. A blockbuster could seek to exploit any genre, even if the record setters seem all to be action-adventure and science-fiction epics. To put more action and special effects in potential blockbusters, computers were increasingly used to enable filmmakers to meld live action with animation. Disney's *Who Framed Roger Rabbit?* (1988) achieved a nearly miraculous interaction of live and cartoon figures; a decade later *Pearl Harbor* (2001) added animated people to the possibilities of expanding computer capability to traditional narrative filmmaking.

The production of the original negative represented less and less of the total cost of releasing the film. And without saturation marketing, particularly through expensive television advertising campaigns, no blockbuster could be created. In pre-production, the marketing strategy was devised simultaneously with the script. Marketing people worked to create consumer products and obtain product placement tie-ins. The quicker the consumer products could be created, such as T-shirts and toys, the more awareness could be built up in the advertising campaign. In addition, product placement allowed the studio to gain money to up-front their products in a blockbuster's narrative, and then tie the products into the overall marketing through shared costs of television advertising.

Blockbusters start their distribution life in the US. One of the more important decisions lies in the choice of a release date; summer (middle May through early September) is best; Christmas (middle November through early January) is the second-best solution. In this game of bluff, the six majors seek an exclusive for the weekend release. The goal for an exclusive is to gain at least 2,000 screens, and preferably 3,000, for simultaneous release. Most sought-after dates (in order) are Memorial Day weekend (last Monday in May), Independence Day weekend (around the 4th of July), Thanksgiving Day weekend (last Thursday in November), and Christmas Day weekend. If an exclusive cannot be captured, then a targeted blockbuster is released. An example of this came in 1999 when *Notting Hill* was released over Memorial Day weekend, despite having to go up against *Star Wars: Episode 1 – The Phantom Menace*. *Notting Hill* was able to succeed because it was targeted toward women, whom the studio bosses assumed would not be interested in the *Star Wars* prequel. And they were right.

Hollywood studios try to set in place their blockbuster media (read: TV) strategies about eight weeks before the opening. Basing these strategies upon extensive market research, moguls spend in proportion to what they figure the picture will gross. In the media buy, television is by far the greatest expense, including network and cable. Newspapers, magazines, radio, and outdoor advertisements are considered supplements.

The television spots define the film's campaign. These thirty-second ads are inserted into programs with the demographics of the audiences the studio bosses deem will attend the potential blockbuster. Here is where stars and narrative are crucial. If the film is intended to appeal to everyone – such as *Titanic* (1997) – then studio executives need to place the advertisements so as to aim it at all people; that means TV programs with the highest ratings, such as the Super Bowl. This is what the industry calls "reach" – seeking the maximum exposure to as many persons as possible. But moviegoers on average are educated, middle-class young people, so shows such as *Sienfeld*, *Friends*, and *Frasier* are almost movie trailers interspersed within a TV narrative because their TV audiences match the target movie audience. With this correlation the studios maximize "frequency" – or how many times potential audience members see the TV ad for the film. The bottom line is that the studio bosses must strategize an optimal plan to reach the target audience with as many "exposures" in the days just before the release into multiplexes. Then the film can generate millions of dollars of ticket sales on the first weekend and be declared a blockbuster.

All this up-front costing and planning can really only be afforded by the six major studios – all vertically integrated operations: Paramount, Warner Bros., Universal, 20th Century-Fox, Disney, and Sony. These six – year in, year out – control almost 80 percent of the movie business in the US, and approximately half the market in Sweden, Germany, and several other nations in Western Europe, not to mention Asia. They keep their "Big Six" club exclusive in part because few can afford the true cost of investing in a blockbuster, in 2001 nearing $150 million. All this spending can be blamed on what Lew Wasserman wrought a quarter of a century ago.

The new markets

Classic price discrimination – releasing a film so as to maximize the revenues from each separate "window" – has long defined Hollywood. Basically, this means that the "Big Six" release films in the following order: theaters, home video, pay-per-view, pay cable, and finally, broadcast and basic cable television. This release line-up is for the US and all other nations. Each window in this sequence is opened to draw out the maximum amount of revenue, and then shut. A new window is opened only when all the value of the previous window has been fully captured.

Many have predicted the end of the theatrical window. But opening a blockbuster in a multiplex is vital, and TV will not kill it, but rather assist it in growing in importance. By the end of the twentieth century, a blockbuster was defined by how well it does in theaters in the US during its first few weeks. Indeed, the goal of the two-month marketing campaign has been to make a film a "first-choice." If not "voted" a blockbuster after three weeks, another potential blockbuster replaces it. The chief executives of the "Big Six" want to create a hit in first-run theaters because history has shown that blockbusters in theaters mean maximum revenues in the later windows. This is why it is no paradox that, in our age of home video, there are more screens in US theaters than at any time in cinema history.

The new markets began in 1972 when Time, Inc. transformed the world of cable television in the US with Home Box Office. For a monthly fee of about $10, cable television subscribers saw recent Hollywood motion pictures – uncut, uninterrupted by commercials, and not sanitized to please network censors. For the first time in the television age, Hollywood had found a way to make TV viewers pay for what they watched in their living rooms. With "pay television," HBO drew back the older movie fan who did not want to go out to a theater, but loved watching second-run films on television at home.

This technological movie-viewing revolution was expanded in 1975 with the beginning of the home-video revolution when Sony introduced its half-inch home videocassette recorder. An enthusiastic public around the world snapped up so many machines that by the close of the twentieth century nearly all homes with TV sets had a VCR nearby.

During the early 1980s Hollywood found a way to make the most of these new technologies. Pay-cable channels copied HBO, and were offered by the dozen. Stores renting and selling videos popped up on every street corner. By the mid-1980s, "ancillary" revenues passed box-office take. Soon, the Internet made buying a tape and having it delivered a simple set of moves of the mouse. By the late 1990s the VCR alone was generating more than $20 billion in rentals and sales in the US, three times the box-office take. As the twentieth century ended, the DVD began to deliver better quality movie images and digital sounds, but more importantly added yet another window to the blockbuster's revenue life.

The average release of a blockbuster to home video (VHS and DVD) comes within seven months of its theatrical release. The distribution and marketing departments of a studio decide upon the release date and advertising for the cable and video release. Cable promotes the films as trailers. The marketing of video usually comprises the creation of in-store advertising campaigns using now familiar icons made famous by the blockbuster theatrical release. The revenues at these stages is more often than not pure profit, as the costs of the film have been fully covered at the theatrical stage.

Successful blockbusters constitute the core of the rental and sell-through market. Studies have shown that there is a correlation between the success of a film at the box office and the success of a film in the home-video market. The action-adventure and comedy genres are specifically known to do well in the home-video market. Video sales are not really a seasonal business except during Christmas, when the sell-through market peaks.

TV is often portrayed as the killer of the Hollywood studio system. Yet here is another example where television windows stand at the core of the "film" business. The multiplication of exhibition windows through various means of TV distribution globally means that "ancillary markets" account for 75 percent of a blockbuster's revenues. Domestic theatrical box-office figures are therefore now, more than ever, only a partial index of a film's financial success performance, even though they continue to be featured in headlines, tables, and lists in the industry's journals. The dirty secret is the studios do not want us to know just how much is made on blockbusters after they leave theaters. Releasing box-office data has become part of the promotion. Once over, the studios gain no advantage by releasing data.

Auteurs and risk

Steven Spielberg's *Jaws* marked the entry of a new, younger generation of Hollywood directors. George Lucas followed. Their ability to produce blockbusters made them central to the blockbuster era. They – among others – can create blockbuster cycles, or what studios call franchises. We know them by their numbers: *Jurassic Park 3* (2001), *Rocky IV* (1985), *Halloween III* (1982), and a score of *Friday the 13ths*. *Jaws* proved that the studio risked not making sequels as it inspired a slew of imitators: werewolves (replacing sharks) in Joe Dante's *The Howling* (1981) and John Landis's *An American Werewolf in London* (1981); vampires in John Badham's *Dracula* (1979) and Tony Scott's *The Hunger* (1983), and so on. Far better was Fox's claim on George Lucas's *Star Wars* sequels and prequels – the ultimate franchise.

Yet even Lucas and Spielberg have had their blockbuster busts. While *Star Wars* minted money, Lucas's *Howard the Duck* (1986) did not. *Jaws* and *E.T.* set records, but Spielberg's *1941* (1979) and *A.I.* (2001) fade into obscurity. There is risk. Not all intended blockbusters become vast money-minting movie machines. During the summer of 1998, for example, *Godzilla* seemed destined to become the newest blockbuster success, based as it was on a well-known "brand" and a marketing campaign the size of its star. The film was released over the 1998 Memorial Day weekend, but ended up with a cumulative US domestic box-office gross of $136 million. Simply because of a Memorial Day weekend haul of just $58 million, the additional $78 million could not prevent it from being labeled a failure.

In retrospect, the problems began a year earlier when the first theatrical trailers and TV advertisements for *Godzilla* were released worldwide. Expectations could not have been higher based upon its $120 million budget. In trying to build up the anticipation that this was going to be one of the biggest blockbuster events ever, Sony kept the title monster out of the public's eye to maintain an air of mystery. As the months went by the advertising got more and more spectacular, costing an estimated $50 million. Sony finally released *Godzilla* to a then-record 3,310 screens across the US, approximately one in ten.

Sony executives looked to recent Memorial Day successful blockbusters – *Men in Black* (1997) and *Mission: Impossible* (1996). How could *Godzilla* not come close to Steven Spielberg's *The Lost World*, which had opened with a cumulative US gross of $93 million over the Memorial Day weekend of the previous year? Similar to the occupants of *The Lost World*, *Godzilla* was a dinosaur-like creature, so Sony executives reasoned *Godzilla* ought to gross in the vicinity of $90 million. Its marketing budget eclipsed that of *The Lost World*, and the expectations that the two filmmakers, Dean Devlin and Roland Emmerich, were going to deliver the goods on this picture were high. Two years earlier, the duo delivered one of the highest grossing pictures of all time, *Independence Day*. Yet the actual take was half that, and by the end of June all industry observers were shaking their heads and looking for a new trend in blockbusters. The risk simply could not be eliminated.

Studios try using market research to obtain sample feedback from the potential audience. Marketing research usually starts with concept-testing, where the research group sees how the audience relates to a specific movie idea. This moves on to testing titles, stars, and even alternative print campaigns. Yet, for all the fancy focus groups, previewing remains at the core of the market research for a blockbuster. At a production preview the production executives work closely with the filmmakers to fine-tune the movie. Often this leads to creative conflict, and indeed it slowed the release of *Titanic* by six months. More often than Hollywood would like to admit, the preview process can end up altering what the final film released contains.

Ultimately, to minimize risk, all six of the major studios function as part of vertically integrated media conglomerates. These conglomerates have stakes in multiple media industries, and so it is rare when one of their divisions is not atop one of the many industries in which they participate.

The Hollywood transformation into the cores of fully vertically integrated mass-media corporations began in July 1969, when Steven J. Ross's Kinney Corp. took over Warner-Seven Arts and renamed it Warner Communications, Inc. Thereafter, through the 1970s, Ross expanded the divisions of the company to embrace all new forms of release. In the process he created the late twentieth-century prototype media conglomerate, as Warner acquired cable TV's Home Box Office and took Hollywood directly into the business of operating cable TV systems. For Ross these new TV technologies were not to be fought but embraced for they were simply more outlets for Warner Bros.' Hollywood studio productions. Ross looked to total vertical integration, the ownership of means of production, distribution, and presentation to the public.

By the early 1990s, Ross had expanded the studio operations of now Time Warner to cover all media outside radio and newspapers. To some, Time Warner seemed to be a "cable TV company" because of its innovation of HBO and Cinemax and multiple system cable operations. To others it was a film studio. *Time* seemed to define it as a magazine company. It was all this and more. Indeed, Ross saw each acquisition as a step to protecting his company's "ancillary markets." He sought to take greater and greater advantage of the power which vertical integration offered: reducing costs of sales and transactions, and thereby increasing profits. His vertically integrated corporation would sell films to "itself," and thus not have to absorb the expenses associated with bidding for product from others. He did not live to see the AOL merger, but surely would have approved of it, as the logic behind the deal was the same as he had been using for decades.

Ross also recognized that conglomeratization enabled Warners to maintain its growing economic power and keep out the competition. Cross-subsidization, in particular, enabled him, with his ever-growing power in more and more media markets, to take profits from a thriving area to invest and innovate in another. Single-line competitors did not have this luxury and so were gradually taken over by the Time Warners of the world.

In the end, vertical integrating media conglomerates generated considerable profits from a wide spectrum of mass media enterprises, including theme parks, recorded music, publishing, and film and television production, distribution, and exhibition. But at the core was the blockbuster. They generated the franchises that vertical integration could optimally milk and that conglomeratization could protect for only the "Big Six." Thus the blockbuster may seem a single product, but in reality it stands at the core of the mighty vertically integrated media conglomerates which define our cultural world as we begin the twenty-first century.

The blockbuster's future

The blockbuster reinvented Hollywood. Its profits so overwhelm the corporation that such financial publications as the *Wall Street Journal* report increases and declines in stock prices simply based on first weekend box-office take. In its quarter-century history, the blockbuster has taken the six major Hollywood studios into a Golden Age of profitability far greater than ever before in movie industry history. With the rise of new technologies – video assisted production, distribution by satellite, exhibition on cable television and directly to the home by satellite – we have entered a business world which can only grow bigger and more powerful.

Because it takes so much up-front investment and time for an independent film to make a profit, independent distributors and moviemakers have a tough time surviving in today's world. Integrated major studios can shoulder the burden of loss while still cranking out multiple pictures a year, one of which is surely to become a blockbuster. For the most part, releasing a movie into the marketplace ends up being a big risk no individual can afford – even a Steven Spielberg or a George Lucas. Thus most so-called independent studios are in reality parts of the "Big Six." So, while Miramax might be known for its cutting-edge films, it is actually only one of many divisions of the vast Disney corporation. In the end Miramax is not independent, but, like all Disney divisions, responsible to Disney chief operating officer, Michael Eisner.

As much as critics pan blockbusters, as we move into the twenty-first century, interest in watching movies has never been higher. Only the technology for presentation seems to change, indeed expanding the possibilities for viewing. All of these changes, from cable to pay-television, from the multiplex to the VCR, from the DVD to the Internet, add up to one clear trend: more and more people are watching more and more movies. And their monies end up in the coffers of the six major studios.

And this is not just in the US. Throughout most of the world Hollywood filmmakers such as George Lucas and Steven Spielberg have became the cultural idols of a generation in the same way novelists had only two decades earlier. Students around the world dream about creating the great blockbuster, becoming a rich and powerful maker of movies, and usually moving to Hollywood in the process.

Looking to history, nothing looms on the horizon to alter this business and industrial practice. In all the technological transformation for movie-viewing, the major movie corporations have lost none of their power. A handful of companies formed more than a half century ago – albeit with new owners – still have hegemony over the creation of the movie blockbusters and their distribution in all technologies throughout the world. Since the end of World War II they have survived the forced selling of their theater chains, the rise of network television, the advent of cable and pay-television, and, most recently, the videocassette revolution. These companies may have new owners, but they show no signs of weakening. Indeed, if anything, they are getting stronger.

Worldwide business at the box office also remains quite healthy, with Paramount and Fox's co-production *Titanic* by the close of 1998 having grossed more than $1.8 billion in tickets over the globe for a single film. In 1998 two of the "Big Six" exceeded $1 billion in world box-office revenues – Viacom's Paramount Pictures and the Disney studio. 20th Century-Fox, Sony, and Warner Bros. gathered in about three-quarters of a billion dollars each.

The future for the blockbuster looks bright. The blockbuster – whether seen in a theater, on pay TV, or as home video – will continue to play a defining role in world media economics. Realistically, as we begin the new century, nothing looms on the horizon that will threaten the oligopolistic power of the major studios and their blockbuster creations. The "Big Six" major Hollywood studios will continue to enjoy the fruits of their formidable economic power, and their influence will keep reaching throughout the world, more powerfully than any other mass medium. The Hollywood oligopoly has learned to thrive in the age of advanced technologies, based on skilled use of media economics.

This oligopoly will continue to operate with its safe and predictable blockbuster narrative formulae. The "Big Six" will compete over small differences rather than important considerations of filmic expression. Kristin Thompson is right; the blockbuster has not changed and will not change Hollywood's classical style. Sequels have a built-in recognition factor, and an emotional appeal that makes the job of profit maximization much easier than trying to locate a new film made by some independent. The homogenization of content and style – within well-accepted limits and properly called the classical Hollywood style – derives from the oligopoly of the "Big Six." And the "Big Six" will continue their power and this style well into the twenty first century making and marketing blockbusters.

A bibliographic essay

This chapter really began twenty years ago when I wrote an essay on Hollywood of the 1970s for *Wide Angle* – "The American Film Industry of the 1970s," (5, 3 [1983], 52–9). In 1984, I was requested to pen a short essay on *Jaws* for the first volume of the *International Dictionary of Films and Filmmakers* (London: St James Press), which opened my eyes to the importance of a film I had seen in Milwaukee's Northridge mall. Marilyn and T. P. Moon and Stephen Heath pointed out that *Jaws* was something new and different.

In my book *Shared Pleasures: A History of Movie Presentation in the United States* (Madison: University of Wisconsin Press, 1992), the blockbuster figured centrally in the changes in movie presentation I sought to analyze. One of my contributions in Geoffrey Nowell-Smith's *The Oxford History of World Cinema* (Oxford: Oxford University Press, 1996) enabled me to reflect on the blockbuster in the early 1990s. My essay in Steve Neale and Murray Smith's *Contemporary Hollywood Cinema* (London: Routledge, 1998) argued in part that Lew Wasserman used the blockbuster strategy as his way to reinvent the Universal studio, and thus the Hollywood industry itself.

My longest and most extensive analysis of the place of the blockbuster in Hollywood can be found in my book (co-authored with Benjamin M. Compaine) *Who Owns the Media?* (Mahwah, NJ: Erlbaum Publishers, 2000) where I devote 40,000 words to analyzing fully the ownership, operation, and implications of the Hollywood film industry as the twentieth century ended. My chapter's 166 endnotes, six corporate profiles, and seventeen tables – generated with the help of Meredith Traber and Daniel Pickett – provide all the citations and notations anyone might desire or need to verify, and dissect, my arguments about the history and economics of the blockbuster's key role in the transformation of Hollywood as it entered the twenty-first century.

4

THE ROLE OF THE AUTEUR IN THE AGE OF THE BLOCKBUSTER

Steven Spielberg and DreamWorks

Warren Buckland

In his polemical discussion of auteurism, André Bazin wrote that it involves "choosing the personal factor in artistic creation as a standard of reference" ([1957] 1985: 255). However, he also distanced himself from the other auteur critics of the 1950s by pointing out the commonplace notion that "the cinema is an art which is both popular and *industrial*" (ibid.: 251; emphasis added). An auteur is a technician or craft worker (principally a director) who attains the status of artist. But is the label of artist merely a form of (self-) invention? What processes are involved in the transformation of a technician into an auteur, especially in the industrial and economic organization of contemporary Hollywood (the "package-unit system")? And is there a correlation between the "package-unit system" of film production and the rise of blockbusters? I shall argue that an auteur in contemporary Hollywood is a director who gains control over all the stages of filmmaking: not just film production, but also distribution and exhibition. In other words, he or she attempts to vertically integrate (or *re*integrate) the various stages of filmmaking. As an example, I shall refer to the Hollywood director most associated with movie blockbusters, Steven Spielberg, focusing on his authorship and relation to the DreamWorks studio he co-founded with Jeffrey Katzenberg and David Geffen on October 12, 1994.

Steven Spielberg and Benjamin Franklin, Francis Coppola, and Mark Twain

The traditional criteria for identifying authorship are internal to films, and center on the auteur's control of the filmmaking process. This internal approach to auteurism can be divided into two categories: the classical auteur, a skilled craft worker who has mastered – and indeed represents – "the tradition"; and the Romantic auteur: a lone, creative genius who works intuitively and mysteriously outside of all traditions. When speaking of Hollywood auteurs, we are referring primarily to auteurs of the classical tradition, who work inside the institution of Hollywood but are able to react against its mass-production techniques and master the filmmaking process to the extent that they can create stylistic and thematic consistencies (an authorial signature) in their films. And – in the case of directors such as Spielberg or Alfred Hitchcock, for example – the classical auteur can gain a reputation by using both *mise-en-scène* and narrational strategies effectively to create a precise audience response. The category of the Romantic auteur is reserved primarily for the (traditionally European) art film director, or American independents who cater to specialized audiences (such as Hal Hartley, Jim Jarmusch, Richard Linklater, and Kevin Smith).

More specifically, an internal approach to auteurism analyzes the filmmaker's craft, his or her "poetics." John Caughie writes that "it is in the *mise en scène* – the disposition of the scene, in the camera movement, in the camera placement, in the movement from shot to shot – that the *auteur* writes his individuality into the film" (Caughie 1981: 12–13). Similarly (and from the perspective of the more rigorous statistical style analysis), Barry Salt identifies a director's style by systematically collecting data on the formal parameters of films, particularly those parameters most directly under the director's control, including duration of the shot, shot scale, camera movement, angle of shot, and strength of the cut (measured in terms of the spatiotemporal displacement from one shot to the next). Salt collects data from these parameters by laboriously analyzing films shot by shot, and by defining a director's style as a distinct patterning of form (Salt 1974).

V. F. Perkins has outlined the director's role in detail (1972: chapter 5). He writes that "the director's most significant area of control is over what happens *within* the image. His control over the action, in detail, organization and emphasis, enables him to produce a personal treatment of the script situation. On occasion the treatment can be so personal as to constitute a reversal of attitudes contained in the script" (ibid.: 74). But he adds that the director does not need to subvert the script to make a personal statement: instead, he or she can intensify part of the script's possibilities, to organize it into (what Clive Bell calls) significant form: "The director has to start from what is known or necessary or likely or, at the very least, possible. From this base he can go on to organize the relationship between action, image and décor, to create meaning through pattern" (ibid.: 94). In contrast to Caughie and Salt, Perkins also emphasizes that it is the director's control of the action and the actors' gestures that partly defines personal style: "the director defines his effects *within* the action" (ibid.: 95), which can be effective and distinctive as long as the director does not impose meaning on or reach beyond the limits of the action.

The gradual shift in Hollywood film production from the "producer-unit system" to the "package-unit system" has redefined the role of the workforce, especially the director. Mastery of the filmmaking process is no longer a sufficient criterion for authorship status: the director also needs to control external factors such as production, money, and the deal-making process. The director needs to become a power broker, a talent worker (which involves mastery of management skills), and must also create a brand image, in order to gain positional advantage over the competition. Christopherson and Storper (1989) call these external criteria "industry-specific" rather than "occupation-specific" skills.[1]

But why are industry-specific skills necessary? Susan Gillman points out the conflict between authorship and the rise of mass publishing in the US:

> Increases in population and literacy, combined with advances in technology and transport, were the enabling conditions for a massive increase in book and journal output following the Civil War. The rapidly expanding business of producing and marketing literary products created what was in some ways a boom for writers. . . . [Yet] the net result was an implied paradox: as the man of letters' name grew more and more widely known and his books were more and more popularly consumed, he became less and less in control of his book/product, his audience/consumer, and his own image . . . The writer's authorial freedom, then, is fatally compromised by the success of his own writings.
>
> (Gillman 1989: 23–4, as quoted in Dillon 1997: 58)

According to Gillman, in the age of mass production, internal authorship – mastery of the writing process – is necessary but no longer sufficient in the creation of authorship. External control – that is, control of the immediate organizational and economic environment – is also necessary. Both Benjamin Franklin and Samuel Clemens (Mark Twain) took great interest in writing as well as printing and publishing. But whereas Franklin was successful both as a writer and a publisher, Clemens's investments in publishing led to bankruptcy (C. L. Webster & Co. went bankrupt in 1894). The literary double Samuel Clemens created (Mark Twain) was a success (he mastered the art of writing, a mark of internal authorship), but as a publisher he was a failure (he was unable to control his external authorship).

In the mass-production system of classical Hollywood, the studios maintained external control of authorship by stamping a distinct studio identity on their films, controlling the hiring, production, marketing, and distribution decisions, creating and maintaining their stars' persona, and so on. Within this system many directors remained anonymous craft workers, or *metteurs en scène*. However, a number of directors mastered the filmmaking process and worked against its mass-production techniques to create stylistic and thematic consistencies in their films, and a few, such as Hitchcock, attempted to become independent filmmakers and promote themselves. However, Hitchcock's two independent productions, *Rope* (1948) and *Under Capricorn* (1949), made little money, and Hitchcock returned to the studios in 1950. And, as Robert Kapsis has documented, in the 1950s Hitchcock successfully promoted himself as an entertainer (the master of the suspense thriller), while in the 1960s he attempted to develop a new self-image by promoting himself (to highbrow film critics) as a serious auteur (Kapsis 1992).

In the following section I shall emphasize how production in Hollywood after the 1940s shifted to the making of fewer but more expensive films, from which studios expected to make huge profits. With emphasis on the individual high-profile film – the blockbuster – to generate all the profits, each one needs to be controlled more strictly in the marketplace, which not only includes exhibition in cinemas throughout the world, but also TV broadcasts, video releases, and merchandizing. Part of Spielberg's decision – and Coppola's before him – to establish his own studio, after running his own film company, Amblin, was to attain control over his films in this rich marketplace. Like a handful of other contemporary Hollywood directors, Spielberg is an auteur, *not* because he is working against the Hollywood industry (as were the auteurs in classical Hollywood), for the industry is no longer governed by mass production. Instead Spielberg is an auteur because he occupies key positions in the industry (producer, director, studio co-owner, franchise licensee); he is therefore attempting to vertically reintegrate the stages of filmmaking – but, unlike classical Hollywood, the integration is under the control of the creative talent, not managers. Whereas Coppola tried to vertically integrate in the 1970s and 1980s – his Zoetrope studios ended up in much the same way as Twain's publishing company – Spielberg has been as successful as Benjamin Franklin. Spielberg's colleague George Lucas is a successful external auteur, but not internal – at least on the evidence of his lack of mastery of *mise-en-scène* and narrational strategies in directing *The Phantom Menace* (1999), a film that succeeded on the basis of Lucas's control of external authorship processes.

Deal-making and the blockbuster

Janet Staiger argues that one of the problems a vertically integrated film industry faced was not only that it broke monopoly or antitrust laws, but also that the major studios were burdened with a self-generated demand – to fill their own theaters (1983: 69). Such a demand encouraged the mass production of films, as did the practice of blind-selling and block-booking. The divorcement of theaters from the majors due to the Paramount Decrees of 1948, plus the outlawing of blind-selling and block-booking, meant that each individual film took on more importance, for it had to be sold to exhibitors on its own merits. Production values of each film increased, and the differentiation (primarily through stars, directors, and special effects) of films from each other intensified. Each film became a prestigious product which, potentially at least, had a longer shelf life, which means it was able to attract more box-office receipts.

Jim Hillier has developed a similar argument: "Releases from the majors settled down at a little over 100 a year in the 1980s as against 350 or more fifty years earlier" (Hillier 1992: 16). Consequently, focus shifted to individual films: "with fewer films to share the ups and downs of profitability, there was a greater need for at least some to make big profits" (ibid.: 10). Each film therefore needed to be treated as an event: "each film needed to be special in some way and marketed as such" (ibid.: 16). In addition, the film needed to be heavily promoted: "from the 1970s, so much more was riding on individual films that immensely larger sums were thought necessary for promotion and publicity" (ibid.: 16).

These industrial and economic changes functioned as incentives to the rise of blockbusters in the film industry. Economists comment that "the growing emphasis on blockbusters reflects a rational adaptation by risk adverse firms to changing market conditions" (Garvin 1981: 2). In the film industry after World War II, those changing market conditions were set off, not only by the Paramount Decrees, but also the rise of competition from TV, as well as the rise of fixed costs (rents, rates, and labor costs, which increased substantially after World War II, thereby increasing a film's breakeven level). The film industry's response to TV is now well known: the invention of CinemaScope, the short-lived 3-D, and the increased use of color. Tino Balio emphasizes that "all these innovations brought people back to the movies. [But] they did not resume their former moviegoing ways before television; customers became selective. As a result, the phenomenon of the "big picture" characterized business more and more" (1985: 433). In other words, the audiences still went to the movies, but only on special occasions, rather than most evenings. The studios therefore realized that the market for films was finite, and thereby cut back on production, but invested heavily in the fewer films being made. This is because a large, expensive production has the potential of overcoming its immense costs by attracting huge audiences and spectacularly large revenues, of becoming the special movie that draws audiences back to the cinema.[2]

Moreover, blockbusters are formulaic because they adopt the same types of self-insurance: a reliance on presold elements (such as a successful novel); well-known performers who play characters embodying simple, clear-cut moral values; elements of spectacle and special effects; and narrative motivation. Furthermore, blockbusters encouraged the introduction of new distribution patterns (from platform release to saturation release) and saturation advertising.

In addition to making fewer films, studios outsourced film production to independent companies. The studios' role was limited to financing and distributing the independently produced films:

> The initial and later incentives to shift to an industrial structure of independent firms releasing through the majors fostered the development of a system of production in which film products were set up on a film-by-film arrangement. . . . While in early 1950 about 25 per cent of the films in production were clearly independent productions (with other films including profit sharing for certain staff personnel), in early 1956 the figure was about 53 per cent, and in early 1959, it was 70 per cent.
>
> (Staiger 1983: 78)[3]

Similarly, Tino Balio writes that "independent production has become assimilated by the majors as an alternative to the studio system of production" (1985: 419).

Despite this shift from the producer-unit system, which mass produced films, to the package-unit system, in which independents produced a few high-cost films, Staiger argues that the package-unit system continues the detailed division of labor of the producer unit system (Staiger, in Bordwell, Staiger, and Thompson 1985: 330–7; esp. 330 and 335). Similarly, Jim Hillier argues that deal-making has led to a restructuring of the Hollywood film industry, not a complete revolution, and concludes that it is still business as usual in Hollywood: "the majors stuck to very cautious, very conservative, very expensive film-making . . . By the mid 1980s, the majors had demonstrated that movie production and distribution was still profitable, and the business was still essentially in their control" (1992: 17). The reason for a lack of an industrial revolution in Hollywood, according to Bordwell and Staiger, is the need to maintain the most cost-efficient form of filmmaking: the classical film style: "Historically, the classical style played a major, if not the central, role in the American film industry and its mode of production . . . the principles of classical filmmaking still hold sway . . . in most cases the desire to maintain and vary the classical style has played the determining part in Hollywood's film practice" (Bordwell and Staiger, in Bordwell, Staiger, and Thompson 1985: 367–8).

While I largely agree with the diagnosis by Bordwell, Staiger, and Hillier that the mode of film *practice* has predominately remained the same in the transition from the producer-unit system to the package-unit system (namely, a classical film practice), I disagree with their argument that the mode of *production*, particularly the division of labor, has also remained the same. Most contemporary Hollywood films begin as independent productions, while the major studios continue to finance and distribute them. Moreover, in many cases the independent production companies are set up to make one film and are dissolved when the film is completed. This results in a temporary network of freelance workers, or independent contractors. Thomas Malone and Robert Laubacher diagnose this shift, with a particular focus on the setting up in the 1990s of electronic networks between members of the new workforce:

> Tasks aren't assigned and controlled through a stable chain of management but rather are carried out autonomously by independent contractors. These electronically connected freelancers – e-lancers – join together into fluid and temporary networks to produce and sell goods and services. When a job is done – after a day, a month, a year – the network dissolves, and its members become independent agents again, circulating through the economy, seeking the next assignment.
>
> (Malone and Laubacher 1998: 146)

The temporary network has become a popular form of organization throughout the business world because it is more flexible and efficient than a permanent corporation. But this does not mean that the large corporations will disappear. What it means is that corporations now outsource their work to temporary networks of individuals or to small, specialized companies. As already noted above, Hollywood studios primarily finance and distribute films. They outsource the production process to temporary networks formed and dissolved by talent agents. These talent agents (or other players, such as an entertainment lawyer or powerful director) act as mediators between the permanent corporations (the studios) and temporary networks of filmmakers. The agent brokers the deal by initiating a project, finding and allocating resources, and/or coordinating the network of freelance workers. The temporary network appears to be particularly suited to the volatile world of contemporary commercial filmmaking. Moreover, temporary networks are established between the stages of pre-production, production, post-production, and distribution-exhibition. By contrast, in the classical Hollywood studio system, each studio (corporation) integrated financing and production, employed (rather than hired) talent and craft workers, and distributed their own films in their own theaters.

Deal-making does not encourage long-term relationships between individuals. Instead, it encourages a short-term outlook, for each temporary network needs to produce a positive (profitable) result. In addition to needing the necessary competence and skills to create such a result, the freelance workers need to specialize in one task and be distinctive to be rehired in another temporary network. In the case of directors in particular, Henry Jenkins has written that: "By treating filmmakers as independent contractors, the new production system places particular emphasis on the development of an idiosyncratic style which helps to increase the market value of individual directors" (Jenkins 1995: 115). Jenkins implies that the deal-making process encourages the auteurist approach to film consumption, since directors are provoked into demonstrating their mastery of the filmmaking process. Moreover, deal-making also encourages a number of directors to control their external authorship, via vertical integration.

Spielberg's authorship

Spielberg's internal authorship can be located in the thematic consistencies across his films: uplifting themes such as love, friendship, and childhood fantasies; themes about human contact with the unknown, ordinary people in extraordinary situations, the individual who loses control of his life, the individual separated from his home, isolation (especially the child's sense of isolation and abandonment by the father); and the serious political and moral themes as found in his later films (*The Color Purple* [1985], *Schindler's List* [1993], *Amistad* [1997], *Saving Private Ryan* [1998]).

Above all, Spielberg's internal authorship can be located in his mastery of *mise-en-scène* and especially narration. The first scene of *The Lost World: Jurassic Park* (1997) is typical. The second shot of the opening sequence is a long take lasting fifty-two seconds. It consists of a complex orchestration of camera movements and a play with off-screen space. The camera pans down from the sky and tracks right, along a coastline. It stops when a yacht comes into view. Almost immediately one of the yacht's crew enters the middle ground, screen right, and the camera shifts focus from the yacht to him. The camera then begins to track left, over the ground it has already covered. The focus shifts again as another crew member carrying a champagne bottle enters from screen right in close-up. He pours the champagne into a glass, which is on a table in the foreground. As the camera continues to track left, a family is now revealed to be taking a picnic on the beach. Cathy, the little girl of the family, takes a sandwich and explores the beach on her own. A separate shot of the father brings the long take to an end.

As Cathy wanders off to a separate part of the beach, Spielberg sets up a new

Figure 4.1 The Lost World: Jurassic Park (1997). The Kobal Collection/Universal/Amblin.

space. Cathy discovers a compsognathus, a small bird-like dinosaur (which is rendered using digital special effects), and begins talking to it. In addition to the photo-realistic appearance of the special effects, Spielberg and Industrial Light and Magic have created the illusion that the compsognathus is a pre-existing entity by creating a match-on-action cut with it. As the compsognathus jumps to get closer to Cathy, Spielberg cuts to another shot, and the action of the compsognathus is completed. In other words, the compsognathus's jump is "carried over" the cut. In one of the shots, we see Cathy feed the compsognathus part of her roast-beef sandwich. This shot demonstrates technical skill as live action and digital animation "interact" (although Cathy's hand partly obscures the point of interaction).

Moreover, Spielberg uses narrational techniques to manipulate the spectator's access to the narrative. As Cathy turns around to call her parents, the camera dollies in on her face, capturing her excitement as she looks off-screen in her parents' direction. In the next shot, the camera cuts ninety degrees, but otherwise repeats the previous shot: the camera dollies in on Cathy's face. However, her expression and mood have changed. She now looks off-screen in the direction of the compsognathus, and the camera captures her worried expression. In the following shot we see that she is surrounded by several more compsognathuses.

At first, it appears that Spielberg's camera has given spectators full access to the relevant narrative events: we see the compsognathus, and we see Cathy's reaction to it. However, while Spielberg was giving us access to Cathy's excited expression, something important was happening off-screen: the introduction of several additional compsognathuses. Moreover, Spielberg delays our access to this narrative information further by repeating a shot of Cathy looking, rather than showing us what is happening off-screen. Spielberg focuses our attention on relevant narrative information but limits our access to the narrative at the same time. This opening scene illustrates Spielberg's very understated but inventive and resourceful use of cutting, camera placement and movement, restricted narration, and off-screen space.

Spielberg's external authorship is his brand identity. To establish a brand identity, a product needs to express an inspiring, overarching vision, must be easily recognizable, must connote trustworthiness, and needs to deliver on its promises. A product can achieve these qualities only by establishing a value-based relationship to its customers – particularly an emotional experience. A brand is equated with the emotional feeling or memorable experience it evokes. The classic example is Coca-Cola which, advertising analysts tell us, "promises consumers a touchstone to the American dream." Rolf Jensen (1999) argues that consumers buy the experiences, promises, and emotions products convey, and he identifies six basic types of emotion essential to advertising: adventure, love and friendship, care, self-identity, peace of mind, and beliefs and convictions.

Spielberg's brand image is closely linked to his internal auteur status, particularly the themes conveyed in his films. Indeed, Jensen's list of six emotions can easily be found in Spielberg's films – and, taken together, they seem to sum up the emotions conveyed in *E.T: The Extra-Terrestrial* (1982). The archetypal status of *E.T.* in Spielberg's canon explains why the logo of his company Amblin consists of the inspiring, overarching visionary image of Elliot and E.T. flying in front of and silhouetted against the full moon.

It is instructive to see how this image has been transformed in the DreamWorks logo. The moon and the young boy remain, but there are subtle shifts in meaning. The logo begins with the moon in its last quarter. The camera slowly tracks right, but the image of the moon is soon exposed as a reflection in water, as a float and fishing line temporarily break up the image. The camera then follows the fishing line upwards, but is partly obscured by clouds. As the clouds clear, we see the crest of the moon again – it is the exact same shape and size as it was before in the reflection, but this time a boy is sitting on the crest, fishing. This is an impossible fantasy image in at least three respects: the crest of the moon is seen as an object in itself (rather than a spherical object partly obscured in shadow); its scale is reduced to its perceived size, rather than its actual size; and the boy sitting on it is not shown in the reflection. The moon crest then partly transforms into the majuscule "D," and the camera tracks right to reveal more letters spelling "Dream." Clouds then obscure the lettering. When the clouds clear, the lettering has receded into the background, and the whole word can now be read: DreamWorks, underlined and supported with the initials of the three founders: SKG.

Figure 4.2 Recirculating *E.T.*, Manhattan, New York, March 2002. Image courtesy Malcolm Croft.

The music is coordinated with the images. The logo begins with a lone classical guitar. When the boy on the moon appears, the guitar is replaced by orchestral strings. As the moon is replaced by "D" and the other letters of "Dream" are revealed, full orchestral music, emphasizing the brass section, is introduced. When the clouds clear to reveal the full name, the classical guitar returns. Finally, the color is almost monochrome, consisting of a dark-blue night sky, but with daytime fluffy clouds, which clearly convey an oneiric atmosphere.

The Amblin image is a fragment of a well-known narrative. The impossible fantasy effect is "motivated" within the story: E.T.'s powers enable Elliott to fly – indeed, to escape from his adult pursuers. The DreamWorks logo is another inspiring, overarching visionary image, consisting of a number of transformations: the image of the moon is suddenly exposed as a reflection; the crest of the moon transforms into the letter "D"; and the spectator's perspective changes twice, disguised on both occasions by the clouds. In the Amblin logo, the boy has a distinct identity: he is a young lonely boy from the suburbs who misses his father but befriends an alien as compensation. His mistrust of adults conveys a universal emotional experience of lost childhood. The boy in the DreamWorks logo is more emblematic, although he connotes a typical middle-American country boy (such as Tom Sawyer) pursuing a popular leisure activity (in this instance I am aligning Spielberg with Twain). The emotional experience that DreamWorks is attempting to convey is an idyllic, idealistic, sentimental Norman Rockwell-type image of America – that is, another universal image of (lost) childhood innocence. It may seem strange, then, that Spielberg's first film for DreamWorks was *Amistad*, yet the debates surrounding the film (for an overview, see Jeffrey 2001) clearly suggest that this is a rose-tinted view of a suppressed part of American history. We could even argue that, in terms of theme and narrative, *Amistad* is a remake of *E.T.*, in which the childhood fantasy element of the latter film, plus its narrative structure, tensions, and trajectory, are overlaid with the political and moral themes of slavery and human freedom.

DreamWorks and vertical integration

In 1994, industry trade papers and other commentators were quick to note that DreamWorks was the first movie studio to be set up in Hollywood for more than seventy years. Such comments suggest that DreamWorks is a vertically integrated studio. I aim in this final section to assess this claim critically.

The troika of Steven Spielberg, Jeffrey Katzenberg, and David Geffen form a multimedia group with multiple core competencies: Spielberg in live-action film-making; Katzenberg with animation, TV, and running a studio; Geffen in music and deal-making. Furthermore, Spielberg invited Walter Parkes and Laurie MacDonald from Amblin to produce live action films for DreamWorks. DreamWorks's founders therefore have a depth of experience and proven track records in creating multi-media products, particularly live-action and animated films. It is also a privately owned company, so it does not have to make quarterly statements to shareholders, enabling Spielberg, Katzenberg, and Geffen to focus on the long-term aim of building up the studio, rather than worry about making immediate profits for shareholders. For a small studio, DreamWorks has large financial capital, since Geffen has negotiated a 1 billion dollar revolving credit facility from Chemical Banking Corp. and has persuaded Microsoft's co-founder Paul Allen to invest $500 million, giving him a 21 percent stake in the company (Dunaief 1995: 1).

DreamWorks is like a contemporary Hollywood studio to the extent that it outsources its filmmaking by offering production finance – with the exception that Spielberg will occasionally act as an in-house director and make a number of films. DreamWorks also distributes films. However, in many cases it co-finances films with other studios, and distributes them only in the US. The co-financing studio or, if it does not have a co-financing deal, Universal distributes the film internationally (as was the case with *Road Trip* [2000], *The Road to El Dorado* [2000], and *Shrek* [2001]). DreamWorks initially tried to imitate old Hollywood by planning to build a studio backlot at Playa Vista, just outside Los Angeles airport, where Howard Hughes had set up his aviation company. However, like Hughes's "spruce goose," the deal never got off the ground, and DreamWorks is currently located on the Universal backlot. DreamWorks has been more successful in imitating classical Hollywood by reworking its genres (e.g. *Gladiator* [2000]), a strategy Spielberg has found useful in the past, especially with his Indiana Jones trilogy (and with the Amblin-produced *Mask of Zorro* [1998]).

It is arguable that the failure of the Playa Vista deal may be a blessing in disguise, for DreamWorks does not have the burden of maintaining the high fixed costs of a "large lumpy object," but can focus instead on pursuing its main overarching vision: to foster creative and imaginative filmmaking (a vision reflected in the DreamWorks logo). At the press conference announcing the formation of DreamWorks, Spielberg said: "Hollywood movie studios were at the zenith when they were driven by point of view and personalities. Together with Jeffrey and David, I want to create a place driven by ideas and the people who have them" (in King 2000: 532). In Tom King's summary, "Spielberg said their plan was to create an unthreatening home for filmmakers to explore and share 'substantially' in every success" (ibid.). DreamWorks is therefore a studio driven by personality, for it offers an informal creative environment that fosters talent – especially directors and writers – who have their own vision and imagination, and do not require constant guidance (and receive a substantial amount of gross participation points in return). This is why DreamWorks has attracted directors such as Robert Zemeckis, Ridley Scott, and Woody Allen.

On the downside, that DreamWorks has no physical environment means it has fewer assets. It is a pure content company with no backlog of films or TV programs on which to make video sales or earn TV royalties. Furthermore, Universal owns the domestic and international distribution rights of the few DreamWorks video and music productions that do currently exist (see Goodridge 2001: 2). DreamWorks's current output of films is small: around ten a year, which allows little margin for error, with the risk of Chemical Banking foreclosing on its loan if the small slate of films do not go into profit. That is, DreamWorks is overdependent on the profitability of its product, for it cannot rely on conglomerate backing, as do the major studios. To address this problem, DreamWorks co-finances many of its films with other studios. For example, Paramount co-financed *Saving Private Ryan*, 20th Century-Fox co-financed *What Lies Beneath* (2000), Universal co-financed *Gladiator*, and Warner Bros. co-financed *A.I.* (2001), which means any profits need to be shared. As additional insurance that its films make a profit, DreamWorks is renowned for spending huge amounts on marketing its films: for example, it spent $40 million marketing *Chicken Run* and *Gladiator* in 2000 (Goodridge 2001: 2). Furthermore, Spielberg has not totally committed himself to DreamWorks (King 2000: 528); he is not under strict contractual obligations (he has signed up to direct only three films for DreamWorks over seven years, an obligation he has kept by directing *Amistad*, *Saving Private Ryan*, and *A.I.*), and he can develop projects with other companies. In financial terms, SKG each put in $33.3 million (a total of 10 percent of the company's assets), but receive 67 percent of the profits and 100 percent of the voting rights (Serwer 1995: 71). And, as indicated above, DreamWorks does not distribute its own films internationally or its videos and music worldwide: this distribution is handled by Universal.

The management of creative freedom in contemporary Hollywood, or control of internal and external authorship via vertical integration, is a high-risk venture, particularly in relation to the high-priced blockbuster. Spielberg has not taken full control because he co-finances and co-distributes his DreamWorks films, and the lack of conglomerate backing leaves the company vulnerable. Plus, the downside of taking control is that one has to pay one's own marketing costs. Industry journalists continually comment on the anomalous status of DreamWorks (Duke 2000; Bart 2001) and speculate as to whether a powerful figure such as Spielberg (who is now worth over $1 billion) can nonetheless still control his own product in Hollywood. Duke asks: "In an era of mega-mergers, is there a viable future for a solo movie company . . .?" (Duke 2000: 1). Only time (and money) will tell.

Notes

1 "A small but important segment of directors, screen actors, and screen writers have developed industry-specific rather than occupation-specific skills in conceiving, packaging, and financing productions" (Christopherson and Storper 1989: 340).

2 A blockbuster can therefore be defined in terms of the presence of two linked variables: the huge sums involved in production and marketing, and the amount of revenues received. A film such as *The Blair Witch Project* (1999), which had low production and marketing values ($35,000 to produce, plus a successful advertising campaign on the Internet), but which made a huge sum of money ($140 million at the US box office), does not, under this definition, count as a blockbuster (figures from the International Movie Database). At the present time, blockbusters are minimally required to reach the magic figure of $100 million at the US box office, although huge productions that cost $100 million or more are expected to reach the $200 million mark.

3 Staiger goes on to argue that, by the late 1950s, "film companies had transferred their mass production techniques to television series" (1983: 78).

References

Balio, Tino (ed.) (1985) *The American Film Industry*, rev. edn, Madison: University of Wisconsin Press.

Bart, Peter (2001) "Hits Aside, How Will the Dream Work?," *Variety*, April 2.

Bazin, André [1957] (1985) "On the *politique des auteurs*," in Jim Hillier (ed.), *Cahiers du Cinema: The 1950s*, Cambridge, MA: Harvard University Press: 248–59.

Bordwell, David, Staiger, Janet, and Thompson, Kristin (1985) *The Classical Hollywood Cinema: Film Style and Mode of Production to 1960*, London: Routledge & Kegan Paul.

Caughie, John (ed.) (1981) *Theories of Authorship*, London: Routledge and British Film Institute.

Christopherson, Susan, and Storper, Michael (1989) "The Effects of Flexible Specialization on Industrial Politics and the Labor Market: The Motion Picture Industry," *Industrial and Labor Relations Review*, 42, 3: 331–47.

Dillon, Elizabeth (1997) "Fear of Formalism: Kant, Twain, and Cultural Studies in American Literature," *Diacritics*, 27, 4: 46–69.

Duke, Paul F. (2000) "D'Works: What Lies Beneath?," *Variety*, July 24–30: 1.

Dunaief, Daniel (1995) "Chemical Wins Starring Role in $1B Loan to Spielberg & Co.'s Multimedia Venture," *American Banker*, 160 (March 31): 1–2.

Garvin, David A. (1981) "Blockbusters: The Economics of Mass Entertainment," *Journal of Cultural Economics*, 5: 1–20.

Gillman, Susan (1989) *Dark Twins: Imposture and Identity in Mark Twain's America*, Chicago: University of Chicago Press.

Goodridge, Mike (2001) "DreamWorks, Universal Extend Distribution Pact," *Screen International*, April 20: 2.

Hillier, Jim (1992) *The New Hollywood*, London: Studio Vista.

Internet Movie Database, "Business Data for *The Blair Witch Project*," online: http://us.imdb.com/Business?0185937.

Jeffrey, Julie Roy (2001) "Amistad (1997): Steven Spielberg's 'True Story,'" *Historical Journal of Film, Radio and Television*, 21, 1: 77–96.

Jenkins, Henry (1995) "Historical Poetics," in Joanne Hollows and Mark Jancovich (eds), *Approaches to Popular Film*, Manchester: Manchester University Press: 99–122.

Jensen, Rolf (1999) *The Dream Society: How the Coming Transformation from Information to Imagination Will Transform your Business*, New York: McGraw-Hill.

Kapsis, Robert (1992) *Hitchcock: The Making of a Reputation*, Chicago: University of Chicago Press.

King, Tom (2000) *The Operator: David Geffen Builds, Buys, and Sells the New Hollywood*, New York: Random House.

Malone, Thomas, and Laubacher, Robert (1998) "The Dawn of the E-Lance Economy," *Harvard Business Review*, 76, 5: 145–52.

Perkins, V. F. (1972) *Film as Film: Understanding and Judging Movies*, Harmondsworth: Penguin Books.

Salt, Barry (1974) "The Statistical Style Analysis of Motion Pictures," *Film Quarterly*, 21, 1: 13–22.

Serwer, Andrew E. (1995) "Analyzing the Dream," *Fortune*, 131 (April 17): 71.

Staiger, Janet (1983) "Individualism Versus Collectivism," *Screen*, 24, 4–5: 68–79.

Part II

EXPLORING SPECTACLE

5

TALKING ABOUT A REVOLUTION

The blockbuster as industrial advertisement

Michael Allen

The blockbuster movie has typically been made up of several elements – a large budget, enhanced production values, star presence, large-scale story material, and display of technical virtuosity – not all of which may be present in any one instance. As arguably the best, or at least the most spectacular, that Hollywood can create, the blockbuster movie has offered an ideal platform for displaying new developments in technical and artistic expertise. This chapter hopes to examine the strategies by which the blockbuster film has periodically been used by Hollywood as an advertisement for newly developed technical processes.

Technological innovation, development and integration are ongoing processes occurring across cinema's history. However, for the purposes of the current argument, three phases of cinema's technological development, in association with the blockbuster movie, will be "arrested" and examined. These are: the transition to sound at the end of the 1920s, the introduction of widescreen in the early 1950s, and the adoption of digital post-production techniques from the late 1980s onwards. It has to be noted immediately that the term "blockbuster" emerged during the 1950s and, as such, must be used conditionally in reference to pre-1950s films. These latter, while employing similar large-scale production values, stars, and technical effects, were not referred to as "blockbusters" at the time of their release. The term should therefore be placed in parentheses in relation to these films.

Finally, a note on structure and intent: a linear chronological history will be avoided in favor of a thematically organized argument. In the process, a number of central issues will be addressed in an effort to understand how the alliance of the blockbuster movie with significant shifts in cinema's technological base has been engineered and implemented both "externally," in terms of trade and public discourses, and "internally," in terms of the textual systems of the films themselves.

Industry players

The technological innovations under review in this chapter were developed and introduced into the American film industry for specific reasons, as a means of renegotiating the industry status of the companies involved. As Douglas Gomery (1985) and Donald Crafton (1999), among others, have argued, Warner Bros. bravely, but strategically, used the new synchronous sound technology developed by Western Electric in the mid-1920s to engineer an expansion of their operations. "The Vitaphone deal was one of several tactics designed to elevate the small outfit to the status of a film major" (Crafton 1999: 71). In the early 1950s, 20th Century-Fox decided to promote the adoption of a new film technology system – CinemaScope, with its widescreen format, color and stereo sound – partly as a means of consolidating its own position in Hollywood. It did so also as a mechanism for forcing necessary change in a film industry that was beginning to experience a real threat at that time from television as the new mass medium for moving-picture entertainment. In the early 1980s, computer software companies had been shunned by Hollywood following the failure of certain key projects, especially *Tron* (1982), which had been perceived as a test case for the potential of the new computer-generated digital effects. By the late 1980s, those companies were keen to reattract interest from an industry which they saw as a potentially major and lucrative market for the digital image-creation programs they had continued to improve and develop across the rest of the decade.

In all of these instances, therefore, there were different reasons for pushing the adoption of new film technologies, whether from a desire to become a more powerful industry player, to stave off the threat posed by a new medium, or to reinterest a disinterested film industry in the new possibilities of computer-based images. In each case, there was a keen desire to make a mark, to make the film industry sit up and take notice of the new image and/or sound-producing technologies these companies and individuals possessed.

The chosen strategy in each case was to ally the chosen technical system with attention-grabbing blockbuster movies which would announce their potential in a spectacular, impossible to ignore, way. Warners chose *Don Juan* (1926) as their first major synchronized sound feature, a large-scale sweeping historical epic starring their then leading man John Barrymore. Fox chose *The Robe* (1953), a film which, though it boasted no major stars, had a biblical story which would provide the perfect means for showcasing the awesome width of the widescreen format as well as the Technicolor and the surround-sound audio dimensions of their CinemaScope system. Digital special effects were tested out in relatively confined instances in several low-key films, such as *The Last Starfighter* (1984; digital creation of the spaceship) and *Willow* (1988; brief morphing sequence which transformed a character from a tortoise to a tiger to a human in a single shot), before becoming foregrounded in *The Abyss* (1989), *Terminator 2: Judgment Day* (1991), and *Jurassic Park* (1993).

Vitaphone, CinemaScope, and digital-effects technologies were therefore used to create a new kind of film product that was demonstrably different and more impressive than that which then currently existed. Only a blockbuster – big, expensive, star-laden – could hope to carry the weight of expectation that a major new type of cinema technology brought with it. The blockbuster, in this context, became the showcase for the new technology, enabling it to be presented as self-evidently significant. If it wasn't, the reasoning went, the industry would not have given it so lavish a public arena in which to announce itself.

Wrapped up in the announcement of a new technology that promises (some would say threatens) to transform the industry is always the question of cost. Both new audio-visual technology systems and blockbuster movies are expensive, often spectacularly or even infamously so, and by their very production expose, or make apparent (again), the true power hierarchy of the industry. Who are the companies who can afford the new systems and can afford to showcase them in big-budget movies? Who cannot? Across the three phases of technological innovation being covered in this chapter, and as the market conditions of the film industry have changed, there has been a progressive shift toward the production of fewer, and more expensive, films using increasingly complex, and equally expensive, new technological systems. Indeed, this was an explicit element in Fox's strategy for selling CinemaScope to Hollywood. "In order to sell to exhibitors the concept of fewer and costlier pictures, Fox concentrated its efforts from the start on promoting the visual and aural merits of its process. According to the studio, the grandeur of CinemaScope could be fully realised only when applied to more expensive properties" (Hincha 1985: 46). The arrival of a major new cinema technology, and its presentation in a blockbuster film, separates the major from the minor players. Those who introduce a new technology in this way stand, at least temporarily, in the top position of power, forcing the industry to change and to adopt the expensive systems controlled by them. The doubled high-expense of blockbuster and technical system creates an elitist hierarchy within the industry: to the victor go the major spoils.

Specific strategies

Having signed the Vitaphone contract in April 1926, Warner Bros. began an organized campaign of announcements concerning their "New Musical Device." As Crafton notes, their first announcement, while not mentioning Vitaphone by name, reflected "a distinct effort to mould the reception of sound in the mind of exhibitors and the public" (Crafton 1999: 71). Later announcements stressed that "the invention is in no sense a 'talking picture' but a method whereby a film can be accompanied by the music cue and other musical and vocal numbers given by means of what is now known as the recording machine, for want of a better name" (*Film Daily*, 26 April, 1926: 1).

Running in parallel with these official "technical announcements" were the beginnings of a campaign to garner public interest in the coming season of Warners releases. One film was particularly focused upon – *Don Juan*, starring John Barrymore. The campaign built public expectation for the film, and situated it firmly as the leading "blockbuster" attraction of the season. On June 4, a full-page ad in *Variety* (p. 7) announced the premiere of the film at Grauman's Chinese Theater. The advert foregrounded John Barrymore as the star while, at the foot of the page, noting that the film was "to be shown with Warner Bros. new musical synchronisation arrangement from the American Bell Telephone Co., Western Electric Co. and Bell Laboratories." On July 21, another full-page ad appeared (p. 13), now putting Vitaphone first, and in much bigger lettering, above Barrymore's name. Indeed, the shift of public expectation from the star to the new technology was made obvious:

> If you think the world has been thrilled before, wait until August 6th when –
> Warner Bros. will present the
> VITAPHONE
> at the Warner Theatre, New York, in conjunction with the
> WORLD PREMIERE SHOWING OF
> "DON JUAN"
> with the world's Greatest Actor
> JOHN BARRYMORE

On August 4, another ad in *Variety* (p. 11) advised the public (and the industry) to "Watch this date! August 6th, 1926. Motion picture history in the making! August 6th 1926 will go down as the most important date in the history of theatres! Watch the newspapers! You'll read about it, hear about it everywhere! It is the date on which Warner Bros. present By Arrangement with The Western Electric Co. and the Bell Telephone Laboratories VITAPHONE." Barrymore now comes after those artists who would be appearing in the shorts that were to form the first part of the evening's presentation. Finally, following the premiere, a two-page ad (pp. 12–13), reading across the paper rather than down it, announced on August 11, the "Greatest Sensation in the History of Motion Pictures. Public Thrilled – Critics Amazed. Audiences Stood and Cheered Warner Bros. Presentation of VITAPHONE." Although Barrymore's name is now bigger (following threats of legal action from the star), it came lower down the page, and the emphasis was still on the technology rather than the star or the film. Overall, however, these various instances show Warners trying to market, as twin attractions in assuring the box-office success of the film, the various elements of the "blockbuster" – stars, epic story, expensive production values – and the promise of the novelty of a new technological process.

Warners' campaign to introduce the Vitaphone to the public and the film industry, therefore, consisted of three phases. In the first, the ground was prepared by relatively cautious announcements that Warners had acquired a potentially significant new piece of cinema technology. In the second, emphasis was placed on the film that was to be the first to feature the technology, in order to position it as an unmissable production and event – as a blockbuster with massive popular appeal. The advertising campaign foregrounded the epic subject matter and the star-appeal of John Barrymore. Only after this had been done did the emphasis gradually shift to focus on the new synchronizing technology, until this became positioned as the main attraction of the entertainment. The untried technology was thereby protected by the box-office assuredness of the blockbuster film.

A similar strategy was undertaken by Fox in its campaign to sell CinemaScope to Hollywood and its audience in the early 1950s. Again, the first emphasis was on the new technical system. An advert in *Variety* on 18 March, 1953 (pp. 10–11), announced "First Demonstrations of CinemaScope for Producers, Exhibitors and the Press. This week, a momentous new era in motion pictures is being launched at our Hollywood studio with the first demonstrations of CinemaScope, the most eagerly anticipated development in the history of entertainment."

Having established the existence and imminent unveiling of a major new cinema technology, 20th Century-Fox then began a parallel programme of advertising and press releases. Between April and July, articles and advertisements in trade papers reported upcoming demonstrations of CinemaScope, then the success of those demonstrations, details of Fox's forthcoming CinemaScope production schedule, and Fox's increasing success in persuading the industry to adopt the system. On June 10, for example, a huge three page advert in *Variety* (pp. 11–13) announced that "At press time 20th Century-Fox had received 3,668 orders from theatres large and small for CinemaScope installations . . . the entire nation is talking about, exhibitors are preparing to launch, producers are moving ahead with CinemaScope." While undoubtedly overemphasized, the strategy of the campaign had been firmly established.

Once again, having successfully hyped the new technical system to the point where there was considerable public expectation and curiosity about it, it had to be given an impressive debut – an arrival whose sense of occasion and spectacle would be seen to justify Fox's claims for it. Fox began this process in late July with fresh advertising announcements, one of which, labelled "a Progress Report from 20th Century-Fox on CinemaScope," described the conclusive impressiveness of:

> 20th Century-Fox's first two CinemaScope productions in Technicolor, *The Robe* and *How to Marry a Millionaire.*

> Seeing CinemaScope put to practical use in full-length features is an exulting experience. On our Miracle Mirror Screen, through the magic of the anamorphic lens, it staggers the imagination and dwarfs the entertainment giants of the past with its overwhelming splendour and technical superiority. Now, through its panoramic range and sweep and the intensity of its dramatic impact that makes the audience participants in the action without the use of glasses, the motion picture truly has come alive.
>
> (*Variety*, 22 July, 1953: 9–11)

This combination of technical system and blockbuster feature content was to be repeated in other Fox adverts throughout the next two months, in the build up to the release of the film. The two elements were made to work in a synergistic fashion to promote simultaneously the wonders of the system and the box-office quality of the film(s) themselves.

The campaign worked. On the day of the premiere on September 16, 1953, *Variety* (p. 1) reported that "tonight's premiere . . . of *The Robe* at the Roxy New York is advance-characterised as a true milestone, a date from which film history may well be measured." Fox kept up the pressure in the weeks following the release of the film. In an orchestrated campaign in *Variety* lasting several weeks, the studio strategically planted sizable advertisements for the CinemaScope system, and its first creation *The Robe*, somewhere on the page, or pages, immediately following the weekly reports of box-office returns. The association of technological change with blockbuster financial success was unmissable, and was instrumental in finally persuading the industry as a whole to adopt the new widescreen format.

As mentioned earlier, digital special effects emerged slowly as a new and significant film production technology, due partly to industry resistance and partly to insecurities as to whether the software programs could actually deliver what they promised. Even by the time of *The Abyss*, focus was still being put on the real life actors and action (especially the grueling underwater diving work) rather than the state-of-the-art special effects. Indeed, director James Cameron was still so unconvinced that these effects could be achieved that he insured himself against their possible failure by duplicating them using traditional techniques.

Terminator 2: Judgment Day was really the first film in which the digital special effects became a feature in their own right. With its huge (and ever mounting) budget, its major star (Arnold Schwarzenegger), its unremitting high-action plot and cutting-edge effects, *Terminator 2* was the archetypal blockbuster film. The combination of blockbuster movie and breakthrough technologies was a feature of publicity and press coverage about the film. When asked about the $100 million budget, seen as the biggest ever at the time, James Cameron commented: "The point is that this is a large-scale action film, and action films with special effects cost money. This film is in that league – an A-picture, a big presentation picture" (Bahiana 1991: 24). The *Hollywood Reporter* noted that, at the press screening of the "megabudget" film, "a packed house cheered and applauded repeatedly at 'T2's' breathtaking special effects and chase sequences" (Grove 1991a: 10). A week later it was quoting Larry Kasanoff, vice-president of Lightstorm Entertainment, the film's production company, as saying about the press reaction:

> It's been pretty extraordinary . . . They're [saying] things like "greatest science fiction movie in history"; "will blow you away"; "redefines the state of special effects." At the same time, he notes, "the information from Tri-Star on the tracking of the movie is phenomenal. We have virtually 100% awareness of [it] in this country a week before we open (Wednesday). There is an extraordinarily high want-to-see [score]."
>
> (Grove 1991b: 10)

The shift from a film that almost incidentally includes digital special effects to a film that centrally features them had been made with *Terminator 2*. Admittedly, the film's blockbuster status as the "must-see" film of the year was due to a combination of classic factors, but the attention given to the special effects in the movie shows how the film was being used to announce the final successful adoption of digital imaging technology. Through the publicity and media hype surrounding the film, people were made to want to see it for the groundbreaking special effects as much as they were the film's other, more traditional, attractions.

The final, and irrefutable, arrival of digital special effects was announced by *Jurassic Park*. In a report in *Variety* on the film as production was underway, Christian Moerk noted that:

> A full year before stomping onto the silver screen, Universal/Amblin's juggernaut creature feature *Jurassic Park* already promises to leave permanent footprints in the special effects industry . . . "They will probably use computer graphics to create the dinosaurs, very few models and no stop-motion animation," says Hoyt Yeatman, co-founder of Dreamquest . . . "There has been a disbelief in the industry that computer graphics alone could create a realistic-looking animal, and that's why this is unique."
>
> (Moerk 1992: 5)

Again, the film's credentials as a blockbuster – Steven Spielberg directing a big-budget, high-action feature based on a best-selling novel by Michael Crichton – was consciously employed as a means of simultaneously building expectation about the never-yet-seen, cutting-edge technological sophistication that would come to be one of the film's major attractions. As with the previous technologies looked at in this work, such effects were not to be wasted on a lesser film, but were to be employed on the best example of a blockbuster movie that Hollywood could create. The motto would seem to be "if you're going to hype it, hype it with effect."

It is significant, in this respect, that the Moerk report notes that, with *Jurassic Park*, "ILM [Industrial Light and Magic; George Lucas's special effects company] is really creating a bit of a brain drain right now. . . . We know that a tremendous number of people in the computer graphics area have been brought in" (Moerk 1992: 5). The biggest, the most expensive, the most labor-intensive: these qualities of the blockbuster movie were overlaid onto the unveiling of new film-technology systems to ensure that the mass popularity produced by the blockbuster movie itself helped to engineer the context by, and through, which the new technology was displayed, discussed, and finally absorbed to become part of accepted practice.

In one important sense, the allying of new, expensive, and often unproven audio-visual technologies with the blockbuster film can be seen as the logical conclusion of the current state of filmmaking in America. The blockbuster mentality that now controls thinking in Hollywood means that fewer and fewer, larger and larger films are made every year. These films have to have an immediate and massive impact on the marketplace, earning hundreds of millions of dollars in a few weeks. If they don't, the financial costs of their failure are correspondingly huge, and often catastrophic. Within this context, gambling upon the effect that the use of a new, untested technological system will have in giving any major production a "must-see" edge over its competitors becomes a bet worth taking, even if that system itself is prohibitively expensive. In this sense, blockbuster movies and new audio-visual technologies form a perfect and necessary partnership.

Stars, blockbusters, and technology

The history of digital "firsts" just outlined brings up another important issue concerning the synergy between the blockbuster movie and the introduction of a new phase of film technology: namely, the role and relationship of the film star to this negotiation. The three digital-effects blockbusters just cited show this relationship in process. As identified at the head of this chapter, star presence is one of the potential elements of the blockbuster. It is by no means essential or inevitable, however, that a blockbuster film production will be built around a major star or stars. As *Variety* noted, the lead actors in *The Abyss* were "not [being] considered by Fox to be powerful marquee draws" (Gold 1989: 11). *Terminator 2: Judgment Day*, on the other hand, prominently featured Arnold Schwarzenegger who, if he was not the huge star that he would later become, was certainly in the top tier. Promotion for the film featured him at least as much as it did the stunning special effects. *Jurassic Park*, as with *The Abyss*, featured no major stars, but made sure that the advance word on the film built expectations that something visually extraordinary was going to be unveiled with the film.

We therefore get a range of strategies for mixing stars (or lack of them), and significant steps forward in special effects. *The Abyss* miscalculated this balance, offering no stars, but keeping the groundbreaking effects back until too late into the film, by which time audiences and critics alike had tired of the story. While the effects were noted in reviews as "spectacular" (*Evening Standard*, October 12, 1991: 33) and "outstanding" (*The Observer*, October 15, 1991: 44), they were not seen as important or impressive enough to save the film. With *Terminator 2*, the still unproven effects were cushioned by the presence of an audience-pulling star in Schwarzenegger. If the effects did not impress, it was possible that he could still carry the film. By the time of *Jurassic Park*, the effects work, while still not 100 percent proven, was sufficiently dependable to allow them effectively to carry the entire film. They are, in fact, the *raison d'être* of the film; without them, the lack of stars and weak story-line would have seriously jeopardized the success of the film, even with Spielberg directing.

So we can see in the example of the final emergence of digital effects into the limelight a particular negotiation between the use of stars both to protect fragile new technologies and to help promote them. This pattern is a repeat of the one which takes place, over a greater time-span, between the coming of sound at the end of the 1920s and of CinemaScope in the early 1950s. In the earlier case, first John Barrymore in *Don Juan* and then Al Jolson in *The Jazz Singer* (1927) were used as main attractions to help confirm the validity of the new synchronized sound technology. Not only would the audience see them perform, and witness the novelty of a new kind of cinema technology, they would see those performances mediated and enhanced *through* that technology.

For Fox and their peers considering the potential of CinemaScope in the early 1950s, the issue was not one of stars so much as technology itself. It was a rival technology – television – that had to be challenged, not a rival studio's roster of star performers. The emphasis, almost inevitably, shifted to the technology itself: what it was, what its technical specifications were, how it looked and sounded. Warners needed Barrymore, and especially Jolson, to demonstrate their new sound system. Fox needed their audiences to want to see the system *itself* as a powerful and seductive alternative to the small, black-and-white, monaural television set. To succeed in this battle for survival, the new widescreen, color, and stereo film technology had to be put into stark, unmediated contrast with its technically impoverished rival. Stars, in the first instance at least, would only have proved a distraction. Having successfully showcased its new technical process in its own and sole right, Fox began using stars to reconfirm its blockbuster potential. Its second feature, *How to Marry a Millionaire* (1953) featured three female stars: Betty Grable, Lauren Bacall, and Marilyn Monroe.

Figure 5.1 Advertising the event: *The Jazz Singer* (1927). The Kobal Collection/ Warner Bros.

Spectacle and narrative

This last point brings up another issue concerning the relationship between spectacle and narrative in terms of both the blockbuster film and any new film technology introduced through it. The accounts in the press and other announcements that have been cited above are some of the *external* ways in which the teaming of blockbuster movie and new technological development is realized and conveyed to interested parties, whether trade or public. A further, more *internal* text also exists. It is quite possible to see the announcement of a new technology occurring on a textual level within the blockbuster film itself, specifically in terms of the relationship between its narrative and spectacular modes of address. But it is also important to see that the way in which the industry and the "commentary machine" anticipate and discuss the arrival of a new phase of technology actually sets up the discourse of expectation and reception of that technology when it finally arrives and can be experienced.

The film text itself can, in this context, be seen to perform, to display its own particular talent, its own specific attractions: "The logic by which the film displays its own image is what we will call 'performance.' . . . The dissipation of narrative conventions works to foreground the performance of the enunciation" (Jacobs and de Cordova 1982: 300). In the films under discussion in this essay, the moment when narrative is suspended and the shift is made to star performance coincides with the presentation of the new technology which is making that performance possible. So, for example, when we hear swords clashing as Barrymore duels in *Don Juan*, or Jolson gets up to perform his first song in *The Jazz Singer*, they are able to do so only by virtue of the film itself foregrounding the new Vitaphone sound recording technology. The spectator enjoys both Jolson's performance *and* the experience of witnessing the presentation of the Vitaphone system. In this way we are presented simultaneously with a moment of diegetic *and* technological spectacle – when the new technology presents itself and says, in effect, look/listen to me. The blockbuster format is ideal for this because of its peculiar balance between spectacle and narrative. A specific, sanctioned space is opened up within which the new technological process can be displayed – more readily and apparently than in a lower-key film, where it could well pass unnoticed because the diegetic rationale wouldn't so readily allow it.

The situation is more complicated when star-actor performance isn't an explicit part of the textual system. In both *The Robe* and a digital effects film such as *Jurassic Park*, the presence of actors who are very much second-tier stars throws even more intense attention onto the innovative technological processes on display as the real focus of the films. In these cases, the presentation of those systems becomes even more marked and apparent because the spectator is distracted to a much lesser extent by star presence or performance, but is instead asked to look at, and/or listen to and appreciate, the technical system alone. We can see this in the presentation of certain panoramic landscapes in *The Robe* or in the first sighting of the dinosaurs in *Jurassic Park*, when the narrative pauses as we, along with the on-screen characters, watch awestruck at the digitally created beasts. Both kinds of image ask us to appreciate them as the result of impressive new image-creation technologies, rather than solely as elements in the narrative drive of the films in which they appear. At such moments, the film is talking about its own process of creation, offering spectacular images as illustration of its new technological possibilities.

Increasingly, therefore, in both critical writing and word of mouth about the blockbuster, as well as in the formal textual systems of the films themselves, we can see the film industry talking about itself in terms of its technical parameters. The transgressive nature of such a revelation is telling in a production and viewing process that has habitually ensured that its mechanisms remain hidden in order to maintain the integrity of its illusionism. This chapter has attempted to explore the reasons why the industry has periodically felt it necessary to expose its mechanisms so completely and explicitly, and, as importantly, why it has used the blockbuster as the preferred vehicle for demonstration of these new mechanisms.

The answer to this question is partly political, to do with industrial in-fighting and power-relations, adjustments, and resistance from outside attacks. Within this context, those who could marshal the most impressive components – financial, star talent, material – could ensure that they would edge ahead of rivals. Size, in this respect, does indeed matter. And partly it is to do with rejuvenating tired industrial processes, markets, and audiences. New attractions need to be injected into stale practices, and in order to jolt the comatose (industrial and commercial) patient back into life, eye-dazzling, ear-catching experiences must be offered. Again, this is the province of the blockbuster movie – the biggest, most lavish, most visually and aurally impressive kind of film Hollywood has to offer.

But ultimately, perhaps, it also has to do with the spectator wanting the pleasure of being caught between knowing and not knowing; between suspension and recognition of disbelief. The phases of technological innovation covered in this chapter have all offered this. We know that it is the Vitaphone record that is making Jolson speak and sing while simultaneously believing that it is him alone doing it. We want to believe that the massive image and surround-sound environment of CinemaScope is the real world while simultaneously knowing that it's all an illusion. We know that molten metal cannot melt and flow through a helicopter window to become a human pilot, but what we most want to do at that moment is to believe the evidence of our own eyes.

The blockbuster writes all of these issues large, pushing them to the limit and beyond. The blockbuster announces itself and its values more explicitly than any other kind of film. Indeed, that is one of the reasons such films are so popular, because they represent the most, if only in a material rather than an artistic sense, that cinema can offer. Moreover the existence, and continuation, of American filmmaking has often been framed both in terms of the blockbuster (value for money, an aural and visual experience not available anywhere else, an immersive and visceral thrill) and in terms of emergent audio-visual technologies that promise to extend and intensify those values. Furthermore, in the high-risk contemporary marketplace the blockbuster fundamentally *depends* upon the new technological pleasures it affords its audience. In revealing and talking about new technologies through the blockbuster, the film industry both (re-)confirms the unique range of pleasures it can offer its audience and signals its continued survival in an increasingly threatening media landscape.

References and bibliography

Bahiana, Ana Maria (1991) "*Terminator 2: Judgment Day*," *Cinema Papers*, 84, August.

Belton, John (1992) *Widescreen Cinema*, Cambridge Mass. and London: Harvard University Press.

Crafton, Donald (1999) *The Talkies: American Cinema's Transition to Sound, 1926–1931*, Berkeley: University of California Press.

Gold, Richard (1989) "It's Sink or Swim Time for 20th Century-Fox; '89 b.o. Fortunes Hinge on 'Abyss,'" *Variety*, 9–15 August.

Gomery, Douglas (1985) "The Coming of Sound: Technological Change in the American Film Industry," in Elizabeth Weis and John Belton (eds), *Film Sound: Theory and Practice*, New York: Columbia University Press.

Grove, Martin A. (1991a) "Hollywood Report," *Hollywood Reporter*, 28 June.

Grove, Martin A. (1991b) "Hollywood Report," *Hollywood Reporter*, 1 July.

Hincha, Richard (1985) "Selling CinemaScope 1953–1956," *Velvet Light Trap*, 21 (summer).

Jacobs, Lea, and de Cordova, Richard (1982) "Spectacle and Narrative Theory," *Quarterly Review of Film Studies*, 7, 1.

Moerk, Christian (1992) "'Jurassic' Looks Like an F/X Classic," *Variety*, 7 September.

6

SPECTACLE, NARRATIVE, AND THE SPECTACULAR HOLLYWOOD BLOCKBUSTER

Geoff King

Spectacle, spectacular imagery; sheer scale, lavishness and (hopefully) quality of big-screen audio-visual sensation: however the blockbuster is defined, qualities such as these have often been close to the center of its appeal, from the early Italian historical epics of the 1910s to today's digital special-effects extravaganzas. Overt, large-scale spectacle is not a major feature of all films that enjoy blockbuster-scale success at the box office. But it is often a major ingredient at the high-budget end of the spectrum and in production and/or distribution-led definitions of the blockbuster. The spectacular variety of blockbuster, on which this chapter focuses, is usually meant to constitute an "event," something that stands out from the cinematic routine. It is sold this way even if the formation of the "event" itself becomes routinized, as is the case in contemporary Hollywood, where the heavily preplanned and presold prospective blockbuster is a central feature around which each year's slate of production revolves, rather than something that departs from the norm. A substantial part of the appeal of many blockbusters lies precisely in the scale of spectacular audio-visual experience that is offered, in contrast to the smaller-scale resources of rival films or media. The definition of the blockbuster in terms of spectacle (as with other attributes such as length and budget) tends to be relative rather than absolute.

Two aspects of the spectacular movie blockbuster are considered in this chapter. The first part looks more closely at the production of spectacular qualities, primarily in terms of visual strategies. Two alternative modes of spectacle are outlined, in relation to shifting contexts of production and consumption: one based on the visual scope of the big-screen experience offered by the cinematic blockbuster, the other related to the impact of visual strategies drawn in recent decades from small-screen media such as advertising and music video. The second part of the chapter focuses on the issue of narrative. If spectacle is so central to a particular kind of blockbuster experience, what is the role of narrative structure? Many have been quick to announce the death, or at least the fading, of narrative in the spectacular context of recent Hollywood blockbuster production, a judgment that, as I and others have argued, is precipitate. To what extent, though, does the spectacular blockbuster adhere to the conventions of "classical" narrative structure? Has it utilized other types of narrative organization; if so, to what extent, and what challenge might this pose more generally to our understanding of the classical Hollywood style?

Spectacle: from large-screen vista to (large *and* small-screen) montage-impact

An epic scale of spectacular representation unavailable in rival media products is one of the promises that has long been made by the would-be blockbuster. From the early 1910s, Italian epics such as *The Fall of Troy* (*La caduta di Troia*, 1910) and *Quo Vadis?* (1913) attracted crowds by offering a scale of events and production values that dwarfed and stood out from more routine cinematic fare (Bowser 1990). The American film industry's response included D. W. Griffith's *Judith of Bethulia* (1913), *The Birth of a Nation* (1915), and *Intolerance* (1916) and the tradition of biblical-historical epic in the studio era most commonly associated with the films of Cecil B. DeMille. Ingredients these early blockbusters have in common include expense, length, a focus on "weighty," "important," or epic-mythical subject matter, and – of more central relevance here – a largeness in the *staging* of the spectacular on-screen events. Great vistas are offered, along with more intimate moments, often involving the reconstruction of epic events on a grand scale: the Civil War battlefield in *The Birth of a Nation*, massive teeming edifices of Babylon in *Intolerance*, the exodus from Egypt in *The Ten Commandments* (1956); the proverbial "cast of thousands," and large outlays on the building of massive sets and/or travel to exotic locations.

An emphasis on spectacular epic production of this kind gained particular prominence in Hollywood in the 1950s and 1960s, decades in which the industry struggled to regain equilibrium in the face of the combined threats of the divorcement of exhibition from production and distribution, the decline in cinemagoing that resulted from broader social changes such as migration to the suburbs, and the rival attractions of television and other leisure pursuits. As a more or less habitual pattern of visiting the cinema declined, the spectacular blockbuster was envisaged as potential savior of Hollywood. Its quality as extra-larger-than-life special event was seen as a way to attract back to the cinema viewers whose more routine attendance could not be guaranteed. Hence, the advent of widescreen formats, among others, institutionalized in the form of 20th Century-Fox's CinemaScope process. Visually, the emphasis was put, again, on sheer scale of imagery: the width of the screen and the vast panoramas it could encompass.

The particular forms of spectacular blockbuster adopted in the 1950s and 1960s ran into difficulties, especially in the later decade, and especially the Roman-historical epic (in the shape of *Cleopatra*, 1963) and the epic musical after what proved to be the deceptive triumph of *The Sound of Music* (1965). The foregrounding of the large-scale, big-screen vista has remained an important ingredient in more recent blockbusters, however, including the successful revisiting of the Roman epic in *Gladiator* (2000). Blockbusters continue to base much of their appeal on the promise of providing a variety of spectacle that befits the nature of the specifically *cinematic* context of exhibition. From *Star Wars* (1977) to *Titanic* (1997), *Pearl Harbor* (2001) and the heavily pretrailed *Lord of the Rings* trilogy (2001, 2002, 2003), epic or fantastic events are designed to play strongly to the audio-visual qualities of the theatrical experience. There appears to be a paradox, however, in the economic basis of contemporary Hollywood's blockbuster production. The large vistas of spectacular attraction are designed to work at their best on the big screen. But the bulk of revenues are currently earned through viewings on the *small* screen, via videotape/disc or broadcast television of one variety or another.

The big-screen vista remains important in Hollywood today. But it has been supplemented, in the creation of overt visual spectacle, by the use of techniques more suited to the creation of spectacular impact within the confines of the small-screen image. At the risk of oversimplification, two varieties of spectacle might be suggested. One has its roots in the creation of impact on the big screen. The other draws on techniques associated in part with small-screen spectacle. In the former case, as in much of the tradition of spectacular blockbuster production, the emphasis is put on the presentation before the viewer of large vistas, at the level of what appears to be the *pro-filmic* reality. For the purpose of this argument, I include here elements of special effects that are not strictly pro-filmic, but that are designed to create that impression (matte paintings or models, for example, or digitally composited images, meant to blend more or less seamlessly with more substantially "real" sets, locations and action). Images such as extreme long shots of the construction of Goshen, the exodus from Egypt, or the parting of the Red Sea in *The Ten Commandments*, or of the ship in *Titanic*, are offered as forms of large-scale spectacle the viewer is invited to sit back and admire on the big screen in a relatively leisurely fashion. This is a form I have described elsewhere as offering a "contemplative" brand of spectacle (King 2000). Time is permitted for a certain amount of scrutiny of the image: admiration of texture or detail produced by lavish expenditure on sets, locations, props and extras, or of the latest illusions available with the use of state-of-the-art special effects. The viewer might as a result be taken more effectively "into" the diegetic world on screen – if the overall effect is a "convincing" representation and helps in the process of "suspending disbelief." Alternatively, or at the same time, the viewer might admire the spectacle *as* impressive construct, testament to the illusionary powers of high-cost, resource-heavy spectacular cinema (for more discussion of this in relation to special effects, see LaValley 1985; Landon 1992; Barker and Brooks 1998; Darley 2000; King 2000). The latter effect, based on the selling of the spectacular capabilities of the medium itself, has always been a significant component of the attraction of large-scale blockbuster production.

What happens, though, when spectacle of this variety is reduced to the spatial limits of the small screen? Widescreen spectacle is particularly vulnerable, either being shown in pan/scan versions, in which only parts of the image are visible and original compositions are subjected to reframing, or "letterbox" screenings that maintain more of the integrity of the frame but reduce still further the scale of the image. The large-scale spectacular qualities of blockbusters such as *The Ten Commandments* and *Titanic* are not entirely destroyed in this process but they are substantially reduced in impact. Other forms of spectacle, however, suffer relatively less in the move from big screen to small – specifically, those based on techniques such as rapid editing or rapid and/or unstable movement of the camera. Constant change of image-content is needed to maintain heightened levels of visual stimulus on the small screen (Ellis 1989), a strategy Hollywood appears to have learned from formats such as advertising and music video.[1] Hyperbolically rapid editing and camera movement have become important sources of heightened spectacular impact in contemporary Hollywood, either replacing or (probably more often) being used in conjunction with images of grander visual scale. This is especially the case in action-oriented blockbuster production, with its basic currency of explosive destruction. The impact of the contemporary action film is often constructed through patterns of rapid montage-effect editing combined with "unstable" camera movement designed to create an impression of subjective immersion in the action, an "impact aesthetic" often increased by the practice of propelling debris and other objects out toward the viewer (for detailed analysis of examples, see King 2000). Particularly notable, given its generic allegiance to the large-vista Roman–biblical tradition, is the use of such techniques as the dominant aesthetic in the action-fighting scenes of *Gladiator* (for more detail, see King 2002a).

A typical strategy today is to combine moments of broader, more expansive spectacle with those of tightly framed explosive-montage-impact effects. The central action sequence in *Pearl Harbor*, for example, offers larger shots, the spectacle of a large number of American ships in various stages of destruction during and after the initial Japanese attack, and closer and more rapidly cut detail – making claims to a more "subjective" location – including the obligatory outward-moving fireball/debris effects and a bomb's-eye-view perspective. What this offers in the realm of heightened spectacle is, in fact, in keeping with a central aspect of the classical Hollywood *decoupage* more generally: a combination of relatively "objective," distanced and closer, quasi-subjective perspectives. The difference, however, is that the more subjective-seeming position is constructed as a variety of spectacular impact (as opposed, for instance, to a less frenzied, more quotidian point-of-view shot).

The appeal of the more "contemplative" end of the spectacular spectrum might be understood in the context of a long tradition of larger-than-life spectacular representation. This includes pre-cinematic forms such as the magic lantern show and the diorama as well as earlier forms of spectacle, both secular and religious in origin. The pleasures offered might include a sense of being taken beyond the scale of everyday life to something suggesting a grandeur, an awe, or a sense of the sublime, even if a format such as blockbuster cinema might offer a rather debased and commercialized version of such an experience. Richard Dyer's attempt to analyze some of the characteristics of the pleasurable/entertaining dimension of the more spectacular varieties of Hollywood cinema (specifically, in his case studies, the musical) offers a useful vocabulary in which to understand some of these pleasures. Of most direct relevance are the qualities of "abundance" and "intensity" identified by Dyer (1992) that can be contrasted with the scarcity and banality that characterizes much of the typical reality of everyday life. The pleasure of experiencing greater-than-life intensity also applies to the high-impact variety of spectacle, a form that offers an intense engagement for the viewer. This is a quality actively discussed as a source of enjoyment by some enthusiasts of the action genre (Barker and Brooks 1998) and also offered by other media targeted at a similar audience, such as action-adventure videogames (King 2002b). The prominence of this format in contemporary Hollywood can be explained by more than just its suitability for translation to the small screen, which may or may not be a consciously exploited causal factor. A more indirect route can also be suggested, given the tendency of Hollywood to embrace styles used in other popular media consumed by its key target audience of younger viewers, including music video, and the employment of directors (such as Michael Bay, director of *Armageddon* [1998] and *Pearl Harbor*) with backgrounds in music video and/or advertising, two of the key training grounds for recent generations of filmmakers.

Whatever the precise causal factors behind – and audience appeals of – the two, a combination of large-scale and more impact-centered spectacle makes sense in the contemporary industrial context. Video and television screenings are the principal sources of revenue, in the longer term. But their potential remains dependent to a large extent – especially at the prestigious, high-budget blockbuster end of the market – on success in the theatrical realm. It is success at the box office, in most cases, that determines the likely scale of revenues to be earned in subsequent forms such as video sales/rentals and sales to pay- and free-to-air television broadcast. Spectacular dimensions that play especially well on the big screen remain important. They help to create the "event movie" impact, in terms of wider media coverage as well as promotion and box office returns, that translates into subsequent success on the small screen for a franchise or a one-off blockbuster.

Narrative still matters

What, though, of narrative in the spectacular blockbuster? It is common parlance in both journalistic criticism and some academic writing to assume or to assert that the emphasis on visual spectacle is at the expense of narrative. "Impressive effects, shame the same effort wasn't put into the plot," is a standard response. The plot of the typical Hollywood spectacular blockbuster may not be terribly challenging or complex; a basic mistake that is often made, however, is to confuse this – a perfectly valid qualitative judgment, but one that could be applied to many other Hollywood films – with the idea that narrative is in some way *absent* or *displaced* by spectacle. It is surprising how often this slippage seems to occur, as if prominent narrative dimensions somehow become invisible once the focus turns to the production of spectacular impact. Different aspects of this argument can be related to the two different versions of spectacle considered above, each of which has been cited as an impediment to narrative. In what follows, I begin by sketching briefly some of these claims and suggesting why they are often mistaken. Having established that narrative remains important, and usually quite central, to the contemporary blockbuster, this section concludes by examining some of the specific qualities of the kind of narrative structure found in the context of spectacular production. My principal focus here will be on the recent spectacular Hollywood blockbuster, rather than earlier examples, as it is here that arguments about the decline of narrative have been concentrated.

Contemporary blockbusters of the large-scale spectacular variety are often lumped together with spin-off forms such as movie-based theme-park rides or videogames. The fact that films are sometimes converted into such formats is used by some commentators as a basis on which to imply that the films themselves exhibit the far less narrative-based qualities of rides or games (see, for example, Bukatman 1998). Narrative is said to be subordinated to the provision of a spectacular "thrill-ride." The logic of this kind of argument is flawed, however, other than as a species of rhetoric, a way to "bash" Hollywood rather than to engage in serious analysis. Even if constructed with one eye on their potential for conversion to ride or videogame, it does not follow in principal that the films should be lacking in narrative dimensions, so different are the requirements of cinema from those of ride or game. Another major strain in these arguments focuses on the prominence of special-effects sequences in the spectacular blockbuster. Narrative dynamics are said to be "bracketed" in many cases by major effects sequences (Pierson 1999), powerful illusions/spectacles that threaten to "overwhelm traditional concerns with character and story" (Darley 2000: 103). The style of visual spectacle and impact that draws on techniques used in advertising and music video, including rapid and emphatic montage-editing, has also been identified as a threat to narrative, most notably in Justin Wyatt's much-cited book on "high concept" in Hollywood (Wyatt 1994).

The fact remains, however, that spectacular Hollywood blockbusters, of both varieties, continue to invest strongly in narrative dynamics, and at more than one level. They tell carefully organized, more or less linear cause/effect stories organized around central characters. They also manifest what a structuralist analysis would term "underlying" narrative structural patterns, on which I have written at length elsewhere (King 2000). Take, for example, *Terminator 2: Judgment Day* (1991), a quintessential example of the recent Hollywood spectacular blockbuster production, and a blockbuster in all contemporary senses of the term (expensive, large-scale, spectacular, and a substantial box-office hit). *Terminator 2* is one of the films regularly cited by commentators such as Pierson and Darley. As such, it is a useful example to revisit in a little more detail, with attention to exactly how it is structured in terms of the relationship between spectacle and narrative.

Terminator 2 is, clearly, a film *driven by* the dimension of spectacle more than that of narrative, which is one reason why it is a good test case. It is safe to assume, I think, that the reason for making the film was to capitalize on the success of *The Terminator* (1984), a modestly budgeted film, in the typical contemporary Hollywood manner of producing a "bigger," "better," more spectacular and special-effects-oriented sequel. The distinctive spectacular attraction of *Terminator 2*, the morphing transformation scenes involving the new-generation shape-shifting T-1000 terminator, was also driven by specific developments in special effects technologies – principally the adaptation and extension of 3-D computer generation techniques used to create the water pseudopod in director James Cameron's earlier

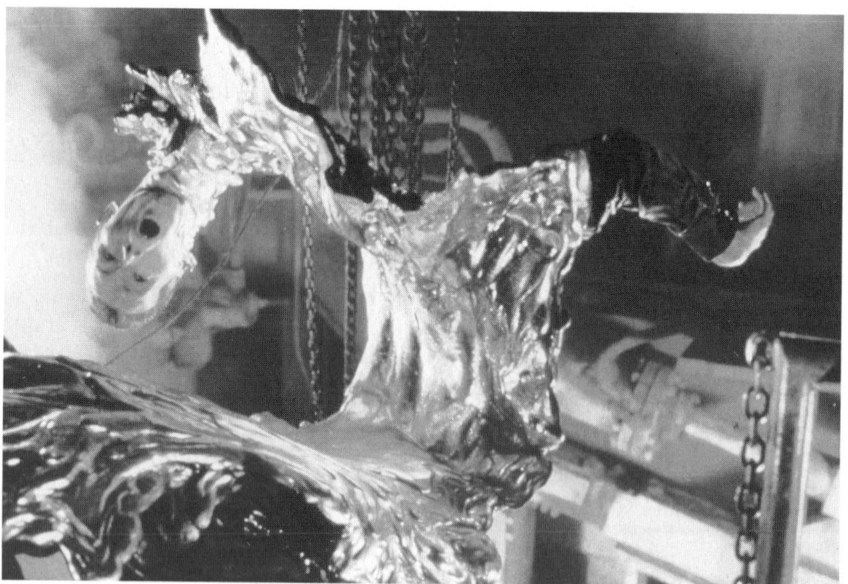

Figure 6.1 *Terminator 2: Judgment Day* (1991). The Kobal Collection/Carolco.

film *The Abyss* (1989). The principle *raison d'être* of *Terminator 2* is the production of special-effects-based spectacle, along with the more conventional action-movie recipe of chase, combat and destruction. *The Terminator* left plenty of undeveloped *narrative* potential – an ending in which the central character Sarah Connor (Linda Hamilton) drives off ready to bear a son who will lead the human resistance in a post-apocalyptic future – but it seems reasonable to conclude that fulfilling this potential was not the major factor in the decision to fashion a sequel. Even if some of the narrative dimensions of the film might be interpreted as responses to socio-cultural issues or anxieties, it is difficult to make any very direct argument to support the claim that these are an identifiable *causal factor* in the appearance of the film.

If *Terminator 2* owes its existence primarily to its potential to create a particular form of spectacular blockbuster attraction, a product of the particular Hollywood regime in place at the time (and very much with us today), it does not follow that, as a result, it is lacking in narrative dynamics, or even that narrative is in a particularly secondary position in the actual structure of the film. The distinction between these two propositions is important, but one that tends to be overlooked in many accounts. *Terminator 2* has strong and carefully orchestrated narrative dimensions. Like most other spectacular blockbusters, it offers a combination of spectacular and narrative appeals, a quality cleared marked from the outset. In its opening moments, *Terminator 2* supplies both large-scale spectacle (images of apocalypse and post-apocalyptic warfare between human and machine) and narrative exposition (a voice-over from Sarah Connor that establishes the narrative context). Outbursts of spectacle and special effects are narratively situated; they serve narrative purposes. The opening vision of apocalypse – repeated later, when located in Sarah's dreams – hangs over the film as its basic, narratively located fulcrum of suspense (will it really occur, or be averted?). Celebrated sequences such as the transformation in which the figure of the T-1000 emerges seamlessly from a checkerboard floor, or when it passes through the metal bars in a hospital hallway, gain their *full* impact also through their location at narratively heightened moments of tension: the ability of the T-1000 to perform such maneuvers directly places the sympathetic characters in danger.

Such sequences are designed to show off the effects. If they are experienced *as* effects, something less than total engrossment in the ongoing events of the diegetic universe must be entailed: the viewer "sits back," as it were, distanced to some extent from the on-screen world, aware of the nature of the image as construct. To interpret this as a spectacular/special-effects *interruption* or bracketing of narrative, however, is to assume a rather one-dimensional model of the experience of film viewing – as if, for example, the *normal* experience of spectatorship was anything close to *total* and undivided engrossment or "suspension of disbelief." The example of special-effects-led spectacle might be used, more helpfully, to illustrate the complex and multidimensional modalities in which any particular film, type of film, or individual sequence is likely to be consumed.[2] If high-definition computer-generated special effects can be experienced simultaneously as "highly realistic and convincing" and as "amazing *illusions* of the highly realistic and convincing," the same kind of oscillations might be available more widely – between that which draws the viewer acceptingly "into" the fictional world on screen and that which marks its more distanced status as pleasurable illusion (the pleasure resulting partly from awareness of its status *as* illusion).

If the major spectacular sequences of *Terminator 2* are themselves narratively situated, the film also exhibits many other features usually associated with the "classical Hollywood" style of narration (as defined by Bordwell 1985). It has a primarily linear, forward-moving structure, across the different narrative threads, based on cause-and-effect relationships between one event and another. It is organized around the qualities and experiences of a distinctive small group of characters who undergo significant development. This would not need to be stated, so obvious does it seem, were it not for some of the sweeping claims made about such films. It does not take any great feats of academic ingenuity, either, to suggest a number of not very deeply "underlying" narrative dynamics of a structural variety, often entailing the establishment and imaginary reconciliation of thematic oppositions. Obvious examples include the theme of "humanity vs. technology" and issues of gender roles and parenting. Plenty has been written about these (for example, Telotte 1995; Tasker 1993), but such dimensions often seem to be lost from sight during discussion of spectacle or special effects. A full and adequate understanding of spectacular blockbusters such as *Terminator 2* requires simultaneous attention to the various dimensions that make up the experience offered to the viewer. The same can be said of films that use the montage-based form of spectacular impact, whether in the form of hyperkinetically edited action sequences or the surface-style oriented music-video aesthetic examined by Wyatt. They still exhibit most if not all of the qualities usually associated, loosely, with "classical Hollywood" narrative and are structured around various thematic oppositions (for more on this in detail, see King 2000 and 2002a).

The continued importance of narrative structure in Hollywood blockbuster-style production has been acknowledged by some recent commentators, in an attempt to redress the balance against assumptions that narrative has been undermined (especially Buckland 1998; Cowie 1998; Thompson 1999). But does narrative have any distinctive characteristics in this context, when combined with an emphasis on the production of spectacular impact? Does it depart in any way from the "classical" version? Spectacular blockbusters of recent decades have sometimes been associated with the more episodic structure of B-movie serials produced in Hollywood in the 1930s and 1940s, a structure in which less emphasis is placed on overarching narrative dynamics. Some of the landmark spectacular blockbusters of the 1970s and 1980s are designed very much with the serial template in mind, obvious examples being *Star Wars* (1977) and *Raiders of the Lost Ark* (1981). As Warren Buckland suggests, the latter can be broken down into a series of six distinct episodes, but these are tied together quite strongly through their position in the development of a feature-length narrative that reaches resolution in the final episode: "The point to make here is that this pattern transcends individual episodes, and is dependent for its very existence on the presence of a feature-length story" (1998: 172). The dynamic is very different from that which results from the shorter serial format, in which a substantial gap occurs between one episode and another.

One quality often associated with recent spectacular blockbuster production is pace. For Thomas Schatz, the distinguishing characteristic of a film such as *Star Wars* is not an absence of narrative drive but a hell-bent and careening form of narrative that emphasizes "plot over character" (1993: 23). This account seems to contradict the claim that the production of spectacular or impact aesthetics has an interruptive or bracketing effect in relation to narrative. The accusation is of lack of narrative depth, rather than of narrative itself (and, whatever the distinctive characteristics of the film, it is hardly the case that character is other than a central component in the armature that drives *Star Wars* or other titles in the franchise). The generation of spectacular impact within what might be described as an incessant, forward-driving narrative-spectacle context is characteristic of many recent Hollywood blockbusters and less-than-blockbuster-scale action films. Exactly *how* major sequences of spectacle or special effects occur within this kind of framework is variable, however, on more than one ground. Large-scale computer-generated effects remain expensive, which is one reason why they are unlikely to overwhelm narrative at present, even if filmmakers were prepared to dispose of the narrative dimension in any substantial manner (which itself seems highly unlikely). *Terminator 2* is a prominent example in this respect, the trademark transformational effects being absent from large stretches of the film.

The rapid succession with which moments of spectacular impact come in some films – a strong example is *Armageddon* – might be seen as a point of distinction from earlier spectacular blockbusters, which tend to be more "stately" in their mode of presentation, moving (in some cases, lumbering) more slowly between larger scale spectacular set-pieces and sequences of greater intimacy. In this sense, it might be said that narrative momentum is "bracketed" a good deal less in the contemporary Hollywood spectacular blockbuster than in some other examples. An alternative might be suggested, in these two different forms of spectacular, between degrees of narrative momentum (forward-moving drive) and narrative depth (complications, ramifications, nuances, etc.), but these are only relative. The trouble with any sweeping judgments, either way, is that narrative/spectacle dynamics vary within as well as between different industrial-historical contexts. Some contemporary spectacular blockbusters are clearly designed to hark back to the "grander" earlier style, prominent examples including *Titanic*, *Gladiator*, and *Pearl Harbor*. The duration and pacing of these films, in particular, is very different from that of the *Star Wars*/*Raiders of the Lost Ark*/*Armageddon* variety. Lengthy scenes of slow-paced, character-based narrative development account for large segments of the running time. For viewers attracted by the promise of spectacle, it might be these sequences that are experienced as the interruptive dimension. The same might be said of *The Ten Commandments*, in which extra-large-scale spectacle is witnessed only on occasion and accounts for a small fraction of the running time (compared, say, to the large-scale scenes of conflict in *The Birth of a Nation*, which are held for more extensive periods). The typical rhythm of the film during its set-pieces is to move quite swiftly from the enormous vista to a more conventionally studio-bound scale of more localized detail at which the principals interact.

Differences can also be identified between films in the same blockbuster franchise. *Jurassic Park 3* (2001), for example, has a structure rather different from that of either of its two predecessors. Less time is spent dwelling on the broader ramifications of the creation of the dinosaurs (a substantial component of the first film, especially) and there is no new twist of a corporate-conspiratorial nature (as there is in the second in the series). There are no human enemies this time. The film, as a result, is some thirty minutes shorter than the first two instalments. Emphasis is put on a forward-driving rescue–survive–escape scenario that delivers a tight succession of spectacular engagements with dinosaurs. This might seem to confirm the suggestion by Timothy Corrigan (1991) that the prevalence of sequels has been a major factor in what he describes as the attenuation of narrative in Hollywood since the mid-1970s in favor of the spectacle provided by the display of cinematic technology. In the sequel, the series film, and the remake, Corrigan argues, "figures of technological or stylistic extravagance . . . detach themselves from the path of character psychology and plot incident" (1991: 170). The main *point* of the blockbuster sequel, in this case as in *Terminator 2*, might be to provide the opportunity to display the latest advances in special-effects capabilities (as well as simply providing "more of the same," as a "thrill ride"). But plenty of narrative structure is still in evidence, even in the relatively stripped-down second-sequel format used by *Jurassic Park 3*. The experience of the special-effects-led spectacle is closely linked to character (including differences in the attitudes and reactions of different characters to the dinosaurs); it also drives the basic "jeopardy" narrative. The narrative structure of events embodies a typical Hollywood moral economy: the fact, for example, that the cavalier young assistant to the dinosaur expert will redeem himself and appear to die in the process (rescuing a young boy from the clutches of a pterodactyl) after being castigated for stealing a pair of eggs from the nest of a velociraptor. Judgments such as that of Corrigan tend to flatten the picture, overstating certain tendencies to the detriment of close understanding of precisely how such films are structured. Broad historical-industrial factors are clearly important in shaping the spectacle/narrative dynamics of blockbusters, but accounts in these terms usually need to be supplemented by more local and specific analysis. Differences of genre, for example – which might include the favoring of different genres on different occasions – seem to play as important a part as shifts from one era to another in accounting for some of the specific qualities found in examples such as *Gladiator* and *Star Wars* or *Jurassic Park 3*.

If some contemporary Hollywood blockbusters are relatively episodic, they are far from alone, historically speaking. As Elizabeth Cowie suggests, episodic structure – in which narrative events are sometimes displaced by set-pieces and not always given clear causal explanation – is found in plenty of products from the "classical" period (for examples see Cowie 1998: 185). This is the case from the levels of "prestige" and spectacular blockbuster production to the B-movie tradition on which one trend in more recent blockbuster filmmaking has drawn. Hollywood production in the studio era, in general, was often not as "classical" as is sometimes implied (most notably in David Bordwell's influential account). Once reasonably coherent narrative became established as a primary basis of organization (by the 1910s) it was constantly subject to combination with all sorts of other appeals, ranging from the presence of larger-than-role star performers to the vicissitudes of melodramatic coincidence and the pleasures of large-scale spectacular attraction (see, for example, Altman 1992; Maltby 1995). This may sometimes be foregrounded to an extra degree in the spectacular blockbuster, but the differences, generally, are relative and of degree rather than absolute. Narrative has never since played less than a substantial role, either, in combination with other dimensions, whether in the most hell-bent or the most heavy-handed and lumbering varieties of spectacular blockbuster production. The experience of spectacle in the blockbuster is usually organized and given resonance by narrative dimensions, in an assortment of different combinations and styles, each of which merits careful analysis in its own right: a weighing up of the balance between narrative and spectacle, their interactions, the specific qualities of each, and the industrial and historical contexts in which a particular format is encouraged.

Notes

1 These devices also have cinematic precedents, of course, most notably the montage style adopted by Sergei Eisenstein.

2 For more on the subject of varying "modalities of response," in reference to special effects sequences and to Hollywood films more generally, see Barker with Austin (2000: 55, 79, 81).

References

Altman, Rick (1992) "Dickens, Griffith, and Film Theory Today," in Jane Gaines (ed.), *Classical Hollywood Narrative: The Paradigm Wars*, Durham, NC: Duke University Press: 9–47.

Barker, Martin, with Austin, Thomas (2000) *From Antz to Titanic: Reinventing Film Analysis*, London: Pluto Press.

Barker, Martin, and Brooks, Kate (1998) *Knowing Audiences: Judge Dredd, Its Friends, Fans and Foes*, Luton: University of Luton Press.

Bordwell, David (1985) "The Classical Hollywood Style, 1917–60," in Bordwell, David, Staiger, Janet, and Thompson, Kristin, *The Classical Hollywood Cinema: Film Style and Mode of Production to 1960*, London: Routledge & Kegan Paul: 1–84.

Bowser, Eileen (1990) *The Transformation of Cinema 1907–1915*, Berkeley: University of California Press.

Buckland, Warren (1998) "A Close Encounter With *Raiders of the Lost Ark*: Notes on Narrative Aspects of the New Hollywood Blockbuster," in Steve Neale and Murray Smith (eds), *Contemporary Hollywood Cinema*, London: Routledge: 166–77.

Bukatman, Scott (1998) "Zooming Out: The End of Offscreen Space," in Jon Lewis (ed.), *The New American Cinema*, Durham, NC: Duke University Press: 248–72.

Corrigan, Timothy (1991) *A Cinema Without Walls: Movies and Culture After Vietnam*, London: Routledge.

Cowie, Elizabeth (1998) "Storytelling: Classical Hollywood Cinema and Classical Narrative," in Steve Neale and Murray Smith (eds), *Contemporary Hollywood Cinema*, London: Routledge: 178–90.

Darley, Andrew (2000) *Digital Visual Culture: Surface Play and Spectacle in New Media Genres*, London: Routledge.

Dyer, Richard (1992) *Only Entertainment*, London: British Film Institute.

Ellis, John (1989) *Visible Fictions: Cinema, Television, Video* (rev. edn), London: Routledge.

King, Geoff (2000) *Spectacular Narratives: Hollywood in the Age of the Blockbuster*, London and New York: I. B. Tauris.

—— (2002a) *New Hollywood Cinema: An Introduction*, London: I. B. Tauris.

—— (2002b) "Die Hard/Try Harder: Narrative, Spectacle and Beyond, From Hollywood to Videogame," in Geoff King and Tanya Krzywinska (eds), *ScreenPlay: Cinema/Videogames/Interfaces*, London: Wallflower Press.

Landon, Brooks (1992) *The Aesthetics of Ambivalence*, Westport, CT: Greenwood Press.

LaValley, Albert J. (1985) "Tradition or Trickery?: The Role of Special Effects in the Science Fiction Film," in George E. Slusser and Eric S. Rabkin (eds), *Shadows of the Magic Lamp: Fantasy and Science Fiction Film*, Carbondale: Southern Illinois University Press: 141–58.

Maltby, Richard (1995) *Hollywood Cinema: An Introduction*, Oxford: Blackwell.

Pierson, Michele (1999) "CGI Effects in Hollywood Science-Fiction Cinema 1989–95: The Wonder Years," *Screen*, 40, 2: 158–76.

Schatz, Thomas (1993) "The New Hollywood," in Jim Collins, Hilary Radner and Ava Preacher Collins (eds), *Film Theory Goes to the Movies*, New York and London: Routledge, 8–36 [reprinted in this volume].

Tasker, Yvonne (1993) *Spectacular Bodies: Gender, Genre and the Action Cinema*, London: Routledge.

Telotte, J. P. (1995) *Replications: A Robotic History of the Science Fiction Film*, Urbana: University of Illinois Press.

Thompson, Kristin (1999) *Storytelling in the New Hollywood*, Cambridge, MA: Harvard University Press.

Wyatt, Justin (1994) *High Concept: Movies and Marketing in Hollywood*, Austin: University of Texas Press.

7

"WANT TO TAKE A RIDE?"

Reflections on the blockbuster experience in *Contact* (1997)

Peter Krämer

In what is arguably one of the most spectacular opening shots in all of film history, the science-fiction epic *Contact* (1997) begins with the camera hovering over the globe, radio stations playing contemporary music on the soundtrack. Then the camera pulls back from Earth into space, the globe and the sun recede into the background, other planets in our solar system pass by, and the radio sounds go back in time, mixing music of previous decades with soundbites from important historical figures. This is followed by silence, while the camera is pulling back further, out of the Milky Way and the cluster of galaxies of which it is part, and further still toward the very edge of the universe, revealing amazing sights of celestial configurations along the way. When the silence, the relentless movement, and the sheer size of the space that is being traversed begin to become oppressive, sounds can be heard again, initially only radio static and then a voice. Finally, the camera concludes its journey by pulling out of the eye of a young girl, who sits at her CB radio calling out, with some urgency, to other radio amateurs: "CQ. This is W9GF0. Come back."

This four-minute "shot" – actually a composite of photographic and computer-generated images and sounds from many different sources, rather than a single recording – is not only an incredibly rich and varied audio-visual design, it also fulfills a number of important functions. First, the shot suggests a significant self-reflexive dimension for the film it opens, with the girl, Ellie Arroway, standing in for the people in the cinema auditorium, all eyes and ears and filled with fantastic dreams and the wish to break out of the confines of the everyday world. Second, the shot sets up the story that the film is going to tell – about Ellie growing up into a scientist dedicated to the radio search for extraterrestrial intelligence (SETI). Third, it introduces some of the film's main themes, such as the relationship between mankind and the universe, between personal longings and technological and scientific endeavors. Finally, it foreshadows *Contact*'s main attraction. Almost two hours into the film, there is another spectacular journey across the universe, reminiscent of the famous climactic trip which formed the main attraction of Stanley Kubrick's *2001: A Space Odyssey* (1968), the film which *Contact* resembles most closely in its thematic preoccupations and intellectual ambitions. When Ellie is invited to go on this trip by her mysterious benefactor, S. R. Hadden, he does so with the words: "Want to take a ride?" Indeed, this is what *Contact* announces itself to be with its amazing opening shot, and how at least one reviewer (in *Variety*) described the film – as "an engrossing ride for most of the way" (reprinted in Elley 2000: 173).

The reviewer and the film's script refer to what is perhaps the most powerful critical metaphor for contemporary blockbuster cinema – the rollercoaster ride (King 2000: 179–80). According to many critics, spectators of blockbuster films are invited to give themselves over to a meticulously designed and expensively constructed mechanism, the main purpose of which is to stimulate them sensually by confronting them with wondrous sights and spectacular action, making their muscles tense and their breath go faster, with adrenaline pumping through their veins, and dizziness taking over before calm is temporarily allowed to set in, suspense, fear, and terror alternating with relief, joy, and elation, screams intermingled with laughter. No matter what they experience and feel during the ride, spectators know that they are perfectly safe, and that at the end they will arrive exactly where they started.

Figure 7.1 *Contact* (1997): Ellie Arroway (Jodie Foster) prepares for the ride of her life. The Kobal Collection/Warner Bros./Southside Amusement Co.

This account of the blockbuster experience accords well with certain aspects of Ellie's "ride" toward the end of *Contact*, a ride which is in fact introduced and executed as the equivalent of a cinematic experience (the transporting device standing in for the film, Ellie for the spectator, the trip for the viewing experience). Extraordinary amounts of money have been spent to create a machine able to remove Ellie from her own world and transport her into another. She is strapped into the passenger seat, and a mysterious light announces the beginning of her journey, which cuts her off from the friends and colleagues she had just been talking with. She goes on a rollicking rollercoaster ride in empty space, punctured by moments of calm in which she submits to the beauty of celestial formations and events on display in front of her eyes. During the longest of these moments, she is magically removed from her seat, floats in the air, and regresses to a younger self: the face of the girl she once was is superimposed on the face of the adult she now is, first one, then the other exclaiming softly: "so beautiful." In a reversal of the very opening of the film, the camera then moves into Ellie's eye and into darkness.

It is at this point that Ellie's trip leaves the rollercoaster model behind. Instead of sensual thrills and visual spectacle, an encounter with an alien creature taking the shape of her own father is at the center of the next part of her journey, which is set on a beach based on a drawing she did as a child of a place she made radio contact with. Overwhelmed by emotions as she is, Ellie still does not lose herself completely: "You're not real," she says to her "father," "None of this is real." At the same time, she is receptive to his words, when he assures her of her parents' love, and of her specialness: "You are capable of such beautiful dreams and such horrible nightmares." This is addressed both to Ellie as an individual and to humanity in general ("You are an interesting species"). The very core of the human condition, according to her "father," is a terrible feeling of isolation: "You feel so lost, so cut off, so alone. Only you're not." His most important message is this: "The only thing . . . that makes the emptiness bearable is each other." Ellie is then transported back to where she started out from, reconnected to her friends and colleagues, and embarks on the long process to make sense of her experience which lasts until the end of the film.

While much about Ellie's journey is subject to debate, one thing is certain. Far from being a purely sensual ride, it has dealt with the very foundations of her being, her individual existence, her relationship with parents and others, and her conception of her place in the universe. In other words, Ellie's journey across the universe, and by implication the journey on which the film *Contact* takes its viewers, has a deeply psychological and spiritual dimension. In its two sustained sequences of audio-visual spectacle, then, the film reflects on the very nature of the blockbuster experience it offers its audience. How do these reflections relate to the story that *Contact* tells? And to what extent is the film a typical blockbuster?

The making of a blockbuster

In terms of its production, *Contact*'s blockbuster credentials are impeccable (according to the criteria provided by Steve Neale's chapter in this volume). *Contact* had a much higher budget ($90 million) than the average Hollywood release (Stevens 2001: 13) and also had an excessive length (150 minutes); it foregrounds special effects, not only during the two journeys across space, but also, for example, by blending footage of President Clinton into the film's action. Like many other megahits the film is based on presold material, in this case a best-selling novel (published in 1985) by America's foremost science popularizer Carl Sagan (Davidson 1999: 341–53, 399–411). *Contact* features Jodie Foster, one of the very few female stars with sustained box-office success across the 1990s. Perhaps most importantly, the film was directed by Oscar winner Robert Zemeckis, Hollywood's most consistently commercially successful director since the mid-1980s. Before that point Zemeckis had directed two minor films produced by Steven Spielberg – *I Wanna Hold your Hand* (1978), which he also co-wrote, and *Used Cars* (1980) – and he had co-written one of Spielberg's rare flops, *1941* (1979). Since the mid-1980s, however, Zemeckis's box-office track record has been astonishing.

With the exception of *Death Becomes Her* (no. 27 in 1992), all of the films Zemeckis directed between the mid-1980s and *Contact* made it into *Variety*'s end-of-year top ten chart of the highest grossing movies:[1] *Romancing the Stone* (no. 9 in 1984), *Back to the Future* (which he also co-wrote, no. 1 in 1985), *Who Framed Roger Rabbit?* (no. 2 in 1988), *Back to the Future II* (based on a story by Zemeckis, no.10 in 1989), *Back to the Future III* (script co-written by Zemeckis, no. 10 in 1990), *Forrest Gump* (no.1 in 1994). After *Contact*, he managed the unique feat of releasing two massive hits in the same year: *What Lies Beneath* was at number 8 in 2000, and *Cast Away* would have made it into the top three if it had not been released so late in the year that more than half of its revenues were generated in 2001. In the Internet Movie Database's October 2001 list of all-time top grossers in the US, Zemeckis had two films in the top twenty five (*Forrest Gump* at no. 6, and *Cast Away* at no. 23) and five films in the top 100, more than any other director apart from Steven Spielberg (who also produced several of Zemeckis's megahits).

Despite his extraordinary success, Zemeckis has a surprisingly low public profile, and there is, for example, not a single book on his life and films. It is, however, possible to make some preliminary statements about his work. Having started out as a scriptwriter, he continues to be heavily involved in the writing process even when he is working with someone else's script. He says: "I've never found a screenplay yet that didn't need massive amounts of what we call rewriting. For me the writing never stops" (Kagan 2000: 39). As one of the most powerful people in Hollywood since the late 1980s (he was, for example, at no. 22 in *Premiere* magazine's May 1996 "Power List"), Zemeckis has certainly been able to select and shape his projects, asserting his authority in relation to studios and stars. While in interviews he emphasizes the importance of character development (Kagan 2000: 39), his films are best known for their spectacular action and their special effects, in particular computer-generated images. In fact, Zemeckis's films since the mid-1980s put the latter in the service of the former. Despite their big-budget spectacle and occasionally epic length, they tell intimate stories, either about childlike men (Marty McFly, Roger Rabbit, Forrest Gump, even to some extent Chuck Noland in *Cast Away*) and their familial or quasi-familial relationships in a largely fantastic (or exotic) universe, or about women and their fantasies, desires, and anxieties (concerning adventurous romance, eternal youth, and murderous husbands) which, quite shockingly, become real. Thus, Zemeckis's hit movies fit into two important trends in contemporary Hollywood. The first is what I have elsewhere labeled "family-adventure movies" which typically revolve around the adventures and (quasi-)familial relations of boys or boyish men and have consistently been the most successful Hollywood films since the late 1970s (Krämer 1998a). The second trend is what one might call women's films, that is, films centered on female characters and/or appealing primarily to female audiences – a type of film that has been marginalized in Hollywood since the late 1960s, yet at the end of 1997 received an enormous boost with the unprecedented success of *Titanic* (Krämer 1998b and 1999).[2]

Contact brings the two strands of Zemeckis's work together by placing a woman at the center of a spectacular and fantastic adventure (including an intermittent romance), which ultimately revolves around her relationship with her parents. Already the film's second shot introduces her father, who responds to Ellie's increasingly desperate radio calls – "Is anybody out there?" – by encouraging her to be patient: "Small moves, Ellie, small moves." She finally receives an answer from Pensacola, Florida, which prompts her, that evening in her bedroom, while getting ready to go to sleep, to ask her father about other distant places she could talk to with her radio: California, Alaska, China, the moon, Jupiter, Saturn. After a pause, she asks: "Dad, could we talk to mom?" "I don't think even the biggest radio could reach that far," he responds. After showing him a colorful picture she has drawn of Pensacola, she then asks her father whether there is life on other planets, to which he replies: "If it is just us, it seems an awful waste of space." Later that night, she sits again at her radio and decides that she needs a bigger antenna, which is followed by a shot of the adult Ellie looking at a huge radio telescope in the jungle (the radio observatory in Arecibo, Puerto Rico), and saying "It'll do."

This sequence reveals the mother's death, together with her father's encouragement, to be at the root of Ellie's attempts to make contact with life beyond the confines of her everyday life, first as a radio amateur and then as a radio astronomer. At the most basic emotional level, her CB activities as a child and her later SETI work are shown to be a search for life after death ("Could we talk to mom?"), and also perhaps for a higher order in the universe which gives meaning to human suffering. Ellie's work as a scientist is thus explained as an emotional and a spiritual quest – an explanation she herself would, of course, deny vehemently. Furthermore, in a move typical for family-adventure movies and women's films, the film's story is set up as the externalization of the protagonist's subjectivity, the magical fulfillment of her wishes ("I need a bigger antenna" – "It'll do"). The film's fantastic story about contact with extra-terrestrials is thus firmly anchored in the everyday experiences and psychology of the central character, whose condition the opening shot, as we have already seen, equates with that of the audience. By inviting the audience to identify with Ellie's predicament as a dreamer and seeker and mourning child, the film aims to tap into some of their fundamental fears and desires, concerning every child's separation from parents (or parental figures), the loss of loved ones, the hope for a reunion overcoming this loss or for something else able to fill the void created by it. This something else, the film suggests, may be rational understanding, vivid memory, religion, and, most immediately, the cinema itself.

In many of the most successful family-adventure movies (e.g. *Star Wars* [1977], *E.T.: The Extra-Terrestrial* [1982], *The Lion King* [1994]), it is the loss of the father which provides the focus for the story (whereas in women's films such as *Ghost* [1990] and *Titanic* it is the loss of the male lover). While *Contact* initially revolves around the death of the mother, the film soon shifts its focus to the lost father. The first sequences with Ellie as an adult replay in many respects the opening childhood sequence. Again, Ellie sits at the radio, only now she listens to the static picked up by the telescope. Again, a supportive male figure is introduced – her fellow scientist, Kent, who is blind and comments on her old-fashioned way of monitoring radio signals ("I think that it is great you still listen") – and then two more men, who represent aspects of her father. The first is her former lecturer (having taken over from her father who was her first science teacher), now head of the National Science Foundation, David Drumlin, who objects to her SETI work as an illegitimate use of resources and of her talent, which will ruin her career as a scientist; indeed he soon stops her research project at Arecibo. The second is the theologian Palmer Joss, who is critical of any scientific project that does not put the interests of humanity first, yet also becomes emotionally involved with Ellie. After they have sex, a rather uncomfortable parallel is established between him and her father: both are calmly passionate men in awe of the wonders of the universe as exemplified by the sky, which her father, in a flashback, talks about in scientific terms (thus stimulating Ellie's interest in astronomy); Joss, on the other hand, talks about the time that he looked at the sky and felt the presence of God. Joss even responds to Ellie's statement that she believes the universe to be full of extraterrestrial civilizations by echoing her father's line: "If it wasn't, it would be an awful waste of space." Ellie then withdraws from him, perhaps because she is afraid to get too attached to people, after she has lost her mother and – we now learn – also her father. A flashback shows her father's death at a time soon after the events of the opening sequence, and Ellie's subsequent rejection of a priest's comforting statements and her now desperate attachment to her CB radio. "Dad, this is Ellie. Come back," she calls out.

The initial attempt to reach her dead mother has thus been replaced with a call to her dead father, and it is this secondary search which in the end meets with success. After Ellie and Kent start a new SETI project in New Mexico with funding by the eccentric billionaire Hadden (another figure set up in close parallel to her father), she receives a signal from the star Vega, which turns out to contain instructions for building a machine apparently able to transport one person across the universe. Drumlin, now converted to her cause, promptly takes over as leader of the project to build that machine and is selected – over Ellie – as its passenger, yet he gets killed in a terrorist attack by a religious fundamentalist. The original machine is destroyed in the process, and when it is revealed that a second one has secretly been built in Japan, Hadden invites Ellie to go. What she experiences is, as we have already seen, indeed a journey to another world, where the immensely powerful extraterrestrials – so as not to overwhelm her with their strangeness – present themselves to her in the shape of her father. In the emotional reunion with her "father," she is given a message of hope, not only for herself, but for humankind at large: the universe is full of intelligent life, and humans will eventually participate in interstellar exchange, but this will take a long time, and Ellie will have to be patient: "Small moves, Ellie."

For now, she has to return to Earth, where her report is met with disbelief, because, from what observers could see, nothing happened at all: the passenger pod never disappeared to go on its journey; it just fell straight into the water. Consequently, Ellie's testimony is discredited, although a scene toward the end does reveal that physical proof for Ellie's journey was found and kept secret by the government. In any case, Ellie herself is enriched by the memory of her great adventure – and so are the countless people who believe in her (thousands of whom greet her outside the Capitol after her testimony). It appears that now Ellie will be able to deal with her childhood loss, and to be open to new emotional attachments (a renewed relationship with Palmer Joss is hinted at) and even spirituality (more about this below). The film's closing scenes show her finally at peace with herself. In front of the New Mexico observatory, she patiently talks to children about science like her father used to talk to her, and when they ask her whether there are "other people out there in the universe," she encourages them to "keep looking for your own answers" and then concludes with her father's line from the opening scene: "I tell you one thing about the universe, though: the universe is a pretty big place. So if it's just us, it seems like an awful waste of space." Thus she combines a basic faith in the meaningfulness of the universe (it is not, after all, a "waste of space") with the skepticism and rationality underpinning scientific inquiry.

The very last scene of the film shows Ellie alone at night in the desert, examining tiny stones in the palm of her hand in the same way her "father" did on the imaginary reconstruction of a Pensacola beach during her trip. As is typical of many of the most successful family-adventure movies, then, at the end the protagonist's original familial issues are resolved and peace of mind is regained (as it is for Luke Skywalker, Elliott, and Simba, for example), and although the lost father never really returns, he is present as a memory (or indeed – like Anakin Skywalker and Mufasa – as a spirit); curiously, though, Ellie's mother is forgotten. What is more, the glittering stones look a bit like the stars in the night sky, and the night sky, which is the film's final image, in turn is like the darkened screen in front of which the audience is sitting. This suggests that the sky that Ellie has been studying all through the film is not distant and alien, but like the palm of her own hand (or indeed like the inside of her own head, as the opening shot implies), and also like the screen which the audience has been examining so intently for the preceding two and a half hours. In the same way that Ellie comes out of this experience as a more rounded and fulfilled person, so, the film suggests, does every spectator, and while for Ellie it is the stars in the sky to which she will turn for further insight and emotional and spiritual nourishment, for the spectator it is first and foremost the cinema screen. Like many family-adventure movies and other blockbusters, *Contact* thus ends up celebrating the power of cinema.

An intellectual blockbuster

Despite its impeccable blockbuster credentials, with Zemeckis mining the most successful narrative formula of recent decades, *Contact* was a relative box-office disappointment. Its domestic revenues of $101 million did not even ensure the film a place in the annual top ten (it was at no. 12 in 1997), and they were far below the gross of Zemeckis's big hits of the last decade: only a third of the amount for *Forrest Gump*, less than half of that for *Cast Away*, and about two-thirds of that for *What Lies Beneath*. One of the main reasons for the film's somewhat disappointing commercial performance was its almost exclusive focus on a female protagonist. Not only do successful family-adventure movies rarely feature women, but science-fiction hits, with the exception of *Aliens* (1986) and *Terminator 2: Judgment Day* (1991), do not do so either. What is more, unlike *Aliens* and *Terminator 2*, *Contact* does not concern itself centrally with the issue of motherhood, nor does it replicate the strong focus of most successful women's films – ranging from *Pretty Woman* (1990) to *Titanic* and *What Lies Beneath* – and of most blockbusting female-centered action-adventure films – ranging from *Romancing the Stone* to *Twister* (1996) – on a romantic relationship.[3] Instead, *Contact* foregrounds intellectual issues and the ways in which the film's protagonist negotiates her intellectual worldview with her emotional and spiritual needs (and in that respect it is in fact closely related to what had been Jodie Foster's biggest previous hit, *The Silence of the Lambs* [1991]).

Indeed, the film and its heroine were perceived by the press primarily in terms of their intellectual orientation. While some critics celebrated this aspect of the film as a welcome departure from the norms of contemporary Hollywood, others felt that it undermined the film's entertainment value, especially for children, usually a primary audience for the kind of family-adventure story *Contact* tells. Andrew Sarris's (1997) review of the film in the *New York Observer*, for example, criticized it as a failed "attempt at an 'intellectual' blockbuster for grown ups," which managed to demonstrate only that "the cinema is more an emotional than an intellectual medium." On the other hand, an *Entertainment Weekly* cover story described *Contact* as an "Event Movie for intellectuals," a "serious" and "unabashedly esoteric" film "packed with cosmic meditations on the duel between Science and God," and asked, with reference to the film's commercial chances: "is Earth prepared?" (Svetkey 1997: 19). Jack Mathews of *Newsday* welcomed *Contact* as "the smartest film in the summer market": "A little intellectual provocation counts for a lot in this summer of braindead action films" (Mathews 1997: B3). Within a few weeks, *Contact* had confirmed its status as an event movie, in the process polarizing critics even more. For Stuart Klawans, writing in *The Nation* (11 August, 1997: 35), it was "perhaps the worst summer film overall," and the *Village Voice* (19 August, 1997: 86) declared it to be the "Summer's Most Obnoxious Movie." At the end of the year the science-fiction magazine *Starlog* insisted again that *Contact* was the "only intellectual genre movie from the past summer" and as such was to be valued and taken seriously (O'Quinn 1997: 78). A similar controversy surrounded Jodie Foster's intellectualized portrayal of Ellie Arroway. Sarris found Ellie to be "a curiously disembodied creature," because Foster seemed "determined to make herself all mind and spirit by draining all the sensual juices out of her hitherto provocative star persona." *Starlog*, on the other hand, saw Foster's performance in *Contact* as "the crowning achievement of her already stellar acting career," precisely because "Foster constantly lets us see Ellie think" (O'Quinn 1997: 78).

What, then, is the protagonist's and the film's intellectual inquiry about? Ostensibly, as we have seen, it centers on the relationship between different worldviews: one driven by feelings, another religious, and the third one scientific. In long dialog sequences, the film again and again brings these worldviews into conflict with each other: for example, when the young Ellie rejects the comforts of religion in favor of a rational analysis of the reasons for her father's death (he did not get to his medicine in time, for which she feels responsible; her rational analysis is thus closely linked to the child's feelings of guilt); or when the adult Ellie competes with Drumlin for the single place in the alien machine and loses out to him in a public hearing because, due to lack of empirical evidence, she does not believe in God and is therefore held to be unrepresentative of humankind. In particular, Ellie's relationship with Palmer Joss is overshadowed by his criticism of science and her rejection of religious beliefs (and indeed it is he who asks the question about her belief in God which leads to Drumlin being selected over her). During their first night together, Joss talks about his religious awakening: "I was lying there, just looking at the sky and then I felt something. . . . All I know is that I wasn't alone, and for the first time in my life, I wasn't scared of nothing, not even dying. It was God." She immediately doubts the validity of his experience and suggests that he just projected an inner need into the outside world when in fact there was nothing out there. At their next meeting, during a debate with the American president on the significance of the message from Vega, she rejects any suggestion that it may have religious implications. If it were of a religious nature, it would have been "a booming voice from the sky," to which Joss replies: "That is exactly what you found." Afterwards, they discuss their differences in more detail. While he argues that science cannot give people what they really need, she argues that humans invented God "so that we wouldn't have to feel so small and alone," and while he says he would not want to live in a world without God, she can not accept God's existence without tangible proof. He responds by asking her whether she loved her father. When she says yes, he demands: "Prove it!" The conversation ends without any agreement.

Having stated their differences very starkly, from here on the film begins to demonstrate the compatibility of emotional, religious, and scientific worldviews. When in a later conversation Joss asks Ellie why she is willing to give up everything, even her life, for the chance to travel across the universe (and it is clear that he asks her because he loves her and does not want to lose her), her answer is meant to convey a total commitment to the pursuit of scientific insight, yet comes across as spiritually motivated: she has always been "searching for something, some reason why we're here." What she finds during her encounter with the extraterrestrials is, of course, the emotional resolution of her childhood trauma and a vision of a higher order in the universe as well as scientific insight. When she returns from her journey and is interrogated about her experience, she is forced to admit that as a scientist she would have to find her own story unbelievable, because there is no physical proof that she ever went anywhere, and because there is indeed – as suggested by her interrogator – a simpler and therefore better explanation for everything that has happened: she hallucinated, and the message from Vega itself was simply a hoax staged by S. R. Hadden. Not being able to defend her experience on scientific grounds, she can confirm and articulate it only in emotional and spiritual terms: "I had an experience. . . . Everything tells me it was real. I was given something wonderful, something that changed me forever, a vision of the universe that tells us undeniably how tiny and insignificant and how rare and precious we all are, a vision that tells us that we belong to something that is greater than ourselves, that we are not, that none of us are alone. I wish I could share that. I wish that everyone, if even for one moment, could feel that awe and humility and hope." This, of course, comes close to Joss's previous description of his experience of God. In the end, then,

Ellie's scientific inquiry has brought her the emotional and spiritual comfort that she was looking for all along. When Joss in his final statement declares to the crowds outside the Capitol that he and Ellie have "one and the same" goal, namely "the pursuit of truth," the film suggests that truth can, and needs to be, found on various levels – emotional, religious, and scientific – and that these levels complement rather than contradict each other.

While this insight may not be particularly profound, it does challenge received scholarly wisdom in relation to the blockbuster experience itself. No matter how rationally constructed a film is (making use of the latest special-effects technology and perhaps of "scientific" market research, and definitely intended to make money), *Contact*'s allegory – which equates Ellie with the spectator, her journey within the film with the journey of the film, the debate about the journey with a debate about the film – suggests that blockbusters aim to put the spectator on an emotional and spiritual journey through the stories they tell and through the creation of extraordinary audio-visual spectacle. Following this suggestion, one might say that successful blockbusters do indeed resonate with the most basic experiences and longings of their audiences, reunite them, albeit only imaginarily, with loved ones, expose them to previously unimaginable beauty, inspire awe, humility, and hope in the face of a higher power, assure them that, while each person is unique and precious, he or she is not alone – and thus help them along on their way toward emotional and spiritual fulfillment.

Conclusion

"Want to take a ride?" is the implicit invitation of all contemporary blockbuster movies. *Contact* delivers the promised ride already in its very first shot, but then goes against the expectations raised by the film's genre, the previous films of its director, and its opening shot by withholding further extended spectacle until close to the end of the film. Instead the film, through intimate family scenes and long, thoughtful dialog sequences, explores the deep seated needs to which such fantastic rides respond and the various ways in which riders on and off the screen may make sense of them. Critics (and, presumably, audiences) were divided in their response to this intellectual blockbuster, the more so as it centered on a woman. For some, the film's entertainment value was destroyed by its reflections on the relationship between feelings, religion, and science; for others it was deepened. For all, however, *Contact* was inextricably linked, by way of contrast and continuity, to Hollywood's big budget, special-effects driven, action-oriented summer movies – as an expensive and pretentious failure to live up to their promise of pure fun, or as a welcome departure from the norm they set.

In this chapter, I have tried to show that *Contact* is perhaps most interesting when understood as a meditation on the blockbuster experience, in particular its spiritual dimension. At the very least, this approach alerts us to the frequency with which Hollywood's biggest hits since the late 1970s have explicitly dealt with spiritual subject matter. There is, for example, the central role played by "the Force" in the *Star Wars* films, and there are Indiana Jones's encounters with divine power at the end of both *Raiders of the Lost Ark* (1981) and *Indiana Jones and the Last Crusade* (1989), and the spirits caught between this world and the next in *Ghost* and *The Sixth Sense* (1999). *Contact*'s reflections on the blockbuster experience also encourage us to investigate the allegorical religious dimension of other megahits, for example *E.T.* (the extraterrestrial as a Jesus figure) and *Terminator 2* (Sarah Connor as a Holy Mary figure). More generally, they suggest that it may be worth relating the blockbuster experience to the religious beliefs and spiritual longings of the baby-boom generation. This generation includes the majority of Hollywood's most successful filmmakers, such as Robert Zemeckis and Steven Spielberg, and also constitutes the largest segment of the American cinema audience. Since the 1970s, an increasing number of baby boomers (and by the 1990s a majority) have been identified by religious scholars as spiritual seekers on a quest for "values and meaning beyond oneself, a way of understanding, inner awareness, and personal integration" (Roof 1999: 35). Many of Hollywood's big hits appear to be informed by, and responsive to, this questing outlook, not only in their stories but also in their moments of intense, overwhelming audio-visual spectacle, such as the two cosmic journeys depicted in *Contact*. Perhaps, then, audio-visual spectacle, usually considered to be the most superficial and meaningless aspect of contemporary Hollywood cinema, sometimes facilitates its most spiritual experiences – much like it used to do in the long defunct tradition of biblical epics.

Notes

Research for this essay in American archives was funded by the Arts and Humanities Research Board.

1 Information about annual box-office charts is taken from "The 1980s: A Reference Guide to Motion Pictures, Television, VCR, and Cable," *Velvet Light Trap*, 27 (1991): 81–2; and the German magazine *steadycam*. Both these sources derive their information from the American trade press. For the year 2000, I have used "Top 250 of 2000," *Variety*, 8 January, 2001: 20.

2 It is also worth pointing out that Zemeckis's films have often dealt explicitly with the power of popular culture: most notably, Beatlemania in *I Wanna Hold your Hand*, romantic adventure fiction in *Romancing the Stone*, classic Hollywood cartoons in *Who Framed Roger Rabbit?*, Jules Verne novels in *Back to the Future III*, and celebrity in *Forrest Gump*. *Contact* emphasizes the importance of television as a news medium.

3 As I have pointed out elsewhere (Krämer 1999: 603–4), there is a powerful narrative model in children's fiction for nonromantic female-centered fantastic adventure stories such as *Contact*. Indeed, Carl Sagan's novel ([1985] 1997: 37, 323, 330) references explicitly the four key examples in this tradition of girl adventurer stories: L. Frank

Baum's *The Wonderful Wizard of Oz* (1900), J. M. Barrie's *Peter Pan* (1904 play, 1911 novel), and Lewis Carroll's *Alice's Adventures in Wonderland* (1865) and *Through the Looking Glass* (1872). Contemporary Hollywood has not been able successfully to revive this tradition, although there are strong resonances in, for example, *Contact*, *Twister*, *How the Grinch Stole Christmas* (2000) and *Monsters Inc.* (2001).

References

Davidson, Keay (1999) *Carl Sagan: A Life*, New York: John Wiley.

Elley, Derek (ed.) (2000) *Variety Movie Guide 2000*, New York: Perigee.

Internet Movie Database, "The Top Grossing Movies of All Time at the USA Box Office," http://us.imdb.com/Charts/usatopmovies, accessed 23 October, 2001.

Kagan, Jeremy (ed.) (2000) *Directors Close Up*, Boston: Focal Press.

King, Geoff (2000) *Spectacular Narratives: Hollywood in the Age of the Blockbuster*, London and New York: I. B. Tauris.

Krämer, Peter (1998a) "Would You Take your Child to See this Film? The Cultural and Social Work of the Family-Adventure Movie," in Steve Neale and Murray Smith (eds), *Contemporary Hollywood Cinema*, London: Routledge: 294–311.

Krämer, Peter (1998b) "Women First: *Titanic* (1997), Action-Adventure Films and Hollywood's Female Audience," *Historical Journal of Film, Radio and Television*, 18, 4: 599–618; reprinted in Kevin S. Sandler and Gaylyn Studlar (eds) (1999) *Titanic: Anatomy of a Blockbuster*, New Brunswick, NJ: Rutgers University Press: 108–31.

Krämer, Peter (1999) "A Powerful Cinema-Going Force? Hollywood and Female Audiences since the 1960s," in Melvyn Stokes and Richard Maltby (eds) *Identifying Hollywood's Audiences: Cultural Identity and the Movies*, London: British Film Institute: 93–108.

Mathews, Jack (1997) "*Contact* Not Quite out of this World," *Newsday*, 11 July: B3, B13.

O'Quinn, Kerry (1997) "Of Hearts and Heads," *Starlog*, December: 78.

Roof, Wade Clark (1999) *Spiritual Marketplace: Baby Boomers and the Remaking of American Religion*, Princeton, NJ: Princeton University Press.

Sagan, Carl ([1985] 1997) *Contact*, London: Orbit.

Sarris, Andrew (1997) "Pity the Aliens! Jodie Foster Has Gone Cold," *New York Observer*, 21 July.

Stevens, Tracy (2001) *International Motion Picture Almanac*, Larchmont, NY: Quigley Publishing.

Svetkey, Benjamin (1997) "Making Contact," *Entertainment Weekly*, 18 July: 19–27.

8

BLOCKBUSTING SOUND

The case of *The Fugitive*

Gianluca Sergi

"We expect them to be loud and noisy."

(Keller 1999: 136)

The summarily dismissive attitude expressed in the above quotation typifies the extent of most critical attention dedicated to sound in blockbusters. It betrays a general tendency to regard the blockbuster as devoid of real filmmaking sophistication and shows an almost contemptuous attitude toward sound. It is my aim in this chapter to explore the role that sound plays in the creation of a blockbuster movie by looking at the specific example of *The Fugitive* (1991).[1] The choice of *The Fugitive* is not based on notions of "quality" or "uniqueness." Simply, it is a very interesting example of how sound can play a key role in helping a movie reach the status of "blockbuster." Although *The Fugitive* can be analyzed in conventional blockbusting terms, as we shall briefly see, it is the attitude of the filmmakers behind the film's soundtrack on which I would primarily like to focus because I believe it is the most effective way to begin to understand the contribution that sound makes.

In conventional terms, *The Fugitive* has some of the typical hallmarks of the blockbuster movie event. The film relies on the services of the biggest star in Hollywood history, at least in terms of box-office results and popular appeal. At the time of writing, Harrison Ford remains the safest bet a film could have: he has appeared in more movies that have broken through the magic $100 million barrier than any other actor in Hollywood history, and the grand total of the box-office performance of his films is also the largest of any actor.[2] In terms of production values, *The Fugitive* boasts that little "extra special" never-before-seen moment that so often helps define a movie as a filmic event.[3] Famously, the film features a real life train crash: no trick folks, this is a real train crashing into a real bus. This stunt alone (amply referred to in all publicity for the film) signals the film's desired scope, despite the relatively limited budget when compared to those of other blockbusters (the reported $44 million budget for *The Fugitive* is dwarfed by *Titanic*'s reported £200 million).

The film also had a "history" behind it. *The Fugitive* is based on an extremely popular series that ran on US television for 120 episodes between 1963 and 1967. The final episode of the series, featuring the "showdown" between Kimble, Gerard, and the one-armed man (i.e. the real killer of Kimble's wife), recorded the highest number of viewers for an episode in US television history.[4]

The film's box-office performance did not disappoint Warner Bros.' hopes. Given a respectable summer release date (August 6, 1993), wisely avoiding head-to-head confrontation with *Jurassic Park*,[5] the movie proved extremely popular: grossing over $360 million worldwide, *The Fugitive* became Warners' highest earner in 1993 (third overall for the industry that year, behind *Jurassic Park* and the surprise hit *Mrs Doubtfire*), eventually going on to become the fifth biggest earner in the studio's history.[6] Unlike the doomed train featured in the film, the movie's status stayed very much on track and went on to achieve several Oscar nominations, including in all three sound categories (sound, sound effects editing, and music), and eventually winning one for Tommy Lee Jones's performance as Lt Samuel Gerard, the detective who doggedly pursues Dr Kimball. The film's remarkable performance during its theatrical run was later confirmed with similarly strong video and, more recently, DVD sales. Indeed, the continuing popularity of the film has recently been highlighted by the release of a second edition of the film on DVD enhanced with new material, deleted scenes, and director's commentary. Almost as a logical corollary to its rise to blockbuster status, *The Fugitive* has had a sequel, *U.S. Marshals* (Stuart Baird 1998),[7] and in 2000 spawned a new TV series reprising Dr Kimball's search for justice.[8]

Critically, the film was received almost unanimously as a success, echoing its popular appeal. Roger Ebert in the *Chicago Sun-Times*, for example, enthusiastically suggests that: "Davis [the film's director] paints with bold visual strokes so that the movie rises above its action-film origins and becomes operatic." He goes on to state: "The [train] crash sequence is as ambitious and electric as any I have seen, with Kimble fleeing for his life while a locomotive bears down on him" (*Chicago Sun-Times*, August 6, 1993). Even those who were less enthusiastic about its merits, such as Desson Howe in the *Washington Post*, seemed willing to acknowledge the film's effectiveness, describing it as a "juggernaut of exaggeration, momentum and thrills – without a single lapse of subtlety – 'Fugitive' is pure energy, a perfect orchestration of heroism, villainy, suspense and comic relief" (*Washington Post*, August 6, 1993). His colleague on the same newspaper, Rita Kempley, goes one further, stating: "Shot on the fly by Andrew Davis, the director who came into his own with *Under Siege*, the yarn is not only gripping, but ripping." In her view, Davis took full advantage, "working from a well-oiled screenplay by Jeb Stuart and David Twohy" (*Washington Post*, August 6, 1993).

It is possible to identify a position, shared by most critics, that would seem to suggest that the success of the movie is ascribable to its "energy." This roughly translates into Davis's "bold visual strokes" that confer an "operatic" quality. Here, no mention is given to the role of sound within the movie. In this sense, the response to *The Fugitive* is rather typical of the critical attention blockbusters (and movies in general) commonly receive. Film criticism has long invested most of its cultural capital in the visual aspects of films and filmmaking. One of the key consequences of this "tyranny of the visual," as a colleague of mine once put it, has been to overlook the role that sound plays in movies in general, and blockbusters in particular.

"Making more of it": *The Fugitive* as the sound blockbuster

> We had a great visual movie, but what we did with that movie was going over the top with sound, but tastefully, not ruining it. Actually, what we ended up doing is making much more of it then it deserved to be. I don't really mean "deserved to be" but more of it than it's there. We took it to a different level.
>
> (Bruce Stambler, supervising sound editor and sound designer on *The Fugitive*)[9]

The above passage signals clearly that the main thrust behind sound in *The Fugitive* was to achieve more than simple "support" for the film's images. In particular, Stambler's extraordinary remark that sound makes "more of it than it's there" deserves attention. What exactly does Stambler mean when he says that sound makes more of it? More importantly, where is the evidence to support his statement?

The Fugitive tells the story of a respected surgeon, Dr Richard Kimble (Harrison Ford), who is wrongly accused of the murder of his wife, Helen. He is found guilty and sentenced to death. Following an unlikely series of events (including a bus crash and a train crash), fate hands him a new opportunity to hunt for the real murderer of his wife, a one-armed man. US Marshal Samuel Gerard (played by Tommy Lee Jones) is dispatched to apprehend Kimble. A cat-and-mouse story-line develops into the central theme of the movie: will Kimble find the murderer before Gerard finds Kimble?

The story-line suggests a rather conventional narrative development: an innocent man is found guilty, escapes, and finally manages to prove his innocence to his tough-but-fair pursuer and the entire world. Given this, it is perhaps not surprising that the film's overall style mostly follows generic conventions.

Indeed, adhering to generic convention would obviously be the safe option.

Looking at it from an aural perspective, when you see a camera flash on screen what you expect to hear is a sound approximating that which a real flash would produce. Nobody expects anything different because generic conventions concerning sound suggest that, ordinarily, sound will map closely what the image is doing, as this quote from Lucasfilm's THX sound website indicates:

> The First Rule of Sound Design: *See a sound; hear a sound.* Every time you see some action on the screen, your mind expects there to be a complementary sound. The support of sound effects helps you "willingly suspend your disbelief" and become immersed in the movie experience.
>
> (Official website for THX: <http://www.thx.com/skywalker/skywalker.html>, accessed September 1, 2001)

Thus, departure cannot be understood as "accidental": a sound designer might stumble across an unexpectedly effective sound, but its use in the final mix is no accident. I would suggest that one of the key indicators of the "going for it" attitude is precisely the willingness to depart from convention as often as possible and feasible in narrative terms. The degree of distance between expectation and actual performance then becomes a measure of the filmmakers' ambition in making more of what is there. In this sense, *The Fugitive* shows great ambition from the very beginning of the movie.

The film opens with the brutal murder of Dr Kimble's wife, Helen. The film credits are interspersed at first with an aerial shot of the Chicago skyline. Reminiscent of Ridley Scott's *Someone to Watch Over Me* (1987), the camera moves slowly across the skyscrapers. (The only difference is one of location: Scott's movie is set in New York.) Suddenly, the film cuts to a shot of a woman being attacked in her own home. The shot is in black and white and slightly slowed down. Cutting between the aerial shots and the struggle between the woman and her assailant goes on until the woman is finally shot dead. At this point, a new cut to a police ambulance arriving at the scene of the crime takes us outside the apartment for a brief moment. The murder sequence finally ends with a point-of-view shot of a police photographer's camera flashing, taking pictures of the crime scene and of the body of the murdered woman.

Ordinarily a sequence like this would be laid down with a rather basic soundtrack. Aerial shots of Chicago would probably have no specific sounds, and music would cover over both credits and aerial shots. The murder scene might require some attention, mostly because of its importance in the overall narrative (it is after all the *raison d'être* of the whole film) and the way it was shot. However, the choices made by Bruce Stambler and John Leveque counter these expectations. At first, the film soundtrack seems to follow the pattern I have just highlighted. Music (composed by James Newton Howard of *E.R.* fame) is laid on in the background. However, this traditional pattern is suddenly and starkly interrupted by the sound of a slamming door – a heavy, metal door sliding shut – which is repeated three times in succession. This somewhat unsettling sound (especially so as we are not provided with its image equivalent) confers a rather "threatening" feel to the otherwise beautiful views of the Chicago skyline. If you compare this opening with Scott's aforementioned *Someone to Watch Over Me* the contrast could not be starker. Scott's movie does not wish to "disturb" the beauty of the images: George and Ira Gershwin's famous title track accompanies the images undisturbed by other sound elements. In *The Fugitive*, the echoing of the slamming door jars tremendously with the images: directionality is used cleverly by bouncing the sound from channel to channel all around the auditorium to prevent pinpointing it to any specific action on screen.

When the shot cuts to the struggle in the home, we would expect to hear the kind of sounds one would associate with the struggle portrayed on screen: screaming, cries for help, objects being thrown about, running steps, etc. Instead, we are confronted with sounds that are manipulated to such an extent that their origins become impossible to pin down. For example, when her assailant throws Dr Kimble's wife to the floor we don't hear the sound of a falling body but that of a long drained clap of thunder. (It is worth noting that there is no indication that it is actually raining.) The gun shot is also "massaged" into something different, more closely resembling a long distant echo of a shot rather than the classic short loud burst we are used to. (Indeed, we are offered an alternative, more conventional version of this later on in the film when the murder scene is relived during the trial.)[10] Throughout the cutting between the shots of Chicago and the murder, a distant police siren is heard echoing through the steel canyons. When the film cuts to the arrival of the ambulance, the soundtrack would appear to acquire more conventional characteristics (i.e. we hear what we see). However, that illusion lasts only a few seconds. As a police officer climbs down from the ambulance, the sound focuses on his rattling keys rather than the noises that in real life would have been more prominent (by this stage there are several police cars and reporters at the scene). The final departure from convention is the sound of the flash of the police photographer, which approaches only remotely that of a camera flash. Its attack is much more aggressive, and its aural characteristics resemble more those of a muffled gunshot.[11] The way sound is edited (i.e. a fast succession of camera flashes) gives this final shot a very aggressive tone. The sequence concludes, once again, with the sound of the slamming door.

While some of these choices are undoubtedly "encouraged" by the images (the murder sequence is shot in slow motion), Stambler and Leveque's choices are so far removed from expectation as to provide a clear indication of the "making more of what's there" attitude. In particular, the "door slamming" sound (there is no visual equivalent in the opening sequence), the police siren (a key aural theme developed throughout the film, as we shall see), and the massaged flash sounds are all substantial departures that suggest careful planning. When I interviewed Bruce Stambler, I put this very point to him:

GIANLUCA SERGI (GS): Immediately after that scene (i.e. the aerial shot of Chicago), there is another interesting example. Usually in films, there seems to be an unwritten rule: if you see it, you hear it. But in the murder scene visuals and sounds are very different. Where does that come from?

BRUCE STAMBLER (BS): It is a process of refinement. It certainly did not start off that way. When you sit down and look at the film, you look at it over, and over, and over, and over again, and you want to stay away from too many "like-sounds" in any given movie and kind of put a signature on stuff. We didn't want to use the sound of a head being cracked open, so you try different things.

GS: Did you show it to someone and they said "Yeah, that works"?

BS: No, we just cut it.

GS: And nobody said "No, I don't think it works"?

BS: Nobody did.

Stambler here states two important aspects: he talks of a "process of refinement," and he highlights the freedom that the sound team enjoyed on *The Fugitive* in terms of decision-making. In other words, he would appear to posit responsibility for sound choice with the sound team, rather than with the director. This presents us with one of the most intriguing questions that arises from a study of sound in movies: who is creatively responsible for this "process of refinement"? If we consider the kind of critical acclaim that film directors customarily receive, one question becomes very relevant: is it legitimate to attribute creative responsibility solely in terms of the film's visual style? If we look at the creative process behind *The Fugitive* we find a situation that would seem to confound such expectations/assumptions, as this further quote from my conversation with Bruce Stambler indicates unequivocally:

> The director actually in my viewpoint has a little bit less of an input. They have more of an overview. For example, in *The Fugitive* I personally struggled with the train crash. I examine every single element because the picture editor doesn't tell you necessarily all that's happening in a scene; the director doesn't tell you either: "It's a train crash!" he'll say, and so will the producer – "It's a train crash!" But there is this series of shit that happens that makes the train crash.

It might be useful to state the obvious once more: the investigation of "aural creative responsibility" can reinforce the concept of directorial input just as forcefully as the case of *The Fugitive* reveals the opposite. I have mentioned *Titanic*:

James Cameron's example is illustrative in this sense. I discussed Cameron's creative input with Gary Rydstrom, who headed the Oscar-winning sound team for Cameron's *Terminator 2: Judgment Day* (1991) and *Titanic*. Rydstrom confirmed Cameron's near-obsessive desire to go through every meaningful sound in his movies. Thus, there is little doubt that Cameron has a very direct and knowledgeable input in creating the soundtrack for his films. This should not lead us to underestimate Rydstrom's creative input, but rather it should act as further reminder of the need to pay more attention to sound because of what it might reveal in terms of creative input and working practices.

Stambler also speaks of the freedom that the sound team enjoyed while working on *The Fugitive*. In contemporary mainstream filmmaking, the concept of the sound team being allowed the space and freedom to "refine" their work is by no means typical. In the case of *The Fugitive*, however, the sound team was given plenty of latitude to experiment and refine, as these words from Stambler confirm:

> When you work with certain people in your job you are very careful to toe the line and if they say "do x" you do x, you don't do x, y, and z, because you are going to get in trouble. Dennis Virkler [picture editor on *The Fugitive*] and the producer Peter MacGregor Scott, here's what they say: "GO for it, make it great." You are not afraid to bring something new, but when you bring your material here [the dubbing stage] and there are fifteen, sixteen people watching you on the stage, you really are subject to quite a bit of ridicule, and you have to be able to take the good and the bad, you know.

Maintaining space: sound and narrative space

One of the areas where the aural process of refinement that Stambler talks about is most evident is the relationship between sound and narrative space. Mainstream cinema conventionally employs camera angle, framing, and lighting to establish a location and/or narrative scenario, and then moves onto the particular. A classic example is an establishing shot followed by a medium shot or a close-up of one of the main characters. A key storytelling device in visual terms, this movement breaks up significantly narrative space into smaller units, from the general to the particular, or vice versa. Sound, however, ordinarily does not follow similar conventions. It would be very difficult for audiences to accept a constant readjustment of aural perspective. A long shot of a scene will call for the creation of a certain soundscape, one of the key elements of which will be aural perspective. The scene immediately after the train crash sequence in *The Fugitive*, where Gerard (Tommy Lee Jones's character) is introduced, provides a useful example. When Gerard arrives on the scene, a long shot establishes clearly, and for the first time, the aftermath of the crash. The camera then follows Gerard and his team as they move through the debris until they finally reveal their identity to a local cop on the scene. The tracking shot employed in this second stage of the sequence focuses on Gerard and his team: framing is kept as tight as possible on this unit. We are barely shown at the edges of the frame a glimpse of the wreckage and the dozens of cops and rescue workers working on it. The passage from long shot overlooking the crash scene to the team walking through the wreckage ends with a medium close-up of the team, after a few quick inserted close-ups of the team members. In this sense, it follows a rather well-established editing pattern (long, medium, close-ups, back to medium) perfectly acceptable in terms of visual conventions. That is, we accept this as one of the possible arrangements of shots and framing that can be employed effectively to illustrate this particular section of the story.

However, sound could not confidently employ an equivalent strategy. If it did, the aural landscape would change tremendously, several times, within the space of a few cuts. To remain with the same example, the complete soundscape of the shot overlooking the crash site could potentially feature hundreds of different sound elements: from sirens to rescue helicopters, from huge cranes to lift the mangled train carriages to the dozens of voices of the rescuers, the noise of their work tools, and so on. From this aurally dense moment, the cut to the team walking through the crash scene would ignore all the sounds not directly pertaining to what is actually visible on screen. In other words, we would hear only the voices of the people on Gerard's team and those of one or two workers visible at the left of the frame. In the case of the close-ups, we would hear only the voice of the character speaking (i.e. no other sound surrounding him/her). This would be far more difficult to accept in the case of sound than it would with the image: audiences have come to expect sound to retain certain elements of the soundscape that is created at the beginning of a scene *throughout* that scene.

This difference should not be understood in terms of "lack." It is not so much that sound lacks the flexibility of the image, or that audiences give filmmakers greater latitude in playing with image editing than they do with sound editing. Rather, sound would seem to be particularly effective in carrying out a fundamental role, namely that of "maintaining" narrative space. Maintenance here is intended in the "servicing" acceptation of the word: a process that ensures that the narrative space created at the beginning of a scene continues to function properly and that it is modified, updated, refined, or extended if the narrative makes it necessary. This is not to be understood as a role either more or less important than that of the image, only substantially different. One of the aims of the soundtrack is to situate the audience *precisely* within narrative space, both in narrative and physical terms. Clearly, using sound as a narrative device to suggest scale and scope can be particularly useful in the case of blockbusters: sound can provide a huge narrative environment despite tight visual shots just as effectively as it can suggest intimacy in large vista-shots *à la* David Lean.[12] In this sense, a film such as Spielberg's *Saving Private Ryan* (1998) is a good example of both: during the Normandy landing Tom Hanks's character slips in and out of the reality surrounding him. While the images continue to portray the overall scale of the event (i.e. hundreds of men trying desperately to reach a safe position on the beach), sound is used at times to isolate the character and provide us with a much more intimate take on his emotional state. At other times, while the shot is kept tight on Hanks, sound maintains narrative space and continuity by reminding us of where we are and what the character is facing.

To state the obvious once again, this crucial property of sound should not be seen as a "natural given": sound does not just "happen" to maintain narrative space. It needs to be carefully designed and structured in order to do so. Thus, the manner in which sound functions in this sense can be seen as a good measure of the filmmakers' attitude toward the film. *The Fugitive* shows clear signs of sophistication in this area. As Gerard enters the movie (immediately after the train crash), a quick burst of his auto's siren announces his arrival. This sound serves the function of singling out Gerard's auto from the several other police cars on the scene: this auto is different, this person is special. The establishing shot of Gerard briefly surveying the scene is accompanied by a very dense soundtrack. This reinforces the scale of the disaster and of the ensuing rescue effort. The sounds we hear are varied in identity (we hear police cars and ambulances, police officers and rescuers, heavy machinery, etc.), but they are diffused around the auditorium mostly in a rather nondirectional fashion (i.e. audiences cannot necessarily identify their point of origin). They all originate generically from the scene that Gerard is surveying. As Gerard and his team walk through the mayhem, sound becomes much more directional (i.e. it becomes possible for the audience to pinpoint exactly where sounds originate: front or rear, left or right, etc.). This shift from nondirectional to directional is one way to "maintain" narrative space and refine it. Physically, as well as in narrative terms, we are placed side by side with Gerard: that is, we are offered the same aural perspective as that of Gerard and his team, while retaining a considerable amount of the previous shot's sound density. This pattern of directionality and density is sustained in the final shot of Gerard speaking to a cop. In other words, whereas the film's image strategy breaks up substantially visual space, its soundtrack provides continuous density and increasing directionality. The effect sought is to place the audience firmly within narrative space while also providing that space with a "tangible" physical presence.

This sequence clearly operates differently from the opening scene. In the case of the latter, a considerable degree of risk is taken by moving away from verisimilitude and realism: sound operates in a way that is not at all "natural" and counters expectation. In the sequence we have just described, sound works in a much more "realistic" fashion: it matches rather closely the action on screen, adhering to what the quote from Lucasfilm indicates as "the first rule of film sound." Effectiveness clearly does not require a substantial departure from convention: there is sophistication in both approaches, and both approaches can be found in the same film serving the narrative without creating any substantial problem in terms of coherence. Indeed, the careful selection and layering of the various sound elements employed in this brief passage is a further indication of that process of refinement to which Stambler refers.[13]

Sound in blockbusters: a different "category of sound"?

Aided, not motivated, by the technological changes of the early and mid-1970s, Hollywood's sound men and women realized quickly the extent to which they could contribute to the creation of a blockbuster movie. There is virtually no blockbuster, from *Jaws* (1975) to *Star Wars* (1977), from *The Lion King* (1994) to *Forrest Gump* (1994) and all the way to *Titanic*, that upon investigation of its soundtrack will not reveal an attitude to filmmaking similar to what Bruce Stambler calls "making more of it than it's there." In this sense, Stambler and Leveque's work on *The Fugitive* is part of a continuing tradition whose boundaries, key features, and significance are still to be properly assessed.

In some important ways, Stambler's words pave the way for a greater appreciation and understanding of film sound at large when he emphasizes the careful and thoughtful process of selection and refinement necessary to create soundtracks as complex as that of *The Fugitive*. Sound can expand and refine narrative space, it can provide overall scale and scope, and it can substantially enhance key areas such as production values and performance. Ultimately, sound can help the narrative achieve continuity and coherence, and can substantially increase the overall impact of the film. There may well be movies where the soundtrack's only aim is to be "loud and noisy," where poor cooperation between filmmakers, lack of attention to detail, or time and financial pressures translate into unimaginative work. However, this should not become a reason to deny sound the attention it deserves.

Investigating sound might help develop a greater understanding of the filmmaking dynamics involved in the creation of a blockbuster. Critics such as Rita Kempley emphasize Andrew Davis's merits in terms of the film's "bold" visual style. What are we to do, then, with the knowledge that Davis actually had little creative input as far as sound is concerned in a film where the latter clearly plays such an important role in the film's dynamics, narrative space, tempo, performance, etc.? The issue here is not whether Davis is a good director, but whether we know enough to be able to express any sort of judgment that is not based solely on consideration of visual style. This is not a matter of directorial fame either: the fact that Davis might not be as well known a director as superstars such as Cameron and Spielberg is less a factor than it might appear. Consider the case of Cameron. Critics and scholars almost unanimously agree that his style is one based on wealth and endless means, a style that one might call "opulent." However, this notion of excess does not match Cameron's attitude to sound, where he appears to have a much more measured approach. In my conversation with Gary Rydstrom, he often remarked on the fact that Cameron's approach to sound could indeed be described almost as "minimalist," where less is more. Sound in *Terminator 2*, for example, operates according to this principle. In the scenes in the mental institution where Sarah Connor is kept, the images suggest a series of cells where inmates suffering from severe mental disorders are kept in captivity. However, despite the obvious potential for extreme aural detail (e.g. patients moaning, screaming, staff talking, air conditioning/heating systems, external sounds, public address announcements, etc.) the soundtrack works to create a rarefied environment where only a few carefully selected sounds are employed. This is but one instance of this approach. What we are to do with this information is where critical attention is clearly most needed.

There is a further intriguing reason to pay closer attention to sound. I have developed my investigation of sound in blockbusters following one basic assumption – that its characteristics in blockbuster movies are in some meaningful way different from those that can be found in "average" mainstream movies. However, in many ways evidence has forced me to review that basic assumption. There is no doubt that the soundtrack in *The Fugitive* is a complex and thoughtful effort that plays a central role in the success of the movie. However, it would be extremely difficult to claim that the features of sound I have been describing are to be found exclusively in the blockbuster domain. Undoubtedly, the availability of better means of production (both in terms of personnel and technology) and more time in post-production are two key ingredients that a larger budget can afford.[14] However, this is not enough to create a whole different "category" of sound. In other words, the difference between sound in mainstream cinema (i.e. the "average" Hollywood production) and blockbuster movies is not as clearly defined as it would need to be if it were to warrant special status.

That elusive Holy Grail of any study of blockbusters, that is, the question of what the difference is between blockbuster movies and "average" mainstream movies, cannot be gauged by investigating sound. There is little doubt that the "making more of it than it's there" attitude serves well the drive for blockbusters. However, there is no evidence that a similar attitude is exclusive to blockbusters. This is perhaps the most important reason why we should investigate sound more: some of our most basic expectations and assumptions concerning how movies work are likely to be severely challenged. I cannot think of a more daunting, yet exciting prospect.

Notes

1 *The Fugitive* (US, 1991): directed by Andrew Davis, sound design and supervising sound editing by Bruce Stambler and John Leveque, music composed by James Newton Howard.

2 It is worth noting that Tom Hanks is getting increasingly closer to Ford's record and will probably overtake Ford soon.

3 Just think of *Titanic*'s (1997) near full-sized replica of the famous ship and the computer-generated dinosaurs of *Jurassic Park* (1993).

4 The record was to be broken by the famous "Who Shot J. R.?" episode of *Dallas* thirteen years later.

5 Spielberg's movie opened in June 1993 and truly "devoured" opposition at the box office.

6 *Batman* (1989) is Warners' biggest ever grossing movie in the US. The only other movies to have grossed more than *The Fugitive* are (in decreasing order): *Twister* (1996), *The Exorcist* (1973 and 2000 reissue), and *Batman Forever* (1995).

7 The sequel did not perform as well as the first movie, gathering about half of *The Fugitive*'s receipts, roughly $90 million worldwide.

8 At the time of writing, it is impossible to gauge its popularity as it is only in its first series. However, twenty episodes have already been commissioned and filmed.

9 All quotes from Bruce Stambler are from a conversation I had with him about *The Fugitive* and other sound matters at Soundstorm (Burbank, California) in July 1999. Wherever possible, I have chosen to leave interview extracts exactly as from the original to keep intact Stambler's train of thought.

10 To "massage" a sound is to change its natural qualities by mixing other sounds with the original recording to obtain something that approximates its original but also takes on a new level of expressiveness. There are countless examples of this common practice scattered throughout contemporary soundtracks. To name but a few in *The Fugitive* alone: the gun shot, the camera flash, Ford's voice when he is chased in the forest, and the sound of the struggle with the one-armed man.

11 This is a well-established "trick of the trade" and has been used in many films; camera flashes, typewriters, and even musical notes are often mixed with gunshot sounds to convey a more aggressive tone. Perhaps the most famous, and effective, example can be found at the end of Alan J. Pakula's *All the President's Men* (1976), when the sound of the two reporters' typewriters slowly changes its aural characteristics and becomes the sound of gunshots – literally translating into sound the popular saying that the pen is mightier than the sword.

12 The availability of multichannel technology from the mid-1970s onwards has allowed filmmakers to explore off-screen sound both in the front and rear of the auditorium, thus expanding narrative space dramatically.

13 Interestingly, a good example of a "less refined" approach can be found in the rescue mission of *U.S. Marshals* (after a plane crash this time). In that instance, the filmmakers seem content to use sound simply to confirm the visuals by mapping images and sounds as conventionally as possible.

14 However, it is important to note that the squeeze on post-production time that a fixed release date might impose can be as much a constraint to sound people as the lack of large budgets. Indeed, it is more likely to be a factor for blockbusters, as they must exploit the most profitable release dates to maximize box-office results.

Reference

Keller, Alexandra (1999) "'Size Does Matter': Notes on *Titanic* and James Cameron as Blockbuster Auteur," in Kevin S. Sandler and Gaylyn Studlar (eds), *Titanic: Anatomy of a Blockbuster*, New Brunswick, NJ: Rutgers University Press: 132–54.

Part III

ESTABLISHING CULTURAL STATUS

9

CIRCULATIONS OF TASTE

Titanic, the Oscars, and the middlebrow

Gillian Roberts

James Cameron's *Titanic* (1997) has become identified with two major indications of success: it is the highest-grossing film in history, and it tied for a record number of Academy Awards. In what follows, I examine issues of taste as they intersect with the Oscars' cultural sanction, and how such intersections impact on blockbusters in general and on *Titanic* in particular. I argue that, despite the Oscars' reluctance to reward blockbusters featuring the action genre, *Titanic* enjoyed great success at the Academy Awards by also appealing to middlebrow expectations. Though its overwhelming Oscar success is not without precedent, the timing of *Titanic*'s multiple victories represents Hollywood's reassertion of legitimacy following the success of independent films in the mid-1990s. The fusion of *Titanic*'s spectacle with the Oscar ceremony for 1997 further demonstrates the film's integral position in Hollywood at that time.

Vincent Canby has described the Academy Awards as "one long commercial for movies, which they make look good" (1987: II.23). Important issues surround the question of what kinds of movies are being celebrated, promoted, and made to look good through the Academy Awards. Emanuel Levy writes that, "through the Oscar Award, the Academy members function as peers, critics, and tastemakers" (1987: 47). Because the Academy consists of film industry members who participate in the Oscar voting processes, the roles of peers and critics are relatively straightforward. But the position of the Academy "as a standard setter" (ibid.: 21) that upholds middlebrow taste deserves further exploration. As Pierre Bourdieu argues, "taste is an acquired disposition to 'differentiate' and 'appreciate'" (1984: 466). Taste is not neutral, however, and judgments reflect those who take it upon themselves to make them: "Taste classifies, and it classifies the classifier" (ibid.: 6). The Oscars, established in 1927, enjoy "almost *universal* acceptance as the most prestigious film award" (Levy 1987: 39; original emphasis), implying that the Academy is perceived as a legitimate classifier and taste-making body.

However, such international scope and high profile have not translated into unchallenged taste. The issue is larger than the annual "heated debates . . . about the 'fairness' of the Academy's choices" (Levy 1987: xvi). For although individual nominations and awards may come under scrutiny, so have the larger tendencies of Oscar celebration. As Levy explains:

> The National Society of Film Critics was founded in 1968 as a "high-brow" association, to counter the "middle-brow" circles whose tastes were considered to be too similar to the Academy's. In the first years of its operation it was accused of being "too harsh" and "snobbish" toward Hollywood's commercial pictures, and too "avant-garde" in its preference for European art films. The National Society stressed that one of its major purposes was "to give annual recognition to the best works in films of the preceding years, without distinction of nationality."
>
> (Levy 1987: 37)

As this passage suggests, the Academy has been classified as celebrating primarily "commercial" Hollywood, middlebrow pictures, at the expense (so the National Society of Film Critics would have argued at their inception) of foreign and art-house cinema.

If the Academy is said to espouse middlebrow aesthetics, where do we locate the middlebrow? Certainly, such definitions are difficult to pin down. As Lawrence W. Levine writes, "'highbrow' . . . was first used in the 1880s to describe intellectual or aesthetic superiority, and 'lowbrow," first used shortly after 1900 to mean someone or something neither 'highly intellectual' nor 'aesthetically refined'" (1988: 221–2); Janice Radway notes that "middlebrow" "did not appear until sometime in the 1920s" (1990: 707). Levine contends that such terms constitute "cultural categories . . . which no one [has] seemed to define with any real precision" (1988: 7). Although I agree with Levine insofar as locating middlebrow culture depends upon its relation to two terms – highbrow and lowbrow – whose own boundaries are not fixed, I wish to use two of Bourdieu's discussions of middlebrow culture that are constructive for discussions of cinema: one involving the context of production, the other concerning issues of aesthetics.

Bourdieu argues that middlebrow culture is bound up in certain kinds of production with corresponding expectations and aims of profit. He writes that "middle-brow art is the product of a productive system dominated by the quest for investment profitability" (1993: 216). The relationship between production and audience is key, as "these works are entirely defined by their public" (ibid.: 125). The aesthetics of middlebrow art are intended to accommodate "the widest possible public" in an effort to appeal to the "average spectator" (ibid.: 126), thereby accumulating as much profit as possible. In the context of blockbuster filmmaking, the "average spectator" is a vital ingredient to success, as such films are "aimed at an undifferentiated popular audience" (Buckland 1998: 166–7). The Academy Awards themselves are aimed at such an audience, presenting their celebration of cinema through the vehicle of a television spectacle directed at a popular viewership.

Generally speaking, the kind of filmmaking celebrated by the Oscars corresponds to Bourdieu's characterization of middlebrow culture, namely as one that offers a negotiation between the accessibility of low culture and the prestige of high culture. According to Bourdieu, middlebrow culture comprises:

> accessible versions of avant-garde experiments or accessible works which pass for avant-garde experiments, film "adaptations" of classic drama and literature, "popular arrangements" of classical music or "orchestral versions" of popular tunes, vocal interpretations of classics in a style evocative of scout choruses or angelic choirs, in short, everything that goes to make up "quality" weeklies and "quality" shows, which are entirely organized to give the impression of bringing legitimate culture within the reach of all, by combining two normally exclusive characteristics, immediate accessibility and the outward signs of cultural legitimacy.
>
> (Bourdieu 1984: 323)

The Academy's role fits Bourdieu's description, for it upholds film as art, particularly the films honored by the Academy. It thereby gives the impression of bringing legitimate culture within the reach of all by bestowing legitimacy on accessible cultural products. The inclusion of non-Hollywood films in Oscar nominations implies a larger playing field than the ultimate winners' list indicates; the presence of the best foreign-language film category, as well as the occasional best picture nomination for a foreign-language film, similarly lends credibility to the Academy, as it incorporates these non-Hollywood products within its rubric of taste. Non-Hollywood victories have both demonstrated that the Academy's tendencies are dynamic, rather than static or monolithic, and reasserted Hollywood's status as point of reference for the Oscars. For example, *Hamlet*'s best picture win for 1948 provoked concern among "moguls and top executives [who] were indeed upset that the Academy voters favored British art films over what they considered American movies" (Levy 1987: 23). Though such an aberration of the Oscar norm indicated that the Academy does negotiate between Hollywood and non-Hollywood filmmaking, responses to the win also reinforced the notion that the Oscar is a Hollywood prize, gone astray in the instance of *Hamlet*.

The status of Hollywood blockbusters at the Academy Awards has altered over the course of Oscar history, just as blockbuster films themselves have undergone shifts and associations. "Blockbuster" itself is a slippery term, but if it is very frequently characterized by large-scale filmmaking, involving expensive budgets, spectacular production values, and a lengthy running time, these factors have often been present in Oscar-winning films. As Levy notes, "most of the Oscar-winning films have been big-budgeted, from the very first one, *Wings*, through *Gone with the Wind* in the 1930s; *Ben-Hur* in the 1950s; *Lawrence of Arabia* and *Tom Jones* in the 1960s; *The Godfather* movies in the 1970s"; further, "over half . . . of the winners have been in excess of the average ninety to 110 minutes" (Levy 1987: 179). These celebrated films correspond to elements of recent action-adventure blockbusters for the qualities mentioned above, but are also distinguished from such films by the "epic" scope of their narratives, which adds an element of prestige not generally associated with today's action films.

Titanic's position within the blockbuster category is assured by its relationship to excess: excess of budget (the most expensive film ever made), particularly in the service of special effects; excess of gross (the highest-grossing film ever released); and, with a running time of 194 minutes, excess of length. Although earlier large-scale productions won the Academy Award for best picture, I wish to argue that *Titanic*'s win, because of the film's reliance on the action genre, represents a departure from Oscar norm. Big-budget Hollywood filmmaking in recent decades has often taken the shape of action films, films that have been absent from the Academy Awards' most high-profile categories. To be more precise, though, action films have not been completely ignored by the Academy; rather, they have been contained by more technical categories. James Cameron's own films exemplify this containment. Although *Aliens* (1986) was nominated for seven Oscars, it won only for best visual effects. Cameron's next two films, *The Abyss* (1989) and *Terminator 2: Judgment Day* (1991), also won in this category. Cameron's work before *Titanic* was therefore celebrated for its technological features, as many other action-oriented blockbusters have been: in the 1990s, successful blockbusters such as *Total Recall* (1990), *Jurassic Park* (1993), *Independence Day* (1996), and *The Matrix* (1999) all received Oscars for best visual effects. However, none of these films won awards outside technical categories. In fact, until *Titanic*, only one film in Oscar history had won both best visual effects and best picture: *Forrest Gump* (1994). *Forrest Gump*'s award for visual effects was in celebration of the film's insertion of Tom Hanks into "real" film footage, which allowed his character to be seen meeting such historical figures as John F. Kennedy and John Lennon. By contrast, *Titanic* depends more on its use of spectacular visual effects than does *Forrest Gump*, and in a way that aligns Cameron's film more closely with the big-budget action vehicles of recent decades. Therefore, where the status of action cinema is concered, *Titanic*'s overwhelming celebration at the Academy Awards constitutes a departure from previous Oscar years. It is to the notion of departure, as it relates specifically to matters of taste, that I now turn my attention.

Titanic was generally viewed as a departure for Cameron, "an artistic achievement for a blockbuster king" (Lacey 1998a: C9). Awards won by Cameron for

Figure 9.1 Do they think they're making a film . . . or a movie?: James Cameron (right) directs Kate Winslet and Leonardo DiCaprio on the set of *Titanic* (1997). The Kobal Collection/20th Century-Fox/Paramount.

Titanic function to uphold this view, as does his response to some aspects of this celebration. In particular, his acceptance speech for the Director's Guild of America award illustrates this sense of elevation of his work: "I used to always say I made movies and not films. *Remains of the Day* [1993] is a film. *Terminator 2* is a movie. Now that I have this, I have to admit that I may have inadvertently made a film" (quoted in Lacey 1998b: C1). Although Cameron's labeling *Titanic* a "film" in opposition to a "movie" arose within the context of another prize, his statement is nevertheless relevant to a discussion of taste and the Oscars. Distinctions of "film" versus "movie" imply the same kind of cultural hierarchy as "highbrow," "middlebrow," and "lowbrow"; where a "film" or a "movie" would fit into these cultural categories would depend upon the text and the critic. That Cameron equated *Terminator 2* with "movie" might indicate that he himself subscribes to the posited departure that *Titanic* represents for his career, as well as to the cultural stratification that underpins such categories as "highbrow," "middlebrow," and "lowbrow." Yet his prefacing his association of *Titanic* and "film" with "Now that I have *this*" indicates an acknowledgment that such extra-textual factors as awards recognition are responsible for cultural categorizations. In one sense, then, it is the awards that make *Titanic* a "film."

In fact, there are other factors, both extra-textual and textual, that also worked to negotiate *Titanic*'s "film" status. Certainly, the release date is significant in these terms. Initially "slated for release" in the summer of 1997, *Titanic* did not reach theaters until December; while at first glance the delay appeared to "cost the studios [Paramount and 20th Century-Fox] dearly" (Baldassarre 1998: 9), this pre-Christmas release inserted the film into a different category, one that anticipated celebration. Summer releases tend to feature blockbuster action films, while Oscar hopefuls are more likely to be released before Christmas. With the later release date, therefore, *Titanic* was primed for Academy notice.

Following *Titanic*'s release, critical reception discussed the film in relation to Cameron's earlier work, acknowledging his status as "a virtuoso at large-scale action-adventure extravaganzas" (Turan 1997: F12). As Matthew Bernstein notes in his study of the film's reception in America, "few reviewers hailed *Titanic* as an unqualified success; most often, the film was deemed to have a flawed romantic melodrama plot, remarkably authentic production values, and an astonishing final hour" (1999: 16). These elements are bound up in *Titanic*'s position as an Oscar-winning blockbuster film and its relationship to taste. Concerning the "flawed romantic melodrama plot," critics consistently returned to *Titanic*'s weak script, written by Cameron. Kenneth Turan was particularly scathing, declaring that "never in the past has a film with a script as lacking as '*Titanic*'s' been so universally (well, almost universally) acclaimed as the acme of the medium" (1998: D2).

If such is the case, then *Titanic*'s cultural elevation through the Oscars must be examined in further depth in terms of middlebrow culture's gestures toward artistic legitimacy. There are elements of *Titanic* that correspond more directly with lowbrow culture than with middlebrow culture. The criticism of Cameron's script as "vulgar" and "cliché-ridden" (Miller 1998: 52) distances the film from the middlebrow insofar as "middlebrow culture is resolutely against vulgarity" (Bourdieu 1984: 326). Further, Herbert J. Gans argues that both the melodrama and action genres typically belong to low culture (1974: 89). But these lowbrow aspects of *Titanic* function alongside elements that operate against the film's "vulgarity," allowing it ultimately to coincide with a middlebrow aesthetic.

Bourdieu includes literary adaptations in his description of middlebrow culture, and I would like to suggest that *Titanic*, as a period piece, carries a similar status to an adaptation. Literary adaptations that are particularly "faithful" to their source material might demonstrate their fidelity by bringing the literary text's language and story to the screen; clearly, many critics believe Cameron to have failed to provide a high standard of language and story in his script. But although many literary adaptations are taken from sources set fairly contemporaneously to the time of the filmmaking – and, indeed, there are also a number of "updated" adaptations that modernize literary works of the past – the period piece, or costume drama, constitutes an important part of the larger genre of literary adaptation. Because of its historical subject matter, discourse similar to that which surrounds the literary adaptation has attached itself to Cameron's film. *Titanic* has been described as "perhaps the most historically accurate film ever made" (quoted in Gristwood 1998: 3), and Cameron's obsessive attention to duplicating minute details of the ship's construction has been well documented; indeed, Laura Miller declares the film to be "ostentatious in its fidelity to the material aspects of the subject," to the point where "it has won the approval of minutia-obsessed *Titanic* buffs" (1998: 52). Just as "in 'period' films, [where] one often senses exhaustive attempts to create an impression of fidelity to, say, Dickens's London or to Jane Austen's village life" (McFarlane 1996: 9), so *Titanic* presents a faithful reproduction of the ship. In this sense, the historic *Titanic* is the material that has been adapted, and is the original against which the "fidelity" of the film is judged. *Titanic*'s authenticity therefore lends it a cultural credibility that critics have found lacking in the screenplay.

In addition, its negotiation of genre and its thematizing of this negotiation effect an elevation of the film with regards to taste. *Titanic* has been described as a "half disaster flick, half period romance," and the present-day frame of the narrative demonstrates the negotiation of the "disaster flick" elements. The juxtaposition of old Rose with the team of scientist-explorers searching for the necklace, the "Heart of the Ocean," presents "something of a storytelling contest" (Negra 1999: 228). Janet Maslin writes that Cameron "treats these explorers as big 90's hotshots, the kind of macho daredevils who could just as easily be found tracking twisters or dinosaurs in a summer action film" (1997: E18). That *Titanic* distinguishes itself from "a summer action film" is demonstrated by the subversion of the expectations of a disaster film: although the film audience is introduced to the disaster through the scientists' high-tech machinery and computer graphics, this initial frame is somewhat defused through Rose's narrative of her personal experience.

Within Rose's personal narrative, references to art collecting also elevate *Titanic* in relation to taste. When Cal, Rose's fiancé, refers to the works of art she has bought as "finger paintings," Rose retorts, "The difference between Cal's taste in art and mine is that I have some." Because Rose has "purchased work by Picasso, Monet, and Degas" (Lehman and Hunt 1999: 97), artists who will become canonized, the film necessarily upholds her taste by pointing out her intuition as far as talent is concerned. Similarly, the film must also endorse Rose's appreciation of Jack's artistic work: as a "prodigy of taste" (Turan 1997: F14), she is already on the right track with Picasso, Monet, and Degas, as art history will ultimately demonstrate. The inclusion of such scenes corresponds directly to Bourdieu's identification of "the references to legitimate culture it [the middlebrow] contains" (1984: 323). Further, in a circulation of taste, the film approves its own maker, for "Jack's drawing of Rose was actually drawn by Cameron" (Munich and Spiegel 1999: 162). Ultimately, therefore, the film attempts to align itself with high art, which carries implications for the artistic status of *Titanic*. The perceived difference between "movie" and "film" has important resonance here: because *Titanic* itself is concerned with high art and taste, the distinction is a significant one according to the film's own terms.

These elements enabled *Titanic*'s celebration at the Academy Awards by allowing the film to transcend the blockbuster action genre. Granted, most of *Titanic*'s Oscars were given in technical categories in which blockbuster action films have been particularly successful in recent years. As David Gritten notes, therefore, the film's Oscar domination was not all that unthinkable, as "the Academy got it about right, applauding *Titanic* only for its strengths" (1998: 20), namely its production values, for which the "critics had unanimous praise" (Bernstein 1999: 21). Gritten also acknowledges that *Titanic*'s having matched *Ben-Hur*'s record of eleven Academy Awards reflects the similarities between the two films: "In many ways, it is a modern equivalent to *Ben-Hur* – long, grandiose and lacking much subtlety, yet tense, thrilling and filled with jaw-dropping, spectacular effects"; further, the lack of recognition for *Titanic*'s screenplay mirrored the fact that it was "one of the few categories in which success also eluded *Ben-Hur*" (1998: 20). *Titanic*'s dominance, therefore, has a precedent in the Academy's celebration for 1959.

Titanic's record number of Academy Awards operates with the film's elements in the elevation of the film's status. Moreover, the two texts of the film and the awards ceremony intersect with respect to exposure and spectacle. The resounding global success of *Titanic* – specifically the extraordinary audience numbers it has drawn – has meant that "hundreds of millions of people will eventually have this experience in common" (Riding 1998: II.1); the film therefore parallels the Academy Awards with its global audience. And, because records seem to follow in *Titanic*'s wake, the Oscar broadcast that so honored the film drew "the biggest audience ever for the annual special" (Carter 1998: E7): "*Titanic*'s popularity was widely recognized as a key factor in its success" (Wyatt and Vlesmas 1999: 39). As a symbol of American show business, the Oscar ceremony "epitomizes . . . where show biz happens to be at that particular moment" (Canby 1983: II.1). For 1997, *Titanic* appeared to dictate Hollywood values through its public reception and Academy recognition. The spectacle of the film corresponded to the glamor of the Oscar ceremonies: "This year, there is a movie whose hefty dimensions meets the Oscar hype" (Lacey 1998b: C1).

Titanic and the Academy Awards did not just make a perfect fit in theory. The two spectacles were fused through the awards presentation as the Oscar stage itself was built to reflect the glamor of *Titanic*:

> Even the stage of the Shrine Auditorium has been redesigned to hark back to old-fashioned elegance, combining set design elements of the less seamy side of *L.A. Confidential* with the ballroom of Titanic. "I'm using old gold mosaic, crushed velvet, silver leaf, a large 50-foot mirror ceiling for a

> Busby Berkeley effect," stage designer Roy Christopher told *Variety*. . . . "Last year was sparer. This year is opulent, with a set that may be likened to an old movie palace in a nineties frame."
>
> (Lacey 1998b: C1)

Titanic became linked to expectations of glamorous film viewing – another "departure" for the action genre – invoked through the movie palace. The film literally set the stage for the Academy Awards; furthermore, both *Titanic* and the Oscar stage can be said to have had "a nineties frame."

Not only the stage, but also the staging and the ceremony for the 1997 Academy Awards afforded *Titanic* the opportunity of increased spectacle. After the filmed sequence that inserted host Billy Crystal into the best picture nominees, a sequence that focused more on *Titanic* than on any other picture, Crystal entered on the bow of a ship. Crystal linked *Titanic*'s features with those of the Oscars: "We are just like that great ship. We are huge, we are expensive, and everybody wants us to go a lot faster." Because 1997 marked the seventieth anniversary of the Academy Awards, Oscar night, even more than usual, was a celebration of itself; the success of *Titanic* was therefore bound up in the Academy's self-celebration, and in some ways became synonymous with the Academy and its expectations. In a clear fusion of *Titanic* and the Oscars, Céline Dion sang the film's theme song, "My Heart Will Go On," while wearing a necklace designed after the "Heart of the Ocean," thereby allowing the awards ceremony to refer continuously to its most celebrated film.

Titanic's Oscar spectacle increased with each nomination and clip that accompanied it, and with each win where a clip of the film accompanied the winner(s) to the stage; further, the winner(s) drew attention to the film in their acceptance speech(es). Cameron was criticized by the press for his acceptance speeches, particularly those for best director and best picture: he "set a standard for orgiastic self-congratulation when he dubbed himself 'king of the world'" ("Familiar Pains on Oscar Night" A22), a far cry from Oscar speeches that usually display a "degree of humility" (Weinraub 1998: E1). But, like Dion's necklace, Cameron's self-appointment as "king of the world" marked a moment of fusion between the film and the ceremonies, the line belonging to Jack in the film (written, of course, by Cameron). When accepting for best picture, Cameron asked "the audience to observe a few moments of silence for the Titanic casualties" ("Familiar Pains on Oscar Night" A22), thereby both occupying the position of directing the winning film and taking on the role of directing the Oscar spectacle. Thus, the blockbuster *Titanic* can be said to have spoken for the Academy Awards, in the sense that the awards celebration was comprised largely of the film's presence, and the ceremony's momentum was shaped increasingly by *Titanic*'s makers.

In terms of the Academy's values reflecting the state of the industry, it is important to remember the previous year, in which independent films were the most celebrated. Juxtaposition of the awards for 1996 and 1997 reveals a power struggle of sorts, serving as a reminder that, while the Academy Awards have identifiable traditions continuing throughout their history, there is an extent to which the Oscars are dynamic. The awards for 1996 constituted a slap in the face to Hollywood studios, as all but one of the best picture nominees were considered "independent" films: of *The English Patient*, *Secrets and Lies*, *Fargo*, *Shine*, and *Jerry Maguire*, only the last was considered a studio product. Many independent companies are "actually owned by conglomerates," but the Academy's preference in 1996 for independent features "seemed not only an implicit criticism of studios but also the very system that created them" (Weinraub 1997: D3). Between 1996 and 1997, therefore, a negotiation of Academy taste is in evidence. But *Titanic*'s victory was viewed as one for Hollywood as well, as, only one year after the dominance of independent films, the "high-tech blockbusters" (ibid.) to which such films had been contrasted made an enormous comeback with *Titanic*'s Oscar sweep: as Gritten declares, "Hollywood has reasserted itself, with *Titanic* proving a perfect rallying point" (1998: 20).

If *Titanic* can be said to epitomize Hollywood filmmaking, it also epitomizes the Academy Awards and their history. Not only did it look "to have been filmed in accordance with old studio practices" (Arroyo 1998: 18), it also allowed Hollywood, "dumbed down by years of brainless blockbusters and sophomoric comedies, forced to relinquish artistic legitimacy to imports and no-budget homegrown curiosities" (Lacey 1998b: C1), to rise to its own occasion and celebrate itself. The implication of such an assertion is that *Titanic* is not a "brainless blockbuster," that it has managed to distinguish itself from the "brainlessness" of other action films to claim "artistic legitimacy." On the one hand, *Titanic*'s translation of its special-effects showcase into a best picture Oscar represents a new direction for the reception of special effects blockbusters; on the other, its status as a period romance alongside its action film elements fits more easily into the middlebrow aesthetic than the futuristic, science-fiction blockbusters that have received recognition through the more technical Oscar categories, but have not swept the Academy Awards in the manner of *Titanic*. As with *Titanic*'s victory, *Gladiator*'s best picture win for 2000 signifies another big-budget spectacle after Oscar dominance "by relatively small, independent-minded films" (Lyman 2001: E7) such as *Shakespeare in Love* (1998) and *American Beauty* (1999); but *Gladiator*, too, uses visual effects (and won the Oscar in this category) to uphold a historical narrative. While *Titanic* has represented a departure in terms of the Academy's classification of artistic legitimacy for visual effects-laden blockbusters, the Academy has not strayed far from standards of the middlebrow, maintaining the circulation of middlebrow taste.

Note

Some material in this chapter was previously published as "Spectacle Matters: *Titanic*, *The Sweet Hereafter*, and the Academy and Genie Awards," *Canadian Review of American Studies*, 30, 3 (2000): 317–38.

References

70th Annual Academy Awards, ABC, 23 March, 1998.

Arroyo, José (1998) "Massive Attack," *Sight and Sound*, February: 16–19.

Baldassarre, Angela (1998) "James Cameron Launches *Titanic*," *Take One*, winter: 6–9.

Bernstein, Matthew (1999) "'Floating Triumphantly': The American Critics on *Titanic*," in Sandler and Studlar 1999: 14–28.

Bourdieu, Pierre (1984) *Distinction: A Social Critique of the Judgement of Taste*, trans. Richard Nice, London: Routledge & Kegan Paul.

—— (1993) *The Field of Cultural Production: Essays on Art and Literature*, ed. Randal Johnson, Cambridge: Polity.

Buckland, Warren (1998) "A Close Encounter with *Raiders of the Lost Ark*: Notes on Narrative Aspects of the New Hollywood Blockbuster," in Steve Neale and Murray Smith (eds), *Contemporary Hollywood Cinema*, London: Routledge: 166–77.

Canby, Vincent (1983) "Why We Watch the Academy Awards," *New York Times*, 17 April: II.1, II.17.

—— (1987) "The Stories Behind the Oscars," *New York Times*, 5 April: II.23.

Carter, Bill (1998) "An Oscar Night to Remember," *New York Times*, 25 March: E7.

"Familiar Pains on Oscar Night" (1998) editorial, *New York Times*, 25 March: A22.

Gans, Herbert J. (1974) *Popular Culture and High Culture: An Analysis and Evaluation of Taste*, New York: Basic Books.

Gristwood, Sarah (1998) "Sink or Swim," *The Guardian*, 2 January: 2.2–3.

Gritten, David (1998) "Titanic Proves Unsinkable After All," *Daily Telegraph*, 25 March: 20.

Lacey, Liam (1998a) "And the Winners Will Be . . .," *Globe and Mail*, 21 March: C9.

—— (1998b) "Overboard!," *Globe and Mail*, 21 March: C1, C9.

Lehman, Peter, and Hunt, Susan (1999) "'Something and Someone Else': The Mind, the Body, and Sexuality in *Titanic*," in Sandler and Studlar (1999): 89–107.

Levine, Lawrence W. (1988) *Highbrow/Lowbrow: The Emergence of Cultural Hierarchy in America*, Cambridge, MA: Harvard University Press.

Levy, Emanuel (1987) *And the Winner Is . . . : the History and Politics of the Oscar® Awards*, New York: Ungar.

Lyman, Rick (2001) "A Night for Big Stars and Big Films," *New York Times*, 27 March: E7.

Maslin, Janet (1997) "A Spectacle as Sweeping as the Sea," *New York Times*, 19 December: E1, E18.

McFarlane, Brian (1996) *Novel to Film: An Introduction to the Theory of Adaptation*, Oxford: Clarendon Press.

Miller, Laura (1998) Review of *Titanic*, *Sight and Sound*, February: 50–2.

Munich, Adrienne, and Spiegel, Maura (1999) "Heart of the Ocean: Diamonds and Democratic Desire in *Titanic*," in Sandler and Studlar (1999): 155–68.

Negra, Diane (1999) "*Titanic*, Survivalism, and the Millennial Myth," in Sandler and Studlar (1999): 220–38.

Radway, Janice (1990) "The Scandal of the Middlebrow: The Book-of-the-Month Club, Class Fracture, and Cultural Authority," *South Atlantic Quarterly*, 89, 4: 703–36.

Riding, Alan (1998) "Why 'Titanic' Conquered the World," *New York Times*, 26 April: II.1, II.28.

Sandler, Kevin S., and Studlar, Gaylyn (eds) (1999) *Titanic: Anatomy of a Blockbuster*, New Brunswick, NJ: Rutgers University Press.

Turan, Kenneth (1997) "'Titanic' Sinks Again (Spectacularly)," *Los Angeles Times*, 19 December: F12, F14.

——(1998) "'Titanic' Is Just the Tip of the Iceberg of Big Flicks with Weak Scripts," *Washington Post*, 24 March: D2.

Weinraub, Bernard (1997) "Hollywood Learns Small is Beautiful," *Globe and Mail*, 25 February: D3.

——(1998) "In Oscars for 'Titanic,' An Omen of More Power for Big-Budget Directors," *New York Times*, 25 March: E1, E12.

Wyatt, Justin, and Vlesmas, Katherine (1999) "The Drama of Recoupment: On the Mass Media Negotiation of *Titanic*," in Sandler and Studlar (1999): 29–45.

10

SEX, CONTROVERSY, BOX-OFFICE

From blockbuster to bonkbuster

Rebecca Feasey

According to Justin Wyatt's influential work on contemporary Hollywood, the high concept blockbuster depends on a simple, catchy tagline which inspires multimedia marketing and merchandizing campaigns in an attempt to lure audiences and separate success from failure at the box office (Wyatt 1994). As Steven Spielberg – one of its founding fathers – once put it, the high concept strategy emphasizes a film's reducibility: "I like movie ideas that you can hold in your hand . . . if a person can tell me the idea in twenty-five words or less, it's going to be a good movie" (quoted in Schatz 1993: 33).

Because high concept is nothing if not a commercial strategy, Hollywood blockbusters have on occasion been designed to exploit what Wyatt refers to as "subject matters in vogue" (Wyatt 1994: 12). "Timely" projects generate publicity and hence profit by courting controversy and discussion. Certainly, this is a difficult balance to maintain, as the mass audience may simply turn its back on material deemed to be too exploitative or sensationalistic. However, during the late 1980s and early 1990s the US film industry produced a cycle of extremely successful films which entered public consciousness precisely by taking on board such "controversial" subjects as homosexuality, promiscuity, and prostitution.

Spearheading this cycle of what may be termed "controversial blockbusters" were such aggressively marketed titles as *Basic Instinct* (1992), *Indecent Proposal* (1993), *Disclosure* (1994), and *Striptease* (1996). At a time when the average cost of a Hollywood feature film was around $29 million, these big-star, big-budget, big-director, and widely released event movies were both very expensive and highly successful at the box office. For example, the $49 million *Basic Instinct* opened on 1,884 screens and ran for thirty weeks between March 20 and October 8, 1992, grossing $118 million; the $38 million *Indecent Proposal* opened on 1,922 screens and ran for twenty-one weeks between April 7 and September 2, 1993, grossing $107 million; the $53 million *Disclosure* opened on 2,168 screens and ran for eighteen weeks between December 9, 1994 and April 20, 1995, grossing $83 million; and the $50 million *Striptease* opened on 1,979 screens and ran for nineteen weeks between June 28 and October 31, 1996, grossing a less impressive $32 million (all figures taken from www.boxofficeguru.com).

Aside from their success, what links each of these films is the fact that all are variants of the contemporary erotic thriller genre. Each attempted to engineer public debate around sexual subject matter by offering fashionable, cutting-edge depictions of dangerous or "scandalous" erotic activity. Most obviously, the famous *Basic Instinct* engages themes of criminality and bisexuality. Yet *Indecent Proposal* also proposes the moral question of what you would do if a handsome stranger offered you or your partner one million dollars for sex; *Disclosure* concerns the inextricable relations between sex, power, and the dangers of the terminally single working woman, and *Striptease* attempts to incite discussion as to the career distinctions between the ecdysiast's art and fucking for money.

Linda Ruth Williams has argued that these examples of the "blockbuster erotic thriller" share much in common with their low-budget/low-profile, straight-to-video skin-flick counterparts (Williams 1993). Indeed, there is at first glance little to distinguish the marketing taglines of *Basic Instinct* ("Flesh Seduces. Passion Kills"), *Indecent Proposal* ("A Husband. A Wife. A Millionaire. A Proposal"), *Disclosure* ("Sex is Power"), and *Striptease* ("Some People Get into Trouble No Matter What They Wear") from the advertising copy for straight-to-video titles such as *Sunset Heat* (1991; "Sex. Money. Murder. It's all a Matter of Degrees"), *Indecent Behavior* (1993; "Sex This Good . . . is Murder"), *Electra* (1995; "Erotic Pleasure Was Never so Deadly"), and *Victim of Desire* (1996; "Some Women Are Desirable . . . Others Are Deadly"). In each of these cases, the film title and reduced narrative idea offer what Williams has elsewhere termed a "come-on" invitation to the spectator (Williams 1996: 106).

The combination of sex with elements of the thriller – or, put differently, the mixing of "fashionable" themes and exploitation tactics – is nothing new. As Barbara Klinger and Eric Schaefer have demonstrated, both exploitation films and adult melodramas were marketed in the 1940s and 1950s through a series of issues then acquiring new cultural significance within postwar American society. The exploitation film was promoted via a series of "in vogue" news stories exposing forbidden cultural phenomena such as artificial insemination and the first male to female sex-change operation (Schaefer 1999), while adult dramas such as *The Lost Weekend* (1945), *Picnic* (1955), *The Man with the Golden Arm* (1955), and *Giant* (1956) were presented through such "timely" themes as adultery, alcoholism, nymphomania, and sterility (Klinger 1994: 36–68). The ways in which such subject matter crosses over between "low" exploitation genres and high-profile Hollywood box-office hits illuminates the potentially slippery cultural status of any movie that attempts to tackle "difficult" and potentially controversial sexual material.

In this chapter, I want to consider how the cycle of 1990s blockbuster erotic thrillers was received by film critics and cultural commentators – in short, by review journalism. Demonstrating that the mere presence of a high concept (topicality, big star, large budget, renowned director, wide theatrical release, etc.) does not guarantee good box office, I consider the different reception fates of one of the successful erotic thriller event movies, namely *Basic Instinct*, and an example of a "failed blockbuster," namely *Showgirls* (1995). In order to illustrate the shifts in cultural status occasioned by critical discussion of these two specific movies, I draw on a range of contemporary film reviews and feature articles from critical, legitimate, popular, and ephemeral media sources. Specifically, I pay particular attention to *Sight and Sound* and *Premiere* as niche film publications, *Empire* and *Total Film* as populist film magazines, *Time* and the *New Statesman* as legitimate news magazines, and the *New York Times* and the *Washington Post* as two of the more respectable urban newspapers in America.

In *Basic Instinct*, Michael Douglas stars as Nick "Shooter" Curran, a troubled detective who investigates the murder of a one-time rock star, and a then-largely unknown Sharon Stone plays Catherine Tramell, the alluring bisexual murder suspect with whom Curran has a dangerous affair. Written by Joe Eszterhas and directed by Paul Verhoeven, the film received an R rating and generated much media interest as a "timely" and, therefore, successful controversial blockbuster that engendered conflicting opinion on the value (or otherwise) of its treatment of issues of sexuality.[1]

Rather than relegating this controversial film to the status of top-shelf soft-core, then, *Basic Instinct*'s promotional strategies and critical reception worked to legitimize this erotic thriller as suitable for the mass audience. Tellingly, much review literature validated the film by presenting it as a metaphor for a period dominated by the AIDS crisis and the perceived "dangers" of the aggressively sexual career woman. For example, the *International Herald Tribune* informed its readers that:

> If *Fatal Attraction* served as a metaphor for the 1980s, with its theme of the dangers of extramarital sex and one night stands, then *Basic Instinct* is a movie of the 1990s. Its underlying theme seems to be the dangers of sex, period.
>
> (Weinraub 1992: 20)

The fact that the *International Herald Tribune* talks about *Basic Instinct* through reference to *Fatal Attraction* (1987) – an earlier, hugely successful entry in the controversial blockbuster cycle – is highly significant. Both films deal with sexual subject matters in vogue, with *Fatal Attraction* being positioned as a crucial intertext for critical understanding of another contemporary erotic thriller and controversial text (i.e. Verhoeven's). As is well known, in *Fatal Attraction* Michael Douglas plays

Figure 10.1 Bonking big time: Michael Douglas and Sharon Stone go at it in *Basic Instinct* (1992). The Kobal Collection/Carolco.

Dan Gallagher, a happily married man who has a weekend fling with a woman who turns out to be psychopathic and violent; as such, the film was received as the first AIDS fear allegory to come out of Hollywood.

Following the example of *Fatal Attraction*, one of the overriding themes that dominates a cross-section of the reviews of *Basic Instinct* is the film's representation of explicit sexual imagery. On the one hand, *Empire* demoted *Basic Instinct* as a routinely conservative big-star, big-budget, big-director sexploitation film, taking issue with graphic scenes of heterosexual activity that were unprecedented for a major studio production. The magazine claims that the movie's "justifiably celebrated humping scenes go just about as far with a pair of mainstream Hollywood performers as it is currently permissible to go" (McIlheney 1992: 20). Similarly, *Time* reported that, "before shooting began, the original producer quit, complaining that Verhoeven was obsessed with showing body parts in various stages of excitement" (Corliss 1992: 56). While much review journalism derided *Basic Instinct* for being "the first mainstream multimillion dollar orgasm movie" (Thompson 1994: 131), so too, other commentaries spoke approvingly of the film's cutting-edge representations of sex and violence. These were taken to be evidence of Verhoeven's unique artistic vision.

Indeed, much review literature discussed *Basic Instinct* as a progressive example of auteurism in contemporary Hollywood by positioning the Dutch-born director as one of the most successful and contentious directors currently working in mainstream cinema. From this perspective, *Premiere* foregrounds *Basic Instinct*'s main themes of sex and death as a continuation of Verhoeven's longstanding artistic preoccupations. We are thus informed that "viciousness is exactly what Verhoeven likes in his sex scenes . . . vicious sex has been central to all of his movies . . . in Holland and . . . in Hollywood" (MacFarquhar 1995: 81). On hearing that "viciousness is exactly what Verhoeven likes in his sex scenes," and that "vicious sex has been central to almost all of his movies," the author here negotiates the cultural status of this particular controversial blockbuster by first positioning the director as an auteur, and then by pointing out how the link between sexual activity and ultraviolence is symptomatic of the Verhoeven oeuvre as a whole. In this way, *Basic Instinct*'s cutting-edge representations of explicit sex and graphic violence are invoked in order simultaneously to demote the film's status as a sexploitation text and to assert its higher cultural value as a legitimate auteurist vision.

Another key theme which review journalism asked its readers to think about was how and why the film links the psychotic killer woman with bisexual activity. Some reports routinely derided *Basic Instinct* for linking bisexuality and homicidal mania and pointed to this blockbuster erotic thriller as evidence of Verhoeven's sexist and homophobic imagination. While the National Organization of Women branded *Basic Instinct* "one of the most blatantly misogynistic films in recent memory," the Gay and Lesbian Alliance Against Defamation charged the film with presenting negative stereotypes that "no self-respecting gay person would put up with" (Grant 1992: 21).[2] According to a *Sight and Sound* feature article, the film equates the psychotic killer woman with bisexual activity to the extent that "every female in the film is not only a possible or actual killer, but also a potential lesbian" (Hoberman 1992: 4). This brief but significant review extract foregrounds the unconscious weight of a culture that has made the lesbian and the female criminal synonymous by displacing women's aggression onto the sexual deviant. In this same way, the academic journal *Film Criticism* presents *Basic Instinct* as a homophobic and misogynist text: we are informed that the film "associates female sexuality and criminality with lesbianism as one more feature of the male perception of the dangerous modern woman" (Deleyto 1997: 24–5).

Conversely, while much review journalism supported public protests by gay and lesbian advocacy groups decrying the film's conservative and phobic representations of psychotic sexual deviancy, critical media discourses also paid attention to what was at times perceived to be *Basic Instinct*'s more "progressive" portrayal of gays. For example, *Vanity Fair* spoke enthusiastically of Verhoeven's new image of woman by informing us not only that Sharon Stone's performance as Catherine Tramell is one of the greatest performances by a woman in screen history, but that this bisexual role is evidence of a "complex, compelling Nietzschean Uberfraulein who owns everything about her own power" (quoted in Scheers 1997: 256). In addition, the *New Statesman* also foregrounds Sharon Stone's depiction of the ice-pick wielding murder suspect Tramell as an empowering image of bisexuality: Claire Beavan, producer of Channel 4's *Out* series, is quoted as taking issue with popular understandings of femininity, consumer-feminism, and lipstick lesbianism by claiming that "a cute dyke with two Ferraris who kills men is a *positive* image" (Picardie 1992: 36). In sum, *Basic Instinct* can be understood from these reports to be a successful controversial blockbuster precisely because of its indeterminate critical status. By generating both positive and negative responses, it circulated as a must-see attraction and a potential conversation piece. Phobic text or progressive auteurist vision? You decide!

By contrast, *Showgirls* is another matter entirely. It, too, was written by Joe Eszterhas and directed by Paul Verhoeven; it, too, was aggressively marketed as a blockbuster erotic thriller (tagline: "Leave your Inhibitions at the Door"). *Showgirls* cost $45 million and opened on 1,388 screens, and yet it ran for only eight weeks between September 22 and November 16, 1995, grossing a paltry $20 million. Clearly, unlike other entries in the controversial erotic thriller cycle, *Showgirls* failed to reach blockbuster status. In fact, it was both a critical and a commercial disaster.

Whereas *Basic Instinct* was cut so as to avoid the NC-17 rating, *Showgirls* was the first movie granted an NC-17 rating from the board of the Motion Picture Association of America to be widely released under this particular classification. The film was awarded the adult certificate for its explicit nudity, graphic language, and representations of sexual violence. *Showgirls* appeared to wear this adult rating as a badge of honor in its marketing campaigns, which in turn encouraged review journalism to exploit the salacious nature of the film by commenting on it in its media coverage. It is important to point out that, because of restrictions placed on advertising potential, producing an NC-17 rated film is generally acknowledged in

Hollywood as a high-risk, low-return venture – one would normally expect a major studio to demand that a director make the cuts necessary to receive an R rating (Mooney 1996: 65). However, in the case of *Showgirls*, an NC-17 was all part of the plan to generate publicity, controversy, and hence profit.[3]

For the benefit of readers who may be unfamiliar with this particular title, *Showgirls* features Kyle McLachlan and a still relatively unknown Elizabeth Berkeley. McLachlan plays Zack Carey, an entertainment director for the luxurious Stardust casino, while Berkeley plays Nomi Malone, a young lap-dancer performing at the seedy Cheetah strip-club. The dancer dreams of becoming a casino chorine, so she plots her way to the star spot over the backs of her rivals and the body of the entertainment director. Although the film was awarded the NC-17 certificate as a more neutral alternative to the pornographic X label, review literature still found it necessary to demote such narrative concerns to the status of the straight-to-video erotic thriller. *Showgirls* was typically presented by critical commentators as, respectively, a "sleazeathon" (Unreich 1999: 97), "sauce-fest" (Empire Editorial Collective 1995: 12), and "trouser arouser" (Russo 1995: 28). While some dismissed it as a "T & B bonkbuster" (Mooney 1996: 61), others warned simply: "dirty movie ahead" (Corliss 1995).

In short, whereas *Basic Instinct* was presented (negatively or positively) by many critics as a legitimate metaphor for the period – a controversial blockbuster event – *Showgirls* was instantly demoted to the disreputable status of its straight-to-video erotic thriller sisters. To be sure, many reviewers picked up on the presence of lascivious themes in their commentaries on the film. Furthermore, such themes could potentially have helped to remove the stigma attached to NC–17 releases on the part of major studios and audiences alike. *Showgirls* was the first major studio production to foreground the safe-sex industry of the 1990s and, from this perspective, might have been validated as a revealing indictment of Las Vegas, Hollywood, and American society, with lap-dancing revealed as a manifestation of consumer sex in the AIDS era. However, rather than prompt public debate concerning the place of lap-dancing in contemporary society, many reviewers simply drew on the direct-to-video erotic thriller tradition as a crucial reference point for what they perceived to be no more than Verhoeven's pseudo soft-core production. Rather than taking interest in a new blockbusting controversy, then, media discourses routinely derided *Showgirls* as a big-budget, big-director, aggressively publicized straight-to-video erotic thriller.

Sub-pornographic references are evident in *Empire*'s feature article entitled "Nice Tits: Shame About the Film." In it, the author plays to a masculine mode of address and appeals to what is commonly termed the structuring male gaze as he informs his reader that *Showgirls*'s marketing campaign consists of "posters of Berkeley showing a good bit of leg, whilst leering come-on lines were plastered across the country" (Mooney 1996: 66). The magazine continues to make assumptions about the demoted cultural competencies, derided sexual repertoires, and soft-core preferences of the film's intended audience, as we are informed elsewhere that *Showgirls* "is likely only to be of interest to bad film enthusiasts and those needing an appetiser to a quick hand-shandy" (Smith 1996). In much the same way, the *Washington Post* refers to both the straight-to-video tradition and the gender of the target audience when it claims that the film is "an overcoat movie for men who don't want to be seen going into a porno theater" (Kempley 1995). *Showgirls* may have been awarded the NC-17 certificate as a more neutral alternative to the X label synonymous in the public mind with pornography. Yet references to overcoat movies and quick hand-shandys foreground the film's status as a "failed" blockbuster. It has now become its Other – namely, a disreputable, straight-to-video experience.

It had been predicted before the film's release that reuniting director Paul Verhoeven with scriptwriter Joe Eszterhas would guarantee domestic and foreign monies at the box office as well as success in ancillary video markets. In this sense, the model of *Basic Instinct* might well have been thought to be an obvious, and credible, intertext for discussion of *Showgirls*'s controversial elements. Yet while the two films were often compared, it is in virtually all cases only so as to deride the cultural status of the latter title. For example, in a review article the *New York Times* informs readers that "*Showgirls* aspires to the sleek seductiveness of *Basic Instinct*" (Maslin 1995), while a *Time* feature article argues that Verhoeven and Eszterhas should have cut *Showgirls* down to the R certificate because "when they made *Basic Instinct*, a sexy R movie, they deployed atmosphere and innuendo. Here, with an NC-17 rating, the lads go slack; they let pubic hair and menstruation jokes do all the work" (Corliss 1995). Both these publications employ *Basic Instinct* as a crucial intertext for *Showgirls* in order to make distinctions between the graphic but respectable sexual violence of the R-rated *Basic Instinct* and the explicit nudity of the NC-17 rated *Showgirls*. In this way, *Basic Instinct* is respected for its aesthetic appeal, controversial material, and ability to push censorship boundaries, while *Showgirls* is criticized for its crude adult rating and coarse aesthetic.

After dismal box-office receipts and following some of the most unenthusiastic reviews in recent memory, then, *Showgirls* must be understood as a public event that failed to generate controversy. From "bonkbuster" (Mooney 1996: 61) to "plopbuster" (Crook and Graham 2001: 55), the film was both a blockbuster joke and a box-office disaster. In fact, the film was considered to be such a critical and commercial tragedy that it was awarded seven Golden Raspberrys in "Tinseltowns's Tackiest Anti-Awards Show." (Founded in 1980 by John Wilson, the Golden Raspberry awards "ritually abuse the year's worst movies . . . with *Showgirls* being singled out for abuse in the year of its release" [ibid.: 70]). Indeed, not only is *Showgirls* presented as failing to draw on the success of *Basic Instinct*; it is also presented as deficient on its own sexually explicit and titillating terms. Rather than foregrounding *Showgirls* as a noteworthy movie alternative and important addition to the erotic thriller blockbusting cycle, much media coverage simply dismissed it for presenting an unforgivably sexless aesthetic. The *New York Times* claimed that "the absence of eroticism turns *Showgirls* into a bare-butted bore" (Maslin 1995), while *Empire* informed its readers that the movie was about "as genuinely arousing as intricately choreographed nude livestock" (Collins 1996: 32). Furthermore, a *Time* feature, entitled "Valley of the Dulls," tells us that "*Showgirls* gets an NC-17 rating and finds a new four letter word for sex; yawn" (Corliss 1995).

In sum, review journalism concurred that *Basic Instinct* constituted a noteworthy blockbuster controversy, an emblematic film and cinematic event for the early 1990s that engendered widespread social debate about its sexually thrilling subject matter. By contrast, although *Showgirls* was similarly marketed as cutting edge and a controversial event movie, these same journalistic sources positioned Verhoeven's 1995 film as the most derided form of popular culture – a movie that failed to excite, arouse, or entertain the viewing public. Because *Showgirls* was aligned with the most debased form of "straight-to-video" entertainment – rather than with the "adult" blockbuster traditions with which it might have been associated – the mass audience was encouraged to keep away from the film for fear of being tarnished with the brush of soft-core porn.

In light of the construction of these kinds of distinctions between legitimate film and exploitation movie, or the granting of high and low cultural values, it might be interesting to think further about the cultural status of other films in the controversial blockbuster cycle. For example, further research on the sexually explicit *Striptease* would be enlightening in the light of *Showgirls*, since critical reviews habitually employed the former film as a crucial intertext for the latter. Indeed, *Striptease*'s marketing pitch informs the viewing public that: "*Striptease* Ain't *Showgirls* . . . Then Again, it Ain't Snow White Either!" Such sexually coded intertextual referencing demonstrates that when the high concept strategy is used to promote films based on subject matters in vogue, the line that separates perceptions of "adult" themes from out-and-out exploitation – and hence success from failure at the box office – may be very thin indeed.

Notes

1 Thomas Austin explains that it was only after watching *Basic Instinct* that one could join in conversations about it. He goes on to explain that having watched a film, the viewer is "socialized" into the collectivity formed around a shared visual event and is therefore able to participate in debates over it (Austin 1999: 157).

2 These authors base their charges of misogyny and homophobia on the fact that three of the four primary female characters in *Basic Instinct* are bisexual or lesbian killers. Roxy/Leilani Serelle slashed her two younger brothers to death with her father's razor. Hazel Dobkin/Dorothy Malone was convicted of killing her husband and her three children, slashing them to death with a knife she had received as a wedding present. Catherine

Tramell/Sharon Stone is implicated in the murders of her parents, one of her lovers, her college professor, and a police detective.

3 Kevin Sandler examines the ways in which MGM/UA maximized the potential *Showgirls* audience by promoting its forbiddenness and raw sexuality in a way previously unseen in any advertising campaign to come out of Hollywood (Sandler 2001: 69–93).

References

Austin, T. (1999) "Desperate to See it: Straight Men Watching *Basic Instinct*," in M. Stokes and R. Maltby (eds), *Identifying Hollywood's Audiences: Cultural Identity and the Movies*, London: British Film Institute: 147–61.

Collins, A. (1996) "New Films: *Showgirls*," *Empire*, 80 (February): 32.

Corliss, R. (1992) "Cinema: What Ever Became of the NC-17?," *Time*, 139, 4 (January): 56.

—— (1995) "Valley of the Dulls," *Time*, 2 October; online: http://www.time.com/time/magazine/archive/1995/951002/951002.cinema.showgirls.

Crook, S., and Graham, J. (2001) "Plopbusters: The Worst Blockbusters Ever Made," *Total Film*, 59 (December): 55–71.

Deleyto, C. (1997) "The Margins of Pleasure: Female Monstrosity and Male Paranoia," *Film Criticism*, 11, 3: 20–42.

Empire Editorial Collective (1995) "Front Desk: Fleshed Out," *Empire*, 78 (December): 12.

Grant, S. (1992) "Sex Crimes," *Time Out*, 22 April: 18–21.

Hoberman, J. (1992) "Fantastic Projections," *Sight and Sound*, 2, 1: 4.

Kempley, R. (1995) "*Showgirls*," *Washington Post*, online: http://www.washingtonpost.com/wp-srv/style/longter.../showgirlsnc17kempley _c02e63.html, accessed June 9, 2000.

Klinger, B. (1994) *Melodrama and Meaning: History, Culture and the Films of Douglas Sirk*, Bloomington: Indiana University Press.

Maslin, J. (1995) "*Showgirls*," *New York Times*, September 22, online: http://www.nytimes.com/library/filmarchive/.

MacFarquhar, L. (1995) "Start the Lava," *Premiere*, 2, 8: 81.

McIlheney, B. (1992) "New Films: *Basic Instinct*," *Empire*, 36 (June): 20.

Mooney, J. (1996) "Nice Tits: Shame About the Film," *Empire*, 80 (February): 61–8.

Picardie, R. (1992) "Mad, Bad and Dangerous to Know," *New Statesman*, 1 May: 36.

Russo, T. (1995) "Preview: *Showgirls*," *Premiere*, 8, 12: 28.

Sandler, K. (2001) "The Naked Truth: *Showgirls* and the Fate of the X/NC-17 Rating," *Cinema Journal*, 40, 3: 69–93.

Schaefer, E. (1999) *Bold! Daring! Shocking! True! A History of Exploitation Films: 1919–1959*, Durham, NC: Duke University Press.

Schatz, T. (1993) "The New Hollywood," in Jim Collins, Hilary Radner, and Ava Preacher Collins (eds), *Film Theory Goes to the Movies*, New York and London: Routledge: 8–36 [reprinted in this volume].

Scheers, R. V. (1997) *Paul Verhoeven*, trans. A. Stevens, London: Faber & Faber.

Smith, A. (1996) "*Showgirls*," *Empire Online*, August, http://www.empir.../review.asp?id=2483&ss=showgirls&sb=t&or=bf&c=&r=0&f.

Thompson, D. (1994) *Sharon Stone: Basic Ambition*, London: Warner Books.

Unreich, R. (1999) "Less is Moore," *Empire*, 88 (October): 97.

Weinraub, B. (1992) "Sex and Death: *Fatal Attraction* for the 90s?," *International Herald Tribune*, 17 March: 20.

Williams, L. R. (1993) "Sisters under the Skin: Video and Blockbuster Erotic Thrillers," in P. Cook and P. Dodd (eds) (1997) *Women and Film: A Sight and Sound Reader*, London: Scarlet Press: 105–14.

—— (1996) "Nothing to Find," *Sight and Sound*, 6, 1: 28–30.

Wyatt, J. (1994) *High Concept: Movies and Marketing in Hollywood*, Austin: University of Texas Press.

11

STAR WARS IN FANDOM, FILM THEORY, AND THE MUSEUM

The cultural status of the cult blockbuster

Matt Hills

Star Wars (1977) has been made to make film history, both positively, within its fan culture (Conrad 1996), and, more often negatively, among film critics. This one film has been engraved as an epitaph for classical Hollywood cinema by film historians (Mathews 1999) and discussed as a marker of merchandizing excess (Fleming 1996; Lukk 1997: 254).

In this chapter, I will suggest that the spectacular visibility of *Star Wars* in narratives of film history can be linked to a range of different bids to establish cultural status on the part of the film's producers, fan-consumers, academic critics, and fan-academic defenders. I will suggest that *Star Wars*'s extra-textual positioning as a blockbuster has led to a series of struggles over cultural status in which its blockbuster status has become unquestionable for many critics and also potentially problematic in the light of its cult status for many fans.

Star Wars's existence as a cult blockbuster has been ushered in by its enduring cultural presence and its enduring fandom. The phrase "cult blockbuster' is used in Thomas Schatz's (1993) unusually sensitive survey of New Hollywood (Schatz 1993: 24; the term is drawn from the work of cult film critic J. Hoberman). I will explore this term later, but for now I want to note that the cult blockbuster seems to challenge established divisions in cultural status: it elevates "the most vital and disreputable genres . . . to cosmic heights" (Hoberman, in Schatz 1993: 24), threatening to revise issues of cultural hierarchy and status. The cult blockbuster is interesting, then, because of the way it does not quite fit into established patterns of high/low cultural status. While elevating "disreputable genres," it also offers the possibility of elevating the blockbuster from its assumed lowly cultural status. Fans of a cult blockbuster may therefore also accrue reflected cultural status, attempting to separate themselves out from the blockbuster's typically devalued "mass" audience. However, as I will show by referring to cult critic Danny Peary's cataloging of

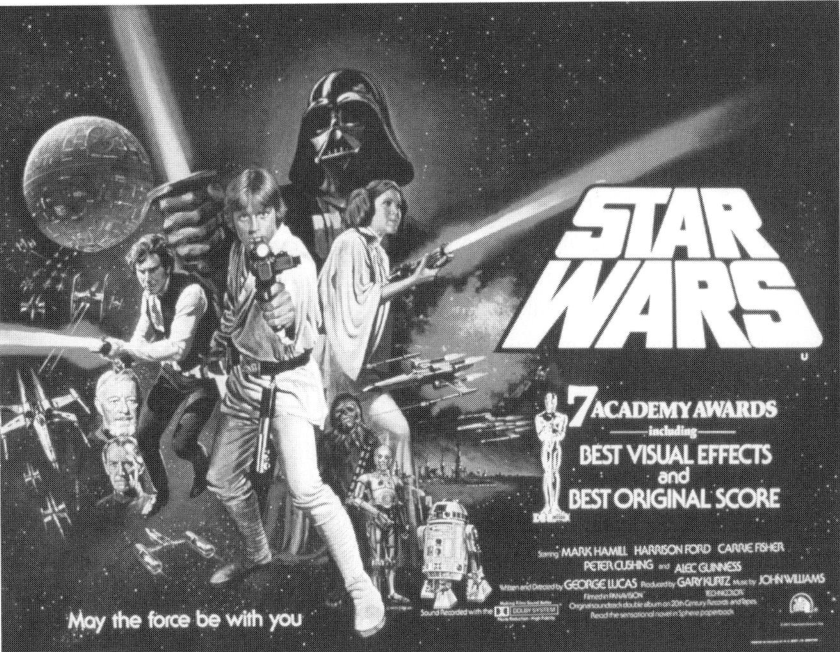

Figure 11.1 *Star Wars* (1977). The Kobal Collection.

cult movies, the conjunction of "cult" and "blockbuster" is also rejected by some cult fans. These fans tend to view cult status as being essentially linked to a *minority* audience. By doing so, they draw on one well-established connotation of the term "cult" within media fandom, even if this connotation (cult = minority) is itself subject to fan conflicts, given the increased mainstreaming of cult media (see Hills 2002).

Another key argument in what follows is that "the blockbuster" is an extra-textual, discursive construction. Texts do *not* present definitive attributes that can allow them to be classified as blockbusters, as if blockbuster status were akin to a textually identifiable film genre – a notion which has, itself, been undermined in recent work (e.g. Jancovich 2001). Instead, the term "blockbuster" depends on the mobilization of certain promotional/economic discourses: we are able to identify the blockbuster only through its placement within a set of industry and reception practices. Being set in motion as a corporate franchise does not *automatically* make a film a blockbuster. And although being a "box-office phenomenon" might be suggested as one nondiscursive defining attribute of the blockbuster, it remains the case that we become aware of this phenomenon only via marketing discourses that construct, define, and reiterate it as such, thereby bidding for cultural status. Certainly, there is an interaction between industrial and discursive constructions. However, my argument is that, ultimately, blockbuster status is constructed, industrially and otherwise, through discursive and extra-textual practices. Blockbuster status, I am suggesting, does not somehow magically belong to or accompany a film on its cultural career: rather, it is conferred and contested within the industrial and audience discourses that surround any given film. Arguably, textually similar films seem to attract the term "blockbuster." However, this is actually not an argument against my position, as it means only that the term blockbuster has, culturally and historically, become associated with specific types of films – its designation may yet be attached to very different types of films in the future. Moreover, if blockbuster status is indeed conferred and contested within struggles over cultural status – typically being linked to one or other term in a culture/economy opposition, as I will go on to show – then the qualifier "cult" provides one way of intervening in, and modifying, these very struggles over the blockbuster's cultural status.

I will consider how accounts of *Star Wars* as a blockbuster – accounts that are a given in much film theory – typically assume that blockbusters can be equated with a denigrated cultural status. I will then examine counterbids for the increased cultural status of *Star Wars*, this time considered as a cult blockbuster; these latter bids typically come from fans or scholar-fans.

To begin with, then, in what ways does the attribution of blockbuster status lead *Star Wars* to be culturally devalued? It has been assumed within much (although not all) film theory that the blockbuster is a necessarily fragmented text, becoming so by virtue of its intertextual stretching across culture. This is implied in Eileen Meehan's (1991) discussion of the "commercial inter-text," and is also central to Barbara Klinger's work on "digression" at the cinema. Klinger implies that New Hollywood's spectators become caught up in intertextual networks determined by marketing concerns:

> We need to recognize . . . how industrial practices constitute an intertextual network which pluralizes the classic text during its circulation as a commodity . . . [and whose] economies of viewing . . . fragment rather than assemble the text.
>
> (Klinger 1991: 125)

For these specific theorists, the blockbuster is implicitly devalued because of its challenge to a singular or "organic" textual site. Furthermore, the commercial omnipresence and merchandized excess of blockbusters is presented as logically determining their narrative incoherence (Wyatt 1994). This assumed loss of textual singularity – a dubious argument, anyway, given the merchandizing that surrounded classical Hollywood cinema – is reinforced by such critics' focus on the commerce of the New Hollywood blockbuster, as opposed to its aesthetics (remembering that this commerce/aesthetics opposition is constructed within their own arguments). The commercial nature of the "*commercial* inter-text" is specifically explored and emphasized. Here, *Star Wars*'s blockbuster "*brand* of spectacle" (King 2000: 75 – my italics) is presented as being all about the economy, and given the culture/economy opposition implicitly drawn on by these critics, the film is supposedly culturally devalued by its close links to commerce.

The power of this discourse is such that it can readily accommodate seemingly opposed statements. The merchandizing surrounding *Star Wars* is, we are told, "not an indiscriminate process, blitzing consumers with stuff that they will inevitably accept" (Fleming 1996: 94). Alternatively, though still invoking a blitz metaphor, we might read of "the carpet-bombing promotion strategy" (King and Krzywinska 2000: 95) of an event movie such as *Star Wars: Episode 1 – The Phantom Menace* (1999). Although discrimination is seemingly exercised in the former case, this discriminatory process proves to revolve around the market-testing of names for *Star Wars* spacecraft, implying after all that Lucas's (artistic, creative) imagination is wholly in thrall to commerce. Similarly, King and Krzywinska's statement also reinforces the sense that marketing has triumphed over "culture." Spectacle versus narrative; merchandizing versus authentic art – each opposition restages a clash between valued culture and devalued economy. Indeed, this replication of common sense discourses of economy versus culture may well account for the success that such theoretical narratives of New Hollywood have enjoyed.

The blockbuster has also been figured theoretically, and in common sense, as rapaciously commercial and minimally "cultural" by virtue of its relationship to time. Martin Barker and Kate Brooks list sixteen associations carried by the term "blockbuster," including: "Blockbusters are hyped, everywhere, 'must see' or they don't exist, yet at the same time evanescent, and leave few traces" (1998: 185). This specific relationship to time is a persistent marker of the blockbuster's reduced cultural status. As Bridget Fowler has suggested, cultural status is, in part, constructed through "the time a product lasts or its felt durability, criteria which are intricately linked to the distinction of either producers or consumers" (Fowler 1997: 161). However, Fowler's discussion of cultural status and durability carries a specific hesitancy; it links value both to "the time a product lasts" (this is seemingly objective) or "its felt durability" (which is marked as subjective). These explanations of cultural status and its links to time are presented as an either/or option: time cannot be *both* an objective measure of cultural status *and* a measure "felt" or constructed by specific cultural groups. Arguably, there is an unresolved tension here between "objective" temporality and "subjective" (i.e. socially constructed) temporalization, or what might be termed "epoch-making" (Bourdieu 1993: 60).

All of this raises the following questions: are blockbusters, as "event movies," bound into an objective time-frame? (Do they empirically come and go in the blink of an eye, displaying Barker and Brooks's "evanescence"?) Or are they discursively articulated to a sense of fleeting eventfulness by film theorists whose cultural capital works to deny any "felt durability" to the commercial and fragmented blockbuster? This either/or, although it may be logically correct, appears to be overwritten within fan culture, where *Star Wars* is valorized both through its empirical temporality (i.e. its enduring cultural presence since 1977) and through an interlinked discursive bid for temporalization (i.e. *Star Wars* is presented as having changed film history, and constructed as a "timeless" mythic narrative).

Film theorists who have sought to devalue *Star Wars* have, on the other hand, neglected the film's empirical temporality, focusing on its commercial and merchandizing excesses and its supposed lack of classical narrative structure. Given that fan cultures and academic cultures are not entirely separate groups, it is only to be expected that some scholar-fans (fans who occupy institutionally and professionally legitimated "academic" posts) will adopt positions between these interpretations. Scholar-fans thus typically allow for *Star Wars*'s empirical temporality (i.e. they emphasize its cultural endurance) but refuse to view this as a matter of the text's "mythic" timelessness, as per the fan culture's bid for cultural status. Scholar-fans also typically de-emphasize the importance of the film's merchandizing, other than as an expression of fans' "grassroots" passion for the meta-text surrounding *Star Wars* (see Brooker 1999: 51–2), while also relating its cultural endurance to its serialized aesthetic-textual structure (Jenkins 2001: 3–4). The "blockbuster as culturally devalued" position is refused in these cases. While an implicit economy/culture opposition is accepted, this time it is culture, as the valued term, that is linked to *Star Wars*; the (fan) culture, not the economy, is considered to be primary. Audience interest can be "helped" by aesthetic textual structures, and hence the economy of *Star Wars* emerges as a by-product of its fans' love for the text.

It could be argued that I am overstating the culture/economy opposition here and elsewhere in this chapter. Of course, there are always grey areas existing between culture and economy when we consider blockbusters (or any other cultural artifact, for that matter). However, my argument is that this structuring opposition is implicitly *written into fan and academic cultures* and thus into their different receptions of *Star Wars*. Grey areas are rendered less grey in fan defences of their favored text's cultural status as well as in academic attacks on *Star Wars* as one of the first of the New Hollywood blockbusters. Not all fans and academics will adopt such positions, as I have already argued in relation to scholar-fans specifically. However, this does not prevent the culture/economy opposition from playing a structural role in fan and academic bids for *Star Wars*'s cultural status, or lack of it.

On the basis of the positions I have summarized so far, it is possible to challenge the cultural devaluation of the cult blockbuster on two fronts. First, the equation of New Hollywood blockbusters with non-narrative spectacle can be challenged, and secondly the "time" of the blockbuster can be examined empirically rather than being read as a reflection of preceding producer/consumer distinctions. The first strategy has been pursued by theorists such as Warren Buckland (1998) and Kristin Thompson (1999: 9), both of whom have queried the orthodox theoretical narrative of New Hollywood blockbusters as a triumph of spectacle, fragmentation and incoherence over classical narrative coherence. Buckland renders the terms of the debate crystal clear: "It is perhaps time to stop condemning the New Hollywood blockbuster and to start, instead, to understand it" (Buckland 1998: 175).

I do not want to revisit this well-trodden academic territory. Instead, I will focus on a less explored aspect; the blockbuster's relationship to time. *Star Wars*'s objective relationship to time obstructs bids for cultural devaluation that are based on viewing blockbusters as inevitably fleeting or "evanescent." Focusing on the cultural status of time, or what might be termed *time-value*, it is apparent that devaluations of the blockbuster based on its "event" status are simply false in the case of *Star Wars* (see Brooker 1999: 52). Considering this relationship between time and the blockbuster, I want to return to Schatz's discussion of the cult blockbuster. Schatz separates out the various connotations of the blockbuster, observing of *Star Wars* that:

> There were countless commercial tie-ins, as well as a multi-billion dollar licensing and merchandising bonanza. *And strictly as a movie franchise it had tremendous legs*.
>
> (Schatz 1993: 24; my italics)

Schatz therefore makes the same accusations as critics seeking to devalue the blockbuster, focusing on tie-ins and merchandizing, but he goes on to address the cultural durability of the movie franchise, listing the reissues, sequel releases, and so on, of the *Star Wars* franchise's first decade (ibid.). It is this call to "objective" temporality rather than "felt durability" that raises questions about the description of *Star Wars* as an "event movie" blockbuster. While it may well carry many of the connotations expected extra-textually of the blockbuster, *Star Wars* cannot be readily aligned with specific devaluations based on planned obsolescence or on popular cultural ephemerality. Narratives circulating around the film within its fan culture also challenge the notion that *Star Wars* was an "event" movie, overwriting connotations of the "event" in relation to the moment of the film's initial release as well as through its endurance: "*Star Wars* was a 'sleeper,' a film whose vast success was in doubt until after it had opened for a while" (Pye and Miles 1999: 81). This type of claim draws on the film's uncertain (i.e. artistic) status, implying that it was not a targeted (i.e. commercial) exercise. Along with the co-existing fan claim, that it "changed the face of commercial cinema" (Conrad 1996: 47), this positions *Star Wars* primarily as "cultural" rather than commercial. Even its impact on commercial cinema, viewed positively as history-making by fans, attributes an artistic "commitment" and integrity to the film and its producers (ibid.).

There is a slippage here from temporality to temporalization or "epoch-making."

Star Wars fan culture moves from recognizing the "objective" endurance of the film, to reading this within a specific constellation of associations with high cultural status. It is in this sense that *Star Wars* has been made to make film history by its fans; its name acts as a valued, positive marker of historical difference, supposedly revolutionizing "effects" spectacles. By consistently marking the end of one "system" or type of film, and ushering in a new episode in film history, *Star Wars makes time*; it accrues cultural status and prestige, for itself and its producers, status which is then reflected on its fan culture as a "consumer community" (Lash 1993: 197–8). This reflection of "symbolic capital" suggests that the knowledgeable *Star Wars* audience may possess a specific (although insecurely consecrated) cultural capital when set against the blockbuster's (typically devalued) "mass" audience. The need to distinguish fan culture from a "mass" audience when the cult alibi of "obscurity" remains impossible results, I would suggest, in the "overconsumption" or repeat viewing of *Star Wars* within its fan culture (see Gomery 1994: 78; Wyatt 1994: 145). Repeat viewing of an obscure cult movie is arguably less vital, because the mere act of having access to this type of movie may, in itself, sufficiently mark out the cult fan's distinction. *Repetition* thus stands in for *rarity* of viewing where the fan distinctions of the cult blockbuster are concerned.

These reworkings of cultural status might be taken to suggest that *Star Wars* represents the death of previous cultural systems of distinction. This extreme position has in fact been presented by John Seabrook (2000). Seabrook coins the term "nobrow" as part of his argument that a seismic shift in cultural distinctions has emerged in recent times, and he offers *Star Wars* as one example of "nobrow":

> The marketing is the culture and the culture the marketing. The space that the marketing of *Star Wars* takes up in the culture, in terms of Buzz, is validation for the fans of the movie – a kind of return on their investment . . . *Star Wars* is both something to buy (marketing) and something to be (culture), through the buying: a *Star Wars* fan.
>
> (Seabrook 2000: 153)

In a nobrow culture, "commercial culture is a potential source of status rather than the thing the elite define themselves against" (Seabrook 2000: 28). However, Seabrook's argument-cum-soundbite that "marketing is the culture and the culture the marketing" neglects the fact that the culture/economy opposition continues to be drawn on in a series of cultural sites, ranging from consecrated and consecrating institutions such as the university to those such as the Smithsonian and the Barbican Art Gallery. It is also significant that fans' cultural productions do not entirely surrender the meaningfulness of a culture/economy separation, even while the very existence of their bids for cultural status through *Star Wars* seems to indicate the collapse of this binary.

This paradox, whereby a binary opposition re-emerges through its own apparent collapse, is evident in Timothy Corrigan's discussion of "the commercial *auteur* and the auteur of commerce" (1991: 107). Although seeming to blur auteurism and commerce, the commercial auteur is the author's name or "signature" marketed as a brand and extra-textually circulated around a film text. It is in this sense that the "signature" of George Lucas has accrued celebrity status or "symbolic capital," being profoundly fetishized by fans (see Brooker 1999: 67) as a marker of authenticity and cultural value. The "*auteur* of commerce," by contrast, is "the more intriguing variation" for Corrigan, as it is here that "a filmmaker attempts to monitor or rework the institutional manipulations of the *auteurist* position within the commerce of the contemporary movie industry" (Corrigan 1991: 107). What this amounts to is a separating out of an economy of culture (where the auteur's name can sell even a blockbuster as a signature event) and a culture of economy (where the auteur seeks to manipulate artistically the conventions of the culture industry).

Although I have so far argued that the cult blockbuster blurs previous lines of distinction and cultural status by culturally elevating the blockbuster, for some cult critics the conjunction of "cult" and "blockbuster" is simply too threatening to their structuring culture/economy opposition. One such critic is Danny Peary, who refuses to grant cult status to *Star Wars* precisely because of its blockbuster (i.e. "mass") appeal:

> Although *Gone with the Wind* [1939] and *Star Wars* have fanatical followings, I have not included them because they are still distributed . . . with the intention of attracting the masses rather than devotees on the fringe of the mass audience; the word cult implies a minority, and the studios are well aware that *Gone with the Wind* and *Star Wars* still attract the *majority* of the movie audience.
>
> (Peary 1982: xiii)

And it is not only Peary who makes this particular move. Theorists such as Meehan (1991) and Jenkins (2001) similarly separate out blockbusters from cult movies. Meehan separates the terms cult and blockbuster by dint of the fact that "Word-of-mouth can break a film designed as a blockbuster, or elevate an obscure movie to the status of a cult film or even a sleeper" (Meehan 1991: 60–1). The possibility which is notably absent here is that *word of mouth may also "elevate" a blockbuster by generating cult status around it*. Note how this possibility confuses the cultural hierarchy implicit in Meehan's position, where blockbusters are designed and "broken" while cult movies are supposedly not designed at all; they are elevated out of obscurity by fan audience activity. Meehan thus denies that cult status can be attached to films positioned as blockbusters, reserving cult status for the necessarily "obscure movie." Equally, when Henry Jenkins discusses *Star Wars* and "enormous cult followings," these followings are related to amateur, student, or fan-produced films (e.g. *George Lucas in Love* and *Troops*) rather than identified as existing around the official films (Jenkins 2001: 2).

So far I have focused largely on struggles over the cultural status of *Star Wars* within, and between, film theory and fan culture. But neither of these repertoires of cultural practices can be detached from the promotional, journalistic, and marketing discourses that also circulate around *Star Wars*. However much it might claim otherwise, *and precisely given that it would claim otherwise*, film theory is structured by the distance that it seeks to claim from the industrial and the commercial. This constructs the illusion that academic work is detached from market-driven concerns. Despite claiming otherwise, both fandom and academia are enmeshed in commercialized systems of meaning. In what follows, I consider briefly how *Star Wars* has been marketed in order to elevate its cultural status, and how fans (and others) have adopted discourses from this ongoing marketing campaign.

The use of promotional discourses to position *Star Wars* as a myth for a "timeless audience" (Mackay 1999: 65) paradoxically links Lucas-as-auteur to a sense of the films as mythologically transcendent, and thus as somehow beyond authorship. It is a strategy for increasing the films' cultural status that has been remarkably successful, finding itself reflected in a vein of academic work on *Star Wars*:

> *Star Wars* is not just an awesome spectacle . . . No, we are instructed that these films have cultural capital; they are relevant to a "timeless" audience because of their mythological themes. Considering *Star Wars* as if it were a modern mythology is an approach that harkens back to the rhetoric around the film during its initial release . . . Film critics, journalists and scholars picked up on this . . . and wrote articles like Andrew Gordon's "*Star Wars*: A Myth for Our Time" . . . The triumph of this point-of-view came in 1987 when Joseph Campbell, architect of the seminal work . . . on mythology *The Hero With a Thousand Faces*, was filmed at Lucas's own Skywalker Ranch in a series of conversations . . . and used *Star Wars* examples when expounding upon the meaning of certain reoccurring mythic archetypes and themes.
>
> (ibid.)

Perhaps not surprisingly, these promotional (and academically licensed) discourses have also been taken up within fandom, suggesting that promotional discourses – especially when mediated by cultural "authorities" such as Campbell – can strongly set the agendas and grounds for fan cultural distinctions. The take-up of these promotional discourses by *Star Wars* fans suggests that fan negotiation with dominant forms of cultural status (revaluing the blockbuster as a cult blockbuster) occurs alongside a degree of dependence on promotional discourses. This dependence emerges not only through a "desperate loyalty to Lucas" (Brooker 2001: 24) but also through fans' active appropriation of discourses such as "*Star Wars*-as-mythology" that have obviously already accrued cultural status. These discourses provide culturally meaningful and seemingly sanctioned ways for fans to legitimate their fandom. Nevertheless, whether fans are described as "actively" or "passively" dependent on the legitimations offered by promotional discourses, the end result remains the same: the relatively uncontested circulation of promotional discourses within *Star Wars* fan culture as well as within sections of academia.

As Mackay notes, the promotional discourse of *Star Wars* as "timeless" has also been actively drawn on by the likes of the Smithsonian and the Barbican, both of which have housed *Star Wars* exhibits, "The Magic of Myth" (1997) and "The Art of *Star Wars*" (2000) respectively. Museum/gallery space therefore represents a further cultural site where the struggle over *Star Wars*'s cultural status can and has been played out. Like the struggle over its cultural status in other fields, such as that of film theory, this contest also hinges on the use of an implied culture/economy opposition. Indeed, journalistic coverage of the Barbican display in the UK acknowledged that, in the case of its *Star Wars* exhibits, there was an implicit challenge to processes of cultural status at work:

> "When you see these works, I don't think you can question their right to be in a museum," says Mark Sladen, curator at the Barbican's art gallery. "They are incredibly beautiful. And, as you are witnessing how icons were generated, they have real cultural significance."
>
> (quoted in Rayment 2000: 25)

"Real cultural significance"; what does this statement refer to? It seems to confer cultural status while lacking any clear referent whatsoever: how does something come to possess "real cultural significance"? The phrase is a simulation of itself, I would argue, since any cultural artifact that possesses "real cultural significance" is unlikely to require such a fragile endorsement. This is a bid for cultural status which appears to hinge on the "authority" of a consecrated institution (the Barbican Art Gallery), but which is nevertheless produced by an institution whose "autonomous" cultural authority is open to challenge, given its commercially motivated endorsement of popular culture. Consider also this quote:

> Through an attribution of *Star Wars* as mythology, the Smithsonian is attempting to raise its cultural worth and importance. They . . . must increase the cultural worth of their object before they use that object . . . to increase their economic worth.
>
> (Mackay 1999: 73–4)

Throughout the twists and turns of *Star Wars*'s devalued and revalued cultural status, a number of points return time and time again. The structuring culture/economy opposition continues to play a role across fan, academic and scholar-fan receptions of the film, whether as a blockbuster or as a cult blockbuster. Working to establish the cultural status of *Star Wars*, the concept of the cult blockbuster challenges the discursive separation of culture and economy without simply collapsing these terms together. The cult blockbuster does not represent a phantom menace, that of the loss of all cultural hierarchies and forms of cultural status. Instead, it offers a new hope: that established patterns of cultural status can be, and have been, reconfigured via the situated agency of fans, theorists, producers, marketers, and journalists. None of us, whether fans, academics, or scholar-fans, can claim to be outside these ongoing struggles over cultural status.

References

Barker, Martin, and Brooks, Kate (1998) *Knowing Audiences: Judge Dredd, Its Friends, Fans and Foes*, Luton: University of Luton Press.

Bourdieu, Pierre (1993) *The Field of Cultural Production*, Cambridge: Polity.

Brooker, Will (1999) "Internet Fandom and the Continuing Narratives of *Star Wars*, *Blade Runner* and *Alien*," in Annette Kuhn (ed.), *Alien Zone II*, London: Verso.

—— (2001) "Readings of Racism: Interpretation, Stereotyping and *The Phantom Menace*," *Continuum*, 15, 1: 15–32.

Buckland, Warren (1998) "A Close Encounter with *Raiders of the Lost Ark*: Notes on Narrative Aspects of the New Hollywood Blockbuster," in Steve Neale and Murray Smith (eds), *Contemporary Hollywood Cinema*, London: Routledge: 166–77.

Conrad, Dean (1996) *Star Wars: The Genesis of a Legend*, London: Valis Books.

Corrigan, Timothy (1991) *A Cinema without Walls: Movies and Culture After Vietnam*, London: Routledge.

Fleming, Dan (1996) *Powerplay: Toys as Popular Culture*, Manchester: Manchester University Press.

Fowler, Bridget (1997) *Pierre Bourdieu and Cultural Theory: Critical Investigations*, London: Sage.

Gomery, Douglas (1994) "Disney's Business History: A Reinterpretation," in Eric Smoodin (ed.), *Disney Discourse: Producing the Magic Kingdom*, New York: Routledge: 71–86.

Hills, Matt (2002) *Fan Cultures*, London: Routledge.

Jancovich, Mark (2001) "Genre and the Audience: Genre Classifications and Cultural Distinctions in the Mediation of *The Silence of the Lambs*," in Melvyn Stokes and Richard Maltby (eds), *Hollywood Spectatorship: Changing Perceptions of Cinema Audiences*, London: British Film Institute: 33–44.

Jenkins, Henry (2001) "Quentin Tarantino's *Star Wars*?: Digital Cinema, Media Convergence and Participatory Culture," online: http://web.mit.edu/21fms/www/faculty/henry3/starwars.html.

King, Geoff, (2000) *Spectacular Narratives: Hollywood in the Age of the Blockbuster*, London and New York: I. B. Tauris.

King, Geoff, and Krzywinska, Tanya (2000) *Science Fiction Cinema: From Outerspace to Cyberspace*, London: Wallflower Press.

Klinger, Barbara (1991) "Digressions at the Cinema: Commodification and Reception in Mass Culture," in James Naremore and Patrick Brantlinger (eds), *Modernity and Mass Culture*, Bloomington: Indiana University Press: 117–34.

Lash, Scott (1993) "Pierre Bourdieu: Cultural Economy and Social Change," in Craig Calhoun, Edward Lipuma, and Moishe Postone (eds), *Bourdieu: Critical Perspectives*, Cambridge: Polity.

Lukk, Tiiu (1997) *Movie Marketing: Opening the Picture and Giving it Legs*, Los Angeles: Silman-James Press.

Mackay, Daniel (1999) "*Star Wars*: The Magic of the Anti-Myth," *Foundation: The International Review of Science Fiction*, 76: 63–75.

Mathews, Jack (1999) "Saber Rattler," in Sally Kline (ed.), *George Lucas Interviews*, Jackson: University Press of Mississippi.

Meehan, Eileen R. (1991) "'Holy Commodity Fetish, Batman!': The Political Economy of a Commercial Intertext," in Roberta E. Pearson and William Uricchio (eds), *The Many Lives of the Batman*, New York: Routledge: 47–65.

Peary, Danny (1982) *Cult Movies*, London: Vermilion.

Pye, Michael, and Miles, Linda (1999) "George Lucas," in Sally Kline (ed.), *George Lucas Interviews*, Jackson: University Press of Mississippi.

Rayment, Tim (2000) "Space Craft," *Sunday Times Magazine*, April 2: 25.

Schatz, Thomas (1993) "The New Hollywood," in Jim Collins, Hilary Radner, and Ava Preacher Collins (eds), *Film Theory Goes to the Movies*, New York and London: Routledge: 8–36 [reprinted in this volume].

Seabrook, John (2000) *Nobrow: The Culture of Marketing and the Marketing of Culture*, London: Methuen.

Thompson, Kristin (1999) *Storytelling in the New Hollywood*, Cambridge, MA: Harvard University Press.

Wyatt, Justin (1994) *High Concept: Movies and Marketing in Hollywood*, Austin: University of Texas Press.

12

THE BEST PLACE TO SEE A FILM

The blockbuster, the multiplex, and the contexts of consumption

Mark Jancovich and Lucy Faire

The term "blockbuster" can be a misleading one. Historically, there have been several different types of blockbusters and each type has been connected to a different type of exhibition. For example, after World War II, the blockbuster referred to prestigious event movies that were associated largely with big, metropolitan picture palaces (Schatz 1993). It is therefore significant that, when the Nottingham Odeon was redesigned in the 1960s, it not only became the first twin-screen cinema in Britain, but the upstairs cinema, Odeon 1, was clearly designed with these films in mind. It was to "show the 70 mm, wide-screen films" while downstairs, in Odeon 2, "continuous performances in ordinary 35 mm" were to be shown. As this suggests, the shows in Odeon 1 would be "on a bookable basis" due to the use of separate performances, a supposed "'first' for Nottingham" (*Guardian Journal*, 30 June, 1965: 4).[1]

More recently, however, the term "blockbuster" has come to be associated with the multiplex, and the two are intimately related. The multiplex has not only transformed the meaning of the blockbuster but was itself a response to developments in the blockbuster. On the one hand, the blockbuster no longer refers solely to the prestigious event movie but has come to mean little more than films that are successful at the box office. On the other hand, as Gomery has noted, the success of multiplex cinemas is specifically based on their ability to use their multiple screens to reap maximum profits from blockbusters. For example, he describes Cineplex, a "Canadian enterprise [that] significantly altered the standards by which North America judged 'going to the movies'" (Gomery 1992: 105), who would "open a popular, well-advertised film on three or four of its screens, and then slowly cut back the number of auditoria as the popularity of the film waned," or, if they found themselves with a major hit on their hands, "they would move it into a half-dozen of their largest auditoria . . . and not miss a single possible customer" (ibid.: 107).

However, while associations between the multiplex and the blockbuster proved financially profitable, and also stimulated renewed interest in cinemagoing as an activity, both remain highly contested objects.

Complaints about the blockbuster are not simply about the films themselves but rather the specific modes of consumption with which they are associated. While different cinemas are contrasted on account of the films that they show, films can also change meaning if shown in different cinemas. For example, in the 1990s, the then director of the Broadway Cinema, Nottingham's regional art film theater, claimed: "There's certainly no way that we're in competition with the city centre mainstream cinemas . . . I just can't conceive of us showing *Jurassic Park* [1993] for instance." Here a blockbuster stands for the difference between the art cinema and the mainstream, but the director then qualifies this remark: "not unless we are doing a season on special effects films or we got Steven Spielberg over to do an introduction to it" (*Nottingham Evening Post* (*NEP*), July 20, 1993). It is not the film itself that is the problem but specific contexts of consumption. *Jurassic Park* might be shown at the Broadway, but only in an educational or intellectual context.

In other words, cinemas are associated with, and come to represent, modes of consumption that are hierarchically ranked and valued. For example, in its strategy for exhibition, the East Midlands Region Media Agencies Partnership (EMRMAP) draws on a specific metaphorical distinction: "Like the restaurant sector, specialist cinemas offer a different menu and a different ambience compared to the 'fast food' multiplexes" (EMRMAP 2001: 23). Nor is such a distinction peculiar to EMRMAP: it draws on a series of discourses and associations that surround the multiplex more generally.

The problems associated with the multiplex are not simply about the films shown. It is often criticized for its relationship to, and effects upon, the city more generally. It is frequently linked with the growth of other out of town developments such as the shopping mall, and is subject to very similar debates (Gomery 1992; Hanson 2000; Jones 2001; Paul 1994; Hubbard forthcoming). According to Miller and his collaborators, the "often contested meanings of these shopping places" can be divided into two main concerns (Miller *et al.* 1998: ix). On the one hand, these shopping malls are seen as a solution to the problems of the inner city – "the now widespread fear of public space" (ibid.: xi) – fears that are often expressed in "highly racialised terms . . . sometimes mediated through notions of dirt and pollution" (ibid.: x). On the other hand, there are also "fears about the increasingly 'artificial' nature of contemporary shopping" (ibid.: xi). As a result, Miller and his colleagues not only discuss concerns about the absence of "natural" light in Brent Cross Shopping Centre but also the middle-class preference shopping area that was perceived as authentic and communal (ibid.: 123). Through these activities and identifications, consumers sought to distinguish themselves from the "ordinary" consumer through a rejection of the supposed commercialism and homogeneity of mass consumption. However, this desire for diversity is not necessarily an appreciation of others; it can be a way of differentiating oneself from the masses.

These concerns were also related to other features of the shopping center and the multiplexes where blockbusters are shown. The success of these developments was precisely that they were geared to customers who not only had access to autos, but had also largely deserted consumption in the town center due to the problems of parking there. However, the auto has increasingly been seen as symbolic of the destruction of the city (Jancovich *et al.* forthcoming). Its demands tear up neighborhoods and pollute the environment, but it also creates social exclusion. As auto ownership has increased, public transport has not only been cut back but has become increasingly associated with the poorest sections of the population. Out-of-town multiplex developments are, in part, seen as safe exactly because only certain sections of the population have the transport necessary to gain access to them.

Furthermore, as leisure and consumption have increasingly moved out to these developments, town centers have declined still further, and these developments have therefore become important symbolically. Unlike in America, where they were produced out of the processes of urban sprawl, most of the British shopping centers and multiplexes have been built on "redundant industrial land" (Gray 1996: 129), and therefore symbolize the transformation of the city from a place of production to one of consumption (Hannigan 1998; Harvey 1991). They represent the literal replacement of industrial factories with cathedrals of consumption that has created a "tale of two cities": a landscape of increased luxury and prosperity for some and extreme poverty for others (Hannigan 1998: 53).

This chapter will therefore examine the contested meanings of the blockbuster by focusing on the meanings of the multiplex as a place. In the process, it will demonstrate the ways in which both films, and the places where they are "ordinarily" consumed, figure within debates over the nature of modernization. The meanings of both the blockbuster and the multiplex are usually organized around a series of related concerns about Americanization, mass consumption, and youth culture, in which these terms can acquire both positive and negative meanings. Drawing on these ideas, the next section will analyze the ways in which the local press have reported on Nottingham's multiplex to examine the public debates over this building. The following section will then discuss the findings of a range of interviews that were conducted as part of a larger project on film consumption within Nottingham.

Selling the multiplex

Nottingham's multiplex, the Showcase, was opened on Thursday June 16, 1988, with eleven screens, which was more than any other cinema in the country at the time. Bowden Wilson of Leicester, the company that had acquired the site, were planning to build a garden center, a DIY store, an auto accessory store, and either a

Figure 12.1 The Showcase multiplex, Nottingham, England. Image courtesy of Mark Jancovich.

public house or a restaurant (*NEP*, February 13, 1987). However, the area became a center of leisure and entertainment rather than retail, and the multiplex was soon joined by the Megabowl and Isis Nightclub.

As with earlier periods of cinema-building, the promotional and publicity materials all stressed the new cinema's modernity and comfort. An advert in the *NEP* claimed that the Showcase would be "very upmarket" (February 4, 1987), while the press claimed that it combined "Comfort . . . Convenience . . . Luxury" with "the healthful comfort of perfectly controlled air-conditioning" (advert in *NEP*, June 17, 1988). Also like earlier cinemas, it was "yet another 'first'" and demonstrated that Nottingham was fully up-to-date (*NEP*, June 17, 1988). Not only was it "Britain's newest and largest cinema" (ibid.), but it would also be part of "one of the most exciting leisure areas in Europe" (*NEP*, October 1, 1987).

The cinema's claims to being modern and innovative were also consolidated through its presentation as an "an all-American operation." According to the "American" manager, American National Amusements, the company that owned the Showcase, was "bringing American standards of quality to Britain in an industry which has a great future" (*NEP*, May 13, 1988). The *NEP* added to these positive associations with America: "the 11-screen cinema is nothing like anyone remembers; nothing like anyone in this country has ever known." The "splendid American venture on the ring road" may have represented an "American invasion of the city," but this was definitely presented as a "good thing" (*NEP*, October 15, 1987).

These reports worked to construct an imaginary America that was consumed through the practice of cinemagoing (Webster 1988; Morley and Robins 1995), particularly the watching of blockbuster movies. For the *NEP*, an interview with the manager claimed that the "'all-American' outlook on life" was encapsulated in the words "movies," "corporate images," "concession stands," "multiplex concepts," and "quality customer service" (*NEP*, October 15, 1987). The cinema was also associated with America through its "glamour." Its "glittering celebrity opening" (*Nottingham Trader*, June 22, 1988) had "a grand reception in grand American style" that gave the guests a "taste of Hollywood" (*NEP*, June 17, 1988).

However, the company was also worried that some Nottingham residents would not appreciate the associations with America and tried to counteract potential problems. They stressed not only that the cinema's American style was synonymous with quality, but that the company would not simply impose itself upon Nottingham:

> Our theatres, with more comfort, more space and more attention to detail, are recognised as the finest in the United States – and that's the standard we're bringing to Nottingham . . . The addition of this kind of enterprise serves as a magnet for and contributes to the development of a myriad of other business enterprises, with the resulting additional employment and revenue to the community. We aim to play a significant role in not only the civic but also the economic affairs of the communities in which we operate.
>
> (*NEP*, October 14, 1987)

It was also stated: "We're not saying British cinemas aren't run well, but we just like to run our business in a certain way" (*NEP*, June 14, 1988).

As a place where blockbuster movies might be watched, the cinema additionally marked its distinction from more traditional cinemas in other ways. For example, it was stressed that there was parking for 850 automobiles and that everyone would find a space. It was also designed in ways that, as can be seen from the comments above, were clearly supposed to signify spectacle, comfort, and luxury, although as we shall see, others have read the multiplex as bland and functional. The "product" was also different: there were no adverts, no smoking, no double features, no interval, and no ice-cream lady (*NEP*, May 23, 1988). However, there was a massive concession stand that dominated the central foyer and which one had to pass to gain access to the auditoria. Food was therefore central in the construction of the Showcase's image, and the selection of foods associates the cinema with America and the mass-produced abundance that it represents (Lyons, n.d.). The cinema management also emphasized that for the first time Nottingham audiences could see films at the same time as the West End of London. The Showcase, it was implied, gave one direct access to Hollywood cinema and, as a result, Nottingham was no longer marginal to London.

Nonetheless, there were several features that question Nottingham's claim to being at the cutting edge of cinema. First, while the Showcase was the first cinema in the UK with eleven screens, it was certainly not the first multiplex. The Point in Milton Keynes, which was opened in 1985, predated the Showcase by three years, and by the end of 1988 there were fourteen multiplexes in Britain. Nor did the Showcase ensure that Nottingham had more choice in venues or screens: there had been more screens in the 1930s and 1940s.

Indeed, while the Showcase's management made claims to the cinema's newness and modernity, it also associated the cinema with this earlier era. The advertising played heavily on the nostalgic glamor of the Hollywood past, even though it sought to assert the Showcase's superiority over that past in certain respects. In short, it tried to negotiate a relationship between the past and future. In a similar way, Lynn Spigel has claimed that her students were able to maintain both a nostalgic desire for the past and a sense of the present as progress from that past, and that they did so in part by imagining the future as an idealized time in which they could reconcile the pleasures associated with both past and present. As she claims: "Nostalgia in this regard is not the opposite of progress, but rather its handmaiden. Like the idea of progress, nostalgia works to simplify history into a time-line of events that lead somewhere better" (Spigel 1995: 29).

The management even enlisted the veteran local film critic Emrys Bryson to endorse the cinema by dedicating an auditorium to him. In response, Bryson is quoted as saying:

> I was worried at first about the effect the Showcase would have, but in fact it cleared out a lot of dead wood and it put the other cinemas on their mettle . . . I think that the multiplexes have actually done a great deal for the cinema industry.
>
> (*NEP*, 25 June, 1998)

While he acknowledged certain anxieties about the multiplex, he ultimately condoned it as embodying both the best of the past and the best of the present.

The meanings of the multiplex

These perceptions of the Showcase were shared by a great many of our respondents. Many saw it as the best of the Nottingham cinemas (Dalbir, aged 14, student),[2] and associated it with America in ways that were wholly positive (Tony, 67, retired teacher). For these respondents, the Showcase was a distinctive and spectacular building. It was "overwhelming" (ibid.) in a positive sense, providing sensorial abundance even to the point of dizzying overload. This abundance was not limited to the spectacle of the building or its food, but also to the range of blockbuster films on offer. It was particularly popular with the groups of Asian youth and with the youth of Southwell, a nearby town, for whom it represented something that was clearly divorced from what they regarded as the provincial location of their everyday lives (cf. interviews with Tarnjit, 16; Dalbir, 14; Subaigh, 11; Suroop, 10; Harprit, 18; Harjot, 10; Bikrumjit, 14; and GCSE English Class, 14–15, Minister School, Southwell). Parents often claimed that their young children loved the place and frequently pleaded to be taken there (Donna, 30, clerical officer; Whitegate Mothers and Toddlers Group). However, while some parents were clearly ambivalent about their children's attachment to the place, its success as a cinema is also closely tied to its function as a "safe environment" for young people. The area was largely cut off from the surrounding city, and its security system meant that youth were not only protected but monitored (GCSE English Class). Safety was an issue for disabled respondents too, who stressed that the Showcase was distinguished by its provision of level access (Joe, 36, volunteer).

However, many adults saw the cinema as an unappealing and alienating space,[3] and those adults who were positive about it were often associated with it through a teenage intermediary. Some elderly respondents, for example, took their grandchildren there, and time spent with their grandchildren colored their feelings about the cinema more generally.[4] Another respondent often went with her son.[5] The Showcase was also seen as a place where the family could do something together, although this situation does not necessarily imply that they occupied the same auditorium. Several respondents said that one of the advantages of the multiplex was precisely that one together could go out as a family, but watch different movies (Donna, 30, clerical officer).

For these respondents, the cinema was not only visually impressive but also welcoming and with friendly staff (John, 55, lecturer; Charlotte, 16, occupation unknown). For others, however, the cinema was a deeply unpleasant and even repellent place whose audience is a mindless mass simply duped by marketing (Stefan, 25, unemployed teacher). For these respondents, the Showcase was not a spectacular and visually impressive building but a characterless and even "placeless" place.[6] However, it was not simply the building that was being discussed here. Thus while some described the showcase as "soulless," "clinical," and "like an airport" (anonymous female, 30, occupation unknown; Lynnette, 26, clerical assistant; Helen, 40, project worker), these descriptions also suggested that it is "impersonal" (Catherine, 25, student). These terms therefore had two implicit meanings: on the one hand they suggested that the place lacked identity, but on the other that it was associated with functionality and rationality – with technology, materialism, and commerce. Furthermore, while Miller and his colleagues found that the supposed "artificiality" of Brent Cross Shopping Centre was frequently framed in terms of the absence of "natural" light, from its first opening, concerns about the Showcase were framed in terms of its "atmosphere."

The air-conditioning units that had been used to sell the place were criticized almost immediately, and customers complained that the cinema was too cold. This was more than simply a complaint about the temperature; it was metaphorically linked to a generalized criticism of the cinema as an emotionally cold place – clinical and impersonal – and to other associations with the atmosphere. Most obviously, many respondents claimed that the cinema had "no atmosphere," by which they meant again that it lacked personality and character and was emotionally cold and empty (Bakersfield and Sneinton Women's Co-Op Guild). However, other respondents complained that the cinema "smells funny" (Dorothy, 61, occupation unknown), or that they experienced a feeling of revulsion at the smell of popcorn which, it was claimed, permeates the cinema (Vic, 59, part-time teacher; Christine, 60, retired secretary; Judith, 60, administrative assistant).

As this reference to popcorn makes clear, this visceral intolerance to the air of the cinema was actually related to broader cultural meanings. One respondent condemned the cinema as "popcorn city" (anonymous female, 41, nurse), and so associated it with low and debased cultural forms and activities. Popcorn has become a symbol for negative evaluations of the Showcase as an American place and, by implication, as a place of popular amusements and "unashamed indulgence in trash" (Barker and Brooks 1998: 195). This is made clear by the frequent references to the cinema as "vulgar" and "brash" (Jackie, 49, part-time student advisor; John, 75, retired), and to the claims that the cinema was part of a process of Americanization (Stefan, 25, unemployed teacher; Neil, 55, welfare worker), a process which, as Duncan Webster has pointed out, is used to displace anxieties about modernity through a deflection of its effects onto an alien invading other (Webster 1988). Thus, America comes to signify the negative features of materialism and mass production in a way that not only lets Britain off the hook but is "mediated through notions of dirt and pollution," even if this process is seen in terms of nation rather than race.

Thus, people complained about the corporate image of National Amusements (anon female, 40, careers advisor), and claimed that they resented being "herded" or "treated like a number" (Helen, 40, project worker; Marc, 25, student). Here the suggestion is that the cinema turns its customers into mere product to be processed – cattle – and it draws on the distinction between the rationalized mass and the authentic community. As a result, many claimed that there is no place to interact with one another or talk about the film afterwards (Brian, 46, probation officer). It is also for this reason that while those who identified with the Showcase used the term "overwhelming" positively, those who disliked the place also referred to it as "overwhelming" (Catherine, 25, student). For these people, it was too big, too overpowering, and hence inhuman. These people complained about the crowds, but also the range of choice which, it was claimed, produced a passive and undiscriminating customer who had no idea of what they were going to see before they arrived at the cinema (Stefan, 25, unemployed teacher; Gray, 1996: 131).

This concern with the undifferentiated mass also shaded over into concerns about the effect of the multiplex upon the city center. For example, the planning officer, Dick Blenkinsop, claimed that he was afraid that the public's choice would be reduced, rather than increased, by the presence of the multiplex, if its presence forced the city center cinemas to close (*NEP*, February 12, 1987). However, the *NEP* displayed considerable optimism in their claim that there would be plenty of customers for the city center cinemas, and that the Odeon was "meeting the challenge not with moans and groans about competition but with typical enthusiasm and verve." The presence of the multiplex was therefore read as "healthy competition" in which the "customer invariably wins" (*NEP*, June 17, 1988). However, the *NEP* also believed that Nottingham was a unique case; that the city was such a vibrant center of leisure and culture that it could easily sustain another large cinema: "No other city outside London offers so much and no other city buzzes with people and activity during the leisure hours in the way that Nottingham does" (ibid.).

While this might sound a lot like boosterism, which it no doubt was, it also seems to have been partly correct. Ironically, it was not the Showcase that killed off the Odeon and the Cannon/ABC. In the late 1990s, there were growing concerns about the impact of out-of-town leisure and retail developments. As a result, while the Odeon and ABC had seen "the arrival in 1989 of National Amusements' edge-of-town Showcase complex," it was the Cornerhouse, a large leisure complex built as part of the new concern with city center development, that was the "straw [that broke] the camel's back" (*NEP*, Weekend, January 27, 2001).

However, no other city in the East Midlands region fared in this way. Nottingham has long established itself as the center of consumption, leisure, and culture within the area, and it has therefore been able to sustain a more diverse film culture than other towns. In Derby, for example, the presence of a multiplex resulted in the removal of all cinemas from the town center with the exception of a small regional film theater, the Metro, while Leicester has two multiplexes, an art house cinema, and two cinemas that specialize in Asian films, one of which is in the town center. Neither was able to sustain a cinema like the Odeon or the Cannon/ABC. Nonetheless, whatever the prevailing tendencies elsewhere, the Showcase only added to the number of screens in Nottingham, although many respondents saw the choice provided by the multiplex as no "real" choice, but only a homogeneous and standardized fare. For these respondents, a more meaningful degree of choice was provided by the supposedly "non-commercial" cinemas.[7]

Conclusion

Cultural distinction ranks not only films, but also the places within which they are consumed.[8] As a result, the multiplex itself has been consumed differently by different social groups, due to the ways in which it has been associated with specific types of cultural consumption. Most obviously, the multiplex frequently figures as a place of mass and undifferentiated consumption as opposed to the art cinema, which figures as a place of diversity and distinction (Jancovich *et al.* forthcoming). Ironically, while both the multiplex and the blockbuster are associated with mass consumption, they are also supposed, as we have already seen, to cater only for specific audiences. Here it is often youth that figures as the key concern and one of the repeated assumptions is that these cinemas and the blockbusting films that they show are aimed at a juvenile audience. However, even here quite incompatible notions of "the juvenile audience" are in operation. On the one hand this audience is associated with the teenager, and on the other it is associated with young children. It is therefore important that we distinguish between different types of multiplex blockbusters: the Disney film aimed at children; the action movie aimed at teenagers; the Spielberg or Lucas feature aimed at a variety of audiences. In other words, while those opposed to the multiplex see it as a place of undifferentiated consumption, the audiences that identify with the place can be seen as far more diverse and differentiated, and may even be fractured and opposed to one another. For example, teenage audiences are often keen to distinguish themselves from the audiences for "children's films," while even teenage audiences are not homogenous but are often deeply combative (Jancovich 2000 and 2002). In other words, it is not that the multiplex audience so often characterized as the blockbuster's audience is an undifferentiated mass, but rather that this is how others have perceived it. As Raymond Williams put it: "There are in fact no masses; there are only ways of seeing people as masses" (Williams 1961: 289).

Notes

1 This chapter is based on a local study of cinemagoing in Nottingham, *Film Consumption and the City: A Historical Case Study in the City of Nottingham*, which was funded by a major research grant from the Arts and Humanities Research Board. The project was directed by Dr Mark Jancovich, and included Lucy Faire, who did most of the archival research, and researchers employed to collect oral histories of cinemagoing.

2 These references are to questionnaires and interviews collected in the Institute of Film Studies at the University of Nottingham. They were conducted by Kate Egan, Rhianydd Murray, and Richard Stevens.

3 One respondent (Stefan, 25, unemployed teacher) even claims that it is a place for gangs and couples!
4 One respondent said that she had taken her grandson to the Showcase on a number of occasions and that she felt that the cinema was much better when you went there with young people (Something Different for Women Club, age range 60 to 75).
5 Another elderly woman thought that the Showcase was marvelous and said that she went there all the time with her son (Clifton Women's Wednesday Club, age range from 60 to 80). Another respondent, who also went to the cinema regularly with her son, also viewed the Showcase positively and goes there every Monday night with a friend (Judith, 39, probation officer).
6 In a similar way, Marc Auge (1995) discusses a range of "placeless" places or "nonplaces," such as airports, motorway service stations, and the like.
7 A similar argument is made by Hanson (2000), as demonstrated by the title of his essay "Spoilt for Choice?"
8 Similar findings have also been made by Janna Jones (2001).

References

Auge, Marc (1995) *Non-Places*, London: Verso.

Barker, Martin, and Brooks, Kate (1998) *Knowing Audiences: Judge Dread, Its Friends, Fans and Foes*, Luton: University of Luton Press.

EMRMAP (East Midlands Region Media Agencies Partnership) (2001) *Draft Business Plan*, February.

Franklin, Ashley (1996) *A Cinema Near You: 100 Years of Going to the Pictures in Derbyshire*, Derby: Breedon.

Gomery, Douglas (1992) *Shared Pleasures: A History of Movie Presentation in the United States*, London: British Film Institute.

Gray, Richard (1996) *Cinemas in Britain: One Hundred Years of Cinema Architecture*, London: Lund Humphries.

Hannigan, John (1998) *Fantasy City: Pleasure and Profit in the Postmodern Metropolis*, London: Routledge.

Hanson, Stuart (2000) "Spoilt for Choice? Multiplexes in the 90s," in Robert Murphy (ed.), *British Cinema of the 90s*, London: British Film Institute: 48–59.

Harvey, David (1991) "The Urban Face of Capitalism," in J. F. Hunt (ed.), *Our Changing Cities*, Baltimore: Johns Hopkins University Press.

Hubbard, Phil (forthcoming) "Going Out (of Town): the New Geographies of British Cinema."

Jancovich, Mark (2000) "A Real Shocker: Authenticity, Genre and the Struggle for Cultural Distinctions," *Continuum*, 14, 1: 23–35.

—— (2002) "Cult Fictions: Cult Movies, Subcultural Capital and the Production of Cultural Distinctions," *Cultural Studies*, 16, 2: 306–22.

Jancovich, Mark and Faire, Lucy, with Stubbings, Sarah (forthcoming) *The Place of the Audience: Cultural Geographies of Film Consumption*, London: British Film Institute.

Jones, Janna (2001) "Finding a Place at the Downtown Picture Palace: The Tampa Theatre, Florida," in Mark Shiel and Tony Fitzmaurice (eds), *Cinema and the City: Film and Urban Societies in a Global Context*, Oxford: Blackwell: 122–33.

Lyons, James (n.d.) "Food Consumption and the Cinema," unpublished manuscript.

Miller, Daniel, Jackson, Peter, Thrift, Nigel, Holbrook, Beverley, and Rowlands, Michael (1998) *Shopping, Place and Identity*, London: Routledge.

Morley, David, and Robins, Kevin (1995) *Spaces of Identity: Global Media, Electronic Landscapes and Cultural Boundaries*, London: Routledge.

Paul, William (1994) "The K-Mart Audience at the Mall Movies," *Film History*, 6: 487–501.

Schatz, Thomas (1993) "The New Hollywood," in Jim Collins, Hilary Radner, and Ava Preacher Collins (eds), *Film Theory Goes to the Movies*, New York and London: Routledge: 8–36 [reprinted in this volume].

Spigel, Lynn (1995) "From the Dark Ages to the Golden Age: Women's Memories and Television Reruns," *Screen*, 36, 1: 16–33.

Webster, Duncan (1988) *Looka Yonder!: The Imaginary America of Populist Culture*, London: Comedia.

Williams, Raymond (1961) *Culture and Society 1780–1950*, London: Penguin.

13

NEITHER ONE THING NOR THE OTHER

Blockbusters at film festivals

Julian Stringer

Judging from the paucity of critical writing on the subject, the received wisdom concerning the relationship between blockbusters and international film festivals is that there is no story to tell – the former evidently avoid the latter, just as the latter shun the former. On the one hand, Hollywood is perceived to be wary of the potential damage a film festival screening can bring, especially if it involves a premiere. As Justin Wyatt and Katherine Vlesmas write of *Titanic*'s (1997) world debut at the Tokyo International Film Festival on November 1, 1997: "Scheduling a premiere overseas prior to a domestic release date was a calculated gamble few studios attempted for a big-budget film: a negative reception could substantially harm the outcome of a North American opening" (Wyatt and Vlesmas 1999: 38). Even when a premiere is not involved, however, Hollywood still has much to lose from sending its biggest movies to the world's major festivals. Because the overseas reception of US blockbusters can indeed never be guaranteed – and because everybody is going to get to hear about the latest Hollywood blockbusters sooner or later anyway – why take the risk?

On the other hand, the festival circuit itself is widely assumed to be hostile to Hollywood in general, and blockbusters in particular. Festivals have become, in the words of Piers Handling of the Toronto Film Festival, an "alternative distribution network" (quoted in Turan 2002: 8) – and that means an alternative to Hollywood. It has been estimated that as many as 70 percent of the films shown at festivals today never find theatrical distributors outside their countries of production. Given such figures, Hollywood is often claimed to be the absolute antithesis of what international film festivals are meant to be all about – namely, offering the rest of the world a chance, exhibiting and evaluating films produced outside the commercial US "mainstream." Many festivals refuse to allow Hollywood blockbusters anywhere near their front door, sensing that, with these kinds of movies already enjoying a distinct market advantage, it would be even more unfair to have them monopolize festival screens as well. Furthermore, the elite or rarefied atmosphere of major competitive events such as those at Berlin, Cannes, and Venice attaches highbrow associations to many of the non-US (frequently so-called auteur) films unspooled at such locations. In this context, the thought of corporate blockbusters collecting festival prizes is enough to make some commentators gag with disgust.

Against such received wisdom, the simple point should be made that the US "mainstream" is very frequently well represented at major international film festivals. More specifically, Hollywood blockbusters have on occasion played a key role in publicizing and promoting such events. Certainly, blockbusting films from the US have sometimes been the recipients of major festival prizes, including the Palme d'Or at Cannes (*Apocalypse Now*, 1979) the Golden Bear for Best Actor at Berlin (Denzel Washington, *Malcolm X*, 1993), and the Golden Bear for Best Actress at Berlin (Juliette Binoche, *The English Patient*, 1997). Summing up the feelings of excitement that may surround the giving of such prestigious awards, Roger Ebert reports in *Two Weeks in the Midday Sun: A Cannes Notebook*: "My peak experiences with Cannes audiences were at the world premieres of Coppola's *Apocalypse Now* and Spielberg's *E.T.* [1982], and in both cases the audiences broke out into tumultuous applause at the end, cheering the directors with an enthusaism usually reserved for opera stars" (Ebert 1987: 93).

Indeed, the Hollywood majors have proved time and again at Cannes and elsewhere that they are more than up to the task of engineering a positive reception (from some quarters at least) for their high-profile event movies. (For further discussion around this subject, see chapter 6 of Beauchamp and Behar 1992: 202–34 ["The Studios and America's Presence in Cannes"].) Positively, blockbusters promise to add an extra level of glitz to what are already sparklingly decadent occasions. This is illustrated in the words of Christian Le Haemonet, French advertising co-ordinator for *Superman – The Movie* (1978), concerning the film's Cannes publicity jaunt: "our plans are the most spectacular. We've hired eight planes with promotional banners, we've rented space for twenty very big posters for the walls of the Carlton Hotel and we've booked between seventy to eighty pages of advertising in the trade papers" (quoted in Petrou 1978: 93).

More negatively, there is always the possibility that such promotional stunts will backfire in full view of the global media spotlight. Publicist Gordon Arnell articulates this dilemma with a further example from the Cannes presentation of *Superman – The Movie*:

> "Overkill can be a real problem," Arnell observed before departing for the Festival, "especially with a very commercial property. The publicity, I mean. 'Love Story' [1970] worked. '[The Great] Gatsby' [1974] and '[King] Kong [1976]' didn't . . . A lot of films have blown out early and

> lived to regret it. Others try to hide their light under a bushel, and then they never really emerge. It's very difficult to find the happy medium."
>
> (quoted in Petrou 1978: 94)

Hollywood blockbusters have on occasion undergone a metamorphosis at festivals, transforming into veritable hate figures. In his account of the 1993 annual event in the south of France, Stephen Walker reports that in this particular festival town there were "Film posters on every hoarding, every building, every wall. *Armaggedon*. *Godzilla*. Bruce Willis. Hugh Grant" (Walker 1999: 153). Operating on a subterranean level far beneath such expensive façades, however, aspiring filmmaker Mike Hakata attempted to sell his £20,000 movie *Two Bad Mice* by chalking the catchy tagline of his publicity campaign on every pavement and street corner: "Fuck *Godzilla*" (ibid.: 188).

It is not the case, then, that blockbusters do not play at film festivals. However, it is the case that the very presence of Hollywood event movies at international jamborees such as Cannes can breed a sense of unease among all concerned. When blockbusters make it to festivals, how should they be positioned? To stick for a moment with the jewel in the crown of festival culture, Cannes is both a famous competitive event and a notoriously exploitative commercial film market. High-profile Hollywood hits thus have an ambivalent status in relation to these two extremes. While the public exhibition of titles such as *The Fifth Element* (1998), *Basic Instinct* (opening-night attraction at the 1992 event), and *E.T.: The Extra-Terrestrial* (premiered at Cannes in 1982) promotes the glamor of the Palme d'Or, Hollywood's annual presence in the south of France also serves as a constant reminder of the wheeling and dealing that drives the huge Marché du Film. As such, the cultural status of Hollywood blockbusters often falls between these two clusters of activity, the former signifying cultural distinction, the latter a naked ambition to make as much money as possible. In short, blockbusters at Cannes are too glamorous to be lumped in with the traffic in lowbrow product that is the market, but not highbrow enough to constitute "international art cinema" in the competition. This situation partly explains why many news reports from Cannes disavow Hollywood movies by fixating on them while simultaneously managing to imply they are something of an embarrassment.

This sense that blockbusters oscillate at festivals between representing the rare and the special ("an enthusiasm usually reserved for opera stars") and the pitifully opportunistic ("Fuck *Godzilla*") manifests itself in other ways as well. On those occasions when they are shown at overseas events, Hollywood blockbusters sometimes share center stage with "big" films produced by other countries. In such instances, the process of negotiating the cultural status of such texts becomes caught up with the issue of the unequal power relations which exist between various film-producing regions of the world. In addition, they become caught up with broader questions concerning the cross-cultural circulation and international translation of popular movies.

As a way of approaching these twin subjects, it is helpful to consider specific examples. Two of the most widely reported films at Cannes in 2002 were spectacular blockbusters. First, the Hollywood megamovie *Star Wars: Episode II – Attack of the Clones* (2002) was sent by director George Lucas for two out-of-competition screenings on May 16 – the same day the film was due to be released across the United States. Second, one of the most expensive Asian movies ever made, *Suriyothai* (2002), was also unveiled for the edification of festival spectators. The exhibition at Cannes of this box-office smash from Thailand was characterized by the *Taipei Times* through the choice of the following highly symbolic language: "Blockbuster Readied for Global Audiences" ("Blockbuster" 2002).

Taking the Hollywood production first, the reason why Lucas chose to show the latest *Star Wars* at the world's most famous film festival is unclear. For a start, it is not as if anyone needs to work very hard to secure global distribution for the latest instalment of this particular blockbusting franchise. Moreover, with *Attack of the Clones* being released in the US on the very same day, the tone of the newspaper reviews and word-of-mouth reports generated as a result of the Cannes screenings would be largely irrelevant – millions would have flocked to see the film at the North American box office already. It is therefore likely that other factors lay behind the decision. Perhaps Lucas wanted to ensure the best possible showcase for the film's enhanced production values and sound designs, or maybe he desired to attract an aura of prestige and worthiness for his newest space adventure.

Whatever the truth concerning *Stars Wars II*, *Suriyothai* is another matter entirely. This historical epic, which reputedly earned a record 600 million baht (US$13.6 million) during its domestic release (compared with US$4.7 million for *Titanic*), needed a festival platform if it was to "breakthrough" internationally. The lessons that other Asian industries could learn from its example were spelled out very clearly in one article published in the Philippines, which observed of the Thai blockbuster's much-anticipated global success:

> The film's domestic gross in dollars translates into . . . a huge fortune by local standards.
>
> And the film's global earnings should push that gross to more than P1B, in Philippine's peso terms. That's much, much more than the P100M that only a few super-blockbusters have made in these parts. And remember, we're talking of only one film.
>
> Sure, *Suriyothai* cost an arm and a leg to produce, but its gross receipts to date have made the huge expenses worth it. And we aren't even factoring in the non-financial benefits of the film's success in terms of prestige, cultural enhancement, national pride and tourism prospects.

> Second lesson to be learned: think global. The Thai film's domestic success may be duplicated or even surpassed by its international release, and it could open doors abroad for other quality Thai productions, which have thus far had limited success only on the festival and art-house circuits.
>
> ("Focus on Asian films" 2002)

In order to succeed internationally, non-US blockbusters – of the "quality" variety, to be sure – have to "open doors abroad," and to do this it is necessary for them to utilize the alternative distribution network that the globalized festival circuit represents. By contrast, if Hollywood blockbusters want to utilize overseas festivals for purposes of enhanced prestige or commercial gain, they need to be sure of the precise opposite – that doors will not be closed in their face.

Another way of thinking about the relative difference between the international visibility and cultural status of Hollywood and non-Hollywood blockbusters is provided by Colin Hoskins, Stuart McFadyen, and Adam Finn in their *Global Television and Film: An Introduction to the Economics of the Business*. They suggest that what they term a "cultural discount" arises for films traded internationally "because viewers in importing markets generally find it difficult to identify with the way of life, values, history, institutions, myths, and physical environment depicted" (1997: 4). They continue:

> A particular television programme, film, or video rooted in one culture, and thus attractive in the home market where viewers share a common knowledge and way of life, will have a diminished appeal elsewhere, as viewers find it difficult to identify with the style, values, beliefs, history, myths, institutions, physical environment, and behavioural patterns. If the programme or film is produced in another language, its appeal will be reduced by the need to employ dubbing or subtitling. Even if the language is the same, accents or idioms may still cause problems.
>
> (ibid.: 32)

On these terms, a Thai blockbuster such as *Suriyothai* carries a relatively high cultural discount in the global marketplace. While it may well enjoy the status of a megahit in its home country, it becomes an unknown quantity once exported elsewhere. The film needs to be explained, or translated, to audiences in countries such as France or the US, where people are on the whole utterly unfamiliar with Thai movies. In order for the film to achieve a modicum of international success, then, *Suriyothai* needs to be positioned in ways that compensate for its high cultural discount. Throughout this process, the film's identity as a "quality" title may or may not be retained.

Of course, exactly the reverse is true for *Star Wars II: Attack of the Clones*. There is no need for any audience in the world to have this film "translated" or explained to them. Indeed, no matter where they are watched, Hollywood blockbusters of this ilk carry the lowest of all cultural discounts. When distributed in overseas markets – at festivals or through other exhibition windows – event movies produced in the US do not need to be indigenized in the same way, or to the same extent, as films produced by other nations. After all, as Joseph D. Phillips reminds us: "US films are the most widely distributed throughout the world . . . the distribution organizations that the major US film companies established to market their product throughout the world are the most extensive and the most effective in the world" (Phillips 1982: 334).

Furthermore, in the specific case of *Star Wars II: Attack of the Clones*, George Lucas benefited from all the competitive advantage that Hollywood supplies. The elements that enabled his film to travel so successfully include its status as a much-anticipated blockbuster; its well-established brand identity as "the new *Star Wars*"; its bigness, relative expensive, and spectacular attractions; the presence of internationally known stars; a presold property (the intertexts of the previous and future titles in the franchise); a famed director renowned as a visual auteur; a simple story that everyone can understand; marketing and merchandizing potential; and the feeling that in general this is a "monumental" film on every level imaginable.

Even though *Suriyothai* and *Attack of the Clones* both played at the Cannes festival in May 2002, then, they did so on a less than equal footing. Their very presence at this most glamorous of all exhibition sites might be viewed in one or other of two different ways. First, that in each case a rare and special blockbuster was coming to town, but that one is very well known and the other is largely unknown. Second, that it is pitiful to see that not just the Americans, but now even the Thais, are cynically dragging a stellar cultural event through the mud by cashing in on the blockbuster's commercial glamor and widespread popularity. Yet despite these similarities, one film remains a "quality" production that requires a lot of explanation if it is to be sold abroad, the other a "typical" product that needs no introduction or strenuous marketing pitch. At the time of writing, *Attack of the Clones* is predictably enough a global megasuccess. It is too early to tell whether or not *Suriyothai* will become any kind of "hit" in the West.

Before moving beyond this specific example, however, it is interesting to note the kinds of activities that have already worked to lower this particular Asian film's already high cultural discount. *Guardian Unlimited* reported two months before the Cannes screening that no less a global luminary than HRH Prince Charles himself had made a request to watch the film: "Perhaps looking for hints to resolve his own family's tribulations, the Prince of Wales has asked to see a Thai film blockbuster rich in royal intrigue, adultery and a queen's sacrifice to save her husband's life" (Aglionby 2002). In addition, it has been widely reported that US blockbuster auteur, Francis Ford Coppola, helped *Suriyothai* director, Chatri Chalerm Yukol, re-edit the film for its Cannes screening, thus presumably overcoming a little more the diminished appeal Thai films are supposed to hold for Western audiences.

In sum, the critical and commercial reception that event movies from the US and elsewhere can expect to receive at international film festivals is highly unpredictable. Such films might be celebrated with garlands of flowers, or told in no uncertain terms to go forth and multiply. However, analysis of recent programming initiatives at one particular event – the London Film Festival – suggests that at the present time there is one kind of movie able both to retain an aura of prestige and rarity and to achieve impressive box-office returns: the "old" Hollywood blockbuster.

Before illustrating this particular argument, it is first necessary briefly to consider some of the specific ways in which contemporary US blockbusters have been exhibited at the London event. What is noticeable about the screening of such films is that no effort has been made to differentiate them from "average" movies; furthermore, no effort has been made to label or promote them as blockbusters. For example, the unspooling of *Die Hard* (1988) at the 1988 London Film Festival was presented in terms which emphasized the film's artistry and authorship. Mention was made of director John McTiernan, the fact that while the film may be an "action thriller" it is nevertheless a "stylish" one, and the aesthetic effects achieved by use of widescreen and a "high-tech building" location (Whitaker 1988: 82). Furthermore, the screening of *Back to the Future* (1985) in 1985 was presented via the republication of a capsule review from *Time* which emphasized such purely thematic details as the film's moments of delightful comedy, the choice of the 1950s as the setting for the action, and the supposed universality of its subject matter: "What movie-goer of any age could resist a sprightly romantic comedy on the Oedipal dilemma?" (Corliss 1985: 57).

Similarly, *Back to the Future II* was described in 1989 as both an auteur and a star vehicle (Robert Zemeckis and Michael J. Fox, respectively), and was presented through "a gala celebrity screening of a film hot off the production lot and only opening in the States a few days before our event" (Whitaker 1989: 5). Finally, *Monsters, Inc.* was shown in 2001 as a "hilariously original" "animated fantasy," with London announcing itself proud to be "the hosts of the European premiere of *Monsters, Inc.* and to welcome its Pixar creators to the Festival" (Wooton 2001a: 10). Once again, it is noticeable that use of the word "blockbuster" is studiously avoided in all of these instances. It is as if the very presence of the term might dissipate the glamor that habitually accrues around festivals such as these.

Put differently, because these contemporary US blockbusters carry a low cultural discount for UK audiences they do not need to be explained or translated. It is enough simply to state why interested parties should pay to watch them at the festival, together with the date, the time, and the venue where they may do so. And further research tends to suggest that this phenomenon is not unique to London. For example, the 1992 Tokyo International Film Festival's description of *Lethal Weapon 3* (1992) is a model of understatement and economy: "Everyone should be fully excited at the explosion at the sky scraper, the wild car chase, and the big fire in which a vacant building gets wholly inflamed. What's more, the two heroes joined by Joe Pesci make things funny all through this film" ("*Lethal Weapon 3*" 1992: 105). Once again, actually naming *Lethal Weapon 3* as a "blockbuster" (or Japanese equivalent?) might potentially compromise the cultural status of the whole festival. Therefore, there is no need to remind readers of the fact that a blockbuster is indeed what this particular film is.

This situation is reversed at London in the case of non-contemporary blockbusters, or those titles produced during the heyday of the Hollywood studio era. Many of these "old" films have been out of circulation for years, and they are now being revived in ways that inscribe elite attractions for attentive festival audiences. (For a more general discussion of this subject, see Stringer forthcoming.) The curious fact here is that old Hollywood blockbusters appear to have more in common with non-US blockbusters than they do with contemporary Hollywood event movies. Old blockbusters also carry a relatively high cultural discount; dated and consequently culturally unfamiliar, they resemble foreign titles in that they too need to be explained and "translated" for modern audiences.

A key way in which this has been done at the London Film Festival is by replicating the movies' original blockbusting attractions. Most obviously, in the early 1980s London established an annual series of Thames Silents, or special events which showcased the public exhibition of classic silent movies prior to their subsequent broadcasts on Thames Television. Throughout the decade, pride of place was reserved for these choice screenings, both in the festival's published programs and in its publicity campaigns more generally. The Thames revivals worked to promote and sell old blockbuster attractions as if they were new prestige pleasures.

Consider in this respect the fact that the revival in 1984 of *The Thief of Bagdad* (1924) was mounted as akin to a roadshow presentation of a silent superspecial, with an orchestral score "specially composed by Carl Davis who will conduct the Philharmonia Orchestra at each performance," and variable ticket prices (£5, £7, £10) "available only from the Dominion, Tottenham Court Road, London W1, until the period November 9–29 when a limited selection will be on sale at the NFT Box Office" (Brownlow 1984: 78). This arrangement contrasts with, say, the screening at the same event of the contemporary box-office hit *Gremlins* (1984), which was shown (like many other titles) at the National Film Theatre, at 2.30 in the afternoon, and for uniform ticket prices (£3.25).

Other films were similarly presented in ways which worked both to lower their potentially quite high cultural discounts and to promote an aura of exclusivity and rarity. *The Big Parade* (1925) was revived in 1985 as "an unprecedented success – it

Figure 13.1 Anna May Wong and Douglas Fairbanks senior in *The Thief of Bagdad* (1924), one of the Thames Silent Classics showcased at the London Film Festival. The Kobal Collection/United Artists.

made more money than any other M-G-M silent, and catapulted King Vidor and John Gilbert to the heights" (Brownlow 1985: 41). *Intolerance* (1916) was recirculated in 1988 as "a remarkable experience . . . No one has risked approaching Griffith's lunatic heights of courage. The walls of Babylon are built nearly a hundred feet high, solidly enough for chariots to run along the top. Despite the thousands of extras and seething battles, the intimate moments are as remarkable as anything in silent cinema" (Brownlow and Gill 1988: 8). In addition, *Sign of the Cross* (1932) was presented in 1989 in "a new print produced from [Cecil B.] DeMille's personal copy of the original 124 minute road show version with intermission released in 1932 . . . Because of the Depression, Paramount limited DeMille to a strict budget of only

£650,000 for what he had envisioned as a super production. He coped brilliantly, planning every shot in advance so that not one penny more was spent than appeared on screen" (Hopkins 1989: 104). Finally, *Ben-Hur* (1925) was presented in 1987 as a spectacular event in need of interpretation for a contemporary audience:

> Surprising as it sounds, there is film-making in *Ben-Hur* almost as impressive as in *Battleship Potemkin* [USSR, 1925], made the same year. Two of the finest action sequences ever put on celluloid – the sea battle and the chariot race – still look magnificent. Add to that the attraction of ten short Technicolor sequences, the story of a Jew revenging himself against the Roman Empire, and some astounding special effects and you will overlook the mannered acting and the occasional langueur. The making of the film helped to break the Goldwyn company and nearly broke MGM. It was shot in Italy and largely re-shot in Culver City. It cost four million dollars – twice as much as any film before it.
>
> (Brownlow and Gill 1987: 70)

As with the other films unspooled during the course of the 1980s Thames Silents series, *Ben-Hur* was exhibited in elite and prestigious circumstances – not just at the more exclusive and rarefied London Palladium, with ticket prices at £5, £8, £10.50, and £13, but also through its first performance on November 25, 1987, as a "Royal Charity Gala in the presence of HRH Princess Alexandra in aid of the British Deaf Association . . . For the Charity first night optional donations of £5.00, £7.00, £14.50 and £17.00 make a total seat price of £10.00, £15.00, £25.00 and £30.00" (ibid.).

It is important to point out that there also appears to have been a shift in the most recent years toward the revival at the London festival of select New Hollywood blockbusters, signalling that the process of recirculating US event movies has a future life at festivals. Both *Doctor Zhivago* (1965) and *The Sound of Music* (1965) were screened in 1995. More symptomatically, perhaps, *Funny Girl* (1968) was presented at the 2001 festival through a catalog description which refused to shrink from the task of naming and claiming this particular film as not only a blockbuster, but also an object of rare value:

> Whatever the cinema's new technology may portend, a big film needs a big screen – and none more so than this welcome reminder of the Hollywood blockbuster musical of the 60s, impeccably and painstakingly restored by Grover Crisp for Columbia Pictures to William Wyler's original Cinemascope, six-track stereo, road-show format, using Technicolor's new dye transfer printing process.
>
> (Jeavons 2001: 63)

In addition, Francis Ford Coppola's new, much expanded (by one hour) version of his 1979 Vietnam War epic *Apocalypse Now*, retitled *Apocalypse Now Redux*, was screened at the 2001 London Film Festival. On original release, this title "was regarded as a fabulous but flawed film that received international acclaim and the Palme d'Or at Cannes but did not deliver the box office or kudos back home in America." Now, with the festival "proud to present the British premiere of *Apocalypse Now Redux* in all its cinematic glory" (Wooton 2001b: 11), London confirms once again that today's globalized festival circuit plays a significant role in the international previewing of blockbusters from old and contemporary Hollywood alike.

What an examination of festival catalogs from London also shows, however, is that non-US "old" blockbusters are much less likely to receive special treatment. For example, by the time the Italian silent spectacular *Cabiria* (1914) was revived at the 1997 event, it was merely one among many of the numerous "Treasures from the Archive" exhibited in the series of that name. Despite the fact that the film's "scale, spectacle, colossal sets and special effects (by Segundo de Chomon) indelibly influenced both Griffith and DeMille – probably its budget too: it was the first production to cost over a million dollars" (Jeavons 1997: 57), *Cabiria* was not distinguished in any discernible way through the kinds of exclusive exhibition arrangements – performances by the Philharmonia Orchestra, variable ticket prices, Royal Charity Galas, etc. – bestowed upon the revival of silent Hollywood's greatest hits.

What conclusions may be drawn from all this? It has already been suggested that, in negotiating the cultural status of event movies, film festivals translate blockbusters in diverse kinds of ways. On the one hand, they can foreground the exhibition of prestige attractions as a mark of quality and rarity. On the other hand, they also hide megahits under a bushel, judging that the economic advantage of screening blockbusters needs to be tempered with awareness of the potential damage they may bring the reputation of any individual event. Most significantly, the successful revival of old Hollywood blockbusters suggests that, if the past is a foreign country, it is a wholly acceptable one – at least where American movies are concerned. However, past and present blockbusters produced outside the US remain for some film festivals merely foreign.

References

Aglionby, John (2002) "Prince Takes Interest in Thailand's Royal Intrigue," *Guardian Unlimited*, online: www.guardian.co.uk/monarchy/story/0,2763,660036,00. html, posted March 1, 2002.

Beauchamp, Cari, and Behar, Henri (1992) *Hollywood on the Riviera: The Inside Story of the Cannes Film Festival*, New York: William Morrow & Company.

"Blockbuster Readied for Global Audience," *Taipei Times*, online: http://taipeitimes.com/news/2002/03/11/story/0000127285, posted March 11, 2002.

Brownlow, Kevin (1984) "*The Thief of Bagdad*," 28th London Film Festival, program brochure: 78.

—— (1985) "*The Big Parade*," 29th London Film Festival, program brochure: 41.

Brownlow, Kevin, and Gill, David (1987) "*Ben-Hur*," 31st London Film Festival, program brochure: 70.

—— (1988) "*Intolerance*," 32nd London Film Festival, program brochure: 8.

Corliss, Richard (1985) "*Back to the Future*," 29th London Film Festival, program brochure: 57 [originally published in *Time*].

Ebert, Roger (1987) *Two Weeks in the Midday Sun: A Cannes Notebook*, Kansas City: Andrew & McMeel.

"Focus on Asian films," INQ7.net, online: www.inq7.net/ent/2002/apr/08/ent_2–1.htm, posted April 8, 2002.

Hopkins, Charles (1989) "*Sign of the Cross*," 33rd London Film Festival, program brochure: 104.

Hoskins, Colin, McFadyen, Stuart, and Finn, Adam (1997) *Global Television and Film: An Introduction to the Economics of the Business*, Oxford: Clarendon Press.

Jeavons, Clyde (1997) "*Cabiria*," 41st London Film Festival, program brochure: 57.

—— (2001) "*Funny Girl*," 45th Regus London Film Festival, program brochure: 63.

"*Lethal Weapon 3*," 1992 Tokyo International Film Festival, program brochure: 105.

Petrou, David Michael (1978) *The Making of Superman the Movie*, London: Universal Books.

Phillips, Joseph D. (1982) "Film Conglomerate Blockbusters: International Appeal and Product Homogenization," in Gorham Kindem (ed.), *The American Movie Industry: The Business of Motion Pictures*, Carbondale: Southern Illinois University Press: 325–35.

Stringer, Julian (forthcoming) "Raiding the Archive: Film Festivals and the Revival of Classic Hollywood," in Paul Grainge (ed.), *Memory and Popular Film*, Manchester: Manchester University Press.

Turan, Kenneth (2002) *Sundance to Saravejo: Film Festivals and the World They Made*, Berkeley: University of California Press.

Walker, Stephen (1999) *King of Cannes: A Journey into the Underbelly of the Movies*, London: William Heinemann.

Whitaker, Sheila (1988) "*Die Hard*," 32nd London Film Festival, program brochure: 82.

—— (1989) "*Back to the Future II*," 33rd London Film Festival, program brochure: 5.

Wooton, Adrian (2001a) "*Monsters Inc.*," 45th Regus London Film Festival, program brochure: 10.

—— (2001b) "*Apocalypse Now Redux*," 45th Regus London Film Festival, program brochure: 11.

Wyatt, Justin, and Vlesmas, Katherine (1999) "The Drama of Recoupment: On the Mass Media Negotiation of *Titanic*," in Gaylyn Studlar and Kevin S. Sandler (eds), *Titanic: Anatomy of a Blockbuster*, New Brunswick, NJ: Rutgers University Press: 29–45.

Part IV

THE BLOCKBUSTER IN THE INTERNATIONAL FRAME

14

"WHAT'S BIG ABOUT THE BIG FILM?"

"De-Westernizing" the blockbuster in Korea and China

Chris Berry

> These kinds of big productions and scenes [in American blockbusters] rely on strong economic backing; money can be seen as the invisible hand controlling the film's production and, in the last instance, its director.
>
> (Wang 1997: 81)

> At one time, I tried to catch up with Hollywood movies, but it was useless. So, I decided to produce movies that appeal to Koreans' native sentiments.
>
> Park Chan-wook, director of *Joint Security Area* (Rhee 2001)

This essay's title is as borrowed and translated as its object of study. "What's Big About the Big Film?" ("*Dapian Shenme Da?*") is a short article by filmmaker and critic Zheng Dongtian (1998). In China today, "*dapian*" or "big film" most frequently appears coupled with "*Meiguo*" or "America" in the phrase "the American big film." It is the closest Chinese equivalent to "blockbuster," and is used in Chinese-language discussions of Hollywood blockbusters. "De-Westernizing" is borrowed from an anthology called *De-Westernizing Media Studies* (Curran and Park 2000). In both the People's Republic of China and the Republic of Korea, the idea of the "blockbuster" has been appropriated into local critical discourse, to refer not only to American blockbusters but also to local productions considered blockbusters. Among South Korean *beul-lok-beo-seu-teo* ("blockbusters"), *Joint Security Area* was the most successful film in Korean cinema history at the time of its 2000 release. Yet the words above of director Park emphasize difference from Hollywood blockbusters at least as much as similarity. In borrowing the idea and practice of the blockbuster and adapting them to local circumstances, at the very moment of perceiving a local "lack" Park simultaneously de-Westernizes it.

This chapter examines both the critical concepts and industry practices surrounding Chinese and Korean blockbusters to argue that the blockbuster is no longer American owned. The idea may be borrowed and translated, but this should not be understood in terms of the original and the copy, where divergence from the original marks failure of authenticity. Instead, in the postcolonial politics and globalized economics of blockbusters, borrowing and translation are only the first step on the road toward agency and creativity. In "Disjuncture and Difference in the Global Cultural Economy," Arjun Appadurai (1996) points out that the dominant analysis of globalization established by Marxist scholars has been that it Americanizes and promotes homogenization. In contrast, Appadurai argues that it heterogenizes. Globalization in his view is not a single process, but a multiplicity of localized events as different cultures are brought into contact. In a similar vein, Lydia Liu (1995) writes of "translingual practice" in these moments of local contact, with translation understood as an active process whereby the foreign is made sense of through the local context of its appropriation.

Such scholarship encourages reorientation of the existing America-centric examination of blockbusters, based on the understanding that blockbusters today are global and plural. Just as modernity and capitalism are no longer seen as Western or singular but as global and plural, so film studies as a discipline needs to drop its Eurocentric blinkers if it wishes really to understand the phenomena it purports to theorize, including that most Western of film forms, the blockbuster. The comparative examination of Chinese and Korean blockbusters in this essay focuses on both critical discourses and filmmaking practices. In both cases, but in different ways, the blockbuster is made sense of and practiced according to local cultural and filmmaking contexts. Steve Neale's essay in this volume on the multiple and contingent meanings of the blockbuster in the United States reveals that pluralizing the blockbuster begins in America itself. But this chapter reveals that the active participation of Chinese and Korean critics and filmmakers in that process makes a difference and constitutes "de-Westernization" as well as pluralization. However, the chapter concludes by noting the impossibility of determining whether this participation constitutes challenge or capitulation, and the importance of grasping de-Westernization within globalization as a fundamentally ambivalent practice.

In both the People's Republic of China and the Republic of Korea, the rise of blockbuster consciousness is linked to dismantling trade protectionism under intense lobbying from the United States and using levers such as "most favored nation" trading status and access to the World Trade Organization. Within the general tide of increased foreign film imports over the last decade and more, Hollywood blockbuster films have commanded attention by virtue of their exceptional bigness – big budgets, big stars, big effects, big publicity campaigns – which is even more strongly marked against local productions than other Hollywood films. Taking Korea first, two different sets of protectionist mechanisms are concerned. One consists of limits on film imports and has disappeared, and the other of limits on foreign film exhibition, which has survived so far. Until the 1980s, importers could obtain a license to import a foreign film only if they produced Korean films. This tie was dissolved in 1985, with the introduction of a new Motion Picture Law (Ho 1986). As a result, the number of imported titles almost doubled, from twenty-seven in 1985 to fifty in 1986 (Korean Film Commission 2002). On July 1, 1987, the same law was revised to allow foreign companies to produce and distribute films directly in South Korea rather than working through local partners (Lee 1988). Between 1987 and 1988, imported titles leaped from 84 to 175, and by 1990 they took 80 percent of the box office (Korean Film Commission 2002). The term "blockbuster" circulates through articles written at this time.

As the Korean film industry felt the pressure from Hollywood imports in the late 1980s and early 1990s, the screen quota was "the only windbreak" (Park 1991). This quota applies not to import, but to exhibition. Since 1996, 106 days per year must be reserved on each screen for local productions, down from a high of 165. (The law specifies 146 days, but includes circumstances in which 40 more can be opened for foreign films.) According to Trade Minister Han Duck-soo, "There are only eight nations in the world, including Spain, that keep such a screen quota system. And their theaters show home-produced movies for about 50 days a year on the average" (*Korea Herald*, July 7, 2000). The United States began demanding removal of this quota system intensely in bilateral talks in 1998 and 1999 during the run-up to Korea's entry into the World Trade Organization. Initially, the South Korean government responded sympathetically (*Korea Herald*, June 29, 1999). But the threatened removal of screen quotas provoked a strong defense campaign by local filmmakers, during which they undertook such dramatic measures as shaving their heads and hunger strikes (Alford 1999; *Korea Herald*, July 2, 1999). This struggle was recorded by Cho Jai-hong in a 1999 documentary film, *Shoot the Sun by Lyric: The Fight for Screen Quotas in South Korea*, which won attention in countries facing similar struggles, such as Taiwan (Yu 1999). The campaign was successful, although Washington continues to push for abolition.

In the People's Republic, import control was exercised through the centralized command economy system during the Maoist era, and until the mid-1990s all film imports and exports remained a monopoly of the government-owned China Film Export and Import Corporation (*Zhongguo Dianying Shuchu Shuru Gongsi*). Therefore, Hollywood companies could not set up their own distribution and exhibition chains inside China. Furthermore, China Film was permitted only to buy outright the local Chinese rights for any import; it could not set up "box office split" deals acquiring rights in return for returning a percentage of box office to the rights-holder. As I learned when working for the corporation in the mid-1980s, this effectively blocked major Hollywood imports; China Film had to use foreign exchange earned from exports to buy them, and its earnings did not meet Hollywood's high prices. In his study of Hollywood's efforts to enter the Chinese film market, Stanley Rosen (2001) cites a flat figure of between $30,000 and $50,000 paid per film in 1992.

In the mid-1990s, China Film – like many other government agencies – was gradually divested of many monopoly rights. Even the government-owned film production companies have the right to import films bought for a flat fee now. However, since 1995, China Film has had a new monopoly: the exclusive right to do "box office split" (*fenzhang*) deals on up to ten films a year (Wang 1996). These films are routinely referred to in the Chinese press as "the ten big films," or the "American big films," and they dominate the Chinese box office. According to a film bureaucrat cited in Rosen's study (2001), they take 70 percent. Scholars to whom I have spoken off the record suggest 85 percent, but that this is too high for the government to admit to. Although China has a screen quota regulation like South Korea's, it is routinely ignored (Rosen 2001).

Blockbusters are made local in South Korea and China in two main ways. First, Hollywood blockbusters are made sense of in reference to local historical, cinematic and economic circumstances. This then shapes the production of South Korean and Chinese films which are also referred to as "blockbusters" but are different in certain ways from their Hollywood namesakes. The localization of the blockbuster is a contested process within both South Korea and China. However, Chinese responses are colored more by refusal of Hollywood blockbusters, and Korean ones by an effort to produce local versions. These responses continue long and different histories of dealing with Western capitalism. The People's Republic has moved away from the "socialism in one country" associated with Maoism, but in theory the new market economy and increased foreign trade is still subordinated to socialist politics. On the other hand, the Republic of Korea has long pursued export-led engagement with the West, and particularly its major patron and protector, the United States. As will be detailed below, within a growing global hegemony of liberal capitalism, the Korean "tactic" has been more economically successful so far.

First, the local discursive environment in South Korea and China has much in common. The familiar debate between free-trade advocates and those expressing concern for local jobs is found in both countries. Concern for local interests is most commonly voiced, but Hollywood is not totally without local supporters. Even an official of the Korean Ministry of Culture and Tourism, which defended the screen quota against the Ministry of Foreign Affairs and Trade's call for a quick phase-out (Hwang 1999a), stated, "In the long term, the protectionist measure doesn't help enhance the local film industry's competitiveness" (Hwang 1999b). Popular support for this position was also aired on bulletin boards (*Korea Herald*, June 29, 1999). Similar voices are heard in China, for example, in an article that sees conspicuous high technology in Hollywood blockbusters as a wake-up call for the Chinese industry (Zhang and Yang 1997: 70), and in one that explicitly rejects the cultural imperialist argument and states that the "ten big films" will spur Chinese filmmakers and promote diversification (Wang 1997: 82–3).

However, in both South Korea and China, the debate is heavily colored by local memories of colonialism and forced modernization. The "encounter with the West" began in both countries with demands for free access to Korean and Chinese markets that resonate all too easily with Hollywood's demands today. In the Chinese case, this is particularly clear in Xie Jin's 1997 Chinese blockbuster (*dapian*), *The Opium War* (*Yapian Zhanzheng*). The film was made when trade was a high-profile issue again, and its dialog emphasizes the contrast between the rhetorics of free trade and fair trade. Where the British demand removal of trade barriers to peddle narcotics in China, the Qing dynasty government insists on trade according to its laws, designed with the welfare of the Chinese people in mind. Zheng Dongtian's (1998) brief essay on *The Opium War* underlines the analogy, however inexact, with the American forcing open of the Chinese market for the contemporary "opium" of Hollywood entertainment. Hence his conclusion that, after considering the history of the Opium Wars, the word "blockbuster" does not roll off the tongue as lightly as it used to. Rosen's (2001) discussion of the ban on screening American films following NATO bombing of the Chinese embassy in Belgrade in 1999, and negative response to American films with Tibetan themes, contains numerous references to cultural imperialism and the argument that American political motives lie behind Hollywood's economic motives.

In Korea, in addition to concern about imports from South Korea's neocolonial protector, the United States, the other country whose films cause worry is its former

Figure 14.1 Made in China: *The Opium War* (1997).

direct colonizer, Japan. Until recently, Korea had legal blocks on the import of cultural products from Japan, but these have also been dismantled. While the first films imported were not successful in the marketplace, recent imports have done well, leading to fears of "another Japanese invasion," as one article puts it (*Korea Herald*, June 30, 2000). Although Hollywood occupies over half the Korean box office, Japan is the second most important foreign supplier, taking 7.1 percent of box office in 2000 (Kim 2000).

Within this overall trade debate colored by memories of colonization, Hollywood blockbusters constitute a prominent topic in both countries. Perhaps this is not surprising: their bigness makes them noticeable. However, various Chinese and Korean commentators observe that they are not only big, but also big beyond the power of local industries to emulate, however much they might wish to do so.

In Korea, all American blockbusters circulated freely before the American push for the removal of the screen quota, meaning there was no need to explain what blockbusters were when the screen quota debate reignited. But in China, sustained contact with blockbusters began only with the box office split deals in 1995. This is when the first cluster of articles using the term "big film" is to be found, and many of them do explain it, placing great emphasis on budgets (Ni 1998; Li 1987: 17). Many writers also carried out comparisons. "At the moment, a thirty million *reminbi* budget [under US$4 million] counts as a 'big film' in China. Actually, in America that would be a 'little film,'" writes Zhang Baiqing (1998), a point echoed by many others. Zhang notes this represents a tenfold increase on the most expensive 1980s films, that some budgets are even higher, and that the increase has been spurred by a desire to emulate Hollywood blockbusters following their Chinese success. However, Zhang's article is also predicated on the financial impossibility of direct emulation, implying that Chinese blockbusters are necessarily different from American blockbusters. In Korea, competition with Hollywood imports stimulated a doubling of the average budget for Korean films from 1995 to the level in 2000 of US$1.7 million (Pacquet 2001), and for Korean blockbusters from over US$2 million to the US$9.1 million budget reported for the 1999 science-fiction film *Yongary* (*Korea Times*, August 5, 1999). However, even this figure does not change the accuracy of critic Chang Suk-yong's observation about an earlier Korean blockbuster: "its production cost is incomparable to Hollywood blockbusters which spend an average 90 billion won ($74 million)" (*Korea Times*, March 11, 1999). As a result, it is commonly remarked that Korean action films have far more drama and dialog and less in the way of special effects and action than their Hollywood equivalents.

This leads to the question of filmmaking responses to the arrival of blockbusters. It could be argued that market domination by Hollywood spectacles in Korea and China means Chinese and Korean filmmakers now operate in the "space of the other," as de Certeau terms it (1984: 36–7), even "at home" in the domestic marketplace.

The discussions above indicate both film industries can muster similar budgets to produce their own "blockbusters," but nonetheless Chinese and Korean responses have been quite different.

Chinese blockbusters have located themselves in the lineage of local pre-existing trends for large budget films, emphasizing difference from Hollywood. Before the discourse of the "big film," there was an earlier discourse of the "epic" or "giant film" (*jupian*). Sometimes, "giant film" does translate to "blockbuster" (e.g. Wang 1994: 79). But usually "giant film" implies something different from American blockbusters. The earliest references to the "giant film" I have been able to trace so far are from 1988 and refer to Ding Yinnan's film *Dr Sun Yatsen* (Zhou 1988; Ding *et al.* 1997; Jin 1987). However, familiar use of the term in these articles suggests it was already well established. *Dr Sun Yatsen* is a revolutionary historical biopic. All commentaries note it had a high budget, spectacular scenes with large casts, and a seriousness of purpose. In the following years, there was a cycle of such films, all referred to as "giant films." Examples include *The Birth of New China* (*Kaiguo Dadian*, 1989), *The Kunlun Column* (*Weida Kunlun*, 1988), *Mao Zedong and his Son* (*Mao Zedong he Ta de Erzi*), *The Decisive Engagement* (*Da Juezhan*, 1991), and *Zhou Enlai* (*Zhou Enlai*), discussed as "giant films" in Si Cun (1990 and 1992) and Shao Dan (1990), among others. This sets up a conceptual distinction between the "giant film" (or "epic") and the "big film" (or "blockbuster"). Blockbusters are, by implication, less serious and lacking in pedagogical purpose. "Giant films" follow what the government refers to as the "main melody" (*zhuxuanlu*), meaning the prioritization of pedagogy, whereas the emphasis on entertainment in "big films" places them outside this category.

Although the cycle of revolutionary epics probably peaked in the early 1990s, it continued past the "box office split" deals and the initiation of the "big film" discourse. However, with the production of *The Opium War* in 1997, the discursive opposition between the "giant film" and the "big film" ends. *The Opium War* is clearly a historical epic, and the events it relates are crucial precursors to revolutionary history. At 100 million *renminbi*, it also had the largest Chinese budget at the time of its production (Zhang 1998) and spectacular scenes with casts of thousands if not special effects. However, in local criticism, *The Opium War* is referred to not as a "giant film," but as a "big film" or blockbuster. This suggests a synthesis of the giant film and the big film that further distinguishes Chinese blockbusters from American blockbusters, in this case in terms of seriousness of purpose. It also suggests a turn away from emphasizing inability to emulate Hollywood perfectly (Ma 1998; Fan 1998) and toward the idea of a qualitatively different and superior Chinese blockbuster.

However, the success of this tactic is in doubt. Although a few Chinese films regularly beat Hollywood blockbusters in the domestic market, most are not "giant" or "big" films, but the urban comedies of Feng Xiaogang and sentimental melodramas now favored by Zhang Yimou. Zhang Baiqing (1998) argues that the limited budgets of Chinese blockbusters generally confine their market to China; they lack the production values to compete internationally. *The Opium War* was intended for export, but according to Zhang, it made back only 80 of its 100 million *renminbi* budget. Furthermore, worthy blockbusters with Chinese characteristics do not seem to have won the hearts of local audiences. Even when American films were withdrawn from exhibition following the bombing of the Belgrade embassy, Chinese audiences simply stayed at home rather than go and see Chinese films (Rosen 2001).

In contrast, Korean blockbusters have led a resurgence of the local industry, both in the domestic market and overseas. While no Chinese film has come close to matching *Titanic*'s (1997) Chinese box-office income of 359.5 million *renminbi* (Rosen 2001), *Titanic*'s Korean box office record of 4.7 million viewers was swiftly overcome by the local 1999 action blockbuster, *Shiri*, which attracted 5.78 million viewers (*Korea Herald*, July 21, 2000), over twenty times the average for a local film (*Korea Herald*, November 24, 1999). *Shiri* itself has since been both taken up for American distribution by Columbia and trumped within Korea by the 2000 action blockbuster *Joint Security Area* (Pacquet 2001).

The new success of high-budget Korean films with better production values and greater emphasis on marketing – far more developed than in China – has increased Korean share of the domestic market to levels unprecedented since import quotas were dropped. As budgets have increased, actual numbers of Korean films produced as a percentage of total number of imports and domestic productions distributed has dropped from 76 percent in 1984 to 14 percent in 1999 (Korean Film Commission 2001). But while the market share taken by Korean films dropped as low as 15.9 percent in 1993 (ibid.), it returned to 35.8 percent in 1999 and to 32.8 percent in 2000 (Kim 2000), meaning that the screen quota was not even necessary in those years. Surveying Stephen Cremin's weekly *Asian Film Library Bulletin* shows Korean films regularly in the Seoul top ten, whereas all ten slots in Taipei are regularly taken by Hollywood films. According to Rhee Tae-rim (2001), "recent Korean movies recorded the highest share of any local movie market worldwide except for France."

Furthermore, this domestic success has been accompanied by exports. 1999 dollar-value film exports were ten times the 1998 level (Pacquet 2001). Both *Shiri* and *Joint Security Area* set new records for the export price of Korean movies to the former colonizer, Japan, with the former selling for $1.3 million and the latter for $2 million (*Korea Herald*, November 29, 2000). *Shiri* even accomplished the unprecedented breakthrough of topping the Hong Kong box office for three consecutive weeks in 1999 (*Korea Times*, April 11, 2000). While this does not match Hollywood, it is a small-scale emulation of Hollywood's deployment of big-budget entertainment to win international audiences.

Figure 14.2 Made in Korea: *Shiri* (1999).

However, Korean critics are very aware that this success is based on imitation of Hollywood blockbusters. Their comments indicate skepticism about director of *Joint Security Area* Park's claim to have abandoned emulation and struck out on his own. Both Im Yeong-ha (2000) and Lee Kyung-Eun (2001: 86–7) distinguish between creative transformation and mere imitation, arguing that the Korean blockbuster is still imitating. Nam In-Young (1998: 164) even says that appending "Korean" to the word "blockbuster" only marks where Korean blockbusters fail in their efforts to imitate Hollywood blockbusters. This leads to the question of how to assess the pluralization and de-Westernization of the blockbuster phenomenon.

No doubt, achieving agency within the world of the blockbuster by participating in production has not led Chinese or Korean filmmakers to produce radically different films challenging the domination of Hollywood blockbusters. However, when the blockbuster becomes a familiar and localized form, can we speak anymore of this as operating in the "space of the other"? Perhaps it is not surprising that Lee

(2001: 83–4) also invokes Homi Bhabha's concept of "colonial mimicry" (1994). In contrast to earlier condemnation of "colonial mimicry" as simply and only capitulation, Bhabha makes two strong counterarguments to demonstrate ambivalence at the heart of the phenomenon. First, it enables a measure of agency in the manner discussed above. Second, the inability of the colonized to become the colonizer – "almost white, but not quite," as Bhabha puts it – exposes the lie of the civilizing mission that justifies colonialism; the very structure of imperialism demands the maintenance of difference at the same time as it holds out the promise of inclusion. Similarly, the necessary pluralization of the blockbuster that occurs with the inability to match Hollywood budgets exposes the fallacy of the "level playing field" egalitarianism that underpins the free-trade rhetoric of globalization.

However, we should also hesitate before retreating into high modernist postures dismissing entertainment. As discussed above, there is little evidence, despite increased popular nationalism, that Chinese audiences are attracted by the worthy pedagogy of blockbusters with Chinese characteristics. On the other hand, both of the most successful Korean blockbusters to date (*Shiri* and *Joint Security Area*) provide a space for examining and exorcizing the anxieties associated with the division of the Korean peninsula. In a discussion of Zhang Yimou's films of the early 1990s, Sheldon Lu (1997: 132) tempers mainland Chinese condemnation of these films as pandering to Western tastes, noting that they also use the Western film marketplace to conduct an offshore critical discourse impossible within China itself. Films such as *Shiri* and *Joint Security Area* may emulate Hollywood and seek out international audiences, but they also use the blockbuster as a site to speak to local Korean issues. Indeed, Christopher Alford (2000) goes so far as to argue, in explaining the recent success of Korean cinema, that "Most important is the increased artistic freedom allowed . . . During the '70s and '80s the ruling military regimes heavily censored the content of films. But the restoration of civilian government in 1992 has culminated in an explosion of creative energies." Of course, discussion of censorship as a possible cause of the comparative failure of Chinese blockbusters and Chinese film in general is foreclosed upon within China's own critical discourses. But, given the similar resources available to both Korean and Chinese filmmakers, this is clearly a crucial factor in accounting for their different responses to the challenge of Hollywood blockbusters. The question of precisely how Korean blockbusters engage local Korean issues and what possibilities and limitations are imposed upon them by adopting the blockbuster strategy is being explored by authors such as Lee Kyeung-Eun (2001). Further exploration of this question and whether or not Chinese filmmakers are able to develop more radically resistant blockbuster formats that find favor with local audiences constitute important further projects in the effort to understand the de-Westernization of the blockbuster and its consequences.

Notes

My thanks to two research assistants and their funders: Lin Yuting in Berkeley, funded by the Center for Chinese Studies at the University of California, and Cho Eunjung in Seoul, funded by the College of Letters and Sciences at Berkeley, located relevant Chinese and Korean materials. My Korean is minimal, so Cho Eunjung helped me understand Korean-language materials. I also benefited greatly from discussions with Professor Kim Soyoung of the Korean National University of the Arts. The Chinese part of this essay was presented at the 2001 Association for Asian Studies Conference in Chicago. I thank other panelists and the audience for their responses, and especially Tina Mai Chen for organizing the panel and provoking me to think about this topic.

References

Alford, C. (1999) "Goliath Balks at David's Quotas 'South Korea Under pressure from the Motion Picture Assn. of American – Theater Quotas,'" *Variety*, 9 August, online: http://www.findarticles.com/cf_0/m1312/12_375/55578547/print.jhtml.

—— (2000) "Local Hits Boost Korean Biz. 'South Korea's Movie Theaters,'" *Variety*, 10 January, online: http://www.findarticles.com/cf_0/m1312/8_377/59111023/print.jhtml.

Appadurai, A. (1996) "Disjuncture and Difference in the Global Cultural Economy," in *Modernity at Large: Cultural Dimensions of Globalization*, Minneapolis: University of Minnesota Press: 27–48 [first published in *Public Culture* 2, 2 (1990): 1–24].

Bhabha, H. (1994) "Of Mimicry and Man: The Ambivalence of Colonial Discourse," in *The Location of Culture*, New York: Routledge: 66–84.

Curran, J. and Park, M. (eds) (2000) *De-Westernizing Media Studies*, New York: Routledge.

de Certeau, M. (1984) *The Practice of Everyday Life*, Berkeley: University of California Press.

Ding, Y., *et al.* (1997) "Film Roundtable: On the Epic Film, *Dr Sun Yatsen*" ("*Yingpian Conghengtan: Jupian <Sun Zhongshan>*"), *Film Art* (*Dianying Yishu*), 2: 3–18.

Fan, H. (1998) "We Should Take it Easy on the Production of Chinese Blockbusters" ("*Guochan Dapian Chuangzuo Yingdang Huanxing*"), *Popular Film* (*Dazhong Dianying*), 5: 16.

Ho, H. (1986) "A Review of the Past and a Look to the Future," in *Korea Cinema '86*, Seoul: Motion Picture Promotion Corporation.

Hwang, J. (1999a) "Film Industry's Plea for Screen Quota Turns Emotional," *Korea Herald*, 18 June, online: http://www.koreaherald.co.kr/SITE/data/html_dir/1999/06/18/199906180002.asp.

—— (1999b) "Debate Flares up over Plan to Reduce Mandatory Showing of Local Movies," *Korea Herald*, 14 June, online: http://www.koreaherald.co.kr/SITE/data/html_dir/1999/06/14/199906140013.asp.

Im, Y. (2000) "Two or Three Things I Want to Ask about the 'Korean Blockbuster'" ("'*Hanguk Hyeong Beullokbeoseuteo' E Daehae Mutgo Sipun Se Gaji Geosdul*"), online: http://www.nkino.com/moviedom/print.asp?id=3585, accessed February 26, 2001.

Jin, X. (1987) "On the Music in *Dr Sun Yatsen* ("*Ping Yingpian <Sun Zhongshan> de Yinyue*")," *Film Art* (*Dianying Yishu*), 11: 42–3.

Kim, M. (2000) "A Year of Money and Accolades for Korean Films," *Korea Herald*, 30 December, online: http://www.koreaherald.co.kr/SITE/data/html_dir/2000/12/30/200012300023.asp.

Korea Herald (June 29, 1999) "Movies and the Free Market," online: http://www.koreaherald.co.kr/SITE/data/html_dir/1999/06/29/199906290019.asp.

——(July 2, 1999) "Film Industry Disputes Free-Market Policy," online: http://www.koreaherald.co.kr/SITE/data/html_dir/1999/07/02/1999907020019.asp.

——(November 24, 1999) "Korean Films Gain Ground on Hollywood to Claim 40 Percent of Local Market Share," online: http://www.koreaherald.co.kr/SITE/data/html_dir/1999/11/24/199911240023.asp.

——(June 30, 2000) "Another Japanese Invasion," online: http://www.koreaherald.co.kr/SITE/data/html_dir/2000/06/30/200006300014.asp.

——(July 7, 2000) "Seoul Agrees to Reduce Domestic Film Quota in Talks with US," online: http://www.koreaherald.co.kr/SITE/data/html_dir/2000/07/07/200007070002.asp.

——(July 21, 2000) "'Shiri' Director Buys Kangnam Theater," online: http://www.koreaherald.co.kr/SITE/data/html_dir/2000/07/21/200007210057.asp.

——(November 29, 2000) "'JSA' Breaks Export Record," online: http://www.koreaherald.co.kr/SITE/data/html_dir/2000/11/29/200011290041asp.

Korea Times (March 11, 1999) "Spy Thriller 'Shiri' Opens New Chapter in Korean Movie Market," online: http://www.koreatimes.co.kr/14_6/199903/t465142.htm.

——(August 5, 1999) "Korea's Godzilla Attacks Hollywood," online: http://www.korealink.co.kr/14_10/199908/t4A5125.htm.

——(April 11, 2000) "Korean Pop Arts Poised to Sweep Asia," online: http://www.korealink.co.kr/14_6/200004/t20000411212127465129.htm.

Korean Film Commission (2002) "Korean Film Database," online: http://www.kofic.or.kr/english.asp, accessed April 9, 2001.

Lee, K. (2001) "From *Shiri* to *JSA*: National Narratives in Korean Blockbusters Dealing with the North and South Korean Issue" ("*<Shiri> Eseo <Kongtong Kyeongbi Guyeok JSA> Kkaji: Nambuk Kwangye-rul Diru-nun Hanguk Hyeong Bulleokbeosuteo Eseo Boyeoji-nun Minjokguk-ga Sosa-e Naehayeo*"), in Choi Min *et al.* (eds), *Film Culture Research 2001* (*Yeonghwamun Hwayeongu 2001*), Seoul: Korean National University of the Arts School of Film and Multi-Media/Dept. Cinema Studies [*Hanguk Yesul Jonghap Hakgyu Yeongsangwon Yeongsangireonkwa*]: 47–90.

Lee, S. (1988) "General Review of Korean Films in 1987," *Korea Cinema '88*, Seoul: Motion Picture Promotion Corporation.

Li, X. (1987) "American Blockbusters: What Do They Spend the Money On?" ("*Meiguo Dapian: Qian Hua zai Nali?*"), *Popular Film* (*Dazhong Dianying*), 10.

Liu, L. (1995) *Translingual Practice: Literature, National Culture, and Translated Modernity – China, 1990–1937*, Stanford, CA: Stanford University Press.

Lu, S. H. (1997) "National Cinema, Cultural Critique, Transnational Capital: The Films of Zhang Yimou," in S.H. Lu (ed.), *Transnational Chinese Cinemas: Identity, Nationhood, Gender*, Honolulu: University of Hawaii Press: 105–36.

Ma, Z. (1998) "Chinese Should Go for Commercial Blockbusters" ("*Zhongguo Ying Zhaohuan Shichang Dapian*")," *Popular Film* (*Dazhong Dianying*), 5: 15.

Nam In-Young (1998) "Blockbuster or Irony: Between Capitalism and Nationalism" ("*Bulleokbeosuteo Tto-nun Aironi: Jabeonju-uiwa Minjokju-ui Sai-wui Jultagi*"), *Kino*, November: 162–5.

Ni, Z. (1998) "*Titanic* Sums up a Century of Cinema" ("*Taitannike Hao: Dianying Gongye de Shijie Zongjie*"), *Popular Film* (*Dazhong Dianying*), 6: 26–7.

Pacquet, D. (2001) "Korean Film Newsletter #9: February 26, 2001," online: http://www.koreanfilm.org/news9.html.

Park, P. (1991) "Korean Films in the 1st Half of 1991," *Korean Cinema 1991*, Seoul: Motion Picture Promotion Corporation.

Rhee, T. (2001) "Are Korean Movies Seeing a Renaissance?," *Korea Times*, 21 January, online: http://www.koreatimes.co.kr/kt_culture/200101/t20010122175346461164.htm.

Rosen, S. (2001) "'The Wolf at the Door': Hollywood and the Film Market in China from 1994–2000," in Eric J. Heikkila and Rafael Pizarro (eds), *Southern California in the World and the World in Southern California*, Los Angeles: Greenwood Press; online: http://www.usc.edu/isd/archives/asianfilm/china/wolf.html, accessed March 27, 2001.

Shao, D. (1990) "The Artistic Appeal of *The Kunlun Column*" ("*<Weiwei Kunlun> de Yishu Moli*"), *Film Art* (*Dianying Yishu*), 2: 143–52.

Si, C. (1990) "On *The Birth of the New China*" ("*<Kaiguo Dadian> Fangtan*"), *Film Art* (*Dianying Yishu*), 1: 165–80.

—— (1992) "Three Revolutionary History Epics" ("*Geming Lishi Jupian Sanpin*"), *Contemporary Film* (*Dangdai Dianying*), 2: 55–9.

Wang, R. (1994) "Hollywood Films and the Hollywood Phenomenon" ("*Haolaiwu Dianying yu Haolaiwu Xianxiang*"), *Contemporary Film* (*Dangdai Dianying*), 1: 79–86.

Wang, T. (1997) "Discussing the Imported 'Ten Big Films' from the Angle of Eastern and Western Cultures" ("*Cong Dongxifang Wenhua de Jiaodu Tan Jinkou 'Shi Dapian'*"), *Film Art* (*Dianying Yishu*), 3: 79–83.

Wang, Z. (1996) "1995 Market Summary for Film Imports" ("*1995 Nian Jinkou Dianying Shichang Zongshu*"), in Zhang Zhaolong (ed.), *China Film Yearbook 1996* (*Zhongguo Dianying Nianjian 1996*), Beijing: China Film Press [*Zhangguo Dianying Chubanshe*]: 203–5.

Yu, S. (1999) "Taiwan's Film Industry Threatened by WTO Entry," *Taipei Times*, November 23, online: http://www.taipeitimes.com/beta/1999/11/23/story/0000011875.

Zhang, B. (1998) "Chinese Blockbusters Need to Get it Together" ("*Zhongguo Dapian Haozi Weizhi*"), *Popular Film* (*Dazhong Dianying*), 5: 14.

Zhang, F. and Yang, J. (1997) "Directions for the Audiovisual Arts in the Era of High Technology" ("*Gao Keji Shidai de Yingshi Yishu Zouxiang*"), *Contemporary Film* (*Dangdai Dianying*), 2: 63–71.

Zheng, D. (1998) "What's Big about the 'Big Film'? – A Memo on Reading *The Opium War*" ("*'Dapian' Shenme Da? – Du* Yapian Zhanzheng *Beiwanglu,*" in China Film Association (*Zhongguo Dianyingjia Xiehui*) (ed.), *On the Cinema of Xie Jin* (*Lun Xie Jin Dianying*), Beijing: China Film Press [*Zhongguo Dianying Chubanshe*]: 569–71.

Zhou, X. (1988) "Discussing Ding Yinnan on the basis of *Dr Sun Yatsen*" ("*Cong <Sun Zhongshan> Lun Ding Yinnan*"), *Contemporary Film* (*Dangdai Dianying*), 3: 79–89.

15

ONCE WERE WARRIORS

New Zealand's first indigenous blockbuster

Kirsten Moana Thompson

> It is impossible to exaggerate the importance of this film. Angry, explosive and powerful, *Once Were Warriors* is a crowning achievement for all those involved . . . a movie which marks a new dawn in New Zealand filmmaking.
>
> (Cook 1994)

New Zealanders have traditionally favored commercial American cinema over their own tiny indigenous cinema. However, in 1994 Lee Tamahori's NZ$2.056 million *Once Were Warriors*, the story of a working-class Maori family fractured by sexual abuse and domestic violence, became New Zealand's first national blockbuster, surpassing that year's US release, *Jurassic Park* (1993). Based on the eponymous best-seller by Alan Duff, it became the first film in New Zealand's history to gross more than $6 million at the domestic box office.[1] (As MacDonnell [1995] puts it, this "controversial novel" became a "blockbuster film".) It was the most financially successful film in the country's history (outdoing even Jane Campion's *The Piano* [1993]), with one in every three New Zealanders seeing it. It had particular financial success in small-town cinemas and provincial locations and became the subject of New Zealand's biggest video-piracy case. Described by one critic as "smash-mouth filmmaking," the emotionally powerful film swept through the festival circuit, winning more than sixty international prizes, including best first film at Venice, Rotterdam, Montreal, Durban, and Australia, and it was sold by the New Zealand Film Commission to more than sixty countries (Horton 1995).

This chapter will examine *Once Were Warriors*'s national reception and dissemination across the New Zealand public sphere, which garnered accolades such as "the great New Zealand film for which we have been waiting" and "epic in scale" (Cook 1994). In examining a low-budget, social realist – or nonspectacular – film that had critical social impact, I hope to complicate contemporary understandings of the blockbuster as a commercial and cultural phenomenon. Steve Neale's essay in this volume identifies narrative, economic, and generic components that

Figure 15.1 *Once Were Warriors* (1994).

have historically defined the US industrial context of the blockbuster. These include spectacle, relative length and expense, and the adoption of special technologies and presentational features in the content and exhibition of the film. Since early in the twentieth century, the American blockbuster has functioned as an important way in which Hollywood differentiates its product in the global marketplace, through high production values, use of stars, and spectacle. By these criteria, *Once Were Warriors*, a low-budget social realist drama with historical and cultural features unique to New Zealand, would not appear to meet any generally accepted definition of a blockbuster. However, I propose that the definition of the blockbuster needs expansion to consider the ways in which the global marketplace, while dominated by American cinema, is also increasingly subject to influences from other cultural formulae. Indeed, the critical and commercial success of Ang Lee's *Crouching Tiger, Hidden Dragon* (2000), not to mention the work of John Woo and Jackie Chan, is one marker of the influence of international acting and production talent on American generic formulae. Significantly, *Once Were Warriors*'s success also launched the Hollywood career of director Lee Tamahori (*Die Another Day* [2002]), thus following the earlier trajectories of New Zealand filmmakers Geoff Murphy, Vincent Ward, Jane Campion, and Peter Jackson. Further, I suggest that the blockbuster's definition as a marker of commercial success and cultural influence can encompass national cinemas outside Hollywood, which, while not matching the scale of American successes such as *Titanic* (1997) or *Gladiator* (2000), can nonetheless produce new understandings of the blockbuster as a critical term in discourses of popular consumption and reception. Through the test case of *Once Were Warriors*'s extraordinary commercial success and cultural influence in its national context, I suggest that the blockbuster need not be defined solely in terms of spectacular content or global success, but rather may also function contingently, as a localized phenomenon of consumption and reception.

The success of *Once Were Warriors* is remarkable, not least because its release competed directly with that of an American film widely accepted as a blockbuster, *Jurassic Park* (released in the New Zealand market in 1994). This is even more marked in a country whose tiny population of 3.4 million has meant that its film industry is not commercially viable in its domestic context. It produces a mere half-dozen films each year with financial support from the New Zealand Film Commission, and is largely dependent on export to European television and international film festivals for success in the art film market. When a domestic film such as *Once Were Warriors* overcomes the longstanding hegemony of American (and British) films in New Zealand to obtain financial success *in its domestic context*, its success takes on added cultural significance, particularly when New Zealand nationalist identifications have historically been located in sport, rather than in film. Although *Once Were Warriors* found international success in the art and festival exhibition circuit, its reception in New Zealand functioned as a site for historical and political debate, and nationalist identification and interrogation – and all this *because* of its sociological subject matter.

Once Were Warriors is a contradictory film, a generic hybrid of social realism and stylized melodrama that also shares certain classical blockbuster attributes of marketing and reception. While its themes and locations are socially realist, its visceral use of music, sound, stylized Polynesian design, and violence collide in what one New Zealand critic has described as "the roller-coaster ride of its narrative" (Simmons 1998: 332). While it does not feature global (read American) stars, or computerized special effects, its extra-textual circulation and synergistic by-products have functioned in ways parallel to Hollywood marketing practices. For example, the film has produced sequels, soundtracks (featuring well-known New Zealand artists Herbs, Moana and the Moahunters, *et al.*), and a musical. *Once Were Warriors* was based on Alan Duff's 1990 controversial best-selling novel which sold more than 50,000 copies – ten times as many as most New Zealand novels. It won the Pen First Book Award and was short-listed for the NZ Book Awards in 1991. Communicado, a successful production house for television and video, which considered a cinematic adaptation of a national best-seller as the ideal project for its entry into the feature film market, purchased the rights to the novel on its publication. The film received financial backing from the New Zealand Film Commission and NZ On Air, and post-production support from the Avalon National Film Unit, and was released with an R13 rating. Its success produced the best-selling literary and cinematic sequels *What Becomes of the Broken Hearted?* (novel, Duff, 1996; film, Ian Mune, 1999). In addition, *Once Were Warriors* was selected in 1996 as one of four films (none of which was *The Piano*) to be represented on stamps to commemorate the centenary of New Zealand cinema.[2]

Added to its commercial and critical success, the film quickly entered New Zealand popular vernacular, with cases of domestic violence and child abuse referred to in the national press as "warriors families," and men acknowledging, "I've got a warriors problem." Indeed, the discursive proliferation of "warriors situations" and other metonymic references to the film by the government, social welfare agencies, and personal confessionals was an indication of the widespread nature of the film's popular consumption and recirculation.[3] After the film's release, women's refuges reported a surge in admissions and police noted a rise in the reports of domestic violence. Jill Hema, a Maori women's refuge coordinator, observed: "South Auckland refuges were overflowing. Women have been coming through saying 'We've seen *Once Were Warriors* and that's me. It's hit home.'" One woman from the Bay of Plenty rang her local paper to explain how she had been beaten by her husband for 20 years. "I felt every punch that she got. That movie was so real, it was just uncanny" (Pryor 1995: 26). As *Once Were Warriors* was in pre-production, a prominent case in the New Zealand news featured the story of a twelve-year-old boy beaten to death by his father. Domestic violence and sexual abuse have been prominent subjects for debate in the public sphere, reflecting the cultural interventions of feminist activism in the country in the last thirty years.[4] In 1993, there were fifty-six deaths in New Zealand from domestic violence. In 1998, statistics showed 10,000 children and 6,000 women spent time in women's refuges (McLeod 2000). One reviewer foregrounded the horrific quality of the film's realism: "*Once Were Warriors* is truly a frightening and powerful film. Forget Elm Street. Ignore Camp Crystal Lake. This takes place in the most frightening place of all, the homes of New Zealanders" (Croot 1994).

The wide cultural dissemination of *Once Were Warriors* can be understood partly through its social utility in dramatizing domestic violence, alcoholism, and sexual abuse. Probation officers, social workers, police, and cabinet ministers used the film as both parable and cultural shorthand to draw attention to New Zealand's social problems (Turia 2000; Sell 1998). In 1998, a resource *kete* (kit) was created by Te Hau Ora O Te Tai Tokerau, a regional health and social services provider for the Maori Affairs Department, which adopted the film's colloquial language and themes to educate men about violent behavior: "Hey Bro', do you give your missus the bash? Has your missus had to go to the doctor as a result of your hidings?" (Gregory 2000). The same year a Conference of Child Abuse and Neglect discussed "the reality of the enduring *Once Were Warriors* lifestyle," and called for renewed *iwi* (tribal) responsibility for abuse among Maori (DuChateau 1998). In 1999, parliament launched a $5 million campaign by the Children, Young Persons, and their Families Agency, which included a television commercial that featured a Maori family, modeled on the Heke family of the film (Perry 1999). Producer Robin Scholes reiterated what many theatrical reviews of the film have also underscored as its educational function: "What I'm most proud of is that people will not be able to leave the cinema and not talk about the film. A lot of people will know the circumstances in which this family lives . . . We believe we have made something which is passionate, which will be controversial, but controversial in a positive sense – it will open up discussion" (Communicado 1994: 5). Indeed, many critics responded to the film's provocative political implications by heralding its importance as social critique: "with messages that are pertinent to Maori, to Pakeha, and to an international audience, no New Zealander can afford to miss this film if he seeks to begin to understand our cultural heritage and the changes forced upon it by today's bleak economic might" (Fisher 1994).

The film's harsh unmitigated portrait of domestic violence, parental neglect, poverty, rape, gang membership, and alcoholism also stirred national discussion about the social effects of colonization for Maori, who are 12 percent of the population, yet disproportionately represented in imprisonment, unemployment, alcoholism, and domestic violence statistics. I suggest that the film figures national identity through the cultural changes in Pakeha–Maori relations over the previous thirty years as well as the economic effects of the National and Labor governments' extensive deregulation and privatization in the 1980s, which disproportionately affected Maori and other Polynesian minorities.

Once Were Warriors tells the story of a Maori family headed by a violent and abusive father, Jake "the Muss" Heke (Temuera Morrison), whose alcoholism and physical violence ultimately destroys his family of five children and his wife, Beth (Rena Owen). The film's stylized drama of violence culminates with Jake's friend Uncle "Bully" secretly raping the eldest daughter, Grace (Mamaengaroa Kerr-Bell), who in despair hangs herself from a tree in the family's backyard. The drama centers on the two principal female characters, Beth and Grace, and the catalyst that Grace's death provides in enabling Beth finally to leave her husband. Jake's identity is literally embodied in his sobriquet, "the Muss" – slang for the muscles he proudly flexes. He is a warrior of bars and parties in which any infraction of respect incurs his "fisthappy" response. Ironically, the film's representational critique of New Zealand masculinity was socially interpreted in contradictory ways. For example, a recent study of prisoners by a psychologist in the Department of Corrections revealed the influence of Jake as an antisocial hero: "A lot of our young Maori now identify with Jake the Muss. They believe that to be Maori you have to be staunch and a 'bro'" (Perry 1999).[5] The eponymous television program developed by Brian Lepou, a social worker who counsels young Maori offenders, interrogates this discourse of "staunch" New Zealand masculinity. *Staunch*, which also stars Mamaengaroa Kerr-

Bell, is one of the many cultural spin-offs that capitalize commercially on popular engagement with the social problems of the film.

Once Were Warriors is not the first Maori film exported to European television or circulated on the art house circuit. Barry Barclay has directed two of them, *Ngati* (1987) and *Te Rua* (1991); the third is Merata Mita's *Mauri* (1988).[6] Like *The Piano* and *Heavenly Creatures* (Peter Jackson, 1994), *Once Were Warriors* foregrounds a deep-seated gender violence endemic in New Zealand's culture, but unlike the former films it situates that violence in the legacy of colonialism. The title's elision of the pronoun "they" by its rhetorical absence (implied in the remaining "were") emphasizes the subject position of colonial identity as the film's allegorical dimension. Such an elision also re-emphasizes, through rhythmic stress, the word "once" with its silent echo of loss, underscored by Beth Heke's final speech of farewell to her husband Jake: "Our people once were warriors, but not like you Jake. They were people with *mana*, pride. People with spirit."

Although many New Zealand films have achieved success in the export market, it was not until the 1993 release of *The Piano* that the country's cinema achieved a certain international prominence, with Jane Campion's and Anna Paquin's Oscars at the 1994 Academy Awards. *The Piano* drew parallels between the interchangeable exchange economy of land and women's bodies in the colonial *mise-en-scène*, at the same time preserving a problematic representation of Maori as exoticized backdrop to that space. Rena Owen (Beth Heke) argued that, as a Maori production (cast and crew), *Once Were Warriors* was a response to such traditions of representation: "This film tells the truth about what happens to a race that has been systematically demoralized, what's left after you've stripped a people of their pride and made them feel like second-class citizens. In *The Piano*, we were monkeys in the background. Here we are seen as we are. Of course, the Maoris bloody loved it" (Clinch 1994).

Coming 154 years after the Treaty of Waitangi, New Zealand's founding national document, *Once Were Warriors* marked a seminal period in the history of New Zealand's race relations, as biculturalism gained increasing strength since the renaissance of Maori language and culture in the 1970s. In 1984, legislation was passed permitting retrospective claims on the Treaty of Waitangi, dating back to when the treaty was signed in 1840. This historic legislation meant that all New Zealand laws relating to land, fisheries, rivers, and forests became subject to constitutional scrutiny in terms of their compatibility with the rights guaranteed to Maori in the treaty. This was largely in response to political pressure effected by protests, marches, and occupations, which saw the return of some Maori lands confiscated illegally by British or New Zealand authorities in the years since national formation. Concomitantly, in the 1970s, and gaining strength in the 1980s and 1990s, Maori language and culture saw a renaissance in the public sphere, aided by the leadership of groups such as Nga Tamatoa and community leadership by Dame

Whina Cooper, Donna Awatere, Ripeka Evans, and others. By the 1990s, Maori language was taught in schools and spoken in courts, and governments under both major political parties (National and Labor) accepted the goal of a bicultural national identity.

In 1914, the New Zealand film industry's first domestic feature, George Tarr's *Hinemoa*, the story of a Maori princess, followed Georges Méliès's 1913 version of the same legend, *Loved by a Maori Chieftess*. Over the next seventy years, the tiny industry would produce forty-two features, some of them produced or directed by American companies, targeting New Zealand's exotic location, Maori culture, and cheap production costs. The beginning of the contemporary domestic film industry has often been cited as the *annus mirabilis* of 1977, when four features were released: *Wild Man* (Geoff Murphy), *Landfall* (Paul Maunder), *Off the Edge* (Mike Firth), and, the most influential of all, Roger Donaldson's *Sleeping Dogs* (starring a young Sam Neill of *Jurassic Park* fame). As a result of industry lobbying and the unexpected commercial success of these independently produced features, and encouraged by Alan Highet, a sympathetic Labor Minister for the Arts, the government agreed to establish the New Zealand Film Commission (NZFC) in 1978. Its directive was "to encourage and also participate in the making, promotion, distribution and exhibition of films . . . enabling the world to see New Zealanders as they see themselves" (Martin and Edwards 1997: 13). Under this Act, the Commission's function was to encourage the production of New Zealand films, broadly defined to encompass narrative content, the nationalities of creators, crew, financiers, and cast, or the use of domestic technical facilities. Initially operating on grants from the Lottery Board and later from taxation sources, the Commission continues to play an instrumental role in the investment in and marketing of New Zealand films. In 1980, the NZFC first participated in the markets at Cannes, underscoring an early recognition of the export market for New Zealand cultural product. In 1981, the New Zealand Film Archive was created, and in 1983, the Short Film Fund.

Between 1980 and 1984, tax advantages led to an explosion in independent financing in feature films, rising from two in 1980 to fourteen in 1984 until the loopholes were closed. Between 1977 and 1987, sixty-nine feature films were produced, which paralleled growth in domestic television production (aided by local content laws), the development of domestic film criticism and industry journals, and the academic study of film.[7] The domestic film industry has long struggled with the dominance of American and British programming in domestic media, which in turn prompted the government's strategies of subsidies and promotion. NZFC reports emphasized the role that domestic films played in local currency support and – given the increasing importance of the global marketplace for New Zealand's economy – the enhancing of the country's international profile. Positioning the national film industry as a unique export commodity aligned with the country's increasing dependency on tourism (which replaced dairy farming as the primary source for overseas funds), the NZFC claimed the films would "[bring] New Zealand to a discriminating and sophisticated world market, with inevitable benefits for both trade and tourism" (Reid 1986: 15). On an investment of NZ$1.508 million for *Once Were Warriors*, the NZFC received a 327 percent return. Further, the current blockbuster success of *Lord of the Rings: The Fellowship of the Ring* (Peter Jackson, 2002) is proving to be a profitable endeavor for the New Zealand government, which invested $4.5 million in tax breaks and subsidies for the production. Prime Minister Helen Clark expects "spin-offs for tourism, computer software, filmmaking, wine and food, and dozens of other local industries" (Oliver 2001: F5). A current New Zealand tourism campaign, "100 % Pure New Zealand," offers this ad copy: "Welcome to Middle-Earth. A place where ancient stories are told and spells woven. Where the craggy peaks, mountain mists and breathtaking vistas inspire adventures only dreamed of" (Cleave 2001: F7).

The opening shot of *Once Were Warriors* foregrounds the pictorial beauty of the "breathtaking vistas" that are so central to this touristic and, now, global blockbusting imagery. But there is something curiously pristine and two-dimensional in this image of the Southern Alps, and with the intrusion of a diegetic truck horn and a crane out, we see that the image is a *trompe-l'oeil* – a billboard, in fact an advertisement for a fictitious company called EnZpower. Not unlike the startling beauty of the opening images of *The Piano*, the image signifies a key visual trope in colonialist ideology (and modernist New Zealand poetry and art), one which continues in contemporary tourist marketing: empty landscapes, ripe for consumption. Yet the dramatic context of this image is anything but bucolic: cluttered in the frame is the long snake of Auckland's Southern Motorway, where garbage and graffiti surround abandoned car wrecks. This environment is urban, harsh, and sprawling – the visual indicator of the Heke family's home, which is right next to the motorway. Tamahori acknowledged this strategic stylization: "I definitely wanted a very hard, almost treeless urban experience that not many people in New Zealand would ever have been aware of or seen" (Communicado 1994: 3).

Lee Tamahori's training in televisual aesthetics[8] transforms the conventions of social realism by creating what he conceived of as a mixture of televisual social realism and "what [he] call[s] cinematic value . . . a cinematic experience" (McKenzie 1995: 65). This cinematic "experience" combines the emotional impact of his subject matter with extensive stylization: a hybrid soundtrack of hard-rock guitar solos and traditional *haka* (war) chants; graphic matches; fast cutting; and a graphic title sequence and "end" which slam the film shut at its narrative conclusion. Stuart Dryburgh's (*The Piano*) cinematography is reminiscent of the warm golden brown of a beer commercial or the brown haze of nicotine smoke, themselves key aspects of the *mise-en-scène*. The rare eruptions of blue (in the opening billboard) and green (at the Marae) heighten the restricted color palette of black, red and brown, traditional colors in Maori aesthetic design. Production designer Mike Kane explained his use of filters to enhance brown skin tones: "We wanted to expose a lot of skin so that we had warm tones contrasting with the cool urban tones of South Auckland" (Communicado 1994: 13).

Perhaps the most prominent form of stylization is Tamahori's bold use of Polynesian *moko* (facial tattoos) in the hyperbolically tattooed Toa Aotearoa gang that the eldest son Nig Heke (Julian Arahanga) joins:

> In the seventies young urbanized Maori in search of powerful symbols of ethnic identity rediscovered the art and Moko found a new generation of skin.
>
> (Barber 2000)

The film's stylized composite of Polynesian tattoos that coat the gang members' bodies iconicized a growing popularity in indigenous aesthetics, another signifier in a resurgent Maori culture. Indeed, among Maori lesbians the chin Moko has also emerged as a new subcultural practice. Hans Neleman's photographic study of tattooed teenagers, gang members, Rastafarians, and government workers, *Moko–Maori Tattoo* (Reid 1986), represented the new popularity of *moko* across gender, class, race, and provincial/urban boundaries – what another journalist called "the birth of Pacific urban chic" (Warner 1995).

Once Were Warriors's indigenous blockbuster reception also crossed overlapping demographic boundaries, including women, youth, Maori and Pakeha, rural and city. By combining the specificity of the local within generic and visual formulae that have been profitable international formulae, *Once Were Warriors* capitalized on a shifting sense of national identity: "The film brought people out of the woodwork, people who never go to the cinema came to see it. The book was read by middle and upper class people, but the working classes flocked to the film" (Stimpson 1995). The film broke provincial records for attendance and was particularly successful among teenagers, a key demographic sector of contemporary film audiences. Rena Owen explained its appeal: "it's the leather, the music, the sound systems, the tattoos, the gangs and the handsome boys that appeal to the teenagers. There's a vibrancy amongst all the kids, everyone from the age of 25 down is seething with their urban lifestyle. If you're that age and you go and see the movie, there are people in there who are like you and speak the language you speak" (Communicado 1994: 5).

Through its generic and stylistic hybridity, *Once Were Warriors* hit on a successful economic formula that enabled New Zealanders to overcome their historic reluctance to support the domestic box-office dollar, what Lawrence Simmons describes as a "productive friction that at a textual level allows the film to interrogate contemporary social reality and appeal to a large commercial audience at the same time" (Simmons 1998: 332). Concomitantly, the film offered a social realist melodrama in which the legacies of racism and social dysfunction are acknowledged and overcome. This generic and cultural hybridity is a marker of contemporary cinema under massive global changes and one, I suggest, that is not completely subjugated by American hegemonic formulae. At a time when national formations of identity were shifting under the burdens of the global economy, the legacies of colonialism, and the debates over the Treaty of Waitangi, *Once Were Warriors* offered a stylized blockbuster fantasy of New Zealand as a racially hybridized culture, uneasily adjusting to its contemporary identity as a Pacific nation.

Notes

1 The film was distributed by Fine Line Features and earned $2.201 million in its US theatrical release. It was released on video in 1995.

2 The other three were *Hinemoa* (George Tarr, 1914), the first New Zealand feature film; *Broken Barrier* (John O'Shea, 1952), a biracial love story; and *Goodbye Pork Pie* (Geoff Murphy, 1980), the first commercially successful film in New Zealand.

3 See, for example, "Lara's story," that of a twenty-year-old Maori woman and domestic abuse survivor. "With every new stone I turned I became stronger. I took time out ... to deal with other issues in my life. I didn't want that '*Once were warriors*' thing for my kids" (Anon 1999: 3).

4 The 1980s included prominent debates over sexual harassment (the "six angry women" incident, in which Mervyn Thompson, drama lecturer at Auckland University, was abducted by six anonymous women and tied to a tree for his alleged sexual harassment of female students) and female sexual abuse statistics (the "one in five" women debate) in *Metro* magazine.

5 The study's sample data is too small to be scientifically reliable, and I cite it merely as evidence for the film's cultural influence across a wide body of the population, which included the incarcerated. The psychologist noted that social alienation and frustration was dealt with through violent aggression: "They also felt that violence enhanced their status and reputation. It also gave them a rush or was cathartic – they were feeling pent-up frustration and finding a target was a release for that."

6 All years are those of New Zealand domestic release; international release dates are usually the following year. There have been other films that dealt explicitly with social issues affecting Maori youth: *Other Halves* (John Laing, 1984), a biracial love affair, and *Kingpin* (Mike Walker, 1985), about juvenile delinquency. *Te Rua* (1991) was a German–New Zealand co-production. A number of other New Zealand films have Maori subject matter, although usually in a peripheral manner.

7 The first New Zealand film journal was *Alternative Film* (1972), followed by the NZFC journals *Rough Cut* (1978) and *NZ Film* (1979), *Illusions* (1986), and *the big picture* (1994). Film criticism was first taught at Victoria University in 1970 and at Auckland University in 1975.

8 Winner of the Mobius (US), Facts (Australia), and Axis (NZ) advertising awards, Tamahori began his career as a commercial artist and photographer. He joined the commercial film industry in the 1970s as a boom operator and became an assistant director in the early 1980s of *Thunderbox*, a popular half-hour drama for television, and several stories in the Ray Bradbury syndicated television series.

References and bibliography

Anon (1994) "Warriors Still on the Warpath," *On Film*, 11, 7: 20.

Anon (1999) "Mortgage Broker Wins Top Business Award," *Business Development News*, 65, July/August: 3.

Anon (2000) "No Sign of Wider Abuse," *Wairarapa Times Age*, August 3.

Anon (2000) "What Tariana Turia Said – in Full," *New Zealand Herald*, August 31.

Anon (2001) "No Easy Answers for At-Risk Families," *New Zealand Herald*, March 10.

Adamson, Judy (1994) "Shocking Picture of Maori Loss," *Northern Herald*, December 1.

Barber, Fiona (2000) "More than Skin Deep," *New Zealand Herald*, February 20.

Barclay, Barry (1998) "The Control of One's Own Image," *Illusions*, 8 (June): 8–14.

Blythe, Martin (1994) *Naming the Other: Images of the Maori in New Zealand Film and Television*, Metuchen, NJ: Scarecrow Press.

Calder, Peter (2000) "Our Films: Flash or Flushable?," *New Zealand Herald*, May 25.

Clark, Harvey (1994) "Hell in Paradise," *New Zealand Herald*, May 13: 4.

Cleave, Louisa (2001) "NZ the Big Picture," *New Zealand Herald*, December 8–9: F7.

Cleave, Peter (1991/2) "Revising the Warrior," *Illusions*, 18 (summer): 27–31.

Clinch, Misty (1994) "Maori, Maori, Quite Contrary," *Daily Mirror*, April 13.

Communicado (1994) press pack for *Once Were Warriors*, Auckland.

Cook, Stephen (1994) "Powerful Warriors Hits Hard," *Northern Advocate*, June 9.

Croot, James (1994) "Frightening and Powerful," *Dunedin Star Movieweek*, June 26: 8.

Dobson, Diana (2001) "CIB is Flying South," *Gisborne Herald*, September 3.

DuChateau, Carroll (1998) "Aggro Culture," *Quote*, May 11: 12–15.

Fisher, Stephen (1994) "Warriors the One We've Waited For," *Evening Standard*, May 28.

Gregory, Angela (2000) "Maori Take Action on Family Violence," *New Zealand Herald*, July 18.

Horton, Gregory (1995) "Film's Forceful, Heartbreaking," *The Herald*, March 3.

MacDonnell, Brian (1995) "*Once Were Warriors*: Controversial Novel Becomes Blockbuster Film," *Metro: Film, Television, Video, Multi-Media*, 101: 7–9.

Major, Wade (1995) "*Once Were Warriors*: Maoriz N the Hood," *Entertainment Today*, March 16: 15.

Martin, Helen, and Edwards, Sam (1997) *New Zealand Film 1912–1996*, Auckland: Oxford University Press.

McKenzie, Stuart (1995) "Warrior Cast: Stuart McKenzie Talks to Lee Tamahori," *Art Forum*, February: 65–6, 104.

McLeod, Scott (2000) "Jian Huang Murder: Run of Mill 'Domestic' Can Easily Turn Tragic," *New Zealand Herald*, March 1.

New Zealand Film Commission (1994) *Once Were Warriors* press pack, Wellington: New Zealand.

Oliver, Paula (2001) "Force of Hobbit: the Spin Off," *New Zealand Herald*, December 8–9: F5.

Olley, Carley (1994) "Punch Drunk on a Raw Message," *New Plymouth Daily News*, June 17.

Perry, Keith (1999) "Violent Maori Males 'Worship Jake Heke,'" *New Zealand Herald*, August 15.

Pihama, Leonie (1996) "Repositioning Maori Representation: Contextualizing *Once Were Warriors*," in Jonathan Dennis and Jan Bieringa (eds), *Film in Aotearoa, New Zealand*, 2nd edn, Wellington: Victoria University Press: 191–4.

Powers, John (1995) "Creeping Oprah-ism," *Vogue*, March: 256.

Pryor, Ian (1995) "Bigger than Spielberg," *Independent on Sunday*, April 16: 26.

Reid, Nicholas (1986) *A Decade of New Zealand Film: From Sleeping Dogs to Came a Hot Friday*, Dunedin: John McIndoe.

Sell, Bronwyn (1998) "Survey Reveals 'Warrior' Drink Cycle," *New Zealand Herald*, February 3.

Simmons, Lawrence (1998) "Ideology and Class Warfare in *Once Were Warriors*," *Southern Review*, 31, 3: 330–42.

Sklar, Robert (1995) "Social Realism with Style: An Interview With Lee Tamahori," *Cinéaste*, 21, 3: 25–7.

Smith, Jane (1999) "Knocked Around in New Zealand: Postcolonialism Goes to the Movies," in Christopher Sharrett (ed.), *Mythologies of Violence in Postmodern Media*, Detroit: Wayne State University Press: 381–95.

Stimpson, Mansel (1995) "Warrior Queen," *What's On in London*, April 12.

Turia, Tariana (2000) transcript of speech to New Zealand Psychological Society conference, Waikato University, August 29, 2000, online: http://www.converge.org.nz/pma/tspeech.htm.

Warner, Kirsten (1995) "When Less is Maori: A New Zealand Film Highlights the Birth of Pacific Urban Chic," *The Guardian*, February 24.

16

TELEVISION FOR THE BIG SCREEN

How *Comodines* became Argentina's first blockbuster phenomenon

Tamara L. Falicov

> You will applaud, with *Comodines* you will applaud. It is one of those police films of an international level of quality that we are all used to. But no. You don't have to read subtitles. It is an Argentine film. It is another film coproduced by *Artear* that the *Clarín* Group is proud to support.
>
> (advertisement in *Clarín*, June 17, 1997)

Introduction: antecedents to the blockbuster era in Argentina

Historically, Argentina's film industry has been marked by periods of volatility in terms of production funding, exhibition, and distribution outlets. Once an industry famed for its "golden age" in the 1930s and 1940s, it later abandoned its large-scale studio system due to structural problems, aggressive marketing by the Hollywood industry, and other factors. From the late 1950s onward, the state was mandated to assist the film industry stay afloat. In 1957, the National Film Institute (Instituto Nacional de Cinematografia) (INC) was established to develop funds to aid in national film production. From the 1960s onward, the film industry shifted away from a commercial studio model to an artisanal, small-scale director-producer model. These typically auteurist films were produced by filmmakers who (in some cases) have gained national and international prestige. Examples of well-known Argentine directors are Leonardo Favio, Adolfo Aristarain, Fernando "Pino" Solanas, Maria Luisa Bemberg, Eliseo Subiela, Hector Olivera, Marcelo Piñeyro, and Luis Puenzo. These filmmakers' aesthetics are typified by a European sensibility, but their screen content is usually set within an Argentine historical context. While some films made by this group accrued respectable box-office returns, the majority did not reach a wide audience. In the words of film scholar and critic

Octavio Getino, "the problem plaguing Argentine cinema is that it is too hermetic and intellectual" (Thieburger and Dupcovsky 1990: 11). In general, these films appealed only to a small, middle- to upper-middle-class group of people.

In the late 1990s, new film legislation paved the way for a wealthy group of investors and producers to join in financing film projects: private television channels, themselves owned by large multimedia conglomerates. These television players were instrumental in helping create a commercial cinema that could compete successfully with US blockbuster movies. This chapter will describe the making of an Argentine blockbuster movie, *Comodines* (1997), how it came to be, and what impact it and other films had on the debates around state financing for national cinema in Argentina. Billed as the "First Hollywood-style movie spoken in Spanish," *Comodines* (the literal translation is "Jokers," but the US release title was *Cops*) beat the all-time record for first week box-office receipts and created sizable hype when it was released.

The term "blockbuster," while not a widely used Anglicism in Argentina, will be used throughout this chapter to describe a new way of producing and marketing films in Argentina. I would argue that a film such as *Comodines*, and others – such as animated films *Dibu, la película* (*Dibu, the Movie*, 1997) and the biggest box-office hit of the decade, *Manuelita,* 1999) – fit Justin Wyatt's (1994) definition of the "high concept" blockbuster product – that is, a market-oriented filmmaking package that focuses, among other things, on surface iconography, or spectacle, and marketing potentiality.

The rise of the Argentine blockbuster

In 1997 four national films together amassed 5 million spectators by the end of that year. In a country where 80 percent of films shown are Hollywood movies, and where close to thirty films on average are produced annually, this was no small feat. These four box-office sensations were action-oriented or youthful films with names such as *Comodines* (*Cops*), an action film, *Dibu, la película*, an animated film for children, *La furia* (*The Fury*), an action thriller, and *Cenizas del Paraiso* (*Ashes from Paradise*), a drama about a love triangle between a young woman and two young brothers. The film that drew in the most fame and hype, however, was *Comodines*, based on a "cops and robbers" television show called *Poliládron* (*Thieves*). It was an action film that simulated a Hollywood police buddy movie such as *Lethal Weapon* (1987) and drew audiences with its well-known actors Carlos Calvo and Adrian Suar, both of television fame. It was not coincidental that *Comodines* was a spin-off from a television show aired on one of Argentina's main television channels, Artear, Channel 13. The film was co-produced by the channel, which thus gave it ample advertising screen time on Artear. This form of film and television integration was one way in which film producers in Argentina could produce and market their films on a comparable scale to that of US studios. In addition, the popularity of these films boosted the strength of the Argentine film industry. In 1997, employment for feature length films increased by 84.2 percent (DEISICA 1997: 34).

This was a watershed year for a new kind of cinema in Argentina – popular, yet in some circles (especially small director-producers) it aroused skepticism and more than a little cynicism. This was because TV channels were not only proprietors of advertising vehicles and production funds; they also had access to other resources such as state subsidies. These corporate beneficiaries of state subsidies often angered small director-producers who depended solely on state loans and subsidies to make their films. In other words, these glossy film productions were all put together with private television support in addition to state film institute financing, rather than according to the traditional model of small independent director-producers receiving state support. Therefore, while some lauded the entrance of television channels in the world of national filmmaking, others such as film director Javier Torre questioned their motives, as well as their overall contribution to national culture, since many of the resulting films were commercial, formulaic, and, in his opinion, not much different from Hollywood fare (interview with author, 1998).

In addition, many low-budget director-producers felt that the new film legislation passed in 1994 to improve funding for film production was compromised with this new alliance of the national film institute and television producers. This government–big business alliance was characteristic of a neoliberal economic policy espoused by President Menem that favored big-business interests over culture and education in the public interest (Belaunzan and Blanco 1993: 6).

Television–film integration in Argentina

In the late 1980s, an economic crisis affected all realms of Argentine society and greatly reduced the scope of cultural production. In 1990, a mere ten films were produced, the lowest figure since 1934. The film sector, in large part, was concerned over the fate of the Argentine industry, and pushed Congress to reform legislation to infuse new sources of funding into the film sector. In 1994, a law dubbed the "New Cinema Law" was passed. This legislation infused more money into the National Film Institute coffers through a surcharge on television ads diverted from the Comité Federal de Radiodifusion (COMFER), the Argentine equivalent of the US Federal Communications Commission (FCC). These monies supplemented the funding already in place from legislation (1968) that allotted 10 percent of all box-office receipts for exhibited films to be earmarked as a source of national film funding. In total, the pool increased fourfold to 50 million pesos (US$50 million). In addition, the National Film Institute (INC) changed its title to the Instituto Nacional de Cinematografia y Artes Audiovisuales (National Film and Audiovisual Arts Institute [INCAA]), to reflect the film industry's integration with television and other audio-visual industries.

Comodines was produced by Pol-Ka Productions, in affiliation with Flehner Films, both production companies that create television programs as well as advertising. These companies worked in conjunction with Artear to gain access to television advertising at minimal cost. Patagonik (another production company, responsible for *Dibu, la película*, *Cenizas del paraíso*, and others) is owned partly by Channel 13 or Artear (Grupo Clarín) and partly by Buena Vista International, or Walt Disney productions. Diego Lerner, the vice-president of Buena Vista Productions, Disney's distribution wing, describes the "synergy" that arose in 1997 when large multimedia companies joined forces to make commercial movies in Argentina:

> This is the first picture [*Cenizas del paraiso* (*Ashes from Paradise*)] that Buena Vista releases with Artear and Patagonik where in addition, we are producers. Believe me that we won't be hush-hush with all of this. Patagonik holds stock in movie theaters, Artear has mass communication resources, and Buena Vista has distribution all over the world . . . There are few resources that we don't already have. If I had to pay for all of the media sources we've obtained through our co-producers associated with the film, it'd be impossible to do this financially. And I'm from Disney.
>
> (Belaunzan 1997: 16)

Distributor Bernardo Zupnik, of his company Filmarte, who distributed *Comodines*, noted that the only manner in which Argentine cinema could compete against Hollywood would be to include the financial strength and resources of television companies and other large multimedia groups (D'Esposito 1997: 27). Issues such as movie promotion, television advertising, and the use of famous actors here only possible for the most part with the inclusion of companies that had the ability to cross-promote media content as well as the means to exhibit and/or distribute the film. The television ad campaign for *Comodines* played extensively on Channel 13, a co-producer of the film.

Television ads, which normally cost between $150,000 to $200,000 a spot, are prohibitively expensive for most small Argentine film producers. In addition, Grupo Clarín owns two large radio stations, Radio Mitre and FM 100. In addition to *Clarín*, the most popular and widely circulated newspaper in Argentina, the holding owns the largest cable television system, Multicanal, which also is used in marketing in-house products (Blanco 1993: 2).

The advertising in *Clarín* reveals what discourses were used to market the film's image. In one ad the headlines beamed: "With *Comodines* we broke with everything. Including box office records." The advertisement stated:

> *Comodines* was transformed into the release that was the most successful in recent times: 172,595 showed up in the first few days. More than

> *Independence Day*, more than *Twister*, more than *Jurassic Park*, more than *Caballos salvajes* and *La furia*. We congratulate all of those who worked to make sure we could all believe in national cinema.
>
> (*Clarín*, June 24, 1997)

For a start, this and other ads capitalized on how they beat earlier US blockbuster film records in the same span of time. By making this comparison, it necessarily elevated the status of the film as comparable to one from Hollywood. This comparison was unusual, given that Argentine critics had often categorized Argentine films separate from US ones, such as when they devised two separate "top ten lists" of films of the year (one for US and others, and the other for national films). (See the cultural magazine *La Maga* for annual lists.)

Directly preceding the abovementioned advertisement were statistics to prove the ad's assertions. *Comodines* was released on June 19, 1997, on nineteen screens. In four days, there were 98,000 viewers. *Independence Day* was released on July 18, 1996, on fifteen screens and amassed 94,000 viewers in four days. *Mission Impossible* opened on July 11, 1996, on eighteen screens and took in 82,000 viewers in four days. Here *Comodines* is framed as the biblical David that beat the behemoth Goliath from the North. Simultaneously, it compares itself with other Argentine films such as Piñeyro's *Caballos salvajes* (*Wild Horses*) (1995) and *La furia* (*The Fury*), one of the 1997 movie hits. One reason this ad may have framed *Comodines* as a "national film" was a nostalgic harkening back to the "golden age" of Argentine cinema in the 1930s and 1940s, when the studio system was alive and well and genre films flourished. One of the discourses surrounding the failure to attract audiences for national films was that national filmmakers were no longer making commercial genre films as they did in the celebrated "halcyon days" of Argentine cinema. Thus, one advertising strategy employed by the producers of *Comodines* was to position themselves as descendants of that era.

The creators of *Comodines*

In an interview, Fernando Blanco, one of the co-founders of Pol-Ka, the production company that masterminded *Comodines*, attributed the film's success to the fact that it was the first serious attempt to mimic Hollywood with a well-known genre, but, at the same time, to fill it with Argentina's own star system, language, and popular appeal (interview, 1998). In another interview with the director of *Comodines*, Jorge Nisco, he admitted his fear in creating a film that was long a part of US turf that was not to be touched by smaller, developing countries such as Argentina. Nisco notes:

> I felt a great risk in directing this film because the public is used to the large scale action pictures from abroad. For that reason we know that the

> expectations would be high, including the critics . . . our goal was to make a similar looking film that could stand alongside the rest of the action movies.
> (Urien 1997: 5)

In order to create complex and true-to-life action scenes, a helicopter explosion and other special effects, there had to be an investment in state-of-the-art film equipment. On Pol-Ka's website, it states that the director of photography, Ricardo de Angelis, "worked with a new camera that was brought to the country from the US company Film Factory." De Angelis was responsible for all of the technical material and worked with seventy people in this sector. In their own words, "The camera, an 'Arri[flex] 535,' was the only one in Argentina and worked to capture the action scenes never before filmed." Further, in terms of sound, Oscar

Figure 16.1 Comodines (1997).

Jadur and David Mantecom worked with Dolby Stereo and all of the sound effects were processed in a studio in the US (see www.pol-ka.com.ar). These statements allude to uses of cutting edge technology, and its links with the United States demonstrates how Pol-Ka worked to distance itself from the "typical" Argentine film. Part of the longstanding stigma associated with national cinema in Argentina has been the perception that these films could not compete with the high production values, sound quality, and acting ability typical of the US and other more developed film industries. Therefore, when producers began making films with special effects, there had to be a consideration of technological capacity. In a continuation of the interview with Jorge Nisco, the director discussed technological issues associated with the film:

Q: Are there big differences in the way special effects are created here compared with the US?

A: Perhaps there they work more in computer effects. For cost reasons, we could not access that technology. For example, perhaps the helicopter explosion seen in the film would have been done via the superimposition of images by computer in the US That is impossible for us. We decided to do this with a model and it worked perfectly.

Q: This idea of two cops that hate each other but later become friends is typical of the movies . . .

A: And the explosions and everything else, yes, it isn't anything new. However, I adhere to what Adrian [Suar] says: "we didn't invent gunpowder, but we know we can manufacture it."

(Urien 1997: 5)

These phrases signal a recognition that until that point in time, Argentina could not compete fully with the more developed countries in terms of high quality special effects. However, Nisco describes this contribution to Argentine cinema by noting that while they were derivative of Hollywood, they gained respect from Argentine audiences in that they were able to master the technology from the developed world and thus were now "modern" and technologically "cutting edge," albeit with some economic limitations. In various articles, the creators of *Comodines* touted their technological prowess of the genre more than any other facet of filmmaking. This, to them, along with the large numbers of box-office returns, signified their contribution to the Argentine national film tradition.

All the world's an ad – the case of *Comodines*

A further development in filmmaking during this period was the introduction of product-placement advertising in Argentine cinema. Although this was a staple form of revenue production in the television industry, until 1997 it had never been attempted on the silver screen. Traditionally, in the Argentine audio-visual industries there has been a separation among the television, film, and advertising sectors. For one, many filmmakers did not like to work with television actors due to an elitist view that television, as a "lesser genre," was not sophisticated enough to commingle with the cinema. By the same token, the issue of product placement within the cinema never intersected, mainly on account of the "noncommercial" and artistic nature of national cinema. This is also because advertisers had never envisioned the national cinema as a large audience vehicle to advertise their products. With *Comodines*, product placement had its debut within a feature length film. This was a natural convergence because *Comodines* was based on a television series. In fact, the producers of *Poliládron* approached their television advertisers to see whether they would be interested in "larger format" ads on film. According to *Comodines* co-producer Fernando Blanco, in Argentina, product placement is called "nontraditional advertising" or "advertising inside the *mise-en-scène* of the program" and is a beneficial way to minimize costs for Argentine television producers. From his perspective, it was "long overdue for films to utilize product placement as they do in US and some European films" (interview with author, 1998). Moreover, in *Comodines*, the level of product visibility reached new heights. In addition to seeing products throughout the film, such as an ad for Topline chewing gum on a television set, or a billboard for Crush soda in the subway, there was a series of television ads as the trailer for the home-video edition. There were ads for products such as Burger King, Coca Cola, the cellular phone company Movicom, and the gasoline company Esso, which were featured with an explanatory intertitle at the beginning stating: "The following companies sponsored the marketing of *Comodines*."

This linkage of advertising with film has created a series of debates in the US regarding the nature of product placement, product tie-ins, and corporate sponsorship. Some critics contend that product placement helps to link the spectator to the movie through the ads shown on the screen to the ads they experience everyday. In this way, product placement works to incorporate the viewer on multiple levels of engagement. Other scholars charge that product placement is gratuitous and excessive. From the positive perspective, film scholars have noted that, on some level, product placement such as product tie-ins and the like can work to "democratize the narrative process by opening up the narrative to audience participation." Thomas Schatz points out that film as a multimarket "intertext" offers myriad spaces for audience engagement, such as video games and other multimedia reiterations (Schatz 1993: 34–6). Certainly, in the case of *Comodines*, this was the first time there was a shift to an "interactive" mode for consumers of product tie-ins. Scratch-off games found in packages of Bimbo white bread (comparable to Wonder bread) and others could be viewed as working to engage viewers with the movie. From a different, more critical vantage point, film scholar Janet Wasko asserts that product placement has no positive effects: the commercialization of products within the *mise-en-scène* of films compromises the integrity of the narrative of the film itself (Wasko 1994). In Argentina, many critics complained that viewers of *Comodines* were bombarded with advertising and that it was untenable. Claudio España, esteemed film critic at the newspaper *La Nación*, wrote:

> In terms of subliminal material, despite the obviousness of the advertising, it becomes unbearable the amount of product placement that taints the image: placards on ambulances, billboards on the main freeway, branding on television, gasoline ads, advertising in restaurants . . . it becomes interminable. (España 1997)

Regardless of one's position on the pros and cons of commercial devices placed within films, it is evident that a title such as *Comodines* broke the mold of national cinema and took the unorthodox position of making a commercial film replete with product placement a viable practice within the realm of national cinema. While it might have been viewed as "crass," "commercial," or "vulgar" (as art house filmmaker Javier Torre and others deem it [interview with author, 1998]), the reality was that the film was made on a budget of $2.5 million (a low sum for Hollywood but high for Argentine standards) and that it had high production values. This may have given others such as potential investors the idea that Argentine cinema could be a worthwhile venture and thus build up a more consistent industry.

The rise of multiplex cinemas

In addition to this prospect of strengthening potential investors for national film production, a trend in multiplex cinema-building created potential spaces for national films that was desperately overdue. Beginning in 1995 and extending into the twenty-first century, there has been a sharp rise in multinational corporate investment in multiplex cinemas throughout most of Latin America. Argentina, as well as other Latin American countries, has witnessed the influx of foreign-owned theater chains such as the US-based Cinemark Theaters, Australia's Village Roadshow and Hoyts theaters, the US's General Cinema, and others. In 1998, Gemma Richardson, marketing vice president of Sony Cinema Products, reported that Latin America now had the world's highest rate of theater growth (Paxman 1998). These movie theaters, located in upscale shopping malls and wealthy neighborhoods in major cities, screen mainly Hollywood films, but occasionally make room for "independent" films from the United States (that is, films from studios such as Miramax, which is actually owned by Disney) as well as Argentina. In 1997 and 1998 the Argentine box office grew 20 percent, and thus has proven to be a lucrative business venture for theater entrepreneurs. Harold Blank, the Buenos

Aires vice-president for Hoyts, the Australian-owned theater which opened its first multiplex in 1998, stated that "Argentina has the highest per-capita income in the region. With 33 million people, I don't see any difficulty with there being 1,000 new screens – and there are 450 already in the pipeline" (ibid.).

Multiplex cinemas have arisen in response to changes in viewership patterns, whereby a segmentation of the market has allowed for particular subgroupings with disposable income to see films or buy products that are specifically tailored to their tastes, rather than "lowest common denominator" films created for a wide cross-section of the population. By creating small theaters and supplying a variety of films for different populations (along age, gender, race, ethnicity, class, and religious lines) the concept of multiplexing is, in theory, a more democratic means of access because it includes a diversity of offerings to different niche audiences. In the film community, there was a hope that, with the opening of film screen spaces, there would be more opportunities to screen Argentine cinema. In reality, however, the popular blockbuster movie *Titanic* (1997), for example, was simultaneously shown on six screens in the multiplex rather than on one or two. Although the presence of these new screens has brought in more revenue to the country in the form of employment, and the INCAA's film development pool has increased in the form of box-office receipts, it is not clear thus far whether these multiplexes will consistently screen national films (those that are not allied with large media companies) and thus expand spaces of exhibition for national filmmakers.

In the case of *Comodines*, however, the film had the advantage of being shown in the newly constructed suburban "shoppings" (as they are called in Argentina) as well as on screens set aside specifically for national cinema. These screen allocations have been part of an effort put forth by the INCAA. So far, the INCAA has been able to purchase two movie theaters to show Argentine and other foreign art films. The Sala Tita Merello is a triplex in a downtown area once in vogue for moviegoing (but no longer), and the newer Teatro de la Comedia is located in a posh neighborhood on Santa Fe Avenue. Although these movie theaters were designed to create a place for national cinema that traditionally had trouble finding an exhibition venue, this did not exclude the commercial national productions that typically had no trouble securing space in mainstream commercial locations. This move has been criticized by film critics such as Sergio Wolf (Wolf 1998: 69). Why was *Comodines* shown on specifically designated screens for national cinema in addition to mainstream commercial movie screens? The film was billed as a national film, but at the same time was differentiated by stressing its technically superior production values.

"Glocal" spaces?

In terms of form and content, *Comodines* is a hybrid film in that the form is a global genre – that is, a TV serial spin-off action film – while the content, though formulaic, utilizes local language, actors, and other local color within a Hollywood narrative structure. By using a typical "action film" template, it was universally palatable to audiences. For example, the film is about two policemen who are forced to work together, but who initially cannot stand to be in each other's company. However, toward the end of the film, they wind up helping one another, and grow to be friends. While it is essentially formulaic, the film makes good use of local actors who are familiar faces on TV, and thus have star power in Argentina. Another local aspect is the use of typical Argentine Spanish (i.e. the use of slang, or *lunfardo*), humor, and a soundtrack consisting of Argentine rock bands that has special appeal to the youth market. Thus, the film takes pains to present itself as comparable to a Hollywood movie, but different enough that national audiences could identify with it and be proud to call it their own.

In what could be called a "global aesthetic," one striking aspect of the film is its choice of scene locations. Although the plot is set in Buenos Aires, most of the action takes place in city spaces that are generally unrecognizable from those of any other large metropolis. Scenes throughout the film are set in generic spaces such as supermarkets, office buildings, the freeway, and a cemetery; and these in a videogame sequence in the opening shot. In short, *Comodines*, while purporting to be distinctly national, is set in what David Harvey calls "globalized spaces," that is, Western, industrialized, and urban spaces that are not specific to any one locale (Harvey 1990: 295). However, for actor and co-producer Adrian Suar, the success of the film was based on feelings of pride that Argentina could successfully compete in making action films with what he considers a different twist:

> We created something dignified. *Comodines* is a cop movie with an American rhythm. Action movies have been shown here for fifty years, but they were never made in Argentina. It isn't same when you see two dudes like myself and Calvo running down Florida Street.
>
> (Scholtz 1997: 3)

Suar mentions how the film takes an "American rhythm" but then reflects how the two protagonists run down a pedestrian shopping street in the downtown area of Buenos Aires. So, for Suar, despite having a US appeal, the film utilizes a distinctly Argentine space (that is, Florida Street) which he thinks gives it a local feel. While I would disagree with this characterization, mainly because the street scene is filmed at night and thus could pass for any other street, it is true that use of local language, star power, and music does give the film a local flavor. It is also the case that, in terms of audience popularity more generally, media scholar Joseph Straubhaar found that use of local actors, humor, and language do prove a natural advantage over films with subtitles (Straubhaar 1991). In other interviews with Suar, he states that he and others hoped to (re)insert Argentina within the commercial film world on the same footing with Hollywood, thus reminiscent of the heyday of the country's studio-system era. Clearly, Suar was interested in bringing audiences the kind of action films that have never characterized Argentine cinema. Thus, proponents of an Argentine blockbuster cinema wanted to modify or expand the definition of national cinema in Argentina.

Conclusion

Although blockbuster movies such as *Comodines* have had the wherewithal and resources to compete with the giant of the North, they have done so with the use of state loans and subsidies. This has been a contentious issue among the small director-producers, who feel that they, the "smaller guys," must now compete unfairly against production companies who are powerful allies with large multimedia conglomerates. Further, members of the film community charge that the original spirit behind cinematic legislation was to provide funds for filmmakers who produced films that did not conform to the dictates of the marketplace. Instead, however, in the 1990s, the INCAA, during President Menem's presidency, conformed more to an "industrial" model of film production, stressing commercial hits and a business approach rather than an "artistic" model favored in the 1980s under President Alfonsín.

Films such as *Comodines* have undoubtedly been proven to boost the economy of the film industry, but they could do so without the "corporate welfare" handed out by the state. In the case of Brazil, Argentina's neighbor to the north, cinema laws stipulate that multimedia conglomerates are not eligible for state subsidies. Therefore, it might take a concerted effort by producer-director filmmakers to push for improved film legislation to rectify this inequality of opportunity for filmmakers in Argentina.

Comodines, though, is a case example of how in the 1990s the Argentine film industry produced films that brought audiences back to see national cinema. Although movies such as this veered away from a tradition of filmmaking that focuses on social issues facing Argentina, it forged a commercial filmmaking style that has boosted employment for the film industry and provided a blockbusting form of movie entertainment with a local twist.

Notes

This article is an expanded and revised version of "Argentine Blockbuster Movies and the Politics of Culture Under Neoliberalism, 1989–98," in *Media, Culture, and Society*, 22 (2000): 327–42.

All translations are those of the author.

Thanks to Sue Carter and Stephen Steigman for their editorial assistance.

References

Belaunzan, Jorge (1997) "El cine argentino es negocio (de la TV)," *La Maga*, July 23: 16.

Belaunzan, Jorge, and Blanco, Eduardo (1993) "El gobierno necesita que en cultura no pase nada," *La Maga*, May 12: 6.

Blanco, Eduardo (1993) "El Grupo Clarín controla o tiene participacion en casi 30 empresas," *La Maga*, November 24: 2–3.

DEISICA (Departamento de Estudios e Investigacion del Sindicato de la Industria Cinematografica Argentina) (1997) *Annual Report*.

D'Esposito, Leonardo (1997) "Asi se construye un exito argentino," *La Maga*, July 2: 27.

España, Claudio (1997) "Un artefacto demasiado controlado," *La Nación*, June 19.

Harvey, David (1990) *The Condition of Postmodernity*, Oxford: Blackwell.

Paxman, Andrew (1998) "Southern Renaissance: Corporate Ventures Multiply Region's Booming Multiplexes," *Variety*, March 23–9: 43–4.

Schatz, Thomas (1993) "The New Hollywood," in Jim Collins, Hilary Radner, and Ava Preacher Collins (eds), *Film Theory Goes to the Movies*, New York and London: Routledge: 8–36 [reprinted in this volume].

Scholtz, Pablo O. (1997) ". . . Y *Comodines* hizo historia," *Clarín*, June 24: 3

Straubhaar, Joseph (1991) "Beyond Media Imperialism: Assymetrical Interdependence and Cultural Proximity," *Critical Studies in Mass Communcation*, 8: 39–59.

Thieburger, Mariano, and Dupcovsky, Diego (1990) "Reportaje: Octavio Getino," *Contra luz: revista de cine*, October: 11–14.

Urien, Paula (1997) "El año del cine argentino," *La Nación*, September 21, supplement: 1–14.

Wasko, Janet (1994) *Hollywood in the Information Age*, Austin: University of Texas Press.

Wolf, Sergio (1998) "El cine argentino en los '90," *Causas y Azares*, 6 (spring): 65–70.

Wyatt, Justin (1994) *High Concept: Movie and Marketing in Hollywood*, Austin: University of Texas Press.

17

LOCATING BOLLYWOOD

Notes on the Hindi blockbuster, 1975 to the present

Andrew Willis

Popular Hindi films have a special place in current British film culture. Screenings of the latest "Bollywood" blockbusters consistently fill those cinemas around the UK that choose to show them. It is certainly possible to argue that in some ways these screenings represent the last bastion of family moviegoing in the UK – that is, films that appeal to different generations as opposed to films that parents are dragged along to because youngsters want to see them. Indeed, the release of *Kabhi Khushi Kabhie Gham* in December 2001 saw the film enter the UK box-office chart at number 3, behind the more traditional blockbuster *Harry Potter and the Philosopher's Stone* (2001) and the Liverpool-set Samuel L. Jackson star vehicle *The 51st State* (2001).

Throughout 2001 Hindi popular cinema was touted in the British media as the next crossover phenomenon. This followed the massive international success of Ang Lee's Mandarin language *Crouching Tiger, Hidden Dragon* (2000) which had suggested a market for subtitled films. Foreign-language Oscar contender *Lagaan* (2001) and the Shah Rukh Kahn produced *Aśoka* (2001) were both critically well received in the mainstream UK media and did reasonably well at the box office. However, the film that really attracted large audiences was much more typical of certain trends in the contemporary Hindi blockbuster. *Kabhi Khushi Kabhie Gham* is a large-scale, star-filled love story. Yet perhaps the most significant part of its blockbuster status is the fact that for some it represents the shift toward creating films that are no longer simply aimed at the indigenous Indian market, but actively seek audiences within the Indian diaspora – in particular, those in the UK, Canada, and the US. This is not surprising when one considers that the audience outside India can now account for around 65 percent of a film's total earnings (Banker 2001: 8). Unlike that for *Crouching Tiger, Hidden Dragon*, the primary market for *Kabhi Khushi Kabhie Gham* in the UK was drawn from the diasporic community. It would be wrong to see the success of this film as needing any crossover into the subtitled

Figure 17.1 *Aśoka* (2001).

market. Indeed, the box-office returns for nonsubtitled screenings of Hindi language films in the UK is substantial.

One of the main elements that reflects these shifts is the creation, on screen, of a mythical India, one which appeals to the nostalgic feelings in the diasporic audience. This serves an important function for young and old Asians in Britain, which is highlighted by the reasons often offered for attending screenings of Hindi films. For example, when Hyphen Films conducted a series of interviews for their introductions to Channel 4's *Bollywood Best* season, shown in the summer of 2001, many people reflected upon why they thought that Hindi popular cinema is important for nonresident Indians (NRIs). One young woman in Birmingham, for example, stated that "growing up in England we need something to remind us of our culture and stuff. Indian films are good at that." Her reflections were reinforced by a young man, also in Birmingham, who explained why he liked visiting the cinema to see Indian films: "a lot of Indian people, like myself, come to see Indian films basically to see our culture. We get to see parts of India, to see some rituals that perhaps we don't perform here anymore, but we do still back home. Ultimately we are Indian and we still have things in common with people from India, and when we see things on the screen we feel closer to home." It is these feelings and desires that the newest type of Hindi blockbuster seems specifically designed to cater for. For example, *Kabhi Khushi Kabhie Gham* involves characters who are displaced to the UK, due to a family fallout, but hold on to their values drawn from India and their being Indian. These characters dialog seems written in a way calculated to appeal to NRIs and other emigrant communities from the subcontinent. The elements that constitute the Hindi blockbuster have slowly shifted and developed over the past ten years in ways that allow the inclusion of material that will appeal to audiences in India but also, crucially, abroad.

By necessity, this study of popular Indian cinema, or more specifically the Hindi blockbuster, will be rather schematic. As Sumita S. Chakravarty argues, "Indian cinema is too diverse, Indian culture too complex, Indian artistic traditions too varied and eclectic for any one study to encompass their whole range" (1993: 17). Certainly, in any analysis of an industry so big, certain generalizations have to be made in order to chart key changes. The Indian film industry is one of the most active in the world. It has produced near to, or more than, 700 feature films annually since the late 1970s, with a peak of 948 in 1990. Of these around 200 have been in Hindi (Rajadhyaksha and Willemen 1999: 31–2), many of which represent Indian cinema's most popular form, the Bollywood blockbuster.

In this chapter I want to consider some of the stylistic and thematic changes that have occurred between the 1970s and 2001. These are changes which have allowed the popular Hindi film industry to break out of the Indian subcontinent and its more traditional markets in East Africa, the Middle East, and Southeast Asia (for more details see Vasudevan 2000b: 131) and find significant audiences in the UK, Canada, and the US.

The Hindi blockbuster is conceived before the camera rolls. A series of decisions are made regarding format, performers, story-line, locations, songs, playback singers, choreographers, etc. Each of these elements is seen as a key component in the creation of a film that will prove successful with audiences. In this sense, the Hindi blockbuster is undoubtedly a "high concept" cinematic form. Changes in the industry and its modes of production over the past thirty years have meant that the Hindi cinema version of "high concept" has quickly transferred from the low-budget productions that constituted the most popular format of the 1970s to the relatively expensive productions of today.

However, before going on it is worth making a few more general observations about Hindi popular cinema. While critical work is appearing that focuses on Hindi popular cinema, much of that on Indian cinema has concentrated on key auteurs from the world of "art" cinema: for example, Ray, Benegal, Sen, and movements such as the "new" Indian cinema. As Ravi S. Vasudevan (2000b: 134) has noted, popular cinema was dismissed "for its derivativeness from American cinema, the melodramatic externality and stereotyping of its characters, and especially for its failure to focus on the psychology of human interaction." Rosie Thomas also acknowledges this and suggests the ways in which popular Indian cinema is often dismissed by critics in the West. She suggests how the latter consider many of these popular films, particularly the blockbusters, as, to put it bluntly, not worth taking seriously. In their responses they often troop out a number of well-established clichés: "the films are said to be nightmarishly lengthy, second-rate copies of Hollywood trash, to be dismissed with patronising amusement or facetious quips" (1985: 117). However, as film studies begins finally to acknowledge the importance of popular cinema from around the world, Bollywood is taking its place as an industry worthy of detailed and sustained critical interest.

Like others from across the world, such as that of Hong Kong, Indian popular cinema does not rely heavily on Western models of realism. This has created problems for some critics – in particular concerning narrative patterns and story-lines – who have traditionally associated attempts at "realism" with seriousness. However, it is vital to acknowledge that these "problems" are also interesting challenges to the dominant Western models of filmmaking. As Thomas notes, the lack of clear story-line can be explained in the context of Indian cinema:

> What is meant by "no story" is, first, that the story-line will be almost totally predictable to the Indian audience, being a repetition, or rather, an unmistakable transformation, of many other Hindi films, and second, that it will be recognised by them as a "ridiculous" pretext for spectacle and emotion.
>
> (1985: 123)

The formula of the Hindi blockbuster

As Gokulsing and Dissanayake (1998) acknowledge, formula is central to Hindi popular cinema. Of course, like any set of cinematic codes and conventions, these change historically and are open to the influence of wider shifts in cultural trends. For example, the big Hindi blockbusters of the 1970s, such as *Sholay* (1975), contained fewer songs than the popular films of the 1950s and 1960s.

Thomas suggests that there are a number of elements that can be labeled as central to the formula of the Hindi blockbuster. As it is designed to appeal to large audiences who have certain expectations, the Hindi blockbuster seeks to deliver these elements. Sometimes this will involve a reworking or refiguring of familiar components. First, it operates in an excessive manner. A crucial part of the escapism so important to the Hindi blockbuster is its willingness to present its stories in a larger than life, almost fantastical way. Thomas also suggests that "spectacular and emotional excess will invariably be privileged over linear narrative development" (1985: 124). This excess is linked to another key element, spectacle.

Again Thomas, in this case talking about *Naseeb* (1981), argues that spectacle is linked to the key elements of the blockbuster, things that are essential to the continued mass appeal of such films: "song and dance, locations, costumes, fights and thrills (or stunts), most of Bombay's top stars" (ibid.). In the examples that I have chosen, it is possible to identify how these key components change subtly over the period encompassed in my study while remaining central to the form of the Hindi blockbuster and its continued popularity.

Thomas goes on to argue that there are certain narratives that are typical of the Hindi popular cinema and that these narrative components are used again and again. Once more this reveals how a formula can change over time while still using the narrative structures audiences are familiar with and, indeed, desire. For example, in the 1970s and 1980s many films, such as the Amitabh Bachchan vehicle *Muqaddar Ka Sikandar* (1978), incorporated children being lost and found, revenge for wrongs, and two men falling in love with the same woman, leading to a sacrifice based on love. All of these things are familiar from earlier eras, though in the 1970s and 1980s they were given a much harder, urban edge. These stories usually revolve around fate, destiny, and issues of duty and kinship and are worked and reworked throughout a number of films. Again, as Thomas suggests, this means that we can assume audiences are more interested in the ways that the films present and explore these expected plot twists than they are concerned with the originality of the plot. Excess and spectacle therefore take priority over narrative originality, with audiences looking for a visually spectacular presentation of a film's themes and ideas. Part of this celebration of excess is present in the most commonly known element of the Hindi blockbuster, the musical, or song-and-dance, number.

The song-and-dance number is a much maligned, but totally central, part of the formula of the Hindi blockbuster. Such numbers often reflect the emotional content of the film; as Thomas argues, "Hindi film songs are usually tightly integrated, through words and mood, within the flow of the film" (1985: 127). More recently, however, while they have remained an integral element in Hindi blockbusters, they have increasingly become part of the wider marketing strategies employed to promote the films. Key numbers are taken out of the films and used on the popular Asian satellite music channels in the build-up to a film's release, heightening public awareness of the film and the stars who appear in the numbers. Because of their use in this context it is possible to identify the influence of pop-music videos on an aesthetic level. As Gokulsing and Dissanayake argue, "the impact of western musical television (MTV) is being increasingly felt in Indian films: their pace, the camera angles, the music, the dance sequences" (1998: 95). In the contemporary blockbuster, songs are also used to unlock the audience's knowledge of other Hindi films and, attached to this, their nostalgia, thus highlighting the cultural importance of Bollywood for, particularly, NRI audiences. For example, in *Kabhi Khushi Kabhie Gham*, "Aati Kya Khandala," from the 1998 hit film *Ghulam*, is used, as well as refrains from older film songs such as "Vande Mataram" and "Jana Gana Mana."

Another of the key factors within Indian popular cinema, as in other popular national cinemas, is stardom. Stars are a vital component in Bollywood blockbusters: indeed, they often contain more than one big star, whose presence is vigorously used to assist in marketing. *Sholay* is certainly reflective of the use of stars in the 1970s, and, usefully, it is also emblematic of some of the changes that were occurring in Hindi popular cinema at the time. As Arnold notes, "a change of direction transformed the romantic song and dance extravaganza into the violent, action-packed thriller" (cited in Gokulsing and Dissanayake 1998: 95). In fact, *Sholay* is perhaps the most typical and well-known example of these changes. It is action-oriented, containing scenes of great energy and spectacle. The film's central characters are antiheroes whose actions are dictated by notions of honor rather than legality, and who operate on the margins of the criminal world. The film presents these characters in a sympathetic way, suggesting that they may have been forced into illegal actions due to the social inequalities they have encountered during their lives. It is also a film that combines more than one star, here Amitabh Bachchan and Dharmendra, in what had became known as "multistarrers." In the mid-1970s and early 1980s, one cornerstone of such Hindi blockbusters was Bachchan, the superstar of Indian cinema and an actor whose mere appearance almost guaranteed blockbuster-size audiences for a new film.

Amitabh Bachchan: *the* superstar

No discussion of the Hindi blockbuster since the 1970s would be complete without some discussion of Amitabh Bachchan. Many of the most typical elements of the blockbuster in the mid-1970s and early 1980s can be found in his films. Frequently referred to as a "one man film industry," he was by far the biggest attraction in Indian popular cinema of the period. Indeed, Bachchan became so omnipresent within Indian culture that he is often referred to in terms that reflect the intertextual nature of his stardom (Sharma 1993). This is particularly the case in relation to his 1981 blockbuster *Silsila*, which drew on gossip about his private life by casting his wife Jaya and alleged lover Reka. Another example of Bachchan's enormous presence in the Indian popular imagination is the coverage in the mass media of his on set injury during the filming of *Coolie* (1983). Indeed, this incident was so much a part of the film that when the final cut was made it included a freeze frame indicating the stunt that went wrong during a fight scene, accompanied by text explaining that the star had almost been killed at this point. (This suggests that audiences came to this film with pre-existing knowledge of the star and his accident.) Indeed, the finished film itself became an example of his heroic status – as he had managed to complete it – and the accident contributed to its being a massive blockbuster.

Figure 17.2 Bollywood legend Amitabh Bachchan.

As noted above, what is striking about Bachchan from the mid-1970s is how far he became an integral part of many large-scale blockbusters. However, it would be dangerous to suggest that his presence was the only reason that these films were successful at the box office. It is worth noting, as Justin Wyatt (1994) does in relation to Hollywood high concept films of the 1990s, that big stars usually have to appear in the right vehicles, ones that reflect the public's notion of their stardom. Bachchan managed to do this throughout the late 1970s and early 1980s, appearing in action titles, romances, and comedies, but he was not the only essential component in the blockbusters of the period.

A very typical Bachchan film, and a blockbuster of the period, is *Amar Akbar Anthony* (1977). It is a good example of the "multistarrer," as it showcases the talents of established stars Rishi Kapoor, Vinod Khanna, and Parveen Babi as well as Bachchan, and contains a number of story-lines, each devoted to one of the stars. Its plot concerns three brothers who are separated while children and brought up not knowing each other – one by a Christian priest, one by a Muslim tailor, and one by a Hindu police officer – with these narrative strands being drawn together as the film moves toward its celebratory climax. The film's final dance number represents a familiar, ideologically optimistic tendency within Hindi popular cinema. The three brothers unite to save Anthony's girlfriend from a forced marriage to one of the evil Robert's henchmen. They appear in disguises: Anthony as a Catholic priest, Akbar as a tailor, and Amar as a one-man band. The way in which they manage to forget their religious differences to work together is significant in a continent where such differences had been marked in recent history. The finale also shows clearly that, while the number of songs present in such films may have been reduced, they are of no less importance. The final song represents the coming together of the characters and their backgrounds, the reuniting of the brothers separated by a mixture of a cruel twist of fate and urban poverty. It is absolutely integrated into the overall structure of the film and is certainly not an additional sidebar to its narrative and ideological drive. Indeed, the plea for unity visually represented by the song is made all the more effective because of its articulation within such a celebratory moment. The dance movements of the three male leads – they walk upstairs in unison with their hands on each other's shoulders – and their singing in harmony, each contributing a line at a time, reveal how the integration is realized within the cinematic construction of the number. Indeed, such an example highlights the importance of the integrated number to the form of the Hindi blockbuster and suggests that it should be read in terms of the overall perspective of the films, rather than simply as something additionally thrown into the mix. Success, and therefore true blockbuster status, depends upon these numbers working within the structure of the film in a manner that fulfills audience knowledge and expectations. The songs are also often used to reflect another key thematic element in the Bachchan blockbuster, namely, an overt sympathy with the poor and downtrodden. This element is perhaps most successfully achieved in the Bachchan blockbuster *Muqaddar Ka Skinner* (1978), but can be seen in a number of other key Bachchan titles, such as *Don* (1978), *Kala Patthar* (1979), and *Hum* (1991).

As the 1980s progressed, the tried and tested elements of the blockbuster began to change. Amitabh Bachchan was elected to parliament in 1984 to represent his hometown of Allahabad for the Congress Party. For a short time this shifted public focus away from his films, and by the late 1980s even his seemingly unassailable star status began to wane. While he was still having successes, such as the popular *Hum* – which contained so many familiar elements from his star persona that Rajadhyaksha and Willemen were moved to call it "a lexicon of Bachchanalia" (1999: 502) – his films were no longer assured blockbuster status. Undoubtedly, because of such factors the blockbuster formula was forced to change. Newer stars were beginning to challenge the older stalwarts, and some older stars, such as Bachchan, were beginning to take roles that reflected their aging and slightly different status within the industry. New trends were clearly emerging in the Hindi blockbuster.

The 1990s: recent trends and diasporic audiences

A key film, and one that represents some of the most significant shifts in the 1990s, is Sooraj Barjatya's *Hum Aapke Hain Koun . . . !* (1994). It contains some of the changes to the blockbuster formula that would be consolidated by a number of the hugely successful films that followed in its wake. *Hum Aapke Hain Koun . . . !* privileges romance over action, it contains more numbers than the 1970s and early 1980s blockbusters, and it featured newer rising stars of the Hindi film industry, in this case Madhuri Dixit and Salman Khan. One of the most popular films ever at the Indian box office, *Hum Aapke Hain Koun . . . !* recentered old-fashioned family values and the family audience after the action and revenge dramas associated with the Bachchan star persona. In doing so it is representative of films that offered little that might be considered controversial and so ushered in a more conservative era in popular Hindi cinema. Interestingly, according to Rajadhyaksha and Willemen (1999: 519), the film is a remake of the 1982 box-office failure *Nadiya Ke Paar*, perhaps revealing how much the tastes of audiences had changed in the period between the two versions of the story.

The film that most clearly shows the shift toward an interest in nonresident Indians, in terms of both subject matter and potential audience, is *Dilwale Dulhania Le Jayenge* (1995). A massive hit, the film opens with Amrish Puri, playing a newsagent who has been resident in London for twenty-two years, feeding the pigeons in Trafalgar Square. In a voice-over he explains how he feels he has been chained to this place by his economic circumstances and that one day he plans to return home to the Punjab. He closes his eyes, and the film's first song and dance number begins with a group of women wearing colorful clothes dancing in a field. This instantly establishes that his memory of the Punjab corresponds with Hindi popular cinema's representations of the place. From the outset the nostalgic representation of the Punjab is presented unquestioningly as "truthful." The opening clearly gives authority to the mythical "India" created by the Hindi film industry. Such versions of this mythical India have become more commonplace in the most recent blockbusters, such as *Mohabbatein* (2000) and *Kabhi Khushi Kabhie Gham*, as they strive to represent an acceptable vision of "home" for NRIs.

The opening sequence of *Dilwale Dulhania Le Jayenge* continues with a crane down to reveal Puri in the field in front of the dancers, still feeding the birds. The placing of the actor within his character's fantasy also works to position his vision of a rural experience as particularly "authentic." This might also explain the popularity of the film with urban Indian audiences, who are invited to see their "home" in this idyllic, almost pre-industrial rural world – a world that does not evoke the corruption of the city, or rather its cinematic representations, in particular those drawn from the urban-set films from the 1970s onward. The lyrics of the song work to reinforce these visual ideas: "come home stranger, your country calls you." The fantasy of rural bliss is eventually shattered by the bells of St Martin-in-the-Fields, a typically British sound, which drown out the music of the song. This is followed by a montage, under the credits, of Puri walking around London to his workplace. The settings are shot in a way that highlights their dullness, and Puri carries an umbrella which, of course, he has to use. Again, this sequence is edited in a way that contrasts his reality in Britain with his colorful, mythic vision of the Punjab. *Dilwale Dulhania Le Jayenge* marks an important move toward the creation of a mythical India in popular Hindi films, one that is constructed as much for those outside India as those within.

By 1998 these family-oriented films had retaken the box office. However, controversial films still found an audience, for example, *Roja* (1992), which looked at terrorist kidnapping in Kashmir, and *Bombay* (1995), which focused on the relationship between a Muslim woman and a Hindu man against the backdrop of urban religious riots. Both of these films were directed by Mani Ratnam, who was best known for working in the Tamil industry. Other films proved controversial because they reflected the changing approaches to issues such as sex. For example, *Khalnayak* (1993) contained the number "Choli Ke Peechay," performed by Madhuri Dixit, which asked the suggestive question "What is beneath my veil, what is under my blouse?"

Typical of the shift back to romantic story-lines in the 1990s is the megahit *Kuch Kuch Hota Hai* (1998). This is a film that clearly aspired to and achieved blockbuster status. It is a useful example for my purposes as it shows a number of important developments in the Hindi blockbuster of the period, while still offering the key components of melodrama, romance, spectacle, exotic locations, comedy, and song and dance. Crucially, the production values on display here are much higher than those of the blockbusters from the 1970s and early 1980s. The camerawork, editing, and sound are all much more polished than in the earlier decades. This can be explained to some degree by technological advances and higher budgets. Like other romantic films of the mid-1990s, it contains a larger number of songs than the more action-driven, male-oriented films of the 1970s and 1980s. Here there are twelve: they are shot in a more flamboyant style, clearly directed toward the demands of satellite channels and influenced by music-video aesthetics.

More significantly, there is a much greater focus on women. Rather than being a tale of two men who fall in love with the same woman, which leads to sacrifice – as in, for example, Feroz Khan's *Qurbani* (1980) – *Kuch Kuch Hota Hai* presents two women who love the same man. One of them, Anjali, is the character who makes the sacrifice, leaving Rhaul and Tina to fall in love and marry. The film also reveals a more general shift away from engaging with contemporary social issues, in particular class, which had been so emblematic of the Bachchan films of the 1970s and 1980s. Here the main characters are young, socially mobile university students, carefree and clearly very middle class (revealed through their designer clothes: DKNY, GAP, Polo, Speedo, etc). The only worry there seems to be in their lives is whom to fall in love with. The central characters, therefore, offer models of aspiration. The world of *Kuch Kuch Hota Hai* is one of fantasy, but here it is one of wealth rather than the earlier fantasy of justice that marks the Bachchan films, where wealth often symbolizes corruption. This element is also reflected in the use of Scottish locations that help create a fantastic, unworldly setting that does not correspond to any "real" experience of any audience.

As noted, the enormous success of the more romantically oriented family films of the late 1990s marked a significant shift in the make-up of the Hindi blockbuster. Romantic stories mixed with comic subplots became the dominant narrative structure. An excellent example of the style of current blockbuster is *Mohabbatein*, a film that was much more successful outside India than at the domestic box office. Released in 2000, it certainly seems to have been conceived as a blockbuster. The film is cast to appeal across the generations using one of the most popular stars of the late 1990s, Shah Rukh Khan, alongside Amitabh Bachchan. The battle between the worldviews of these characters constitutes the moral center of the film. The bringing together of these two enormous stars is a strategy familiar from the multi-starrers of the 1970s and 1980s and, of course, can be seen as a strategy to appeal to different parts of the mass audience, which is itself made up of different generations. This strategy was repeated with three generations of stars when Hrithik Roshan joined Bachchan and Khan in *Kabhi Khushi Kabhie Gham*. However, Bachchan's presence might also be designed to appeal to those outside India, who see him still as the epitome of the Hindi film star. If, as argued earlier through the example of interviews with young British Asians, NRIs' experiences of India and its culture are filtered through cinema, then films wishing to appeal to that audience would logically include the iconic figure of Bachchan. As "real" memories of "home" are replaced by cinematic images, Bachchan – and the place he occupies within popular culture – becomes even more important.

There are other elements in *Mohabbatein* that contribute to its status as a blockbuster. The film has seven songs with music written by the team behind the successful *Kuch Kuch Hota Hai* (1998), Jatin-Lalit. Setting the film in a university also reflects an attempt to repeat the formula of the earlier, enormously popular film. What is striking in this case is the use of English locations, in particular, Oxford University and Longleat House (which are used for Gurukul University). The sheer size of this film recalls the shifts in the Hollywood blockbuster in the early 1960s, a time when producers were forever trying to top the films that had been successful before. Here everything has the feel of being calculated to be bigger and more spectacular and impressive than earlier blockbusters – for example, the replacing of the one central romantic story of the earlier films with the triple story of the young students and their search for love.

Another striking feature of the film is the level of intertextuality. Again, this is something which has been creeping into Hindi popular cinema since the 1970s. Early on in *Mohabbatein*, there are two moments that clearly reflect this trend and celebrate Hindi popular cinema and the audience's knowledge and memories of it. First, there is the introductory appearance of Bachchan as the strict principal, Shankar. As the young men look out of their bedroom window they see a figure, cloaked and standing next to a lake in the university grounds. The camera tracks toward him from the back as he looks toward the rising sun, a movement which is intercut with a close-up of his hands and a close-up of his mouth. There is then an extreme close-up of his eyes. These are the eyes that are so familiar to all Hindi cinemagoers, as they were a trademark of his earlier screen persona. By this point the audience has no doubt who this is. There is then a cut as he turns toward the camera in slow motion and throws his cloak over his shoulder and begins to walk. This scene dramatically introduces the character through a clever use of audience knowledge of the actor and the seriousness of his status within Indian popular culture. Indeed, his character is someone who has to come to terms with a changing world, just as the actor himself has had to do as he has begun to play much older characters. The values with which Bachchan is most closely associated as a star are no longer central to Hindi popular cinema, and in this role he seems to be aware of this shift in the films and in his own stardom. The music that accompanies his introduction is somber and serious compared with the light romantic fare that dominates the rest of the film. Significantly, Bachchan himself once commented upon the character in a manner reflective of the changes he is experiencing in the Hindi blockbuster and his place within the popular Hindi film industry: "He will have to change. The old generation will have to change their old traditions, so that a new generation can create a new tradition."

Shortly after this scene, the second significant intertextual moment occurs. The comic subplot of *Mohabbatein* focuses on café owner Kake's attempts to woo Preeto. In the introduction to these characters, Kake sings the romantic theme song to the megahit *Kuch Kuch Hota Hai*. Again, this constitutes a clear invitation to the audience to celebrate their knowledge of popular cinema and the songs that they all know. The use of this refrain so early in the film also works as a guarantor to the audience that *Mohabbatein* aims to deliver the same sort of romantic family entertainment provided by the earlier hit. Increasingly, the use of familiar songs, drawn from the history of Hindi cinema, has become a staple of the contemporary blockbuster.

Mohabbatein also reveals how the issues that are central to the film are channeled through individuals rather than through a social class, as in the Bachchan films of the earlier era. It can be argued that this shift is made apparent in the fantasy settings of these later films. *Mohabbatein* uses English locations for the university, *Kuch Kuch Hota Hai* uses Scottish ones. Again, as noted earlier, this contrasts with the films of the 1970s and 1980s which offered audiences recognizable environments within which stories unfolded. The more recent blockbusters create a fantasy world that, through the use of non-Indian locations, does not correspond to a social reality. The socially recognizable settings have now been replaced with ones that highlight the fantasy of the films. Of course, not all Hindi popular cinema follows this model. However, it is possible to argue that the Hindi blockbuster of the early twenty-first century is moving more and more in this direction – indeed, one might observe that the formula for success now demands it. However, as always, this formula will slowly change. Whatever direction the Hindi blockbuster takes in the future, one thing is certain: these films are now enormously sophisticated pieces of filmmaking that deliver entertainment to audiences all over the globe. As such, they are undoubtedly among the most popular blockbusters ever produced by any film industry in the world.

References and bibliography

Banker, Ashok (2001) *Bollywood*, Hertfordshire: Pocket Essentials.

Chakravarty, Sumita S. (1993) *National Identity in Indian Popular Cinema, 1947–1987*, Austin: University of Texas Press.

Deme, Steve (2000) *Movies, Masculinity and Modernity: An Ethnography of Men's Filmgoing in India*, Westport, CT: Greenwood Press.

Dissanayake, Wimal (1993) "The Concept of Evil and Social Order in Indian Melodrama: An Evolving Dialectic," in Wimal Dissanayake (ed.), *Melodrama and Asian Cinema*, Cambridge: Cambridge University Press: 189–204.

Gandy, Behroze, and Thomas, Rosie (1991) "Three Indian Film Stars," in Christine Gledhill (ed.), *Stardom: Industry of Desire*, London: Routledge: 107–31.

Gokulsing, K. Moti, and Dissanayake, Wimal (1998) *Indian Popular Cinema: A Narrative of Cultural Change*, Stoke-on-Trent: Trentham Books.

Kabir, Nasreen Munni (2001) *Bollywood: The Indian Cinema Story*, London: Channel 4 Books.

Mishra, Vijay (1985) "Towards a Theoretical Critique of Bombay Cinema," *Screen*, 26, 3–4: 133–46.

Rajadhyaksha, Ashish, and Willemen, Paul (1999) *Encyclopaedia of Indian Cinema*, London: British Film Institute.

Rao, Leela (1989) "Woman in Indian Films: A Paradigm of Continuity and Change," *Media, Culture and Society*, 11: 443–58.

Sharma, Ashwani (1993) "Blood, Sweat and Tears: Amitabh Bachchan, Urban Demi-God," in Pat Kirkham and Janet Thumin (eds), *You Tarzan: Masculinity, Movies and Men*, London: Lawrence & Wishart: 167–80.

Thomas, Rosie (1985) "Indian Cinema: Pleasures and Popularity," *Screen*, 6, 3–4: 116–32.

Vasudevan, Ravi S. (1989) "The Melodramatic Mode and the Commercial Hindi Cinema: Notes on Film History, Narrative and Performance in the 1950s," *Screen*, 30, 3: 29–50.

Vasudevan, Ravi S. (ed.) (2000a) *Making Meaning in Indian Cinema*, New Delhi: Oxford University Press.

Vasudevan, Ravi S. (2000b) "The Politics of Cultural Address in a 'Transitional' Cinema," in Christine Gledhill and Linda Williams (eds), *Reinventing Film Studies*, London: Arnold: 130–64.

Wyatt, Justin (1994) *High Concept: Movies and Marketing in Hollywood*, Austin: University of Texas Press.

INDEX

Note: Page numbers in **bold** denote an illustration. An "n" following a number denotes a note.